30106022827827

AF745239

The Long History *of* NEW MEDIA

HTTP://THELONGHISTORYOFNEWMEDIA.NET

Steve Jones
General Editor

Vol. 76

PETER LANG
New York • Washington, D.C./Baltimore • Bern
Frankfurt • Berlin • Brussels • Vienna • Oxford

The Long History of NEW MEDIA

Technology, Historiography, and Contextualizing Newness

EDITED BY DAVID W. PARK,
NICHOLAS W. JANKOWSKI, STEVE JONES

PETER LANG
New York • Washington, D.C./Baltimore • Bern
Frankfurt • Berlin • Brussels • Vienna • Oxford

Library of Congress Cataloging-in-Publication Data

The long history of new media: technology, historiography,
and contextualizing newness / edited by David W. Park,
Nicholas W. Jankowski, Steve Jones.
p. cm. — (Digital formations; v. 76)
Includes bibliographical references and index.
1. Digital media—Technological innovations.
2. Digital media—Social aspects. 3. Digital media and culture.
I. Park, David W. II. Jankowski, Nick. III. Jones, Steve.
P94.6.L66 302.23'1—dc22 2011013899
ISBN 978-1-4331-1441-0 (hardcover)
ISBN 978-1-4331-1440-3 (paperback)
ISSN 1526-3169

Bibliographic information published by **Die Deutsche Nationalbibliothek**.
Die Deutsche Nationalbibliothek lists this publication in the "Deutsche
Nationalbibliografie"; detailed bibliographic data is available
on the Internet at http://dnb.d-nb.de/.

FSC
Mixed Sources
Product group from well-managed
forests, controlled sources and
recycled wood or fiber

Cert no. SCS-COC-002464
www.fsc.org
©1996 Forest Stewardship Council

The paper in this book meets the guidelines for permanence and durability
of the Committee on Production Guidelines for Book Longevity
of the Council of Library Resources.

© 2011 Peter Lang Publishing, Inc., New York
29 Broadway, 18th floor, New York, NY 10006
www.peterlang.com

All rights reserved.
Reprint or reproduction, even partially, in all forms such as microfilm,
xerography, microfiche, microcard, and offset strictly prohibited.

Printed in the United States of America

Contents

Acknowledgments

This volume is the result of a long effort to bring together the worlds of new media scholarship and media history scholarship. As such, it benefits directly and indirectly from no small number of peers and fellow-travelers.

The originating impulses for the volume come from the International Communication Association (ICA) pre-conference titled "The Long History of New Media," which was held in May of 2008 at McGill University. This pre-conference was made a success through the organizational and professional support provided by Jonathan Sterne and Jennifer Marleau at McGill. Michael Haley at ICA also lent crucial assistance for what was also the first meeting of the ICA Communication History Interest Group, attended by an impressive array of new media scholars.

A second ICA pre-conference, titled "The Future Is Prologue" and held at the University of Illinois-Chicago in May of 2009, furthered the goals set out in the first pre-conference, and brought us in touch with even more quality scholarship in the world of new media history. This pre-conference would not have happened without the material assistance of Zizi Papacharissi, Mamie Gray, and Dace Kezbers in UIC's Department of Communication, and Maxine Brown, Dana Plepys, Andrew Johnson, and Jason Leigh in UIC's Electronic Visualization Laboratory.

Working together on the journal *New Media & Society* (*NM&S*) is what brought us, the editors of this volume, in contact with each other several years ago. This extended collaboration on *NM&S* has been supported by SAGE Publications staff, particularly Mila Steele and Caroline Sparrow, who also were instrumental in preparation of a theme issue of *NM&S* based on contributions to the first ICA preconference, a publishing event that greatly stimulated preparation of this volume.

At Peter Lang Publishing, Mary Savigar and Bernadette Shade always knew how to keep things under control and how to make everything fit together. We are appreciative of the support and flexibility they provided.

The volume has developed in an atmosphere of thought maintained by conversation. In addition to the authors whose work appears in this book, the editors wish to thank those whose conversations with us continue to keep us curious. In particular, we wish to thank Anne Beaulieu, Mark Brewin, Esther Dyson, Jim Griffin, Larry Gross, Charles van den Heuvel, Jeff Pooley, Lee Rainie, Peter Simonson, Clifford Tatum, and Paul Wouters.

Finally, we thank our families for their unflagging support: Sarah; Mirelle and Mylene; and Jodi, Ella, and Mack.

—Dave Park, Nick Jankowski, and Steve Jones

Introduction
History and New Media

David W. Park, Nicholas W. Jankowski and Steve Jones

In the study of media, it seems now well established that there is little "new" about "new media." As the name of this volume implies, "new"-ness is not itself new. Indeed, one of the most central and least controversial themes in the study of media history (as well as many other kinds of history) is the idea that we've been here before, that novelty is more ordinary than rare. This idea is both familiar and misleading. For while the intersection of history with new media involves themes that are familiar to those who have studied the phonetic alphabet, print, and broadcast media, the comparisons we often draw between histories of different media do not imply that we are simply re-running that which has come before. The history of new media presents us with something more significant than merely another opportunity to see familiar distinctions being reasserted. To be arch about it: newness is not always old news. This volume is not to be mistaken for one that concerns itself only with the history of media technology, or, for that matter, only with the history of media technology now (in the early 21st century) considered to be new. As editors of this volume, we take a more catholic approach, accepting at the outset that histories of media currently deemed to be new are worth pursuing, but also asserting that such a history of a currently new medium would be little more than the beginning of things that could be done when we collide the terms "new media" and "history."

This volume is based on the belief that media and history are so intimately connected that the emergence of what can be called "new media" does something more than merely provide us with new media whose histories can be described. The history of new media challenges us to: become more reflexive in our understanding of how history operates, reconsider the meaning of "newness" as it relates to media and to broader themes in historical thought, reflect on how media operate in terms of information recording and storage, approach social thought with a renewed sense of how the theoretical relates to the historical, and contextualize what is taken as new so as to establish broader and suggestive continuities in the history of communication.

Each section of this volume pays heed to the basic idea that the long history of new media need not be undertaken with only today's sense of newness or with prepackaged definitions of what media are.

By compiling this volume of essays on the history of new media, we are also proposing that history has a special role to play in the study of new media. The linkage between history and new media is not difficult to make. After all, the "new" in new media must always be understood to be historically constructed. The new is also constructed with an eye on the future, or more correctly, an eye on what we think the future will be. James Carey described how the future has often functioned as "cause for a revitalization of optimism," as "the fulfillment of a particular ideology or idealism," and as a "participation ritual of technological exorcism."[1] It is not difficult to notice how new media have been incorporated into visions of the future that act much as Carey describes. And the power that is given to the future is usually associated with the "new" in new media. Not only does this mean that the new media of today will be the traditional media of tomorrow, an emphasis on the history of the future gives us an understanding of what this newness can be said to represent.

Book Structure

Part I of this volume, "Newness Contextualized," collects chapters that address the idea of newness itself. Newness presents obvious challenges to all historians, but for those who attempt to understand media historically, the idea of the new presents us with a heightened need for circumspection. In an article in the journal theme issue from which this collection of essays emerged, Benjamin Peters[2] has pointed out that much of what we take for the canon of media history focuses on the early history of media. In this sense, media history (with its focus on constitutive moments) comes to us as a kind of prepackaged new media history. It is worth stepping back from this to inquire about the role that newness plays in media and in our histories of the media. If nothing else, this perspective leads us to ask: where are the histories of "middle" and "late" periods for media? A sober reflection on newness demonstrates the partiality of our existing histories and summons us to consider the historical dimension of all communication.

In keeping with this idea, the chapters in this section explicitly consider the meaning of newness. In pursuit of this, Devon Powers ("The End of New Music?") demonstrates how music has been historically constructed in terms of novelty and shows how the logic of newness shifts with changes in media and in industry, with important lessons for those who are interested in the history of attention. Noah Arceneaux ("'All You'll Need Is a Mobile Couch'") and Stephanie Ricker Schulte ("Cutting the Cord and 'Crying Socialist Wolf'") examine the histories of mobile television and public Wi-Fi connectivity, respectively. Their careful attention to visions of renewal by way of the technological sublime undone by material and discursive constraints helps to demonstrate how newness plays out in its second and subsequent acts. Christian Thorsten Callisen and Barbara Adkins ("Pre-digital Virtuality") put the entire idea of new media into helpful perspective in their analysis of continuities between the communication in the Republic of Letters and contemporary scholarly communication. They suggest that any presumed newness must be understood in terms of the broad playing field of praxis.

The "media" component of "new media" also has much to do with history. Here we hope that readers will attend to the numerous meanings of the term "media." A historical emphasis in the study of new media involves addressing media not as clearly defined objects, but as shifting practices, discourses, technical configurations, and cultures. Carolyn Marvin has asserted that media "are not fixed natural objects; they have no natural edges,"[3] and newness is one of the things about media that shows us how historically and culturally constructed they are. Writing in the late 20th century, Ithiel de Sola Pool asserted that we were in the midst of a technologically centered communication revolution, meaning that "we have reached a historical corner."[4] The idea that newness itself is a socially constructed process, that there are no natural edges in media, reminds us that historical corners like the one Pool asserted was facing us in the late 20th century are not brute facts but are claims that come from particular parties. The fact that media historians themselves are deeply implicated in the process of assertions of newness should prompt us to avoid presuming that the idea of the "new" implies much that is substantial in the object itself and quite a bit about our relationship to the object.

Marvin tells us that "the introduction of new media is a special historical occasion when patterns anchored in older media that have provided the stable currency of social exchange are reexamined, challenged, and defended."[5] Marvin's language is important. It is not that the introduction of new media allows us simply to redraw the boundaries with no regard for the past and its reproduction into the future, but that the introduction of new media is often linked to adjustments in material practice that can prompt a level of reflexivity in the ideas we use to understand ongoing social processes. To find examples of reexamination, we could turn to the field of communication, where it is not much exaggeration to say that the technological changes in communication processes that are often summed up simply through reference to the Internet prompted perhaps less reexamination of persistent ideas than we might have preferred. When we consider the interrelationships between the history of the media and the history of the theories we use to understand the media,[6] we see a complicated picture in which hopes, dreams, ideological presuppositions, global politics, and much else come to shape the questioning at work.

It is this kind of concern with the interrelationships between the history of media and the history of theories of the media that is addressed in Part II of this volume, "New Media History and Theory." Here, D. Travers Scott ("Sound Studies for Historians of New Media") lays out a sweeping project for how ideas from sound studies can be applied in the context of new media history, reminding us, amongst other things, that media are not just a set of technologies for reading. Zizi Papacharissi and Elaine J. Yuan ("What If the Internet Did Not Speak English?") and Dmitry Epstein ("The Analog History of the 'Digital Divide'") share a critical understanding of some of the Western assumptions of how media function that have been imported tacitly into the study of new media, and they offer productive strategies for us to get beyond such tendencies. Teresa M. Harrison ("The Evolving Medium Is the Message") performs the difficult feat of taking Marshall McLuhan's ideas at face value, and she considers the neuroscience implied in McLuhan's ideas as they relate to grander narratives in media history. Michael Dick ("Twenty Years of Unnecessary Forward Slashes") takes a very small part of the media landscape (the forward slashes in web addresses) and develops an outline for web history that promises to get web history past some of its less complicated narratives of progress.

If newness has been an important dimension in the history of media, it stands to reason that one way to address the idea of newness would be to work comparatively. Comparative histories of media carry with them the hope for a kind of parallax effect, whereby the similarities and differences between media emerge from explicit comparison, so that our perspective on each medium is put into a system with other perspectives. This effect is not dissimilar from what Kenneth Burke coined "perspective by incongruity,"[7] a method he hoped would make the familiar strange, for the purpose of fuller recognition. Simply by working through comparison, the historian is invited to construct typologies and theories. This is potentially dangerous, for as John Nerone avers, "communication history displays a galloping theoretical incoherence."[8] If this theoretical incoherence can be frustrating to some of the more properly professional impulses in media research, it can also be fruitful to think with, and the tendency for comparative new media histories seems well positioned for generating new ways to think about some familiar new media practices.

We find this hope spelled out in the chapters in Part III, "Comparative Approaches." Again, the point is not merely to show that we've been here before. The point is to create the fuller sense of the history of media that becomes possible only when considering more than one set of media practices or when revolving practices around words that have their own multimedia history. Peter Schaefer ("Interface") shows us how a word as familiar as "interface" comes loaded with a surprising story of origin, and more scientific and cultural meaning than we often imagine is at work. Brian O'Neill ("The Long History of Digital Radio") demonstrates how digital radio in Europe is experienced as both a forward- and backward-looking medium, to some degree stalled as a result of its relation to other contemporary media. Benjamin Peters and Deborah Lubken ("New Media in Crises") take two disparate examples—fire alarm systems and distributed computer networks—as case studies for elaborating the role of newness in media history and for calling our attention to the social structures around these media. Holly Kruse ("Pipeline as Network") compares how the oft-ignored pneumatic tube compares with other networked communication, and she addresses the power systems at play in pneumatic tube systems. Gerard Goggin ("Telephone Media") addresses the histories of the telephone and how the telephone in its many iterations has bumped up against numerous other media practices.

Moreover, the consideration of the intersection of "new media" and "history" should give us an appreciation of how new media today may represent new means of conducting historical inquiry. As those who work in the emerging subfield of digital history have already demonstrated forcefully,[9] many contemporary new media allow us to rethink how we go about the most basic tasks involved in historical research. This gives us an important reminder of how history itself has always been performed through a specific set of mediated practices. Contemporary new media provide new ways to: record, compile, analyze, and share information and culture.

Beyond this, it is important to remember, as Lisa Gitelman says, that "media are reflexive historical subjects." She continues:

> Our sense of history—of facticity in relation to the past—is inextricable from our experience of inscription, of writing, print, photography, sound recording, cinema, and now (one must wonder) digital media that save text, image, and sound. . . . Inquiring into the history of a medium that helped to construct that inquiring itself is sort of like attempting to stand in the same river twice: impossible, but it is important to try, at least so the (historicity of the) grounds of inquiry become clear.[10]

In this sense, there is a kind of reflexivity in the inquiries pursued here, as "media" and "history" have more to do with each other than one might at first suspect. This kind of approach may take us a long way from considering media merely as independent variables or as bearers of utopian or dystopian agency in and of themselves. This concern for how new media relate to practices in recording meaning, or to practices in historical inquiry, can be found in John Durham Peters's discussion of how history can be considered as a type of transmission. The historical record is always mediated through and by time, and always involves treating something as the transmission of the past to the present.[11] All of this is reflected in Part IV of this volume, "New Media and Historiography."

This section commences with Meghan Dougherty and Steven M. Schneider ("Web Historiography and the Emergence of New Archival Forms") reimagining the archive as it lends itself to web history, with a focus on the potential for collaborative archival work. Fernando Bermejo ("The Evolution of Audience Labor") shows how new media relate to long-standing practices in audience measurement, with a focus on the kinds of traces we leave behind in new media. Niels Brügger ("Digital History and a Register of Websites") outlines how any web archive might need to be organized before analysis can be performed. Adriana de Souza e Silva and Daniel M. Sutko ("Placing Location-Aware Media in a History of the Virtual") analyze a similar kind of trace, that of geographic location as it relates to well-developed trends in media history. Finally, Simon Popple ("'It's Not Really Our Content'") considers the meaning of web-based archives for cinema history.

Concluding Remarks

History is not new to the scholarly consideration of the media. Some of the scholars and intellectuals who are most closely associated with the study of media (and new media) dealt with media in historical terms. One need only point to Harold Innis, Marshall McLuhan, Lewis Mumford, Elizabeth Eisenstein, and James Carey for examples of influential figures who have addressed the intersection of history and the media.[12] However, just because there are examples of historians of the media who have come before does not mean that it will be easy to stake out space for historical inquiry into the media in the future. Historical inquiry in the field of communication has never really developed institutionally to match the kind of professionalization one finds in, for instance, subfields of history itself. Though there are influential intellectual lodestars such as Innis to guide our inquiry, communication history lacks a clear disciplinary identity. Nerone looks to the lack of a clear disciplinary identity in communication history and surmises that this work "will not gain the respect of other more disciplinary historians."[13] This may be the case for new media history as well, at least for the foreseeable future. However, this need not be a problem. Strong disciplinary identities bring with them not only solid footing and well-rehearsed epistemological standpoints. They also come with their own blind spots, verification-oriented research projects that offer little in the way of innovation, and potentially stifling conditions for the new media researcher. The history of new media, as found here, partakes of some of the freedom and dexterity that is granted to those on the margins. The emphasis on history here will (we hope) bring the fruits of the historical enterprise into conversation with other disciplines, and with a host of ideas. In this sense, perhaps there is something new here.

This volume develops the intersection of "new media" and "history" in a manner that emphasizes a number of interrelated themes. First, the volume has been developed in an attempt to nurture our awareness of how media operate not only as subjects for historical inquiry but also as the substance of all history. This can be found most obviously in the section dedicated to historiography, but the echoes of this basic insight resonate across the volume. Second, this volume sets a course for an approach to history that is, we hope, less tied to print and writing (silent, visual media) than many other historical approaches. In this sense, the volume is inspired by developments in contemporary new media, with their bundles of sensory outputs. History is not only written and read. It is also seen, heard, and felt. The history of new media will require an awareness of the varieties of media experience. Third, this volume underlines the potential for new media history to take newness seriously. Getting beyond the naïve celebration of novelty is a start, but more important than this is the potential for new media history to invigorate the study of media with ideas and theories that grapple with newness, difference, and change. There is no need simply to test or verify the ideas that have propelled the study of media for decades. The intersection of "history" and "new media" is a place where historical work can demonstrate its powers of invention.

Notes

1. Carey, *Communication as Culture,* 174.
2. Peters, "And Lead Us Not."
3. Marvin, *When Old Technologies Were New,* 8.
4. Pool, *Technologies without Boundaries,* 3.
5. Marvin, *When Old Technologies Were New,* 4.
6. For an excellent example of this, see Czitrom, *Media and the American Mind.*
7. Burke, *Attitudes toward History,* 308.
8. Nerone, "The Future," 259.
9. See Rosenzweig, "Scarcity or Abundance?"
10. Gitelman, *Always Already New,* 20-21.

11. Peters, "History as a Communication Problem," 24.
12. The canonical references here would be Innis, *The Bias of Communication;* McLuhan, *The Gutenberg Galaxy;* Mumford, *Technics and Civilization;* Eisenstein, *The Printing Press;* and Carey, *Communication as Culture.*
13. Nerone, "The Future," 260.

Works Cited

Burke, Kenneth. *Attitudes toward History.* 3rd ed. Berkeley: University of California Press, 1984.

Carey, James W. *Communication as Culture: Essays on Media and Society*. Boston: Unwin Hyman, 1989.

Czitrom, Daniel. *Media and the American Mind: From Morse to McLuhan*. Chapel Hill: University of North Carolina Press, 1982.

Eisenstein, Elizabeth L. *The Printing Press as an Agent of Change: Communications and Cultural Transformations in Early Modern Europe*. New York: Cambridge University Press, 1979.

Gitelman, Lisa. *Always Already New: Media, History, and the Data of Culture*. Cambridge, MA: The MIT University Press, 2006.

Innis, Harold A. *The Bias of Communication*. Toronto: University of Toronto Press, 1951.

Marvin, Carolyn. *When Old Technologies Were New: Thinking About Electric Communication in the Late Nineteenth Century*. New York: Oxford University Press, 1988.

McLuhan, Marshall. *The Gutenberg Galaxy: The Making of Typographic Man*. Toronto: University of Toronto Press, 1962.

Mumford, Lewis. *Technics and Civilization*. New York: Harcourt, Brace & Co, 1934.

Nerone, John. "The Future of Communication History." *Critical Studies in Media Communication* 23, no. 3 (2006): 254–262.

Peters, Benjamin. "And Lead Us Not into Thinking the New Is New: A Bibliographic Case for New Media History." *New Media & Society* 11, nos. 1 & 2 (2009): 13–30.

Peters, John Durham. "History as a Communication Problem," In *Explorations in Communication and History*, edited by Barbie Zelizer, 19–34. London: Routledge, 2008.

Pool, Ithiel de Sola. *Technologies without Boundaries: On Telecommunications in a Global Age*. Cambridge, MA: Harvard University Press, 1990.

Rosenzweig, Roy. "Scarcity or Abundance? Preserving the Past in a Digital Era." *The American Historical Review* 108, no. 3 (2008): 735–762.

Part I:

Newness Contextualized

chapter one

The End of New Music? Digital Media, History, and the Idea of Attention

Devon Powers

Introduction

When Michael Jackson died on June 25, 2009, his music underwent a resurrection. If something sentimental—mourning, nostalgia—drove the impromptu dance parties, "Bad"-blaring car stereos, and 24/7 media tributes of the subsequent days and weeks, Jacksonmania also fed something more practical: a fattening bottom line. During the week of July 11, the first in which the *Billboard* charts could measure the impact of his death, Jackson's solo work as well as that from The Jackson 5 occupied nine of the top ten slots for pop albums, five of the top ten digital album downloads, and the top nineteen "Hot 100 Recurrents"—a dominance never before seen in pop music. That week, Jackson became the first catalog artist to outsell a newly released artist since Soundscan started keeping records in 1991.[1] The Jackson trend continued with such force that by the end of 2009, Soundscan named MJ the year's top-selling album artist, and his 2003 *Number Ones* the third top-selling album—beating out queen-of-publicity Lady GaGa and bested only by two other media darlings, Taylor Swift and Susan Boyle.

Certainly the death of a celebrity as famous and controversial as Jackson has all the trappings of a watershed cultural moment, and his posthumous dominion over the pop music market may be understood strictly in those terms. Yet at the same time, it transpired during a time of tremendous flux within the popular music industries, with digital media technologies participating in the rapid revision of the practices of making, distributing, and obtaining music. In this light, Jackson's massive oeuvre and enduring power to generate spectacle transform from abstract cultural legacies to concrete objects of worth and as such raise questions not just about contemporary musical consumption but also the history and historiography of popular music. What does it mean—for the music industry, for scholarly interest in popular music, for popular music history—when a catalog artist experiences such a revival? From a historical vantage, the implications of that question transcend George Lipsitz's observation that music serves as a "conversation in which no one has the first or last word"[2]; music's dialogic nature does not adequately explain how or why discrete music from the past gains contemporary currency nor how we should think about it when it does. These are the questions I seek to explore: how what is changing—and enduring—about popular music provides opportunities for rethinking how to theorize the present and past of music. Rather than an exploration of Jackson, though, what I offer is a meditation about newness and oldness, present and past tense, and the complicated fashion in which they relate to music, especially when situated within new media.

My argument has two related though distinct foci. First, I want to suggest that traditional meanings attached to the idea of "newness," especially within the popular music industries, have begun to lose their utility. This point recognizes the knotty chronology mediated music creates in general, as well as acknowledges how the digitization of music further jumbles this already complex temporality. Since these problems affect not just the music industry but also the kinds of scholarly questions that arise in reference to it—of particular concern, questions about history—my second goal is to suggest that scholarship should concentrate more on the idea of attention, a concept frequently at the fulcrum of discussions of media and music in historical and contemporary circumstances yet remarkably undertheorized. While attention has had some currency within business literature since the onset of the "information age,"[3] those of us interested in popular music and history and/of new media deserve to bestow attention with much more, well, attention. As a mode of perceptual activity, a form of value, and a precipitate of the circulation of culture, attention is useful not just in supplying innovative explanations for how and why music gains prominence at any particular historical moment but also in taking seriously the numerous scholarly calls to factor the notion of circulation more thoroughly into our analyses.[4]

Since the dawn of recorded music, its ability to be both of the moment and of the past has been a source of marvel, contemplation, and eeriness. Thomas Edison's early experiments into recorded sound are a requisite part of music's historical treatment, and it has been frequently noted that what he envisioned as a way to hold speech from the past became something quite different once its primary purpose became contemporary song[5]; paradoxically, a medium intended to record history became a chief disseminator of what was current. Moreover, as recordings came to dominate how music was sold, the record acquired its own ontology; while it had never been a wholly benign document of a live performance, over time recording morphed into a deliberate sonic creation for which there was not necessarily an "original."[6] Following Lisa Gitelman, I make this point to underscore music's similarity to other media in that it is *mediated,* historical not only in its ability to capture a particular moment from the past but also in the technology of its capture.[7] At the same time, Jeremy Wallach's argument for "sonic materialism" understands music recordings to hold cultural, social, and economic relevances that are importantly rooted in their "ability to produce material sonic presences."[8] These presences of music happen in time, singular events and tangible experiences as much as they may also be repetitions and revisitations of writing, recording, or listening that has already happened. They are "now" and "past," new and old simultaneously.

Despite this tangled existence—which, in essence, reckons with the ephemerality of sound—newness persists as an important value for music. We thirst to hear our favorite artists' new songs; we add new music to our collections, even if the songs are not recent releases; we attend shows where artists test new material. Remixes of other artists' hits; restorations of musical genres; remasterings of previous recordings; reissues of classic tunes—each of these is also new, though in each case the word carries different connotations. "New" music is also a scholarly category, not just in terms that formally get applied to genres (such as new classical or neo-soul), but also in how "new" demarcates endeavors which are historical from those which are contemporarily oriented and the methods, goals, and audiences that follow for each.

Instead of following any of these paths toward a definition of new music, though, I want to consider how the complexity itself is illuminating. What it reveals is the conceptual elasticity of "newness"—a term ostensibly marking time, but which also negotiates relationships between and among selves, culture, and the economy. As such, newness is as much a discursive construction as it is a temporal or ontological one, and this is one way to conceive of Ben Peters's provocative description of new media as "media we do not yet know how to talk about."[9] Thus, newness becomes a useful discourse precisely for the means it offers to talk about objects—media, music, and so on—when we are uncertain about them; newness can be called a discourse of *possibility*. We might ask then: under what circumstances, and to what ends, does music come to be understood as new?

A preliminary answer to this question emerges through considering how novelty, in its broadest sense, aids in the perpetuation of capitalism. Karl Marx and Friedrich Engels are worth repeating here. As they write in *The Communist Manifesto*,

> The bourgeoisie cannot exist without constantly revolutionising [*sic*] the instruments of production, and thereby the relations of production, and with them the whole relations of society. . . . All fixed, fast-frozen relations, with their train of ancient and venerable prejudices and opinions, are swept away, all new-formed ones become antiquated before they can ossify. All that is solid melts into air.[10]

Since Marx, this line of thinking has been adapted to explain a wide number of economic dynamics, including co-optation, "creative destruction," and "flexible accumulation," to name just three.[11] Given popular music's long-standing commercial imperative, novelty likewise has assumed a key, if unsurprising, role in the music industry—a requisite that dates back to the earliest days of the U.S. popular music industry. For example, Tin Pan Alley song publishers "had to promote a steady taste for the new among consumers," counteracting the "durable, established appeal" of widely familiar, public, ownerless songs.[12] In encouraging audiences to consume much more music (and, in turn, to own it), Tin Pan Alley laid a foundation that continued to fuel musical production over the course of the 20th century. The creation and exploitation of new musical "products"—artists, songs, albums, genres—developed into a surefire tactic for expanding and extending profit, so much so that, ironically, the industry often tended toward overproduction, characterized by a small number of successful recordings propping up a vastly larger number of failures.[13] Andrew Leyshon and colleagues also observe that the musical economy has traditionally built itself "through a combination of per-unit pricing and the enforcement of copyright law,"[14] both of which emphasize the economic necessity of newness, whether physical or conceptual.

As the above examples reveal, an economy structured to profit from musical newness requires not just material products but also discourse that naturalizes and makes meaningful its continued production. This discursive work happens both inside the recording industry as well as within its correlated intermediaries—and, to a great degree, justifies the need for those intermediaries. For the sake of brevity I'll point briefly to just two examples: the charts and music journalism. The charts, for instance, have long served as an important barometer of musical popularity, regularly invoked as a proxy for consumer taste (including, with full acknowledgment of the irony, at the beginning of the present chapter). As a "complex signifier of relationships among business, musicians, music and consumers" that outlines "not only what is popular but also what is popularity,"[15] the charts continually renew, reinforcing the conviction (and the requirement) that both taste and musical culture be ever on the forward march. Moreover, the construction of the charts, both in customary printed form and their "2.0" counterparts, embed the value of novelty into their very construction. The Jackson example from this chapter's beginning is a case in point: ineligible for placement on *Billboard's* "Hot 100" chart due to the time since their initial release, Jackson's singles were relegated to the "Hot 100 Recurrents" chart—created to account for music that was briskly selling yet was more than eighteen months old.[16] Compounding this, the charts are pointed only toward activity that has transpired in the previous week, denying any cumulative relationship between one week and the next and quickly forgetting their history.

Music journalism's stake in exaltation of the new seeps into even the most mundane activities, such as the general practice of reviewing albums that have been recently released or the pegging of reportage to seasons or timely events. This bent toward the new exists not solely because music reporters have a stake in the reproduction of the musical economy, though it certainly coincides with the industry's economic needs. More important, music journalism imbues those new musical products with taste, significance, and reputation, themselves vital registers of value that over time have become deeply insinuated into the promotional practices of the music industry.[17]

This last point, however, begins to reveal the unstable foundations upon which discourses of newness rely. An economy intent on generating new music materially and discursively must distinguish each new musical product from the next through attachments to other kinds of meaning; indeed, the work of intermediaries of all stripes is often put to this purpose.[18] Yet these other justifications for the attractiveness of novelty—meaning, significance, and the like—are often much more enduring than the sheer fact of being "new." While newness alone might identify a space of *possibility*, durability and attachment must arise from elsewhere.

So far, I've been driving toward a simple point: that "new" music is not just *created*, but also *constructed*, and that it collects a range of other values as it enters the marketplace. However, the difficulties that emerge as a result of these facts become acute in light of how music's mediation further problematizes its ability to be neatly "new." For starters, cementing "new" music—whether in a chart, an album review, or a recording—is precisely what allows that music to go out of style and be replaced. In this way, new music depends, both discursively and materially, upon old music, regardless of whether or not that dependence is articulated. In some ways, this point reconfigures Jean Baudrillard's argument in "The Ideological Genesis of Needs," where he notes that within capitalism, needs are "nothing but the exponential function—the rationalization—of the fundamental processes of production and reproduction of distinctive material."[19] However, a second issue that materiality in general and mediation in particular create for new music is not taken into account in Baudrillard's conception: namely, that that which has been replaced does not simply disappear, never again to be valued. The preservation afforded by mediation allows for affective and instrumental value alike to put otherwise inert relics toward novel, lucrative ends. A fundamental question thus arises: can discourses of newness latch onto "old" objects as easily as to "new" objects?

Practices of the music industry over the past half century would strongly suggest that the answer is yes, and that the economic imperative for "new music" has also somewhat paradoxically created a strong incentive to monetize music from the past. For example, Keir Keightley has explored how in the mid-20th-century music industry, the record industry's adoption of long-playing records (LPs) allowed recording artists to enjoy longer careers while the labels benefited from the extended sale of an artist's back catalog.[20] Over the 1950s and '60s, as "industrial strategies that [sought] to stabilize profitability over the long term" solidified, the move toward LPs underscored the need for the industry to encourage consumers to "resist novelty and 'mindless' consumption."[21] In turn, these changes further transformed the musical economy by setting in motion *material* realities, such as the physical creation of new copies of "old" records. LPs dramatically increased "the variety of music that was now continuously available for sale,"[22] instilling previously untapped revenue streams right alongside, and deeply reliant on, practices of remembrance and history.

As the LP helped elevate the album as the dominant form of enduring musical media (and in some genres, a work of art[23]), other corners of the music industries also discovered ways to profit off the past. After the glory days of the 1960s settled into the leaner 1970s, so began practices such as oldies radio stations, reunion tours, and self-identified cover albums,[24] all of which banked on the ability for old music to be made novel again. I adapt Paul Grainge's work on the film and television industries to consider these structures as part of an "economy of pastness": history rendered not only trendy but viably circulative via "specific technological transformations and strategies of niche marketing."[25] As a result, contemporary music and old, already grappling temporally and affectively, tussled for economic viability—both "new" in the sense of generating possible revenue streams and more physical objects as well as the trappings of newness via intermediary forces such as chart placement, journalistic coverage, and the like.

While the logic of newness persisted in the music industry, then, it likewise relied on a logic of persistence: that media can be renewed and repurposed. By this, I mean something more practical than a Jamesonian notion of bricolage or pastiche—this is not the reappearance of the past as fodder for the ahistorically retro but rather the necessity of the past as a partial driver of our economic present and future. This signals, however, that the point where I began in this section—how economic imperatives prompt the quest for newness—has long been mythic in part. That newness also has a discursive component means that it is fungible, adhering to products from the present as well as the past, in ways that paradoxically quake the very foundations upon which discourses of newness rest. If anything can be new, why make anything new? The contemporary music landscape, infused as it is by digital technology, renders this myth of newness increasingly difficult to defend.

As I suggest above, discourses of newness imply a constant march toward uncharted vistas and a constant replenishing of core capitalist worth and, as such, have been central to the reproduction of music's economy. In practice, though, the music industry has complicated its fervent quest for novelty, turning to old music in order to profit from the plentiful repositories of value that are the new's precipitate: meaning and affect, but also all those mediated objects which may be recycled, resold, and renewed. This creates complications and confusions—such as attempts to render music "new" irrespective of its historical temporality or discourses that establish contemporary releases as "instant classics"—and these issues dilute the very demand for newness they were intended to bolster.

Over the past half century, as the dominant medium for selling recorded music has changed several times, these quandaries have intensified. In each shift, not only has previously unrecorded music made its debut on the new format, but music has also been a key element of the "economy of pastness" and a fertile site for remediation. I employ the term "remediation" in two fashions: quite literally as "re-mediation," that is, the distribution of content via a novel technology, as well as in the conceptual sense articulated by Jay David Bolter and Richard Grusin, where remediation is "a double logic" directed toward both hypermediacy and immediacy.[26] Though their focus is by and large on visual phenomena,[27] remediation is conceptually useful. It offers, for one, a way to think about the common occurrences of reissuing and remastering music, which involve rendering previously recorded music to fit with updated sonic technologies and aural norms. As Greg Milner describes, these efforts strive toward "perfecting sound," and though they deny their own historicity, they are historically contingent; this mirrors how remediation desires to "achieve immediacy by ignoring or denying the presence of the medium and the act of mediation"[28] even as it is technologically enabled. Remediation as a cultural paradigm thus intensifies the historical, temporal, material, and affective entanglements that make "the new" harder and harder to specify.

In addition, newness has been undermined because of the decreasing economic value of music altogether. This goes far beyond earlier crises brought on by musical overproduction. For example, in a dynamic Anahid Kassabian has identified as "ubiquitous music," the prevalence of music in everyday life has dramatically increased—for example, in retail spaces, advertisements, and video games.[29] At first blush, this prevalence highlights the social significance of music as well as the economic value that may flow from it; music is a path toward making money both for the music producers as well as those who benefit from association with it. Likewise, this would seem to suggest ever-growing revenue opportunities for old music as the carriers of affect that can translate productively to other realms.

However, the preponderance of music in everyday life can also undermine these values. As Kassabian notes, "music is being heard often, if not most often, as a secondary activity."[30] Leyshon and colleagues are more forceful in their proclamation that "music has become an increasingly important part of the infrastructure of capitalist society, now an essential crutch to all manner of acts of consumption" but that "this development has actually served to *weaken* the music industry as popular music is decreasingly valued for itself, but is, instead, increasingly valued more for the ways in which it is consumed in relation to other things."[31] This point once again refers to the differing terrains of valuation described before, but alongside a fundamental question emerges: what does it mean if the recording industry cannot profit in the same way from new music? As we witness a profoundly troubled industry at present, this theoretical question gains practicality. Clearly, the ways that the music industries create and market musical newness must change in the face of this depletion of value, at the same time that even more music is required to pervade all of the environments in which it is now a desirable feature. The contemporary implications of this should be obvious, but there are historical ones to be parsed as well. Chief among them is how the diminishing utility of newness likewise impacts the meaning, use, circulation, and definition of historical music.

To explain this last point, let me make an analogy between the remediation and omnipresence of music and some concerns that arise in thinking generally about new media, temporality, and history. In her 2006 book, *Always Already New: Media, History, and the Data of Culture,* Lisa Gitelman observes that an enigmatic quality of digital media, particularly online, is its thorough denial of its own moment of creation—what she calls its "continual, continuous present tense."[32] She further observes that "it is not that the web resists history per se, only that electronic documents compel attention to themselves as differently—often dubiously—historical, where history always happens at the levels of—at least—data, metadata, program, and platform."[33] Since these levels are often either obscure to the everyday user or effaced in the flurry of updates and revisions that typify our online experiences, this offers yet another way of thinking about how the digital environment itself may create a situation in which so much appears to be new that, in effect, the novelty of newness wears thin or is of minimal value. In turn, this all-over presence of "present" complicates the practice of doing history at the same time that it may "pose the question of history itself."[34]

In a digital environment, practices of intermediation that once helped to perpetuate the consumption of musical novelty (and, in turn, set boundaries between the past and present) likewise suffer from this tyranny of the present tense. Let me again turn to music journalism and music charts as categorical examples. Music blogs began to appear in the early 2000s as part of the rapidly expanding blogosphere and soon began to duplicate, then threaten, many of the traditional functions of music journalism—especially given their added capability of serving as nodes of musical distribution. This distributive turn, matched with fans' desires to acquire music without paying, fundamentally disrupted the economics of newness in the music industry in some very important ways. No longer wedded to industry-prescribed ideas of purchase, "leaking" music—circulating music online before an official release date, sometimes even in a rudimentary mix—has come to be a standard practice, so much so that artists have been known to leak their own music in order to gain the ancillary benefits of pre-release.[35] Furthermore, because blogs are driven not just by advertising but also by exuberant fandom, there is often intense competition to post a hotly desired track first.[36] Blogs also may distribute music from any time, functioning not just as sites for unofficial pre-releases, but also unanticipated re-releases—a necessity for a medium characterized by a perpetual need to update.

Charting systems have been similarly changed. In the three major categories of exclusively online music charts—iTunes and other retail establishments; social networks; and music blog aggregators—there exists what I call a "hype value," which ranks music according to what is garnering excitement at the moment rather than sheer sales or industry-regulated debuts. For instance, iTunes charts consider sales within a period of time rather than cumulative sales, and there is no way for an everyday user to access the past history of iTunes charts, other than recording them herself or using *Billboard* charts as a loose proxy. A music blog aggregator such as Hype Machine is, as the name suggests, even more attuned to the value of hype, allowing songs to stay on its charts for only three days and constantly updating what's hot based on blogosphere activity. Yet at the same time, it and other services like it are oddly agnostic on the question of industry-determined notions of musical newness, by allowing music that has "leaked," older music that is at the moment gaining attention, or remixes to chart right alongside recently debuted material. These chart-style rankings thus not only obliterate their histories, but as Gitelman observes, "pose the question of history itself."[37]

The tangle of questions I have raised in the above is directed toward a single argument: that a discourse of newness cannot reign supreme within the digital media environment, and this shift should compel us to seek out other categories of analysis—not just to speak about the dire straits of the music industry but also to follow our own critical and historical impulses. The current moment, when industry-regimented norms of newness are giving way to something unknown, is a prime opportunity to underscore how precarious the idea(l) of novelty has always been. What needs to emerge in its place is a way of describing the dynamics through which music moves, attains significance, and generates revenue.

Within this context, I am arguing for the concept of attention to become more prominent as a category of scholarly analysis. I follow Thomas Davenport and John Beck to define "attention" as "focused mental engagement on a particular item of information"; as they describe, a spectator must both "narrow" his attention on a particular object and then determine whether or not to act.[38] However, I am less wedded to their explanation of an "attention economy," where "capital, labor, information, and knowledge are all in plentiful supply" and "what's in short supply is human attention."[39] Such a conception suggests that there is some finite amount of attention to be given and that we are now at a point in time where there is less of it. Instead, I argue that attention is a mode of perception and a "quantity" that may be used to measure value and is performed as material and discourses circulate in time and space. Each of these factors contributes to its ascendancy as a unit of economic analysis.

As the industrial structures that regulate new production fall prey to unruly marketplaces, and the imperatives of our current media environment purport to be without histories, we exist within what Zygmunt Bauman has described as "liquid modernity"[40]—a fluid state where society's guidelines, modes of interaction, and ways of understanding undergo near-constant revision. Eran Fisher identifies this as a "flat, decentralized sphere of ever-flowing, multiple, and ad hoc assemblages" that is the spirit of our networked age.[41] For both scholars, these arrangements configure contemporary capitalism, the period that has given rise to the unpredictable musical economy alluded to in these pages. Rather than a regimented process of production and consumption, then, a much more erratic formation emerges, impacting not only how we produce and consume but also the temporality in which it occurs. Bauman notes that "instantaneity . . . makes every moment seem infinitely capacious; and infinite capacity means that there are no limits to what could be squeezed out of any moment—however brief or 'fleeting.'"[42] This "capaciousness" is the precondition for the economic relevance of attention: moments awaiting perceptual focus, longing to be filled by whatever may cycle through them, laden with the expectation that *something* will happen.

The cycling-through of objects, culture, practices, etc., that mark our "liquid" age underscores the connection between circulation and attention and the critical role of both in media analyses of all stripes. Benjamin Lee and Edward LiPuma explain that "the circulation of [cultural forms] . . . always presupposes the existence of their respective interpretive communities, with their own forms of interpretation and evaluation."[43] As these forms take advantage of "capaciousness" in their movement through time and space, they also presume—and promise, if not always deliver—the attention of particular constituencies. It is in this way that the understanding of attention is central to grasping the most far-reaching changes presented in a digital media environment.

Various observations in business, information technology, and popular literature have touched upon these changes through discussions of qualities such as the "wealth of networks,"[44] "tipping points,"[45] the "long tail,"[46] and other dynamics that characterize online interaction. Rather than rehearse this literature, the remainder of this chapter shall consider how an awareness of the capacities of digital media might be put toward establishing attention as a conceptual framework for popular music historiography.

Attention as Perception

Jonathan Crary argues that the perceptual modality of attention is historical, associated with modernity, and predicated upon its binary opposite—that is, distraction, inattention, or lack of focus.[47] He estimates that "attention becomes a specifically modern problem only because of the *historical* obliteration of the possibility of thinking the idea of presence in perception; attention will be both a simulation of presence and a makeshift, pragmatic substitute in the face of its impossibility."[48] Attention therefore holds an important place in the comprehension of the capitalist economy:

> At the moment when the dynamic logic of capital began to dramatically undermine any stable or enduring structure of perception, this logic simultaneously attempted to impose a disciplinary regime of attentiveness. . . . It is possible to see one crucial aspect of modernity as an ongoing crisis of attentiveness, in which the changing configurations of capitalism continually push attention and distraction to new limits and thresholds, with an endless sequence of new products, sources of stimulation, and streams of information, and then responds with new methods of managing and regulating perception.[49]

As Crary describes, attention is at its root paradoxical—fluid and rigid, focused and distracted, in need of constant stimulus and the epitome of willful concentration. Moreover, his assessment considers that a key reason for new things is their ability to attract attention. That attention is in "ongoing crisis" thus means it is an opportunity, one that might create material as well as cultural resources. We therefore should not think about the mental processes of attention—the functions of our senses, our brains, and our bodies—without considering their social construction and economic management.

These issues may be put toward an enriched understanding of music history. One place to begin is with a deeper engagement with how audiences at different historical periods and in diverse cultural contexts learn to attend. Scholarship in the area of sound studies has begun this important work,[50] but there is more to be done, especially in applying these insights to consider how innovations in musical style, sound technology, circulation and distribution, etc., inspire different kinds of attending practices over time. Likewise, to the degree that music has served as a blueprint for attention in other arenas or been utilized to manage affective response and behavior as a result of "inattentive" listening, attention can highlight the long-standing importance of popular music for capitalism and the state from another direction.

Attention as a Valuable Quantity

Attention is also a way of speaking about, structuring, and monitoring perceptual experiences so that they may be quantified. This is most evident in media industries' practices of determining the exposure of different goods, through ratings, "mindshare," and the like.[51] In the new media environment, new tools for measuring attention have emerged, and alongside them new definitions of what it means to attend and new strategies for monetizing that attention. This importantly raises the question of interactivity, which we might in this particular context define as strategies designed to involve the user in the harnessing of her attention. Likewise, as scholars such as Marc Andrejevic have attested, in digital media environments the act of paying attention may lend itself to surveillance, revealing more and more information about our habits and preferences.[52]

The contemporary capabilities are worthy of historicization in at least two ways. First, they raise the possibility of new kinds of historical evidence presently being created in attempts to measure attention. For instance, the data on listening collected by music services such as iTunes or Last.FM come to mind as one example of these new types of evidence.[53] Second, they are a useful reminder that media companies have long strived to obtain data on the attending practices of their consumers. How, as popular music historians, can we make sense of the evolution of these "new media" techniques? Moreover, how have these data been quantified and put to use in the development of the music industry?

Conclusion: Attention as a Precipitate of Circulation

To apply the aforementioned quotation from Lee and LiPuma to the present case, the circulation of music is a phenomenon which itself presumes an attending audience and in that process creates that audience. These are insights which have played a role in scholarship on radio but might be adapted to fit other realms of popular music historiography, buoyed by insights from the digital media context. For instance, considering how the movement of music creates contexts for consumption accounts for the phenomenological aspects of music consumption—that it happens in real time but also that notions of what it means to "happen" are themselves shaped by the observer. Attention therefore provides an entry point into thinking about how music is deployed to create particular audiences at particular moments, in ways that might be used to build future audiences or construct upcoming events.

Put differently, this last point underscores how attention is not only phenomenological but also promotional, used to generate even more attention and circulation.[54] Yet, because all attention is not qualitatively the same, it only partly achieves the uses to which it is put as an instrument for measuring the relative value of cultural objects. Richard Caves supports this point when he notes that for cultural goods, "'buzz'—a critical mass of favorable, or at least involved, discussion—is treasured among those who promote the sale of creative goods."[55] That buzz need only be "involved" rather than "favorable" leads to two conclusions. First, buzz (and its cousin, hype) is recursive and self-fulfilling. But second, buzz may result in diverse styles of attention at any given moment—that is, it may be meaningful and engaged, or it may be somewhat more distracted.

Thus, if attention is a phenomenon that happens in time, it therefore can be observed as a phenomenon. Here we might take a page from Elizabeth Currid and Sarah Williams, whose work uses photographic images of space to determine how much "buzz" certain cultural events produced.[56] As historians, we might adopt similar strategies, also keeping in mind that buzz begets buzz, and that these phenomena create spaces for attention and inattention simultaneously.

The ideas above are certainly not exhaustive. But what they suggest is that considering attention may be a way to incorporate contemporary methodological practices toward historical ends as well as to see the history being generated in the here and now. It might be the case, even, that a focus on attention as it relates to our own historiography goes part of the way in achieving this task. As Leo Treitler explains in *Music and the Historical Imagination,* historians of music are always required to consider "music's insistence on its presentness."[57] He continues elsewhere:

> All music, except that which has not yet been composed, or performed, or thought of, is music of the past. On the other hand, all music insofar as it is or might be the object of the historian's attention, is in the historian's present as tradition. . . . It isn't the pastness of our objects that distinguishes them as historical, or us as historians. It is our interest in them as objects (or acts) in tradition.[58]

Our own attending practices as historians can thus be models for the reconceptualization of how attention is central to understanding what history is. We have always been, as Treitler suggests, historians of the present. The possibilities and quandaries of digital media thus bring an added challenge: to become "presentarians" of the past. We must abandon stark contrasts between new and old to recognize—finally, fully—the requirement of conceiving of media as something that is always already both and neither.

Notes

1. Sisario, "In Death as in Life."
2. Lipsitz, *Time Passages,* 99.
3. Davenport and Beck, *The Attention Economy;* Smith, "Designing Organizations"; Goldhaber, "The Attention Economy."
4. See, for example, Jones, "Music That Moves"; Lee and LiPuma, "Cultures of Circulation."
5. Milner, *Perfecting Sound Forever;* Sterne, *The Audible Past;* Millard, *America on Record.*
6. Milner, *Perfecting Sound Forever.*
7. Gitelman, *Always Already New,* 5.
8. Wallach, "Poetics," 35, 37.
9. Peters, "And Lead Us Not," 18.
10. Marx and Engels, "Manifesto," 476.
11. On co-optation, see, for example, Frank, *The Conquest of Cool.* On "creative destruction," see, for example, Schumpeter "The Process of Creative Destruction." On "flexible accumulation," see, for example, Harvey, *The Condition of Postmodernity.*
12. Suisman, *Selling Sounds,* 57.
13. Hirsch, "Processing Fads and Fashions"; Denisoff, *Solid Gold.*
14. Leyshon et al., "On the Reproduction," 186.
15. Hakanen, "Counting Down," 97.
16. Sisario, "In Death as in Life."
17. Jones and Featherly, "Re-viewing Rock Writing"; Powers, "Bruce Springsteen."
18. Negus, "The Work of Cultural Intermediaries"; Bourdieu, *Distinctions.*
19. Baudrillard, "The Ideological Genesis of Needs," 71.
20. Keightley, "Long Play," 375–376.
21. Ibid., 380, 382.
22. Ibid., 384.
23. For example, see Bailey, "Faithful or Foolish," 142–143.
24. Bailey, "Faithful or Foolish"; Shane, "Modern Radio Formats," 7; Powers, "Rock Criticism," 262.
25. Grainge, "Nostalgia and Style," 28, 29.
26. Bolter and Grusin, *Remediation,* 5.
27. To wit, even the authors' points about music focus on the visuality of remediation. See ibid., 42–43.
28. Bolter and Grusin, *Remediation,* 11.
29. Kassabian, "Ubiquitous Listening,"138.
30. Ibid., 131.
31. Leyshon et al., "On the Reproduction," 182–183.
32. Gitelman, *Always Already New,* 145.
33. Ibid., 147.
34. Ibid.
35. Harvey, "To Hold."
36. Wasik, *And Then There's This,* 49–50.
37. Gitelman, *Always Already New,* 147.

38. Davenport and Beck, *The Attention Economy,* 20–21.
39. Ibid., 2.
40. Bauman, *Liquid Modernity.*
41. Fisher, *Media and New Capitalism,* 6.
42. Bauman, *Liquid Modernity,* 125.
43. Lee and LiPuma, "Cultures of Circulation," 192.
44. Benkler, *The Wealth of Networks.*
45. Gladwell, *The Tipping Point.*
46. Anderson, *The Long Tail.*
47. Crary, *Suspensions of Perception,* 1.
48. Ibid., 3, emphasis in original.
49. Ibid., 13–14.
50. For example, see Sterne, *The Audible Past;* Milner, *Perfecting Sound Forever.*
51. See, for instance, Bermejo, "Audience Manufacture."
52. Andrejevic, "The Work of Being Watched."
53. Much of this information is currently proprietary, protected under corporate privacy policies. However, in the case of Last.FM and services such as iLike on Facebook, interesting aspects of this information are public.
54. One example of this is the musical promotional service Tweet for a Track (http://www.tweetforatrack.com), which allows users to obtain music for free in exchange for mentioning it via Twitter or Facebook.
55. Caves, *Creative Industries,* 181.
56. Currid and Williams, "The Geography of Buzz."
57. Treitler, *Music and the Historical Imagination,* 1.
58. Ibid., 47.

Works Cited

Anderson, Chris. *The Longer Long Tail: Why the Future of Business Is Selling Less of More.* New York: Hyperion, 2008.

Andrejevic, Marc. "The Work of Being Watched: Interactive Media and the Exploitation of Self-Disclosure." *Critical Studies in Media Communication* 19, no. 2 (2002): 230–248.

Bailey, Steve. "Faithful or Foolish: The Emergence of the 'Ironic Cover Album' and Rock Culture." *Popular Music & Society* 26, no. 2 (2003): 141–159.

Baudrillard, Jean. "The Ideological Genesis of Needs." In *The Consumer Society Reader,* edited by Juliet B. Schor and Douglas B. Holt, 57–80. New York: The New Press, 2000.

Bauman, Zygmunt. *Liquid Modernity.* Cambridge, UK: Polity Press, 2000.

Benkler, Yochai. *The Wealth of Networks: How Social Production Transforms Markets and Freedom.* New Haven, CT: Yale University Press, 2006.

Bermejo, Fernando. "Audience Manufacture in Historical Perspective: From Broadcasting to Google." *New Media & Society* 11, nos. 1 & 2 (2009): 133–154.

Bolter, Jay David, and Richard Grusin. *Remediation: Understanding New Media.* Cambridge, MA: MIT Press, 2000.

Bourdieu, Pierre. *Distinctions: A Social Critique of the Judgment of Taste*. Cambridge, MA: Harvard University Press, 1984.

Caves, Richard. *Creative Industries: Contracts between Art and Commerce.* Cambridge, MA: Harvard University Press, 2000.

Crary, Jonathan. *Suspensions of Perception: Attention, Spectacle, and Modern Culture.* Cambridge, MA: MIT Press, 1999.

Currid, Elizabeth, and Williams, Sarah. "The Geography of Buzz: Art, Culture, and the Social Milieu in Los Angeles and New York." *Journal of Economic Geography* 10, no. 3 (2010): 423–451.

Davenport, Thomas, and Beck, John. *The Attention Economy: Understanding the New Currency of Business.* Cambridge, MA: Harvard Business Press, 2001.

Denisoff, R. Serge. *Solid Gold: The Popular Record Industry.* New Brunswick, NJ: Transaction Books, 1975.

Fisher, Eran. *Media and New Capitalism in the Digital Age: The Spirit of Networks.* New York: Palgrave Macmillan, 2010.

Frank, Thomas. *The Conquest of Cool: Business Culture, Counterculture, and the Rise of Hip Consumerism.* Chicago: University of Chicago Press, 1998.

Gitelman, Lisa. *Always Already New: Media, History, and the Data of Culture.* Cambridge, MA: MIT Press, 2006.

Gladwell, Malcolm. *The Tipping Point: How Little Things Can Make a Big Difference.* New York: Little, Brown and Company, 2002.

Goldhaber, Michael. "The Attention Economy and the Net." *First Monday* 2, no. 4 (1997). Accessed May 21, 2010. http://firstmonday.org/htbin/cgiwrap/bin/ojs/index.php/fm/article/view/519/440.

Grainge, Paul. "Nostalgia and Style in Retro America: Moods, Modes, and Media Recycling." *Journal of American and Comparative Cultures* 23, no. 1 (2000): 27–34.

Hakanen, Ernest. "Counting Down to Number One: The Evolution of the Meaning of Popular Music Charts." *Popular Music* 17, no. 1 (1998): 95–111.

Harvey, David. *The Condition of Postmodernity: An Enquiry into the Origins of Cultural Change.* Cambridge, MA: Blackwell, 1990.

Harvey, Eric. "To Hold You in Time: Animal Collective Fandom and the Pre-history of a Digital Music Commodity." Paper presented at the International Association for the Study of Popular Music conference, April 8–11 2010.

Hirsch, Paul. "Processing Fads and Fashions: An Organization-Set Analysis of Cultural Industry Systems." *The American Journal of Sociology* 77, no. 4 (1972): 639–659.

Jones, Steve. "Music That Moves: Popular Music, Distribution and Network Technologies." *Cultural Studies* 16, no. 2 (2002): 213–232.

———, and Kevin Featherly. "Re-viewing Rock Writing: Narratives of Popular Music Criticism." In *Pop Music and the Press,* edited by Steve Jones, 19–40. Philadelphia: Temple University Press, 2002.

Kassabian, Anahid. "Ubiquitous Listening." In *Popular Music Studies,* edited by David Hesmondhalgh and Keith Negus, 131–142. London: Arnold, 2002.

Keightley, Keir. "Long Play: Adult-Oriented Popular Music and the Temporal Logics of the Post-war Sound Recording Industry in the USA." *Media, Culture & Society* 26, no. 3 (2004): 375–391.

Lee, Benjamin, and LiPuma, Edward. "Cultures of Circulation: The Imaginations of Modernity." *Public Culture* 14 no. 1 (2002): 191–213.

Leyshon, Andrew, Peter Webb, Shaun French, Nigel Thrift, and Louise Crewe. "On the Reproduction of the Musical Economy after the Internet." *Media, Culture & Society* 27, no. 2 (2005): 177–209.

Lipsitz, George. *Time Passages: Collective Memory and American Popular Culture.* Minneapolis: University of Minnesota Press, 1991.

Marx, Karl and Engels, Friedrich. "Manifesto of the Communist Party." In *The Marx-Engels Reader,* edited by Robert C. Tucker, 473–500. New York: W.W. Norton and Company.

Millard, Andre. *America on Record: A History of Recorded Sound.* New York: Cambridge University Press, 1995.

Milner, Greg. *Perfecting Sound Forever: An Aural History of Recorded Music.* New York: Farber and Farber, 2009.

Negus, Keith. "The Work of Cultural Intermediaries and the Enduring Distance between Production and Consumption." *Cultural Studies* 16, no. 4 (2002): 501–515.

Peters, Ben. "And Lead Us Not into Thinking the New Is New: A Bibliographic Case for New Media History." *New Media & Society* 11, nos. 1 & 2 (2009): 13–30.

Powers, Devon. "Bruce Springsteen, Rock Criticism, and the Music Business: Towards a Theory and History of Hype." *Popular Music & Society* 34, no. 3 (2011): 1–17.

———. "Rock Criticism and Intellectual History at the *Village Voice.*" Ph.D. diss., New York University, 2008.

Schumpeter, Joseph A. "The Process of Creative Destruction." In *Capitalism, Socialism, and Democracy,* by Joseph A. Schumpeter, 81–86. New York: Routledge, 1994.

Shane, Ed. "Modern Radio Formats: Trends and Possibilities." *Journal of Radio Studies* 3 (1995–1996): 3–9.

Sisario, Ben. "In Death as in Life, Michael Jackson Sets Music Sales Records." *New York Times,* July 2, 2009.

Smith, Herbert. "Designing Organizations for an Information-Rich World." In *Computers, Communications, and the Public Interest,* edited by Martin Greenberger, 37–72. Baltimore: Johns Hopkins University Press, 1971.

Sterne, Jonathan. *The Audible Past: Cultural Origins of Sound Recording.* Raleigh, NC: Duke University Press, 2003.

Suisman, David. *Selling Sounds: The Commercial Revolution in American Music.* Cambridge, MA: Harvard University Press, 2009.

Treitler, Leo. *Music and the Historical Imagination.* Cambridge, MA: Harvard University Press, 1989.

Wallach, Jeremy. "The Poetics of Electrosonic Presence: Recorded Music and the Materiality of Sound." *Journal of Popular Music Studies* 15, no. 2 (2003), 34–64.

Wasik, Bill. *And Then There's This: How Stories Live and Die in Viral Culture.* New York: Viking, 2009.

chapter two

"All You'll Need Is a Mobile Couch"

The History of Mobile Television in the United States

Noah Arceneuax

Introduction

As with other forms of emerging media, the development of mobile television has been shaped by a tension between the old and the new. This tension appears in debates about the appropriate content for this medium: does it require new programs customized for the viewing patterns and screen sizes associated with portable phones, or does "mobile television" simply entail traditional, linear programming beamed to miniaturized screens? The quote that serves as the title of this chapter also illustrates this tension between past and present.[1] During the second half of the 20th century, the popular press depicted television consumption as an inherently sedentary activity. The addition of television capabilities to portable phones was thus a point of friction for early observers as it conflated physical mobility with presumably passive viewing. Those individuals actively working in the industry perhaps feel this tension most profoundly as they seek to construct a new form of media but must do so upon foundations established in the past.

The technology for delivering video content to mobile phones has existed for more than a decade, though consumer adoption has not met the initial enthusiastic predictions. Frustration over the slow growth of this industry has been a recurring refrain within the trade press, and in 2008 the Mobile TV World Summit opened with a panel grimly titled "The Death of Mobile TV?"[2] Users have thus far not demonstrated any strong desire for such content or have been unwilling to pay the required fees to do so, a situation no doubt exacerbated by the recent economic recession. As with other forms of mobile communication, the diffusion of this technology has been slower in the United States than in other countries, and it is thus not surprising to find that prior studies of mobile television have devoted most of their attention to other parts of the globe.[3]

This current study is a modest step towards filling this gap in scholarship, outlining some of the regulatory, legal, technical, and economic factors that have influenced the development of mobile television in the United States. The analysis is based on information from popular and trade press articles, previous academic studies, and interviews with several individuals from the mobile television industry, with a focus on the different technologies for disseminating a video signal.[4] Particular attention is given to "legacy issues," the complex web of business deals, technical standards, and regulations created for earlier technologies that present formidable obstacles for new forms of media. The limited success of those services that broadcast television to mobile receivers, using traditional terrestrial broadcasting technologies, in contrast to those services that offer individualized streams to each user, so-called unicasting, can also be read as a possible path for the future of television itself, not merely the mobile variant.

Before proceeding with this analysis of mobile television's history, some clarifications are necessary. The terms *mobile*, *television* as well as the compound *mobile television* are inherently unstable. Scholars of television itself have debated the appropriate definition for their object of study as it has been analyzed as a particular set of industrial relations, a technology, a cultural practice, or some combination thereof.[5] Ongoing technological developments further complicate a precise definition of this medium. Despite such instability, most individuals still speak of "watching television" in a manner distinct from the consumption of other forms of video.[6] This research began from the starting point that *television* and *video* are not synonymous, though it proved impossible to clearly separate these concepts when information about *mobile television* in particular was examined. Industry analysts, wireless companies, and users themselves have used the terms interchangeably too often to make any distinction meaningful.[7] For the purpose of this chapter, then, *mobile television* denotes both the transmission of live events, experienced by the user in a linear fashion, as well as pre-recorded content.

Mobile is also an elusive term. Portable, battery-operated television receivers of the past could certainly be characterized in this manner, such as the handheld Sony Watchman, introduced in 1982. A *Washington Post* article about this device expressed the combination of amusement, wonder, and skepticism often bestowed upon new technologies. The author noted that "Dick Tracy's dream" had come true, referring to the comic-strip detective's mobile videophone, but also the absurdity of trying to read any text that appeared on screen.[8] A number of companies came out with miniature receivers in the 1980s, including watch-phones with liquid crystal displays, though they found limited success outside a small core of early adopters. Television broadcasting was not optimized for these devices, and their image and sound quality were uniformly panned. The one positive, recurring message within the popular press coverage of these devices, however, was their appeal for sports enthusiasts.[9] It seemed that viewers were willing to suffer the slings and arrows of unreadable text, blurry images, and tinny sound if it meant they could follow their beloved team.

The emphasis in this chapter is specifically on the addition of television reception capabilities to portable phones. Content producers in the past did not design separate channels for portable televisions, as they are doing now. Mobile television, according to this current analysis, pertains to new techniques of broadcasting in which the signal is customized for the screen size, battery power, and reception capabilities of properly enabled phones and can for these reasons be categorized as a medium distinct from traditional television. Video receivers in vehicles represent another aspect of the phenomenon (as well as representing the amorphous nature of the electronic experience now denoted by the term *television*) though space limitations preclude a proper assessment of this topic.

At the time of this writing, it is not clear which technologies and economic models will dominate the mobile television industry in the future. Exemplifying the fluctuating nature of this emerging medium, one of the previously dominant services in this field, Flo TV, announced its demise while this chapter was in the revision stage.[10] Further changes will no doubt occur before this work eventually finds its way to the bound, printed page. The material presented here should thus be perceived as a historical snapshot, with observations that will hopefully continue to resonate in the coming years. Several acronyms are used in this chapter, as it is impossible to discuss mobile media without addressing the alphabet soup of technical standards that has developed. Unless necessary for the discussion, these acronyms have not been fully spelled out.

Mobile Television in the United States

Different technologies for broadcasting television to mobile devices have been developed around the world; DVB-H dominates in Europe, South Korea utilizes DMB, while the most developed market in the world, Japan, relies upon ISDB-T. A handset designed to receive one signal will not receive another although technically it would be possible to create such a device. This situation recalls the original era of mechanical television when different companies, each promoting their own versions of visual broadcasting, transmitted low-resolution, silent, black-and-white images.[11] A receiver built for one type of signal could not receive a transmission from a rival station.

These international technologies are mentioned here in order to highlight the atypical nature of the United States. The American television industry is currently testing ATSC-M/H, yet another method for broadcasting to portable receivers. As part of the transition to digital television in the United States, broadcasters switched to a transmission system known as ATSC (so named for the Advanced Television Systems Committee), with the mobile variation of this format established in 2009.[12] Existing television stations can utilize a small portion of their current spectrum allocation to deliver their signal to mobile devices. Because television stations have been given their spectrum allocations free of charge, the policies of Federal Communications Commission (FCC) make it difficult to monetize these airwaves via a subscription-based service. Observers have therefore spoken of this new system of broadcasting as free, with advertising providing the revenue, though some form of user subscription is technically possible. The Open Mobile Video Coalition (OMVC), a consortium of some of the largest broadcasters and technology companies, is supporting the new standard with consumer trials in several U.S. cities.[13]

Until recently, San Diego-based Qualcomm used a portion of the old analog television spectrum, channel 55, to broadcast television to mobile devices using its own proprietary technology: Flo (forward link only) TV. The president of Flo TV praised broadcasting as an efficient method for delivering electronic content, stating that the cost remains constant if there are "one or one million users."[14] By partnering with the cellular providers Verizon and AT&T, Flo TV also offered some forms of interactivity; Flo TV delivered the content to the viewers, and the phone networks carried information back to the source. Users of other cellular networks could not receive the service on their handsets, indicating the significant gatekeeping role that cellular providers have had, and continue to have, upon the development of mobile content. Qualcomm did not release subscriber numbers, though one 2009 report estimated the number at one million.[15]

MobiTV uses an alternative distribution method for video known as unicasting. With this system, cellular providers use their existing wireless networks to offer a modified form of Internet-protocol TV. Because a dedicated connection must be made with each subscriber, which ties up a small slice of the spectrum, detractors claim this to be an inefficient delivery method. In the worst-case scenario, too much bandwidth devoted to video content could clog the network. AT&T's difficulty in supplying reliable service to iPhones is a related example, as these devices consume far more bandwidth than earlier mobile phones. To its benefit, unicasting offers users more control of the viewing experience and is inherently interactive. In a recent report touting its broadcasts of the World Cup, MobiTV boasted of ten million subscribers.[16]

For the same reasons that establishing a precise definition of *mobile television* is difficult, ascertaining the number of viewers in the United States is equally problematic. The subscriber estimates cited above do not account for individuals with web-capable phones who access video content online, using traditional Internet technologies. Also omitted are users of Slingbox, a television accessory that streams the channels from a user's home television to other devices, including phones. One report from the Nielsen Company stated that 20.3 million viewers watched some form of mobile video during the first quarter of 2010.[17] Given that there are more than 300 million viewers for standard television, the mobile variant has considerable room to grow if users indeed show a desire for such services.

Turf Wars in the Air

The technologies of broadcasting and mobile telephony both utilize the electromagnetic spectrum, and decisions regarding the allocation of this resource have fundamentally shaped the respective industries. As mobile television overlaps both of these previously separate phenomena, an overview of spectrum allocation is necessary. With a touch of hyperbole, the *New York Times* called arguments over spectrum "the twenty-first century's equivalent of the nineteenth century's wars between ranchers and farmers."[18]

The government's policy of spectrum allocation dates to the Radio Act of 1912, the first significant attempt to regulate wireless telegraphy in the United States. The stated goal of these regulations was to prevent users from overlapping, and canceling out, one another's transmissions, though decisions regarding spectrum allocation have also determined, in many instances, which broadcasters thrived and which ones failed.[19] The allocation of television broadcasting to very-high frequency waves (VHF) in the 1940s, along with the decision to give stations a six mega-hertz slice of the spectrum, had a profound influence on the television industry as the situation allowed only a limited number of stations in any given city.[20] Contributing to the spectrum scarcity were the "white spaces," or empty portions of the spectrum placed between each channel. This arrangement was necessary due to the poor reception capabilities of the earliest receivers, and this space has remained unused.

These early FCC decisions regarding television are more than a matter of historic interest, as these parameters continue to shape the media landscape. With the development of color and then digital television broadcasting, the government would not grant approval until systems were developed that could conform to the original spectrum boundaries.[21] The digital television system that was ultimately adopted, ATSC, can deliver a high-definition signal using less than six megahertz, though local stations claim they nonetheless require the same amount of spectrum as before to offer such services as alternate channels and mobile content. To cynical observers, the adoption of the ATSC-M/H standard is less about delivering robust content to consumers and more about the television industry solidifying "squatters' rights" claims to its spectrum allocation.

Wireless companies were beneficiaries of the 2009 transition to digital television, as the FCC simultaneously cleared out channels 52–69, part of the ultra-high frequency (UHF) spectrum. AT&T and Verizon acquired most of the newly available frequencies at significant cost, though wireless companies are growing so rapidly that they continually seek additional spectrum. This recent re-allocation is only the latest skirmish in the ongoing squabble between mobile phone companies and television stations. The idea for subdividing radio frequencies into smaller "cells," a technique for maximizing the on-air traffic on a particular channel, had existed for decades before the FCC authorized the launch of America's first cell phone systems in 1983.[22] The FCC's reluctance to take spectrum away from television was a critical factor in this delay. As wireless companies plan for the delivery of more types of content, including mobile television, arguments over spectrum allocation (especially the unused white spaces) have intensified.

Early Attempts

According to Jim Brailean, one of the founders of PacketVideo, his company offered the first public demonstration of a video-capable phone at an industry trade show in Denver in 1999.[23] Brailean, who had been working to achieve this feat for years, recalled that the phone was onstage connected to a Cassiopeia, one of the first models of a personal digital assistant (PDA). The video originated from a camera in the company's San Diego office and was sent to the phone via a cable, with the PDA serving as a larger display screen. This scenario is suggestive of a possible path for mobile television's future development. A small, portable device may function as the receiver though the content could be displayed elsewhere.

Many colleagues were skeptical that PacketVideo could ever successfully stream video to a phone. An engineer who had worked on the AT&T picture-phone of the 1960s urged Brailean to abandon his idea.[24] This earlier invention relied upon existing phone lines to deliver video along with voice communication though consumer adoption failed for reasons that are still debated.[25] AT&T and others in the industry interpreted the commercial failure as a signal of consumer disinterest.

Brailean recalled that other individuals were equally pessimistic: "We used to hear all the time, 'What are people going to do? Watch TV on their phone?' We thought yes."[26]

Following this demonstration, PacketVideo began working with several companies, both in the United States and internationally, though it would be a few years before any American cellular operator adopted mobile video as a regular service. The shortage of video-capable phones was one reason for the delay, combined with the burst of the technology bubble in the early 2000s.

The year 2005 saw a marked increase in mobile television, with Verizon offering a video on-demand service (VCast), relying upon PacketVideo technology. The video clips were delivered over the company's own wireless network. The same year also saw a growth of "mobile virtual network operators," known in the industry as MVNOs. These entities do not control any spectrum of their own but instead license spectrum from an established cellular provider. In addition to traditional text and voice communication, several of these MVNOs also offered video and multimedia content to their subscribers. ESPN launched such a service, emphasizing its sports programming, with a promotional campaign during the 2006 Super Bowl.[27] Amp'd Mobile was an MVNO backed by the MTV network and Universal Music that targeted younger subscribers.[28] *Li'l Bush*, an animated series that debuted on the service, later migrated to the Comedy Central network, perhaps the first instance of a program originating on mobile television before moving to a traditional network. Neither of these companies was successful, with ESPN Mobile continuing to operate as a content, rather than service, provider.

Broadcasting to Mobiles

Prior to the current experiments with ATSC-M/H, there were at least three earlier attempts to launch mobile television broadcasting systems in the United States. Two of these companies, Modeo and HiWire, utilized DVB-H technology, the Nokia-backed system that is dominant in Europe. The difference between DVB-H and ATSC-M/H, however, proved to be an obstacle for commercial adoption of both projects.

Modeo, which first tested its system in Pittsburgh in 2005, operated in the 1.6 giga-hertz range of the spectrum.[29] Michael Schueppert, the founder of Modeo, knew that American television was already transitioning towards the system of ATSC broadcasting, though there was never any thought about modifying this system for the new service. ATSC was designed to replicate the characteristics of NTSC, the older form of analog broadcasting. In the original scenario, television receivers were envisioned as stationary devices that received signals from rooftop antennas, and ATSC was similarly optimized. Portable televisions, which constantly change location and are often operated inside buildings, could thus not receive ATSC signals very well. DVB-H, in Schueppert's opinion, is a better method for delivering video to mobile devices as it relies on COFDM (coded orthogonal frequency division multiplexing). COFDM is a technique for squeezing a large amount of data into a limited range of frequencies, and digital broadcasting systems outside of the United States rely upon COFDM. When the FCC originally evaluated which system of digital television to adopt, there was heated debate between those who wanted some form of COFDM and those who supported ATSC, which does not utilize this transmitting technique.[30] The government eventually sided with the latter, as ATSC requires less power (and thus less money) to distribute a signal over large geographic areas. The debate continued even after the FCC endorsed ATSC in 1996, with *Broadcast Engineering* noting that the vitriolic exchanges rivaled the feud of the Hatfields and the McCoys.[31]

One downside of Modeo's service was the expense necessary to build a national broadcast network. Its rival Qualcomm, which had already begun the original Flo TV service, meanwhile displayed the deep pockets and willingness to fund its own broadcast network, even before consumer demand had materialized. It was also apparent in 2006 that whenever the FCC did develop a standard that television stations would use for mobile content, this standard would have to be within the ATSC family. Modeo's incompatible COFDM system could thus be at a disadvantage. (Recall that the ATSC-M/H standard now under development does not require the creation of a new broadcast network and functions within the existing spectrum allocation.) After the service was officially discontinued in 2007, Modeo's parent company sold its spectrum for approximately ten times what it had cost in 2004.[32]

HiWire, the next major attempt to launch DVB-H in the United States, conducted an extensive trial in Las Vegas in 2006, using two UHF channels, 54 and 59, to deliver more than a dozen cable television channels to mobile handsets.[33] It proved impossible to get broadcast television networks to participate in the trial, with only PBS agreeing to supply content. Scott Wills, the founder of HiWire, said that distribution rights complicated the situation, noting that "nobody knew if they had the right to do this or not."[34]

Even so HiWire was able to operate in the 700 mega-hertz portion of the spectrum, previously the exclusive domain of the television industry, because its parent company, Aloha Partners, had acquired the rights to these two UHF channels a few years before. At the time, some markets still had UHF television stations with legacy rights to these channels, so offering any kind of national service (television or wireless communication) would not have been possible. After acquiring the rights, Aloha Partners then lobbied Congress for the passage of the DTV Transition Bill, which was signed in 2006. Included in the bill was a mandate that many UHF channels be re-allocated entirely away from television, including the same channels that Aloha possessed. These frequencies possess excellent propagation characteristics and would now be available across the entire nation. HiWire's frequencies were now even more desirable, and Aloha sold this spectrum to AT&T for approximately 2.5 billion dollars.[35] In this regard, both HiWire and Modeo managed to be financially successful even if their respective systems were never adopted.

Qualcomm's version of mobile television also utilized COFDM (just as DVB-H does), though it was a distinct system. As both the manufacturer of the chips necessary to receive the FloTV signal and the provider of the video content, Qualcomm's position closely paralleled that of radio stations of the 1920s. Companies that manufactured radio receivers established many of the first stations, supplying the media content as a way to boost sales of their hardware. Qualcomm previously found great success by inventing CDMA (code division multiple access) technology in the late 1980s.[36] This technology denotes a method for maximizing the traffic on a particular frequency and is now one of the two principal platforms through which wireless communication is conducted (GSM being the other). Perhaps Qualcomm was looking to repeat this feat: to develop a platform that becomes a global standard and then to license the necessary software to as many companies as possible.

After Qualcomm acquired rights to channel 55 in 2003, it publicly demonstrated the technology in 2006, under the original name MediaFlo.[37] In 2007, Verizon offered the service to its subscribers, marketed as VCast TV. A national rollout was impossible, as some cities still had UHF channels on channel 55. AT&T added the service in 2008, and in the middle of 2009, coinciding with the transition to digital television, Flo TV was able to expand into many new markets that had been previously off-limits because of existing television stations. Subscribers could receive approximately twenty different channels, though not all of them were available at all times of the day. This juggling of content was done to squeeze as many channels as possible into the same space needed to send a single television channel in the 1940s.

Late in 2009, Qualcomm also released a stand-alone mobile television receiver, not tied to any phone. Verizon and AT&T handsets capable of receiving the Flo TV signal had not sold as well as hoped, so Qualcomm hoped to expand the subscriber base by selling directly to consumers.[38] An ad during the 2010 Super Bowl promoted the device, echoing ESPN's MVNO launch from a few years before. The company also advertised heavily during the 2010 NBA play-offs with spots that emphasized the ability to view sporting events at any time or place. Qualcomm has publicly admitted to investing approximately 1.5 billion dollars in the Flo service, and so far has not shown the willingness to sell off its spectrum, as Modeo and

HiWire did.[39] In October 2010, Qualcomm announced that it was shutting down Flo TV, with the rebranded services offered to Verizon and AT&T subscribers continuing for an unknown period of time.[40]

MobiTV

A 2010 analysis of the global mobile television industry noted that unicasting "has in many cases ceased to be a viable option, at least in terms of live streaming."[41] A 2007 report from the Mobile DTV Alliance also endorsed broadcasting as the preferred distribution method for mobile television.[42] MobiTV's success is thus a startling exception to such predictions. Sprint added the service to some of its phones in 2003, a feat that was considered such an engineering breakthrough that the Academy of Television Arts & Sciences rewarded it with an Emmy.[43] MobiTV has since established relationships with the other major cellular providers in the United States: AT&T, Verizon, and T-Mobile. A user must have an appropriately enabled handset and pay the necessary fee, and in most instances the service has been relabeled and users may not realize they are accessing the MobiTV service. Owners of iPhones or Android phones can additionally pay to download MobiTV applications, outside of what is offered by the cellular provider.

Paul Scanlan, co-founder and president of MobiTV, recalled one effort to convince Sprint of the viability of its service.[44] After being met with rejections and disbelief that a phone could play video, MobiTV mailed a phone to an executive. Upon opening the box, the executive was stunned that the phone screen was indeed displaying video, choppy low-resolution video to be sure, but moving images nonetheless. The video originated from a television in MobiTV's office and was sent over a wireless data network.

The low frame rate of the early service, which was more akin to a slide show, has increased dramatically over the past few years, as has the number of channels that MobiTV offers. Originally, television networks were reluctant to allow their content to be delivered this way, though Scanlan was able to get approximately twelve channels in 2003, including NBC and Discovery. Two channels were cobbled together by MobiTV in order to supply content that was deemed well suited for mobiles: a music video channel and an animation channel. Regarding justification for the animation channel, Scanlan referred to the "pass back" factor, with parents handing the device to children in the backseat. Some of the channels carry live content, while others are time shifted or otherwise served on demand. At the time of the interview, Scanlan stated that the selection of Pope Benedict, the death of Michael Jackson, and the inauguration of Barack Obama revealed dramatic spikes in audience viewing.

The service now operates like a cable television provider, deriving revenue from monthly subscription fees and advertising revenue. MobiTV sells approximately one-third of the advertising inventory on its channels, with the content providers controlling the rest. Some premium channels cost an additional fee. Scanlan notes that the emphasis has been on premium channels, as free services have not yet developed the critical mass to make advertising viable as the sole revenue stream. The MobiTV service has also been modified and reformatted by each cellular provider, with channel selections and subscription rates varying between companies.

As noted at the start of this chapter, mobile television viewing has not reached the levels predicted years ago, though the medium has developed enough for ASCAP (the American Society of Composers, Authors, and Publishers) to attempt to lay claim to some of the revenue it could develop. MobiTV and ASCAP spent two years in court, arguing over the appropriate royalty payments for music that appeared on the television channels.[45] The rate requested by ASCAP was based on a formula different from the one for traditional television or cable broadcasters, with the organization asking for 41 million dollars to cover an eight-year period. Per a judge's ruling on the case, however, MobiTV will instead pay a more modest $300,000. An enforcement of the original figure could have very well forced the closure of MobiTV.

Conclusion

While the goal of this research has been to analyze the past developments, it is impossible to conclude without some speculation as well. The failure of FloTV, when considered alongside other attempts to broadcast television to mobile devices, suggests that mobile viewers are not interested in consuming whatever video content happens to be on at any given moment. Instead, users prefer the individualized, customized viewing experiences associated with video on-demand, which is precisely the benefit of the unicasting services of MobiTV and others.

The one type of video content that does not conform to this dynamic is the transmission of live events, such as the inauguration of President Obama or sporting events. The repeated intersection of sports and mobile television was an unforeseen, though definitely noticeable, discovery of this research. Terrestrial broadcasting to mobile receivers, to extrapolate then, might be limited in the future to key live events, with other forms of video content delivered on-demand per user request. Under this scenario, mobile television programming would come full circle to the original aesthetic promoted for radio broadcasting in the 1920s: namely, an emphasis on the transmission of live events. Government regulators and those in the broadcast industry promoted the "live" nature of broadcasting as something that phonograph records or cinema could never deliver, going so far as to forbid the use of phonograph records for some radio stations all together.[46] With modern-day viewers able to watch entertainment and news programs whenever they want, through a variety of means, perhaps all forms of broadcast television, not simply the mobile variant, will return to this model of programming.

Another historical repetition is the rise of the next generation of media gatekeepers. Among television scholars, the term *post-network era* has gained currency as a way to describe the 21st-century transformations of the television industry.[47] The growth of video recorders, online outlets, and specialized cable channels has eroded the centralized power possessed by the original networks (a situation made possible by FCC spectrum allocation). Viewers are no longer subject to the hegemony of time slots and can watch content whenever and wherever they choose. When the evolving medium of mobile television is added to the sprawling, interconnected world of modern electronics, perhaps it would be more accurate to refer to a *new network era*. The various cellular providers have become new gatekeepers, and their decisions about which handsets and services to support are a fundamental parameter for the development of mobile media.

This examination of mobile television's evolution also offers specific examples of a more generalizable dynamic regarding all new forms of emerging media. Technologies are not governed by any autonomous logic but are instead intrinsically shaped and molded by human decisions, including ones based on situations that are no longer applicable. FloTV and the other mobile broadcasting systems, for example, had to conform to spectrum allocations optimized for 1940s-era technology. The underlying foundation for American digital television itself, ATSC, was similarly designed for an older paradigm of television consumption (fixed receivers with rooftop antennas), while distribution rights drafted in the pre-mobile landscape have determined what types of content could be offered to mobile viewers. These and other examples indicate that the actions of the past continue to mold, shape, and influence the shape of media yet to come.

Notes

1. Smith, "All You'll Need Is a Mobile Couch."
2. Orgad, "Mobile TV," 197.
3. See, for example, Curwen and Whalley, "Mobile Television"; see also Marcus, Roibas, and Sala, *Mobile TV.*
4. See the appendix at end of this chapter.
5. Brunsdon, "What Is the 'Television?'"
6. Lotz, *The Television Will Be Revolutionized,* 21.

7. Another academic study of mobile TV arrived at the same conclusion. See Montpetit, Klym, and Blain, "The Future of Mobile TV."
8. Shales, "Watchman Cometh."
9. For one example, see Williams, "Tiny TV's Take a Giant Step," 4.
10. Kapko, "Qualcomm Cuts Its Losses on Flo TV."
11. Udelson, *The Great Television Race.*
12. "ATSC Adopts Mobile Digital TV Standard."
13. See official site of OMVC, http://www.openmobilevideo.com.
14. King, "Qualcomm Flo TV Needs Wider Adoption, More Services."
15. Little, "Mobile TV."
16. Shields, "MobiTV World Cup Streams."
17. Nielsen Company, "Three Screen Report, Q1 2010."
18. Labaton, "Turf Fight for the Airways."
19. McChesney, *Telecommunications, Mass Media, and Democracy.*
20. Boddy, "Launching Television."
21. Slotten, *Radio and Television Regulation,* 189–231; Huff, *Regulating the Future,* 137.
22. Brodsky, *The History of Wireless,* 169–180.
23. Interview with Jim Brailean.
24. Balint, "Cell Phone-Video Pioneer Held on."
25. Lipartito, "Picturephone and the Information Age."
26. Interview with Jim Brailean.
27. Hill, "Mobile ESPN Throws in the Towel."
28. Whitney, "Digital Dealmaker."
29. Interview with Michael Schueppert.
30. Huff, *Regulating the Future,* 174.
31. "Pinning Down Mobile TV."
32. Pearce, "Crown Castle Pulls Plug on Modeo."
33. Interview with Scott Wills.
34. Ibid.
35. Kapko, "MediaFLO Alone on Top in Mobile Broadcast TV."
36. Dave Mock, *The Qualcomm Equation.*
37. Interview with Mona Klausing and Tony Lutz.
38. King, "Qualcomm Flo TV Needs Wider Adoption, More Services."
39. Ibid.
40. Kapko, "Qualcomm Cuts Its Losses on Flo TV."
41. Schuurman, De Marez, and Evens, "Content for Mobile Television," 145.
42. Interview with Yoram Solomon; the title of the report was "The Economics of Mobile Broadcast TV."
43. Graham, "TV on Cellphones?"
44. Interview with Paul Scanlan.
45. Duryee, "MobiTV Wins Royalty Case."
46. Bensman, *The Beginning of Broadcast Regulation,* 74–78.
47. Lotz, *Beyond Prime Time.*

Appendix: List of Interviews

Jim Brailean, Co-Founder and CEO of PacketVideo, personal interviews, May 6 and June 4, 2010.

Mona Klausing, Senior Manager, Public Relations; and Tony Lutz, Director Product Management, Qualcomm MediaFlo Technologies, personal interview, April 29, 2010.

Nagaraj Nandhakumar, Senior Vice-President Advanced Technology, LG Electronics, personal interview, July 12, 2010.

Paul Scanlan, Co-Founder and President of MobiTV, personal interviews, May 10 and 26, 2010.

Michael Schueppert, Founder and Former President of Modeo, personal interviews, May 6 and 26, 2010.

Yoram Solomon, Former President of Mobile DTV Alliance, personal interview, May 14, 2010.

Scott Wills, Former President of HiWire, personal interview, June 2, 2010.

Works Cited

"ATSC Adopts Mobile Digital TV Standard." *Digital TV News*, October 16, 2009. Accessed October 11, 2010. http://www.digitaltvnews.net/content/?p=10887.

Balint, Kathryn. "Cell Phone-Video Pioneer Held On." *San Diego Union-Tribune*, May 17, 2005.

Bensman, Marvin. *The Beginning of Broadcast Regulation in the Twentieth Century*. Jefferson, NC: McFarland & Company, 2000.

Boddy, William. "Launching Television: RCA, the FCC, and the Battle for Frequency Allocations, 1940–1947." *Historical Journal of Film, Radio, and Television* 9, no. 1 (1989): 45–57.

Brodsky, Ira. *The History of Wireless: How Creative Minds Produced Technology for the Masses*. St. Louis, MO: Telescope Books, 2008.

Brunsdon, Charlotte. "What Is the 'Television' of Television Studies?" In *The Television Studies Book,* edited by David Lusted and Christine Geraghty, 95–113. London: Arnold, 1997.

Curwen, Peter, and Jason Whalley. "Mobile Television: Technological and Regulatory Issues." *info* 10, no. 1 (2008): 40–64.

Duryee, Tricia. "MobiTV Wins Royalty Case to Standardize Streaming Fees in Mobile." *Moconews.net*, May 14, 2010. Accessed October 11, 2010. http://moconews.net/article/419-mobitv-wins-royalty-case-to-standardized-streaming-fees-in-mobile/.

Graham, Jefferson. "TV on cellphones? Funny but profitable." USAtoday.com, September 27, 2005. Accessed March 16, 2011. http://www.usatoday.com/tech/products/services/2005-09-27-mobitv_x.htm.

Hill, Kelly. "Mobile ESPN Throws in the Towel." *RCR Wireless News*, October 2, 2006. Accessed October 11, 2010. http://www.rcrwireless.com/article/20061002/SUB/610020713/Mobile-ESPN-throws-in-towel.

Huff, W. A. Kelly. *Regulating the Future: Broadcasting Technology and Government Control.* Westport, CT: Greenwood Press, 2001.

Kapko, Matt. "MediaFLO Alone on Top in Mobile Broadcast TV." *RCR Wireless News*, October 15, 2007. Accessed October 11, 2010. http://www.rcrwireless.com/ARTICLE/20071012/SUB/71012022/mediaflo-alone-on-top-in-mobile-broadcast-tv.

———. "Qualcomm Cuts Its Losses on Flo TV." *RCR Wireless News*, October 4, 2010. Accessed October 11, 2010. http://www.rcrwireless.com/article/20101004/CONTENT_MOBILE_MARKETING/101009984/Qualcomm-cuts-its-losses-on-FLO-TV.

King, Ian. "Qualcomm Flo TV Needs Wider Adoption, More Services." *Bloomberg Business Week*, June 16, 2010. Accessed October 12, 2010. http://www.businessweek.com/news/2010–06–16/qualcomm-flo-tv-needs-wider-adoption-more-services-update2-.html.

Labaton, Stephen. "Turf Fight for the Airways." *New York Times*, March 28, 2001.

Lipartito, Kenneth. "Picturephone and the Information Age: The Social Meaning of Failure. *Technology and Culture* 44, no. 1 (2003): 50–81.

Little, Arthur D. (Research Firm). "Mobile TV: Turning on or Switching 0ff?" 2009. Accessed October 11, 2010. www.adl.com/mobiletv.

Lotz, Amanda, ed. *Beyond Prime Time: Television Programming in the Post-network Era.* New York: Routledge, 2009.

———. *The Television Will Be Revolutionized.* New York: New York University Press, 2007.

Marcus, Aaron, Anxo Cereijo Roibas, and Riccardo Sala, eds. *Mobile TV: Customizing Content and Experience.* London: Springer-Verlag, 2010.

McChesney, Robert. *Telecommunications, Mass Media, and Democracy: The Battle for the Control of U.S. Broadcasting, 1928–1935.* New York: Oxford University Press, 1993.

Mock, Dave. *The Qualcomm Equation.* New York: Amacom, 2005.

Montpetit, Marie-Jose, Natalie Klym, and Emmanuel Blain. "The Future of Mobile TV: When Mobile TV Meets the Internet and Social Networking." In *Mobile TV: Customizing Content and Experience*, edited by Aaron Marcus, Anxo Cereijo Roibas, and Riccardo Sala, 305–326. London: Springer-Verlag, 2010.

Nielsen Company. "Three Screen Report, Q1 2010." Accessed October 11, 2010. http://en-us.nielsen.com/content/nielsen/en_us/insights/nielsen_a2m2_three.html.

Orgad, Shani. "Mobile TV: Old and New in the Construction of an Emergent Technology." *Convergence* 15, no. 2 (2009): 197–214.

Pearce, James. "Crown Castle Pulls Plug on Modeo: Sells Spectrum to Private Equity." *Moconews.net*, July 23, 2007. Accessed October 11, 2010. http://moconews.net/article/419-crown-castle-sells-modeo-to-private-equity/.

"Pinning Down Mobile TV." *Broadcast Engineering*, June 1, 2007. Accessed October 11, 2010. http://broadcastengineering.com/products/broadcasting_pinning_down_mobile/.

Schuurman, Dmitri, Lieven De Marez, and Tom Evens. "Content for Mobile Television: Issues Regarding a New Mass Medium within Today's ICT Environment." In *Mobile TV: Customizing Content and Experience*, edited by Aaron Marcus, Anxo Cereijo Roibas, and Riccardo Sala, 143–163. London: Springer-Verlag, 2010.

Shales, Tom. "Watchman Cometh: Any Series Is a Mini-series on Sony's New Teensy TV." *The Washington Post*, December 8, 1982.

Shields, Mike. "MobiTV World Cup Streams Top 88 Million Minutes." *MediaWeek*, July 7, 2010.

Slotten, Hugh R. *Radio and Television Regulation: Broadcast Technology in the United States, 1920–1960.* Baltimore: Johns Hopkins University Press, 2000.

Smith, Brad. "All You'll Need Is a Mobile Couch." *Wireless Week*, January 10, 2000.

Udelson, Joseph H. *The Great Television Race: A History of the American Television Industry, 1925–1941.* Tuscaloosa: University of Alabama Press, 1982.

Whitney, Daisy. "Digital Dealmaker." *Television Week*, May 29, 2006.

Williams, Stephen. "Tiny TV's Take a Giant Step." *Newsday*, May 22, 1988.

chapter three

Cutting the Cord and "Crying Socialist Wolf"

Unwiring the Public and Producing the Third Place

Stephanie Ricker Schulte

Introduction

In 2004, the mayor of Philadelphia revealed a plan to blanket a 135-square-mile area with Wi-Fi (short for "wireless fidelity").[1] Mayor John Street characterized his $10 million initiative as an "effort to build a 21st century infrastructure" meant to "revitalize the economically depressed city, particularly its decaying inner-city neighborhoods."[2] Philadelphia was the first large American city to attempt to bridge the digital divide with Wi-Fi.[3] Despite public support for the plan, Verizon "cried socialist wolf," launching an aggressive lobbying campaign and eventually petitioning the state legislature to block the initiative on the grounds it "distorted private competition."[4] In the end, the battle over Wi-Fi in Philadelphia resulted in a compromise. The municipality moved forward with its plan, but private corporations retained "right of first refusal over a municipality's ability to provide broadband services."[5] In fourteen states, including Texas and Missouri, state legislatures also restricted local governments from offering broadband services.[6] Pro-corporate forces won out by in part arguing as the New Millennium Research Council think tank did: "*Wi-Fi is not a public good* and is not an economically efficient or publicly desired product."[7] The verdicts seem surprising given the celebratory rhetoric widely available about the Internet at the time. News media, policy makers, provider corporations, and futurists assumed Wi-Fi Internet would revolutionize work, the

LEEDS UNIVERSITY LIBRARY

economy, and democracy by connecting all citizens to a great new online public sphere. In 1999 the *Economist* noted the "remarkable unanimity" that Wi-Fi would "lead to a computing revolution that dwarfs the one initiated by the PC."[8]

This chapter investigates how this disconnection happened—how Wi-Fi was on the one hand hyped as nurturing and *necessary* for national health and on the other hand deemed not a "public good." The chapter dives into the recent historical archive to trace the narratives (preceding and shaping the discussion of smart phones) that circulated about Wi-Fi technology as it began to spread widely in the late 1990s and early 2000s. This historical inquiry illustrates that because Wi-Fi uses public spectrum and is used in private spaces like cafés as well as public spaces like parks, its expansion required negotiation between government agencies, Internet providers, computer companies, small businesses, and users. By outlining the central tensions in this historical moment of negotiation, this chapter studies the ways Wi-Fi was made meaningful by a number of actors, including journalists, policy makers, providers, businesses, and users. Ultimately, this work illustrates that the battles over Wi-Fi were rooted in historical debates about the function of the public sphere: Should it be designed for economic productivity or civic engagement? Therefore, the public debate about Wi-Fi was also a debate about how to reconcile capitalism and democracy, deeply embedded in tensions about how to be both citizens and consumers.

By no means is this an exhaustive study of all popular representations of Wi-Fi. It is instead a study of popular representations as they emerge in a variety of venues with different intended audiences. Investigating diverse sources together is one way of beginning to sketch the shape of discourse, to outline the "uncoordinated conjunctures" that "have the knitted-together power of a discourse."[9] In this process, this chapter does history as media scholar Lisa Gitelman suggests, by "putting together narratives about events based on interpreting the 'indexical survivals' or inscriptions that form a fragmentary record of the past."[10] It not only illustrates the intersectionality in the cultural and policy spheres but also provides a testament to the productive power of ideas. In *Mobile Communication and Society,* Manuel Castells and colleagues survey current social research in global meta-analysis of the "transformation of human communication by the rise and diffusion of wireless digital communication technologies."[11] This chapter adds a layer of history and cultural production to Castells's work by discussing how the assumptions made about the public sphere, economic productivity, national security, citizenship, and consumership produce both the communication infrastructure itself as well as the policies surrounding it.

The Emergence of Wi-Fi

First introduced in 1997, "Wi-Fi" refers to services or products that use a standard means (IEEE802.11) and transmitters to connect to the Internet remotely.[12] "Wi-Fi" beat out "FlankSpeed" and "DragonFly" to become the user-friendly version of "IEEE802.11b compliant."[13] The first several years of the 21st century marked not only the spread of Wi-Fi but also the hype about it. The years when it was what Gitelman calls "new"—when we "knew" Wi-Fi was coming but did not yet know what it would be or become—were the crucial years that determined its future shape.[14] During these years, a series of debates about its expansion took place in news media and policy spheres: Who would use it? How would they use it? Who would pay for it? What effects would it have?

The history of Wi-Fi is deeply embedded in the political history of the 1980s and 1990s. In their "Brief History of Wi-Fi," *Economist* journalists wrote that the "government seems actively to have guided innovation," quoting a telecom expert as saying, "Wi-Fi is a creature of regulation, created more by lawyers than by engineers." Although it was invented in 1968 in San Diego by Irwin Jacobs, a professor, it was not technologically viable until 1985, when the Federal Communications Commission (FCC) made available parts of the spectrum the so-called garage bands—previously marked for noncommunication activities, such as microwave ovens that use radio waves to heat food. In this landmark decision, this spectrum became available for communication "on the condition that any devices using these bands would have to steer around interference from other equipment."[15] Although some precedent existed, the policy shift was unconventional given that very little spectrum was available without a license. Thus, the FCC made it possible for and encouraged "communication entrepreneurs to develop technology utilizing the garbage band frequencies without need for intrusive government regulation."[16] Although digital divide inequalities persisted, by 2006, 219 million Americans had Wi-Fi access and 98 percent of Americans lived in counties with multiple Wi-Fi providers.[17] By 2007, over 206,000 hot spots (or spaces) existed worldwide in 135 countries.[18]

The Wi-Fi-compatible Apple iBook computer with its "AirPort" standard feature was instrumental in the rapid growth and mainstreaming of Wi-Fi use. In the wake of its 1999 release, other computer manufacturers offered Wi-Fi capability options.[19] With the simplification and resulting popularization of connecting came increasing demand for wired public spaces. In the early 2000s, a number of public and private entities began creating hot spots with Wi-Fi. In 2001, Starbucks provided coffee customers with Wi-Fi access in major cities in the United States and Europe.[20] Starbucks reportedly made this move in recognition that 90 percent of its customers "were Internet users" and because Wi-Fi would give Starbucks a "great opportunity to enhance our existing customers' in-store experience as well as attract new customers to our retail locations."[21] Although the technology was new, the idea was not. In the 1600s and 1700s, cafés "charged for coffee but gave away access to reading materials," and Wi-Fi allowed contemporary cafés to "follow the same model."[22] Because some of the first places in which Wi-Fi was publicly available were cafés, Wi-Fi was inserted into a historical narrative about reading, public space, and democracy.

Although Wi-Fi was imagined by Starbucks and others as a worm-on-the-hook, so to speak, for businesses to attract customers, it was simultaneously imagined as a burden on small business owners, who felt pressured to maintain expensive Wi-Fi networks in order to compete with neighbors.[23] By 2009, Wi-Fi access was an important factor in how people choose cafés, but in 2003 "almost no one" had yet experienced any "measurable increase in business from merely offering Wi-Fi."[24] Café owners did not yet see the payoff of their investment in Wi-Fi technology, although they felt obligated to provide it for their customers. News organizations noted the similarities between this gold-rush mentality—as café owners and Wi-Fi providers rushed to gobble up Wi-Fi real estate—and the dot.com era of the 1990s.[25]

The increase in demand for and early investment in Wi-Fi helped physically reshape spaces.[26] Many early news reports about Wi-Fi focused in particular on the reconfiguration of communal spaces. They noted, for example, how restaurant owners "installed rows of new electrical outlets [and] rearranged seating."[27] Cafés became increasingly designed around the electrical needs of computing instead of face-to-face conversations. Journalists reported that users treated electrical outlets as "public property" and "seldom asked for permission" to use the outlets or string extension cords through restaurants; customers fought over plugs and hot spot locations, leaving expensive equipment vulnerable to theft when they went to the bathroom because the risk was worth securing the electrical outlet. Others risked starting fires by plugging multiple cords into outlets behind furniture and picture frames.[28] Indeed, the popularization of the term "hot spot" as a way of "describing a physical space in common language speaks to the importance of these digital information networks" and the ways they increase the attractivity of particular locations.[29] Thus, news stories not only presented Wi-Fi itself as a contest between café owners but also imagined electrical outlets as a site of contest between customers. These reports worked to construct Wi-Fi (and the electricity needed to use it) as a hot commodity and as a scarce-but-desirable resource.

The sometimes-rough adoption of Wi-Fi was envisioned as making work more bearable by extending office productivity into shared spaces and thereby merging office productivity with leisure. For example, a *Daily News* article in 2007 opened with this anecdote: "Enjoying a gentle breeze in Bryant Park in a polo shirt, cargo shorts and sneakers, Robert Farrell didn't look like a man putting in a day of work." The journalist quoted Farrell as saying, "As long as I have an Internet connection, my business is right here."[30] In their 2004 cover story about Wi-Fi, *Newsweek* featured an image of Yuri Gitman riding his wireless-equipped "Magicbike" on a rooftop. With this bike, Gitman could "bring free Net connectivity anywhere his spirit moves him" or share that signal and "amplify wireless networks, creating mobile networks."[31] The imagery of liberated workers had remarkable lasting power in news media representations. For example, in 2008 the *Washington Post* reported that "workers and residents might find that they won't need to leave their buildings for a breath of fresh air anymore, because they might already be working outside."[32] Wi-Fi's ostensible power to offer the flexibility to work outdoors was imagined as a boon to the health of the workforce.

This increased productivity was important in the post-9/11, post-dot.com moment, when policy makers and news media focused on security and reinvigorating the national economy. After the terrorist attacks, Wi-Fi became a means to both monitor public spaces and back up communication systems in case of another attack. New stories chronicled how police installed Wi-Fi cameras and sensors in London, providing video "good enough to be admissible in court," used handheld scanners to ticket cars in New York City, and monitored busses and subways in Toronto.[33] The *New York Times* reported that Wi-Fi "would keep Lower Manhattan's computers and phones connected with the rest of the world in the event of a major disruption downtown," functioning "like a backup generator in a building."[34] This security-based logic rehearses that of the 1960s investments in Internet technology during the Cold War: Wi-Fi would keep America safe.

In addition, Wi-Fi was also hoped to have the power to shore up emotional and economic weaknesses. New York City's Wi-Fi networks emerged "at a time when there's a lot of doom and gloom over Lower Manhattan," and was imagined as "demonstrat[ing] that downtown does have a future."[35] Wi-Fi would re-urbanize cities, transforming dead downtowns into vibrant and versatile "smart cities."[36] "Nomadic teleworkers would become more productive due to their happier and more flexible working conditions, and the "white-collar army of the unemployed" would be reinvigorated as they turned cafés into "offices and job-searching centers."[37] Not only could already-employed workers work perpetually and more efficiently (even bicycling on rooftops!), but Wi-Fi would also tap the unemployed in the service of national economic productivity and urban renewal.

Public Space and the Third Place

A "third place" trope emerged alongside and as part of celebratory news media stories presenting Wi-Fi as worker liberation and national savior. Borrowing the term from sociologist Ray Oldenburg's *The Great Good Place,* published in 1989, academics, news media reporters, and policy makers used the term to describe the way Wi-Fi technology was reconfiguring public spaces into a "third place," a space between home (first place) and office (second place). Oldenburg argues this space rectifies a psychologically unhealthy "home-to-work-and-back-again shuttle" by offering a deliberately public space to "lend a public balance to the increased privatization of home life." Oldenburg credits these places with not only psychological health but also the health of democracy, and since he views their number as waning, the stakes are high for Oldenburg.[38] Starbucks intentionally set out to become a third place.[39] The company's chairman claimed success when he reported customers use Starbucks as "an extension of their porch, an extension of their office."[40]

In engaging the term "third place," news media and academics glossed over the ways Wi-Fi operated in service of capital. For the most part, the celebratory rhetoric did not address the question of overwork in the context of Wi-Fi Internet access. A notable exception is Lynn Spigel, who asked if the *freedom* to work anywhere is also an *imperative* to do so. She argued that the "current value placed on interactivity should be understood as part of a social milieu in which people are asked to work more of the time, in more locations and where being idle is suspect."[41] Indeed, research shows that more access to Internet connections—through work, home, and mobile technologies—increases the time people report working. In a 2008 Pew Center survey, half of the respondents said mobile technologies meant they worked more hours and that the technologies made it more difficult to disconnect from work.[42] Communication scholars have written about this phenomenon as "displacement," a "temporal concept, defined by a difference in time or time usage; the amount of time in media activity fundamentally alters the amount of time available for other events."[43]

With the emergence of Wi-Fi, labor becomes a public performance. Building on Thorstein Veblen's term "conspicuous consumption," which describes wealth performance in public consumption behaviors, Spigel argues Wi-Fi enables "conspicuous production," her term for perpetual and performative public production when a person "is meant to be seen working all the time.[44] This "performative communication" involves individuals in public "flagging themselves as wired agents, with mobile phones, laptops, PDAs" and "demonstrate[s] their labor value as social actors in a networked world."[45] In this sense, the breadth of competition spread beyond the fight for coverage or outlets into competitive public performance—who worked the hardest, the most, and using the most high-tech tools?

Although most news media and academic works have not addressed the question of overwork, many have focused on shifts in human interaction enabled by the spread of the technology, deeming—in opposition to Oldenburg's hopes—the emergence of the third place as potentially problematic. One article reported that the "politeness police are losing the battle against digital rudeness," or against what the director of the Etiquette School of Palo Alto called the "McManners generation . . . technologically astute but etiquette challenged." As futurist Paul Saffo argued, "Probably the last time technology annoyed us this much was the early days of the automobile."[46] The Canadian *Globe and Mail* called for social self-control when it published the "New Digital Etiquette" in 2005. Rules included to make a purchase if using free Wi-Fi, and to avoid stringing power cables in walkways, monopolizing wall sockets, and making loud calls.[47] As researcher Laura Forlano would likely argue, the suggestion in particular about loud calls reverses in the public-private dynamic because "while the indoor caféspace would be regarded as relatively more private as compared to city sidewalks and streets, people [go] into more public spaces in order to make their phone calls."[48] Also, because many corporations prevent employees from accessing personal e-mail accounts and social networking sites in workplaces, Wi-Fi allows individuals to "explicitly go into public spaces such as parks and cafés in order to do personal activities."[49]

This Wi-Fi-enabled behavioral shift—the shift in which public space became primarily for private and individuated work—frightened academics, who feared that a functioning public sphere would be lost. A healthy public sphere has long been assumed a prerequisite for democracy.[50] For Jürgen Habermas, the public sphere was the domain in which people interacted about public issues. The public sphere "sustains public as opposed to private opinion"; Habermas feared the public sphere was becoming functionally undemocratic and "refeudalized."[51] Because the public sphere is a "realm of integration of perceptions and understandings of common issues," if the public sphere does not function well, a society does not function well.[52] The public sphere is so important because it is how democracies create unity through dissent: "In the public sphere, citizens hardly agree about what political choices are best, but they perceive in common what the political choices are to be made."[53]

Thus, media scholars are concerned about what happens to the health of the public sphere when people focus not on other people but instead on media devices.[54] Political scientist Bruce Bimber noted that the "information revolution raises many important normative questions about the health of democracy" and concerns about the "deintegration" of the public sphere.[55] James Katz and Mark Aakhus have argued that "public space is destroyed and even colonized by private talk that interferes with organic interactions or that prevents public interaction."[56] More communication venues do not necessarily mean better communication and may in fact mean inferior communication. As Bimber argued, the "indisputable progressive nature of technology toward more speed, power, and efficiency does not in and of itself signal social or political progress."[57]

Many café owners agreed. Instead of installing additional outlets and offering Wi-Fi as Starbucks did, some cafés covered over outlets to force customers to talk to one another and preserve the public sphere, enforce what some might call "Old Analog Etiquette."[58] As one café owner described, "we just really feel it's important for people to talk to one another."[59] This owner idealizes face-to-face communication in much the same way as communication scholars such as Habermas do. In this view, Wi-Fi decreases the functionality of the public sphere and, presumably, threatens the health of communities and democracy itself. Some questions even persisted in these early years about whether Wi-Fi threatened not only the health of democracy but also actual health. In 2005 the public health department in Salzburg, Austria, advised legislators to ban Wi-Fi from public schools because of concerns about health risks, citing headaches, concentration difficulties, restlessness, and memory problems.[60]

Although imagined as responsible for problematic shifts in the public sphere, the promise of Wi-Fi technology offered in policy and news media narratives paradoxically also provided an antidote. This antidote tapped "excited rhetoric" that characterized early theories about how the Internet would replace other physical space, such as the "information superhighway" and "knowledge society" notions popular in 1990s policy debates and news media reports.[61] Not only would Wi-Fi be key to revitalizing America's economic growth in the post-9/11 economic downturn, but it would also create a new, virtual public sphere. In this new public sphere, individuals could engage civically by informing themselves, by grassroots organizing, and by forming new communities. Wi-Fi would redefine community, not destroy it. As Barry Wellman has noted, mobile communication can shift community ties from space-located individuals to what he calls "truly personal communities."[62] "Public interaction" would not become dysfunctional but would simply be transported into "disembodied private space" or to "nonplaces."[63] Wi-Fi Internet access would help create a digital democratic sphere, a layer of public space existing alongside the public sphere imagined as key to the health of democracy. In this vision, enabled by Oldenburg's "third place" notion, Wi-Fi was tinged with egalitarianism as a not-supposed-to-be-privatized space tasked with supporting individual psychological, communal, and democratic health. This egalitarianism tempered the hyper-competition-focused coverage of Wi-Fi as enhancing productivity.

Connecting and Unwiring Citizens

Historical analysis of coverage about Wi-Fi reveals a focus on Wi-Fi as a right of citizenship. As early as 2001, Internet entrepreneur Brewster Kahle used a transmitter on his house to transmit free high-speed Wi-Fi access to San Francisco's Presidio Park "on the grounds that free access is now every American citizen's inalienable right."[64] Marcos Lara, who created and ran the Bryant Park network, was quoted in the *Daily News* as saying, "This is not the first time big thinkers sat down and thought that information dissemination to the masses was a good thing . . . that happened one other time and that was with the public library system. This is the public library system of our generation."[65] The president of NYC Wi-Fi, a nonprofit that also manages hot spots, said that "just as you get benches and trees and shade for free, you should get free Internet as well."[66] To some extent, European citizens shared this sentiment. In particular, Estonian citizens "embrace Wi-Fi technology almost as a democratic right" and "Estonians see a link between easy—or free—access to information and their new democracy" because according to a technology adviser to the prime minister, "In Estonia cyberspace belongs to all. That's democracy."[67] In July 2010, Finland became the first country to make broadband access a literal legal right of citizenship.[68]

Although the U.S. government has not declared Internet access a right of citizenship, it has a long history of policies that come close. The FCC has long identified broadband access as critical for American civic participation and necessary for global competiveness.[69] In 2009, the FCC developed a "National Broadband Plan" designed to attain universal broadband access for citizens. The plan assumed increasing access would also "create jobs or provide significant public benefits" and "maximize our nation's economic growth, catalyze investment, spur job creation, and ensure our global competitiveness."[70] As of 2010, "both wired and wireless" broadband rose to the top of the Obama administration's and the FCC's priorities.[71]

Driving the sense of anxiety behind the plan is, among other things, the threat of growing connectivity in China. In 2008 China overtook the United States in the gross number of Internet users. Although the American population still boasted a higher percentage of connectivity than China, China's mammoth population holds growth potentials unattainable in the United States, and South Korea leads the world in broadband connectivity.[72] The FCC argued that even at 95 percent penetration, the United States was "behind where it needs to be on broadband to maintain its global competitiveness and drive economic growth."[73] Connecting broadband access with the future health of the economy in effect raised the stakes and anxiety levels about Wi-Fi.

To attain the goal of universal broadband, the FCC suggested Wi-Fi as a solution, arguing, "Wireless technologies may offer unique advantages and quick-to-market solutions for the delivery of high-speed services."[74] Wi-Fi offered a solution to the persistent "last mile" problem—connecting individual houses to the main lines that follow road paths—and promised to connect "recalcitrant or remote areas that have so far resisted broadband."[75] The FCC's plan also suggests the government use its successful historical investment in telephones as a model, even suggesting a reform to the Universal Service Fund, the nonprofit fund (supported by FCC-mandated telecommunication provider contributions) that helps people get telephone connection.[76]

But the historical record of political thought about Wi-Fi also reveals fear of a looming danger: Wi-Fi may help other countries proportionally more in the battle for Internet domination. Because Wi-Fi can operate without universal electricity, countries that invested in wires may find themselves behind as the "developing" world "fast-tracks" connectivity. In Bangladesh, 15 percent owned cell phones with Wi-Fi Internet by 2008 in rural remote villages that had "never before had access to phones of any kind."[77] MIT's Media Lab installed Wi-Fi transmitters on inter-village busses in India: "When vehicles stop to pick up passengers, computer users within range can use the signal to download files or send email."[78] Thus, the political thinking about Wi-Fi was and is complex. While the rhetoric about bridging the digital divide is in part about connecting citizens and strengthening democracy, the rhetoric is also rife with anxieties about American external control of Internet technologies and global capitalism.

Conclusion

Representations in news media and academic studies that presented Wi-Fi as key for national economic power, for civic engagement, and as essential to creating the public space necessary for a healthy democracy enabled visions of Wi-Fi as a public good. It is no surprise, then, that policy makers in Philadelphia focused attention on providing Wi-Fi to their constituents. However, in a post–9/11 era dominated by global and economic insecurity, corporate Internet providers could successfully argue corporations and not governments should control investments in Wi-Fi networks because they could provide the least financial risk, the best security, and the quickest spread of Wi-Fi access. In Philadelphia, Earthlink suggested using private funds to build the network and then sell access to the municipal government.

But this compromise failed. Earthlink halted service, reporting it was "unable to sign up enough customers."[79] In June 2008 Earthlink "pulled the plug on its experiment with municipal Wi-Fi in Philadelphia."[80] Earthlink had promised a cheap, high-speed system able to replace wired systems, but the signal was unavailable in most homes because older buildings hampered signals sent by transmitters with only a 300-foot range. As the *Philadelphia Inquirer* put it, "The technology simply isn't designed to go through walls, and even a fully built-out network won't change that fact."[81] As it turns out, initial critics of the mayor's proposal were correct.[82] City councilor Frank Rizzo wrote an op-ed that compared believing that the wireless system would work to "believing the moon is made of green cheese."[83]

Before this failure in 2008, the story of Philadelphia's Wi-Fi told in news media and academic publications was the story of a municipal government overcoming adversity.[84] Abhijit Jain, Munir Mandviwalla, and Rajiv Banker wrote that the project indicated governments could create and follow through with change.[85] The *Economist* reported, "The city, and the idea of privately funded municipal Internet, won."[86] Narratives that presented the city as victorious revealed a paradox. The government in Philadelphia *lost* in that it surrendered its power to decide whether it could offer Wi-Fi. Policy makers had to ask corporate permission. Yet, this severely compromised victory was imagined as a success, underscoring how historically unusual municipal victories are against corporate lobbies.

But more important to this chapter than the network's success or failure is the way the battle itself signals the ways Wi-Fi was and is intertwined in debates about the public sphere and about democratic and economic health. The compromise became a success (until it wasn't) in part because of developing sentiment in federal and local government initiatives that Wi-Fi Internet access is a public good and a right of citizenship and was bolstered by news media and academic works that engage third place rhetoric. This rhetoric rehearses the notion that the Internet can and should function as a replacement public sphere for the dysfunctional one it helped produce. Misuse or warping of the original term "third place" and focus on economic productivity constructed Wi-Fi as a development good for democracy and capitalism.

The significance of the Philadelphia example is that policy makers learned it could give away spectrum and facilitate the development of a somewhat functional Wi-Fi system without much risk to public funds. Although they shifted responsibility of Wi-Fi development to corporate powers and relieved themselves of responsibility to provide citizens access, policy makers could argue they were protecting the public good by serving both corporate and civic interests—enhancing national security, economic productivity, and serving the underserved by bridging the digital divide. Philadelphia's Wi-Fi battle provided a "glimpse of what will be possible with future Wi-Fi technologies. It has changed the way regulators and technologists think about spectrum policy."[87]

In sum, academic, news media, and policy visions of wireless share a common assumption: Wi-Fi will create better consumers and better citizens and pave a road to a bright capitalistic and democratic future. Yet, historical analysis of debates about what shape Wi-Fi will take, who will pay for it, and what it will do to the public sphere reveal deep-seated issues with the way Americans reconcile visions of capitalism and democracy. Thus, the notion of universal broadband access, enabled through Wi-Fi, serves both desires in that Americans imagine egalitarian access and increased productivity. If universal Wi-Fi access is a problem for democracy, which relies on leisure time in public for political and social interaction, it also creates a new public sphere to shore up democratic health. Ultimately, this historical analysis of debates about Wi-Fi in both cultural and policy spheres illustrates the ways communication technology participates in long-standing public debates, in this particular case in debates about the incompatibility of democracy and capitalism. Wi-Fi technology offered policy makers, citizens, and corporations means to conceptually reconcile the two, to serve the public good but not risk public funds, to serve the nation as consumers and citizens, and to shore up economic and national security. The conflict continues in current debates between Google, Verizon, and the FCC about net neutrality, perpetuating questions about what the Internet is and whose interests it should serve. On the one hand, for the FCC the Internet is a public good necessary to democracy. On the other, for Google and Verizon it is a commodity. Internet and Wi-Fi technologies continue to be central in conversations about who Americans are—consumers or citizens—and what America is—a democracy or a capitalist engine.

Notes

1. Christensen, "'Wi-Fi'ght Them," 695. The author thanks David Park, Nick Jankowski, Steve Jones, Allison Perlman, Laurel Clark, and Julie Passanante Elman.
2. McCarthy, "U.S. City Cuts Strings," A3.
3. "Wi-Fi for the Masses," 5.
4. Ibid.
5. Christensen, "'Wi-Fi'ght Them," 683.
6. "Let Towns, Cities Provide," D2.
7. Cox et al., *Not in the Public Interest,* viii, emphasis added.
8. "Mobile Telecoms. Unbound," 62.
9. McAlister, *Epic Encounters,* 307.
10. Gitelman, *Always Already New,* 129.
11. Castells et al., *Mobile Communication,* 3.
12. Kleinman, "Café Culture."
13. "A Brief History," 26–27.

14. Gitelman, *Always Already New.*
15. "A Brief History," 26–27.
16. Christensen, "'Wi-Fi'ght Them," 683.
17. "A Brief History," 26–27; FCC estimates cited in CTIA, *The Mobile Connection.*
18. Hayes and Lemstra, "Licence-Exempt."
19. "A Brief History," 26–27.
20. Markoff, "Starbucks," 4; Cassy, "e-finance," 22.
21. Cassy, "e-finance," 22.
22. "Internet in a Cup."
23. Richtel, "HP Makes Wi-Fi Push," 16; Richter, "Wired Downtown," 4Q.
24. Seventy-five percent of New Yorkers chose locations based on Wi-Fi. See Forlano, "WiFi Geographies," 348; and Miller, "The Wi-Fi Bubble," 36.
25. Miller, "The Wi-Fi Bubble," 36.
26. Forlano, "WiFi Geographies," 350.
27. Patriquin, "Cafés Offering Internet," B9.
28. Marriott, "Power Users," G1; Barse and Grubman, "Sipping," C10; Harrison, "Here's Dennis," D4.
29. Forlano, "WiFi Geographies," 351.
30. Carty, "Work, Unplugged," 6.
31. Levy, "Something in the Air," 45–68; Gallagher, "Using a Bicycle," C4.
32. Pearson, "Free Wireless," GZ05.
33. Stone, Itoi, and Flynn, "Wireless World," 60; Granatstein, "Network," 7.
34. Holusha, "A Plan," K4.
35. Wyatt, "More Wireless," D4.
36. Markoff, "More Cities," C7; Levinthal, "Surf's Up," 1B; Hamilton, "Wireless Internet," C01; Hau, "Free Wi-Fi," 9; Donnelly, "Connected City," 5; Molloy, "Smart Cities," 19.
37. "Make Mine a Latte."
38. Oldenburg, *The Great Good Place.*
39. "Trouble Brewing."
40. Clark, "Free Net Access," 4.
41. Spigel, "Designing," 415.
42. Madden and Jones, "Networked Workers."
43. Gumpert and Drucker, "The Perfections," 374–375.
44. Spigel, "Designing," 403–426.
45. Ibid., 416.
46. Bourdreau, "The Net World," 55.
47. Patriquin, "Cafés Offering Internet," B9.
48. Forlano, "WiFi Geographies," 349.
49. Ibid.
50. Drucker and Gumpert, "Public Space," 294–310; Habermas, *The Structural Transformation;* Anderson, *Imagined Communities.*
51. Bimber, *Information,* 244, summarizing Habermas, *The Structural Transformation.*
52. Bimber, *Information,* 244.
53. Ibid.

54. Ling, *The Mobile Connection.*
55. Bimber, *Information,* 243.
56. Katz and Aakhus, *Perpetual Contact,* 18.
57. Bimber, *Information,* 249.
58. Dolan and Daniel, "The Daily Grind," A19.
59. Miller, "Starbucks," 20.
60. Hamilton and Gombu, "Health Agency to Look at Wi-Fi," B2. Carr suggested Internet use had similar cognitive effects. See Carr, *The Shallows.*
61. Graham, "Beyond the Dazzling Light," 16–25.
62. Wellman, "Physical Place," 240
63. For "disembodied," see Gumpert and Drucker, "Mobile Communication"; for "nonplaces," see Auge, *Non-places.*
64. Denton, "Enthusiasts of New Technology," 37.
65. Carty, "Work, Unplugged," 6.
66. Ibid.
67. Underhill, "Freedom in the Airwaves."
68. "Finland Makes Broadband."
69. Forty-one percent of Americans lacked broadband in 2000. See U.S. FCC, *Inquiry: Second.*
70. U.S. FCC, *The National Broadband Plan.*
71. U.S. FCC, *Inquiry: Sixth;* U.S. FCC, "Chairman."
72. MacLeod, "China Vaults Past."
73. U.S. FCC, *Inquiry: Sixth.*
74. U.S. FCC, *Inquiry: Second.*
75. Levy, "Something in the Air," 45–68.
76. U.S. FCC, *Inquiry: Sixth.*
77. Molloy, "Smart Cities," 19.
78. Levy, "Something in the Air," 45–68.
79. "Wireless Philadelphia," A18.
80. Kerkstra, "Philadelphia," B04.
81. Kerkstra, "Local Investors," B6.
82. Cox et al., *Not in the Public Interest,* viii.
83. McCarthy, "U.S. City Cuts Strings," A3.
84. Christensen, "'Wi-Fi'ght Them"; Jain, Mandviwalla, and Banker, "Government."
85. Jain, Mandviwalla, and Banker, "Government."
86. "Wi-Fi for the Masses," 5.
87. "A Brief History," 26–27.

Works Cited

Anderson, Benedict. *Imagined Communities: Reflections on the Origin and Spread of Nationalism.* New York: Verso, 1983.

Auge, Marc. *Non-places: Introduction to an Anthropology of Supermodernity.* London: Verso, 1995.

Barse, Gigi, and Cathy Grubman. "Sipping through the Workday: An Office Alternative Is Brewing." *Washington Post,* March 12, 2002, C10.

Bimber, Bruce. *Information and American Democracy: Technology in the Evolution of Political Power.* Cambridge: Cambridge University Press, 2003.

Bourdreau, John. "The Net World Can't Stop for Etiquette." *Australian,* June 20, 2000, 55.

"A Brief History of Wi-Fi." *Economist,* June 12, 2004, 26–27.

Carr, Nicholas. *The Shallows: What the Internet Is Doing to Our Brains.* New York: Norton & Company, 2010.

Carty, Daniel. "Work, Unplugged: With Wi-Fi Hotspots Growing, Laptoppers Can Do Their Jobs amid the Great Outdoors." *Daily News,* July 9, 2007, 6.

Cassy, John. "e-finance: Starbucks Seeks Online Loyalty: Linger over the Latte with Your Laptop." *Guardian,* January 4, 2001, 22.

Castells, Manuel, Mireia Fernandez-Ardevol, Jack Linchuan Qui, and Araba Sey. *Mobile Communication and Society: A Global Perspective.* Cambridge: MIT Press, 2007.

Christensen, Adam. "'Wi-Fi'ght Them When You Can Join Them? How the Philadelphia Compromise May Have Saved Municipally Owned Telecommunications Services." *Federal Communications Law Journal* 58, no. 3 (2006): 683–705.

Clark, Anthony. "Free Net Access with a Coffee at Starbucks." *Engineering Times,* September 2, 2002, 4.

Cox, Braden, Tom Giovanetti, David P. McClure, Steven Titch, Ron Rizzuto, and David G. Tuerck. *Not in the Public Interest—The Myth of Municipal Wi-Fi Networks.* Washington, DC: New Millennium Research Council, 2005.

CTIA. *The Mobile Connection: Wireless Broadband.* Accessed July 20, 2010. http://www.ctia.org/advocacy/research/index.cfm/AID/10315

Denton, Nick. "Enthusiasts of New Technology." *Management Today,* April 30, 2001, 37.

Dolan, Deirdre, and Jennifer Daniel. "The Daily Grind." *New York Times,* November 28, 2009, A19.

Donnelly, Brian. "Connected City: Edinburgh Goes Wireless." *Herald,* May 18, 2006, 5.

Drucker, Susan, and Gary Gumpert. "Public Space and Communication: The Zoning of Public Interaction." *Communication Theory* 1 no. 4 (1991): 294–310.

"Finland Makes Broadband a 'Legal Right.'" *BBC News,* July 1, 2010. Accessed July 30, 2010. http://www.bbc.co.uk/news/10461048.

Forlano, Laura. "WiFi Geographies: When Code Meets Place." *Information Society* 25 (2010): 1–9.

Gallagher, David. "Using a Bicycle to Uplink on a Download Platform." *New York Times,* December 15, 2003, C4.

Gitelman, Lisa. *Always Already New: Media, History, and the Data of Culture.* Cambridge: MIT Press, 2006.

Graham, Steven. "Beyond the Dazzling Light: From Dreams of Transcendence to the 'Remediation' of Urban Life." *New Media & Society* 16 (2004): 16–25.

Granatstein, Rob. "Network Could Be Invitation to Big Brother." *Toronto Sun,* July 15, 2006, 7.

Gumpert, Gary, and Susan Drucker. "Mobile Communication in the Twenty-First Century or Everybody, Everywhere, at Any Time." In *Displacing Place: Mobile Communication in the Twenty-first Century,* edited by Sharon Kleinman, 7–20. New York: Peter Lang Publishing, 2007.

———, and Susan Drucker. "The Perfections of Sustainability and Imperfections in the Digital Community: Paradoxes of Connection." *In Digital Cities III,* edited by Peter van den Besselaar, Makoto Tanabe, and Toru Ishida, 374–375. New York: Springer-Verlag, 2004.

Habermas, Jürgen. *The Structural Transformation of the Public Sphere: An Inquiry into a Category of Bourgeois Society.* Cambridge: MIT Press, 1991.

Hamilton, Tyler. "Wireless Internet Goes Live Downtown." *Toronto Star*, September 7, 2006, C01.

——— and Phinjo Gombu. "Health Agency to Look at Wi-Fi." *Toronto Star*, March 10, 2006, B2.

Harrison, Crayton. "Here's Dennis: Real Estate Agent Is His Own Roving Billboard." *Dallas Morning News,* March 11, 2004, D4.

Hau, Louis. "Free Wi-Fi Coming to Tampa's Downtown." *St. Petersburg Times,* December 31, 2004, 9.

Hayes, Vic, and Wolter Lemstra. "Licence-Exempt: The Emergence of Wi-Fi." *info* 11 (2009): 57–71.

Holusha, John. "A Plan for Wireless Telecommunications Network." *New York Times,* April 25, 2004, K4.

"Internet in a Cup." *Economist,* December 20, 2003.

Jain, Abhijit, Munir Mandviwalla, and Rajiv Banker. "Government as Catalyst: Can It Work Again with Wireless Internet Access?" *Public Administration Review* 67, no. 6 (2007): 993–-1006.

Katz, James, and Mark Aakhus. *Perpetual Contact: Mobile Communications, Private Talk, Public Performance.* Cambridge: Cambridge University Press, 2002.

Kerkstra, Patrick. "Local Investors to Bring Free WiFi to Philadelphia." *Philadelphia Inquirer,* June 18, 2008, B6.

———. "Philadelphia to Buy Municipal WiFi Network for City Business." *Philadelphia Inquirer,* December 17, 2009, B04.

Kleinman, Sharon. "Café Culture in France and the United States: A Comparative Ethnographic Study of the Use of Mobile Information and Communication Technologies." *Atlantic Journal of Communication* 14, no. 4 (2006): 191–210.

"Let Towns, Cities Provide Cheap, Everywhere Broadband." *Toronto Star,* February 28, 2005, D2.

Levinthal, Dave. "Surf's Up: City Adding Free Wi-Fi Dallas: Wireless Internet Access May Hit Libraries, Parks by Year's End." *Dallas Morning News,* February 6, 2006, 1B.

Levy, Steven. "Something in the Air," *Newsweek,* June 7, 2004, 45–68.

Ling, Rich. *The Mobile Connection: The Cell Phone's Impact on Society.* San Francisco: Morgan Kaufmann, 2004.

MacLeod, Calum. "China Vaults Past USA in Internet Users." *USA Today*, April 21, 2008. Accessed July 30, 2010. http://www.usatoday.com/tech/world/2008–04–20–Internetusers_N.htm.

Madden, Mary, and Sydney Jones. "Networked Workers." *Pew Center for Internet and American Life*, September 24, 2008. Accessed July 20, 2010. http://www.pewInternet.org/Reports/2008/Networked-Workers.aspx.

"Make Mine a Latte." *Economist*, June 14, 2003.

Markoff, John. "More Cities Set up Wireless Networks." *New York Times*, January 6, 2003, C7.

———. "Starbucks and Microsoft Plan Coffeehouse Web Access." *New York Times*, January 4, 2001, 4.

Marriott, Michel. "Power Users, Ready for Refill." *New York Times*, January 6, 2005, G1.

McAlister, Melani. *Epic Encounters: Culture, Media, and U.S. Interests in the Middle East since 1945*. Berkeley: University of California Press, 2001.

McCarthy, Shawn. "U.S. City Cuts Strings from Corporations' Net: Not Everyone Happy About Philadelphia's Public Wireless System." *Globe and Mail*, May 7, 2005, A3.

Miller, Claire Cain. "Starbucks Takes Battle with Rivals to Cyberspace: Offer of Free Wi-Fi Access to Customers Comes with New Attitude on Lingering." *International Herald Tribune*, June 16, 2010, 20.

Miller, Karen Lowry. "The Wi-Fi Bubble." *Newsweek*, August 4, 2003, 36.

"Mobile Telecoms. Unbound." *Economist*, February 13, 1999, 62.

Molloy, Fran. "Smart Cities." *Age*, January 24, 2008, 19.

Oldenburg, Ray. *The Great Good Place: Cafés, Coffee Shops, Community Centers, Beauty Parlors, General Stores, Bars, Hangouts, and How They Get You through the Day*. New York: Paragon House, 1989.

Patriquin, Martin. "Cafés Offering Internet Access Face Low-Tech Growing Pains; Rows of Electrical Outlets, Shifted Seating Aimed at Meeting Gadgetry Demands." *Globe and Mail*, June 23, 2005, B9.

Pearson, Bradford. "Free Wireless Internet Access Available in Downtown Bethesda." *Washington Post*, July 24, 2008, GZ05.

Richtel, Matt. "HP Makes Wi-Fi Push: Firm to Install and Maintain Networks." *International Herald Tribune*, June 17, 2004, 16.

Richter, Maurice. "Wired Downtown, without the Wires; Town Square Looks to Add Wireless Internet Access." *Dallas Morning News*, February 11, 2005, 4Q.

Spigel, Lynn. "Designing the Smart House: Posthuman Domesticity and Conspicuous Production." *European Journal of Cultural Studies* 8, no. 4 (2005): 403–426.

Stone, Brad, Kay Itoi, and Emily Flynn. "Wireless World." *Newsweek*, June 7, 2004, 60.

"Trouble Brewing: Brand Management." *Economist*, March 3, 2007.

Underhill, William. "Freedom in the Airwaves." *Newsweek*, June 7, 2004.

U.S. Federal Communications Commission. "Chairman Julius Genachowski Statement on Obama Administration's Wireless Broadband Initiative," June 28, 2010. Press Release. Accessed July 22, 2010. http://www.fcc.gov/commissioners/genachowski/statements2010.html.

———. *Inquiry Concerning the Deployment of Advanced Telecommunications Capability: Second Report.* Washington, DC: FCC 00–290, 2000. Accessed July 22, 2010. http://www.fcc.gov/Bureaus/Common_Carrier/Orders/2000/fcc00290.pdf.

———. *Inquiry Concerning the Deployment of Advanced Telecommunications Capability: Sixth Broadband Deployment Report to the Federal Communications Commission.* Washington, DC: FCC 10–129, 2010. Accessed July 30, 2010. http://www.fcc.gov/Daily_Releases/Daily_Business/2010/ . . . /FCC–10–129A1.pdf.

———. *The National Broadband Plan: Connecting America.* Accessed July 30, 2010. http://www.broadband.gov.

Wellman, Barry. "Physical Place and Cyber Place: The Rise of Networked Individualism." *International Journal of Urban and Regional Research* 25 (June 2001): 227–252.

"Wi-Fi for the Masses: City-Wide Wireless Internet." *Economist,* March 3, 2007, 5.

"Wireless Philadelphia: Bye-bye, Wi-Fi." *Philadelphia Inquirer,* May 15, 2008, A18.

Wyatt, Edward. "More Wireless Internet Access Set for Lower Manhattan Parks." *New York Times,* April 4, 2003, D4.

chapter four

Pre-digital Virtuality

Early Modern Scholars and the Republic of Letters

Christian Thorsten Callisen and Barbara Adkins

Introduction

Contemporary research on scholarly communication points to the crucial contribution of digital technologies to both "the formal and informal activities associated with the use and dissemination of information through public and private channels."[1] Addressing this issue, Christine Borgman identifies five ways in which digital technologies have apparently influenced and changed scholarly communication.[2] These include the ability to:

- Communicate with more people more often than was possible before the advent of digital technologies;
- Engage in communication that is not only greater in volume and speed but also cheaper;
- Use and distribute documents in new ways;
- Use new methods of communication including e-mail, online discussion, and online presentations;
- Increase the amount of both informal and formal communication.

In this context, it is often assumed that the development of the Internet and opportunities for virtual communication account for many of the qualities of scholarly communication in the "digital age." However, as Borgman points out, current systems and practices of communication, although facilitated digitally, constitute a "rich and complex sociotechnical system formed over a period of centuries"[3] and thus cannot be considered entirely novel. Despite such qualifications, a significant body of scholarship on aspects of virtual communication continues to assume an implicit and essential association between digital web-based environments and virtuality. In this context, according to Rob Shields, "virtual" comes to mean "simulated."[4]

There is little doubt that at least some of the properties of contemporary digital virtuality are a response to the experiences enabled by digital technologies and advanced telecommunications. However, in the context of a sociotechnical system in which, as Shields reminds us, "the digital virtuality of the global Internet, simulations and virtual reality is only the latest incarnation of the virtual,"[5] it is important to examine possible precursors to virtual communication in the online realm. In so doing, we can better understand exactly how the virtual is constructed, and thus find ourselves in a stronger position to identify what truly is unique about digital virtuality. This opens up the question of historical precedent in relation to virtual interaction that is required "to distinguish what is truly novel about the 'information age' from what is transient hype."[6]

With the importance of such historical precedent in mind, this chapter investigates the construction of a pre-digital virtual community, known by its citizens as the "Republic of Letters." Following Jeffrey Haydu, we "make use of the past" to identify continuities in the virtuality involved in scholarly communication in the Republic of Letters and contemporary web-based scholarly interaction. Haydu suggests that one of the most productive ways to learn from the past is to see our history as a sequence of "reiterated problem-solving."[7] We therefore examine the Republic of Letters as a virtual community and consider the techniques of virtuality that individuals within this community employed in order to overcome distances of space and time. This approach allows us to investigate the kind of virtuality present in the Republic of Letters to assist in our understanding of the way this historical case constituted a precursor to contemporary forms of virtuality in scholarly communication. This can contribute to our understanding of how web-based interaction constitutes a distinctive form of scholarly communication and also what these contemporary forms might owe to more general social and political dynamics that persist across historical periods. However, before introducing the Republic of Letters, it would be prudent to reflect further on the concept of virtuality in relation to history and to social and cultural capacities.

Virtuality and History

Shields draws from philosophers such as Henri Bergson, Marcel Proust, and Gilles Deleuze, identifying the virtual as a "real idealization, such as memory, dream or intention."[8] He distinguishes the virtual realm as one concerned with the "ideally real," from actual contexts on the one hand, and abstractions that pertain only to possibilities on the other. The key property that positions the virtual conceptually is its relationship to a concrete object or event. Thus, the past is virtually real because "there is an actual past of events which were once the concrete present and which are now really existing memories."[9] As intangible memories the past may be actualized in a concrete event of remembering.

While intangible ideas such as memories may be actualized unassisted in an everyday conversation, historically, specific techniques have also assisted in bringing intangible ideas into concrete presence. Techniques of the virtual are described as those that "create the illusion of presence through props, simulations, partial presences and rituals . . . which invoke the past and make absent others present."[10] The technologies that enable the employment of these techniques have a significant historical lineage, and forms of virtual life have existed in various forms over a considerable period. For Shields, this provides for questions concerning the crucial role of cultural capacities and processes entailed in producing valued outcomes such as knowledge sharing and communication of new insights.

A key consideration in understanding these cultural capacities in the context of the emerging role of virtual relationships in history is the changing role and place of space and time in relationships of presence and co-presence. These relationships traditionally have been the focus of phenomenological sociology. In his review of the phenomenology of Alfred Schutz for the purposes of understanding contemporary Internet-based interaction, Shanyang Zhao points to his characterization of the contemporaneous lifeworld as constituted by two realms: the realm of consociates "where the individual interacts with others face-to-face in conditions of copresence, and the realm of contemporaries where the individual interacts with others non-face-to-face in conditions of noncopresence."[11] Schutz and his colleagues had also alluded to the role of mediation to describe the possibility of individuals sharing a community of time without sharing a community of space, and Zhao builds on this idea to propose that these mediated relationships now characterize a third realm of the lifeworld, enabled by information and communication technologies, within which "consociated contemporaries" are able to interact. The importance of this third domain is that it is a context in which "presence" can be experienced without the requirement of space-time co-location, where it can be understood as a "state in which virtual . . . objects can be experienced as actual objects in either sensory or nonsensory ways."[12] Presence is thus a crucial mechanism through which the real idealizations in the virtual domain can be made actual in tangible performances.

In a recent study of comments and discussion on the photosharing website, Flickr, Barbara Adkins and Jason Nasarczyk examined how presence was achieved through participants' commitment to an ongoing interaction order in which their photographs, and the techniques, knowledge, and experiences associated with them, were shared and discussed.[13] The quasi-conversational features of interaction, and participants' attention to the ritual aspects of conduct, led to their experience of asynchronously produced discussion as occurring in a "time envelope."[14] Central to the constitution of an interaction order sustaining a sense of presence were the courtesies, protocols, and rituals that the participants observed with respect to acknowledging and deferring to epistemic rights and authority regarding the knowledge to which individuals claimed or displayed access. This aspect of maintaining an interaction order in common is particularly relevant to our examination of scholarly communication. Pierre Bourdieu's analysis of the scholastic field points to the centrality of such recognition relationships to the maintenance of existing scientific orders, and, conversely, the importance of withholding recognition in the subversion and challenging of existing orders.[15]

These observations regarding the key dimensions of presence in online environments point to how participants appropriate opportunities to establish relationships of presence across space and time boundaries, including the rituals and courtesies central to the negotiation of knowledge-based relationships. However, this raises the question of the specificity of these relationships to the application of digital technologies in the scholastic field. Wolfgang Behringer has argued that the early modern era (circa 1500–1800) represented a period of revolutionary change with respect to communication relationships in Europe and their influence on scholarly and research relationships.[16] The invention of printing did not, by itself, contribute to the expansion of knowledge and knowledge relationships.[17] Rather, this expansion was attributable to printing in conjunction with media for the transmission and distribution of information and printed material, particularly the development of transport infrastructure and the services—postal and courier—that these enabled. For Behringer, this system formed the basis of a "space of flows" (à la Manuel Castells) based on enhanced capacities for speed, new organizations, and schedules with respect to temporal ordering of communication, and ongoing developments in printing, including the periodic press and periodic journals.

This period therefore represents an opportunity to investigate the relationships that enabled ideas to be performed and actualized as the foundation for a greatly intensified flow of scholarly exchange. We now turn to a review of the Republic of Letters as a community of scholars experiencing and responding to changes in both communication media and in the scholarly field.

The Republic of Letters

The Republic of Letters is the name given to a community that enabled early modern scholars to interact and share ideas with each other despite being separated by divisions of geography, politics, and religion.[18] The name, a translation of the Latin *respublica literaria*, stems from the Ciceronian definition of a *respublica* (literally public things or public affairs—the public good) based on law and common interests and from the Augustinian definition of a *respublica* based on love. Hence, the *respublica literaria* represented "a society united both by *love* of the same goods [letters], and by law and common interests."[19] It began in the early fifteenth century as a scholarly community of *eruditi homines* (learned people) "transcending frontiers and generations" and united by "the bond of letters."[20] By the turn of the eighteenth century, it had fully crystallized in its citizens' minds as an institution that embraced all people, regardless of ethnicity, religion, or sex, and which allowed (at least in theory) all these individuals to express themselves without fear of recrimination or censorship.

This community served to link scholars throughout the known world—across Britain and Europe, and as far afield as the Middle East and the Americas. In a world without television or international newspapers, and before the widespread dissemination of research via scholarly journals, the correspondence network of the Republic of Letters was essential to any aspiring scholar, allowing one to connect with individuals and ideas that might otherwise have been inaccessible. Of course, for this community to function, it was not enough for individuals to draw information from it; they also needed to contribute to the flow of correspondence throughout the network. To this end, a number of de facto standards emerged, which meant that individuals could be excluded from the community if they did not meet their obligations. First and foremost, relationships within the Republic of Letters were reciprocal. This meant that one did not simply begin correspondence with another person; rather, they entered an arrangement of *commercium literarum* (exchange of letters).[21] This meant that, if one contacted someone else in the Republic of Letters to request information or assistance, there was an expectation that the favor would, in time, be repaid.

Obligations within the Republic of Letters included not only the reciprocal sharing of information but also of gifts.[22] Letters were often sent with attachments—perhaps some books or pamphlets, or an edition of the recipient's own work suitably annotated with suggestions and emendations by the sender, or by other gifts of scholarly interest to the recipient. These might have included antiquities, portraits, seeds, dried flowers, or even cadavers or animals. If one received a book from a correspondent, one was therefore expected to return the gift, usually with a physical artifact, but sometimes by other means—perhaps a dedication of one's own work in thanks for support, encouragement, and information, or the offer of an introduction to another citizen of the Republic. As already noted, such introductions were critical for a scholar in early modern Europe. They offered one not only a "foot in the door" of this erudite community but status within the community as well as access to information and resources that would otherwise have remained unobtainable. The gifts and exchanges, in turn, served to strengthen the recognition relationships which were engendered and maintained via ongoing correspondence.

While the epistolary networks of the Republic of Letters reached across a vast geographic area, these networks themselves centered on certain people and locations. As today, schools of thought often emerged and evolved around the work of influential individuals. These people were almost always based in one of the "capitals" of the Republic—cities that afforded their inhabitants access to great libraries, to the patronage of wealthy aristocrats, and to printing presses, the publicity engines of early modern Europe. By being introduced to such an influential individual, scholars not only opened themselves up to additional sources of information and scholarship but also to the correspondence networks emanating from the individual's pen. These individuals frequently acted as conduits for information across Europe, forwarding letters and books as requested, and providing focal points for the dissemination of information. Thus Hugo Grotius utilized the brothers Dupuy in Paris as a kind of epistolary freight-forwarding service,[23] and Theodor Jansson van Almeloveen found it worthwhile to curry the favor of Friedrich Carpzov, the editor of a journal whose position afforded "to him an extensive network of correspondents who kept him up to date with developments in the Republic of Letters."[24]

However, gaining access to such an individual was not as easy as simply writing a letter. One might have a better chance of success by having a mutual associate "put in a good word" with the desired contact before writing to that individual personally. And when it came to making the first direct contact, one had to be careful to ensure that one displayed the appropriate traits—and adopted the appropriate persona through the acknowledgment of, and deference to, epistemic rights and authority—in order to endear oneself to the corresponding party.[25]

So in this manner the Republic of Letters functioned as a "real idealization" of *intention*: all the activities of its citizens were geared toward gaining and maintaining status within it. It is perhaps not coincidental that this community arose in the scholarly milieu. As today, the "game" of academia involved meeting the right people, making the right impression, and ensuring that one's work was read by as many other scholars as possible. And as already observed, performing these activities appropriately contributed to the construction of recognition relationships that are crucial to the maintenance of scientific orders. Here we come to the second aspect of the Republic of Letters—the notion of (*res*)*publica*, which was as integral a part of this community as the correspondence that bound it.

In his 1637 *Discourse on Method*, René Descartes wrote of the importance of communicating one's research to the public. In the Latin edition of this work the word "public" was translated, with Descartes's approval, as *respublica literaria*.[26] This example helps to illustrate the great focus on the public nature of the Republic of Letters: its citizens had an *obligation* to disseminate their work to the rest of the Republic, and their motivation ought to be for the public good in general. As a result, not only were citizens of the Republic expected to publish their research, but printed editions of correspondence also emerged in order that their discussions might be shared with as large an audience as possible. These appeared in the sixteenth and seventeenth centuries, and compilations of epistles—sometimes edited by the citizens themselves—were often published during a person's lifetime.[27]

As we shall see, the practice of acknowledging and deferring to the epistemic rights of citizens of the Republic of Letters is clearly embedded in their correspondence and forms a component of the common assumptions that are central conditions for subscribing to the Republic of Letters as an idealized community. These observations also resonate with Bourdieu's theorization of the scientific field as based on a "feel for the game" of scholarly communication and the recognition of exchanges on which it continues to rest. Thus while scholars may have taken up extremely different positions on scholarly matters, their debates and conflicts masked an underlying commonality—a tacit consensus on what was worth fighting about. This remains as a key condition under which scholarly fields exist as "ideally real."

The Republic of Letters therefore functioned in the service of the public, facilitating contact across great distances and providing its citizens with the opportunity to engage in research and to voice controversial ideas despite the myriad challenges of an expensive and (at times) unreliable postal system, governmental and ecclesiastical censorship, and violent and prolonged wars. They developed relationships with people they had never met and established corporeal friendships with people that they had first come into contact with through correspondence in the Republic of Letters. But this community could not exist based only on a common orientation toward the public good; it needed to be supported by physical technologies that allowed the transmission of the correspondence which bound it, and by techniques of virtuality that allowed the realization of this community in the minds of its citizens.

Despite growing interest from historians since the 1980s, research regarding the Republic of Letters is still in its relatively early stages and, as such, our understanding of early modern communications technologies, exactly how they were used and by whom, is necessarily limited. Even so, it is possible to conclude that citizens of the Republic had at least five avenues available to them: travelers, couriers, paid messengers, the official postal service, and diplomatic pouch.[28] Although we lack sufficient data to make a firm assessment, it appears that during this period the official postal service remained prohibitively expensive for private use, and the most common method of corresponding was via travelers. Early modern Europe was a highly mobile society, and people—scholars, diplomats, merchants, pilgrims—often traveled between cities. In the mid-1500s a letter could reach London from Rome—traversing approximately one thousand miles as the crow flies, the Alps, and the English Channel—in less than four weeks, and shorter distances could be covered much more quickly,[29] while improvements to road networks throughout the early modern period meant the continual amelioration of distance.[30] One important advantage for the Republic of Letters of this method of corresponding was that it enabled the contents of the letter to be circulated amongst a wider group of people. Paul Dibon points out that letters were rarely sealed,[31] so sending one with a traveler meant that he or she could read it, as well as sharing the details of its contents with other interested parties along the way.

The intimate details of these communications networks do not interest us here; the points to recognize are that "technology" is not synonymous with "digital" and, although technologies are certainly necessary for people to communicate across great distances, communications themselves are fashioned by the individuals involved and governed by the social and cultural mores under which those individuals operate. We shall now examine how citizens of the Republic of Letters used their correspondence to fashion a sense of virtual community.

Techniques of Virtuality

As noted above, Shields refers to "props, simulations, partial presences . . . and rituals" as techniques of the virtual. Here, we separate these four categories, arguing that (partial) presences do not comprise a technique of the virtual per se but are invoked by the props, simulations, and rituals that individuals employ when operating in a virtual environment. Shields's description of partial presences as, for example, "a voice conveyed by telephone or thoughts written in a book"[32] is here reconfigured as imagined presences. These presences are invoked by a recipient based on his or her interpretation, made possible by the sender's use of techniques of virtuality. Thus, thoughts written in a letter become a channel by which the author's presence may be invoked by the reader—thus becoming the ideal realization of a dream—rather than a channel by which the author might impose their presence. It is not enough for the thoughts to be put to paper, or for words to be spoken into a mouthpiece, in the case of the telephone; the reader or listener must *process* this information, receiving it, considering it, and, finally, articulating the imagined presence of their correspondent. In this manner one is able to establish co-presence, a relationship wherein correspondents are "reciprocally oriented toward each other, mutually available and accessible to each other, tuned in to and in touch with each other."[33]

Zhao and his colleague David Elesh argue that co-presence is but one thing that is required for sociality. The other is "co-location," which they define as a spatial relationship, wherein the co-located parties are in proximity to each other (either physically or through a medium such as the Internet), and in which one can experience another.[34] In this sense, both the Internet and the Republic of Letters afford their users co-location: via the media of electronic correspondence and handwritten communication, respectively, people are in proximity to each other. Correspondents are no longer merely contemporaries but "consociated contemporaries," communicating with each other within a "time envelope." In a sense, they can reach out and touch each other by sending an e-mail or a letter, or by "poking" through Facebook or via a request that a friend "put in a good word" for one in their own correspondence with a desired contact. Such solicitations or "pokes" might be intended to prompt further interaction from the other party, but they by no means guarantee it. For that, co-presence is required and thus common interests, etiquette (or "netiquette"), and accessibility come into play. Let us consider some examples of techniques of virtuality that were employed by correspondents in the Republic of Letters to establish this sense of co-presence and thus to enable sociality despite corporeal separation.

Props, if understood as physical supports, may be considered the closest approximation to Shields's notion of partial presences, as they were utilized specifically to provide the recipient of a letter with a visible reminder of its author. For example, much as one might today end a post to an online discussion forum with a personalized "signature" containing a pithy quote, colorful fonts, and perhaps a picture of oneself or a favorite pet, a correspondent in the Republic of Letters might adopt specific practices to present their correspondence as unique. In this manner, the physical artifacts of a letter, such as the paper it was written on, the wax used to seal it, or the handwriting of its author, were used to assert the author's individuality, to personalize the letter, and to offer the recipient a physical reminder of their correspondent. These artifacts did not function to impose a partial presence on the recipient but rather to "[inspire] a search for an imaginary compensation for physical absence."[35] Thus, visual props served as supports upon which other techniques of virtuality—simulations and rituals—could build. In this sense, they served to initiate co-location, by offering a sense of individuality across time and space, even if that sense of individuality had to then be processed and interpreted to be understood by the recipient.

Correspondence within the Republic of Letters also utilized literary props to help establish co-location. The most obvious of these is the commonplace habit of telling the recipient of a letter which letters were being replied to, or of mentioning another letter for which a reply was outstanding.[36] As it was usual for people to keep copies of the letters they had sent, this allowed one to extract the appropriate letter and have it to hand while reading the response or writing one. In this manner, citizens of the Republic were able to position their correspondence as part of an ongoing conversation, using props to aid in a simulation by which partial presences could be invoked.

Simulations were integral to the living of a virtual life in the Republic of Letters. By writing "as if" they were interlocutors in a conversation, correspondents could occupy an imaginary space that was independent of their corporeal environment despite temporal delays in communication. In this space, they achieved both co-location and co-presence, as here they were able to, as one contemporary observed, "meet, and melt, and mix."[37] In conversation, presuppositions make it clear that the parties share common experiences and peculiar cultural circumstances, thus occupying a privileged space from which others are excluded.[38] Consider:

> My friend William Penn calld here t'other day; he told me Lord Sunderland is gon into the Country, full of Discontents; fearing the trimming was not carried farr enough, & doubting the majority of next parliament may not be Whiggs. If so, . . . tis a Melancholy prospect for somebody; for I remember the fate of Spencer, who was hangd at Hereford, with this inscription out a Psalm sett upon the Gallowes, Quid gloriaris in Malitia Potens?[39] You sent me the first newes of the Master of the Horse which is incomparable; He is, I think, a more ridiculous Beast himself, than Caligulas Incitatus, to be joynd with him in the Consulship.
>
> My Wife is yours & your Ladys most humble servant. neice Cotterell has left us for a month; And as to little Mad cap, you hav conjurd up a spirit you will hardly know how to lay; For she is looking every day, when any visit comes, for Mr St John with his snuff box full of Fairies.[40]

This extract contains so many presuppositions that someone who did not witness earlier turns of the ongoing conversation is unlikely to understand the vast majority of the message that Sir William is attempting to convey, even if they are familiar with some of the events under discussion. In the first sentence, there is an assumption that the reader knows who William Penn is, and why he might be in a position to provide news about ongoing intrigues in the English parliament. This news itself contains several other presuppositions: who Lord Sunderland is and why it would be significant that he had gone "into the Country" (and where and what, for that matter, "the Country" is), what a Whig is, why Lord Sunderland's fears of "the trimming [not being] carried farr enough" would bode ill "for somebody," and how all of these details relate to "the fate of Spencer, who was hangd at Hereford."

All of these presuppositions circulate around the shared experience of contemporary political intrigues, though this letter also reflects the cultural milieu within which these men were communicating. The quotation from Psalm 51 assumes a knowledge of Latin and, more specifically, of the Bible in Latin, while the reference to "Caligulas Incitatus" assumes a familiarity with classical literature. For, unless one were familiar with Suetonius's *Twelve Caesars*, it is unlikely that one would know that the ancient Roman emperor Caligula was said to have made his favorite horse, Incitatus, a consul in the Roman government.

In the final portion of the extract, we have more presuppositions that surround shared experiences. There is an assumption that the reader will know who "neice Cotterell" and "little Mad cap" are, while "the snuff box full of Fairies" refers specifically to an earlier turn in the conversation, which itself relies on an entirely different series of presuppositions:

> Pray let her [little Mad cap] know I have received a letter from fairy Land, King oberon is very much her servant, and designs to sail hither with twenty thousand of his subjects in an oyster shell, the first time I go to Easthamstead Ile put his majesty & all his army in my snuff box and carry'em to wait on her Ladyship. the blew Bird is out of Love, & Grognon is alive again.[41]

In all these letters we find other aspects that indicate the *simulation* of conversation. There are greetings, farewells, and the communication of well wishes from mutual acquaintances, just as there are when one visits a friend for tea. In this manner, correspondents in the Republic of Letters wrote to each other as interlocutors in a conversation. By behaving "as if" they were speaking to each other, they were able to simulate physical co-location (with the use of visual and literary props, as already discussed), as well as opening themselves up to co-presence, making themselves "mutually available and accessible to each other, tuned in to and in touch with each other."

The third technique of virtuality to be considered is the use of rituals. We understand a ritual to be "a custom, habit, or practice"[42] that is used "to shift . . . perceptions and understandings in a coordinated and actual manner." Rituals "*actualize* the virtual."[43] Accordingly, just as a coronation ceremony embodies the idea of a king or queen in the form of an individual person, rituals within the Republic of Letters served to actualize specific ideas and roles. Consider the following exchange:

> Of all afflictions being separated from one's friends is one of the greatest; and of all the pleasures such an absence will allow, writing to and hearing from'em is most sensible.[44]

> Your extreamely kind & obliging Lettre from Geneva the 23. passt O.S.[45] was long upon the way, yet found me at last in this solitary place, where I have almost lost the sight

> of the world & the world of me; But yet I cannot quit the onely satisfaction of Life, which is the seeing & hearing from a few valuable friends, among whome your own goodnesse & merit has plac'd you in the cheif rank.[46]

Here, the correspondents engage in a ritual of exchange wherein the use of letters as a substitute for conversation is openly acknowledged. Coupled with literary props and simulation, this positions the author and recipient as interlocutors in a conversation and helps to actualize the imagined community within which they operate. Henry St John's use of the adjective "sensible"—"perceptible by the senses"[47]—in the first of these extracts is particularly telling, as it tacitly recognizes that, in the absence of corporeal proximity, a letter—a physical artifact—is the best substitute for conversation. Likewise, Sir William's response refers to "seeing & hearing from" his friends, not just to receiving a message or a piece of news. The employment of ritual allows the two men to make real their conversation as if they were proximate, despite the physical distance between them.

We have already mentioned some other rituals that were employed in the Republic of Letters—the practice of seeking an introduction to someone before writing to them directly, for example—and still others are implicit in the standards of publicity and reciprocity that supported the community. For example, in 1719, after reading that Pierre Des Maiseaux was working on a history of scholarly journals, Denis-François Camusat wrote to him to let him know that he "had already conceived the design of such a book" and therefore felt it appropriate to ask Des Maiseaux

> for all the elucidation that it is so easy for you to give me. I do not doubt, Monsieur, that with your *lumières*, very assiduous study & with an exact research into all the facts which could embellish a work of this type, I will in the end do a passable job.[48]

Here, in the process of writing to Des Maiseaux to request the use of his research in his own endeavors, Camusat engages in much virtual fawning. He defers to Des Maiseaux's reputation in the Republic of Letters by emphasizing his own inferior position while also taking advantage of the common orientation of the Republic toward the common weal in order to make what today might be regarded as a rather audacious request. Elsewhere we find this deference articulated in the habit of signing letters as, for example, "your obedient humble servant," "yours most affectionately and most attentively," or "completely and utterly yours." Such rituals, embodied as rhetorical commonplaces, served to reinforce the sense of respect and community within the Republic of Letters. These rituals also worked to make concrete the simulation of conversation in these letters via the maintenance of an interaction order between the corresponding parties. Other rituals, such as those to be found in examples of unsolicited letters within the community, were less overt.

We have already mentioned that people often sought introductions to others within the Republic of Letters, yet such an introduction could not always be gained. In these instances, one might have to resort to sending an unsolicited letter to a desired correspondent, especially if one was a young scholar who could not yet take advantage of his or her own network to develop connections with others. In these instances, we find the employment of ritual to emphasize the obligations associated with membership in the Republic of Letters in an attempt to maximize the success of contact:

> Excuse, Monsieur, the liberty I am taking, but I am availing myself of the Privileges accorded in the Republic of Letters, which authorize one to seek out the help one needs.[49]

> Is it permitted for me to write you a very long Letter the first time I have the honor to write to you? I flatter myself, Monsieur, the Rep. of Letters has its rights, & what others would consider an impoliteness, I assure myself, Monsieur, you will interpret as a mark of trust.[50]

In both of these examples, the author "goes through the motions" of excusing his behavior. In the first extract, Jacques-Georges de Chaufepié does so by specifically asking that his conduct be excused, while in the second, Jean-Pierre de Crousaz adopts the posture of the fawning would-be protégé, asking for permission to write such a long letter on their first occasion of correspondence. Each of them then "laughs off" the need for excuses by drawing on the "Privileges" and "rights" of the Republic of Letters, subtly emphasizing that the unwritten laws of the virtual community within which they are interacting not only permit them to make such solicitations, which would be deemed unseemly in other social circles, but also oblige their correspondents to reply. Here, ritual serves again to actualize the idea of liberty that the Republic of Letters embodies. In their virtual community, citizens of the Republic could do and say things that they could not do elsewhere.

Shields's techniques of virtuality—rituals, props, simulations—and Zhao and Elesh's understanding of co-location and co-presence, and the related construction of consociated contemporaries via mediated communication, thus allow us to consider the construction of virtuality between individuals independent of the media that those individuals use to communicate. In order to overcome the problem of spatial, and subsequently temporal, distance, scholars in early modern Europe employed specific tools in order to construct a virtual community within which they could interact. Without instantaneous communication, and without corporeal, audile, or visual contact, they were still able to function as if they were engaging in conversation. This understanding of virtuality has implications for contemporary research that attempts to identify the affordances of modern technologies for social interaction.

Conclusion

Our introduction suggested that the increase in volume, speed, and diversity of communication in the "digital age" has led to many scholars assuming an implicit link between these advances and the advent of digital technology itself. It also pointed out that a growing body of scholars cautions against this assumption, noting that the sociotechnical system underpinning such communication has itself been formed over many centuries. Benjamin Peters offers a simile to help illustrate the evolving natures of communication media. He suggests that, just as words change their meaning over time, so do media.[51] In the case of our historical comparison, the medium of letter-writing holds a different meaning for a correspondent in the twenty-first century than one in the seventeenth. However, the meaning itself has not disappeared—the "old" medium has adopted a new role and its meaning has been preserved in "new" media. For this reason, it is important to separate *what* is being communicated (the communication itself) from *how* it is being communicated (the medium).

When such an approach is adopted, it becomes apparent that, although the instantaneity of modern electronic media certainly has the potential to increase the volume and frequency of communication, the communication itself remains consistent with older forms. Axel Bruns, acknowledging the possibility of historical precursors to the knowledge production process he terms "produsage," summarizes this point thusly:

> The new informational networks which support produsage are crucial in achieving a wide-scale, equipotential access to the environments and projects of produsage, of course, *but they serve only to extend their reach and speed up their processes*; slower, offline, geographically more limited precursors to produsage may be found just as well in the processes of academic peer review or the exchange of folk culture and vernacular knowledge in pre–mass media environments, for example.[52]

Therefore, if one is to effectively identify the affordances of modern technologies and communications media, one must identify what is different about *what* is being communicated. At that point, the fundamental differences in social dynamics can be identified, and further consideration given to *how* electronic media engender, or enable, these differences.

It is certain that there *is* something novel about the myriad electronic technologies that we interact with and use to transmit information on a day-to-day basis. Despite this, it would be prudent to heed warnings of technological determinism when attempting to define the affordances of these technologies. While various studies point to increased volumes of communication, and to opportunities for the transmission of data such as pictures or video across the globe almost instantaneously, many of these fail to identify what else is different about these forms of communication. Having a conversation with someone using a webcam or via e-mail is fundamentally no different from having a conversation using a telephone or via hand-written letter. The same information can be shared, the same assumptions made, and techniques of virtuality can be employed to compensate for a lack of audile, visual, or tactile connection. As such, perhaps we should be asking not what information digital technologies allow us to transmit, but how this information changes the fundamental dynamics of our social interactions: What is different about the information being shared; what is different about the techniques that people employ to construct the virtual; and how does this change the comportment of individuals in their relationships with others?

Notes

1. Borgman, *Scholarship*, 48. This chapter is a revised version of a paper presented at the 11th annual conference for the Association of Internet Researchers; see Callisen and Adkins, "Old Face of 'New' Social Networks."
2. Borgman, *Scholarship*, chap. 4.
3. Ibid., 48.
4. Shields, *Virtual,* 46.
5. Ibid., xvi.
6. McNeely and Wolverton, *Reinventing Knowledge,* xx.
7. Haydu, "Making Use of the Past."
8. Shields, *Virtual,* 28.
9. Ibid., 29.
10. Ibid., 41.
11. Zhao, "Consociated Contemporaries," 92.
12. Lee, "Presence," 37.
13. Adkins and Nasarczyk, "Asynchronicity."
14. Knorr Cetina, "Synthetic Situation," 80.
15. Bourdieu, "Specificity of the Scientific Field," 34.
16. Behringer, "Communications Revolutions."
17. See also Briggs and Burke, *Social History,* chap. 2.
18. For useful synopses, see Grafton, *Worlds Made by Words,* chap. 1; and Maber, "Texts, Travel, and Flying Machines." For more detail, see Goldgar, *Impolite Learning.*

19. Fumaroli, "Republic of Letters," 137–138, emphasis and interpolation in original.
20. Ibid., 136–137.
21. For discussion, see Dibon, "Communication"; and Maber, "Knowledge as Commodity."
22. On the following, see especially Austin and Anderson, "Faith, Friendship and Learning"; Hunt and Shell, "Book as Gift"; Mauelshagen, "Networks of Trust"; and Stegeman, "Scholarly Correspondence."
23. Dibon, "Communication," 49.
24. Stegeman, "Scholarly Correspondence," 232.
25. These rituals are described in Stegeman, "Scholarly Correspondence."
26. Dibon, "Communication," 47; Fumaroli, "Republic of Letters," 136.
27. Burke, "Erasmus," 5; McNeely and Wolverton, *Reinventing Knowledge,* 130.
28. See further Callisen and Adkins, "The Old Face of "New" Social Networks," 12–15, and references cited there.
29. Briggs and Burke, *Social History*, 22.
30. Behringer, "Communications Revolutions."
31. Dibon, "Communication," 49, 50.
32. Shields, *Virtual,* 41.
33. Zhao and Elesh, "Copresence," 570–571.
34. Ibid., 569.
35. Mauelshagen, "Networks of Trust," 17.
36. Maber, "Texts, Travel, and Flying Machines," 240.
37. Howell, *Epistolæ Ho-Elianæ,* sig. A3r.
38. Goffman, "Felicity's Condition."
39. Psalm 51:3: "Why dost thou glory in malice . . . ?" *(KJV).*
40. Sir William Trumbull to Henry St John, June 30, 1702, in Lashmore-Davies, "Correspondence," 94–95.
41. St John to Sir William, June 20, 1702, in Lashmore-Davies, "Correspondence," 92.
42. See "rite," in *Oxford English Dictionary.*
43. Shields, *Virtual,* 35–36, emphasis in original.
44. St John to Sir William, May 23, 1698, in Lashmore-Davies, "Correspondence," 23.
45. "Old Style," in reference to the date.
46. Sir William to St John, June 28, 1698, in Lashmore-Davies, "Correspondence," 25.
47. See "sensible," in *Oxford English Dictionary.*
48. Denis-François Camusat to Pierre Des Maiseaux, April 19, 1719, quoted in Goldgar, *Impolite Learning,* 14–15.
49. Jacques-Georges de Chaufepié to Prosper Marchand, February 8, 1751, quoted in Goldgar, *Impolite Learning,* 21.
50. Jean-Pierre de Crousaz to Pierre Coste [1731], quoted in Goldgar, *Impolite Learning,* 21.
51. Peters, "And Lead Us Not," 22–23.
52. Bruns, *Blogs,* 387, emphasis added.

Works Cited

Adkins, Barbara, and Jason Nasarczyk. "Asynchronicity and the 'Time Envelope' of Online Annotation: The Case of the Photosharing Website, Flickr." *Australian Journal of Communication* 35, no. 3 (2009): 115–140.

Austin, Kenneth, and Wendy Anderson. "Faith, Friendship and Learning: Intercultural Communication in the Republic of Letters." *Language and Intercultural Communication* 10, no. 1 (2010): 17–31.

Behringer, Wolfgang. "Communications Revolutions: A Historiographical Concept." Translated by Richard Deveson. *German History* 24, no. 3 (2006): 333–374.

Borgman, Christine L. *Scholarship in the Digital Age: Information, Infrastructure and the Internet.* Cambridge, MA: MIT Press, 2007.

Bourdieu, Pierre. "The Specificity of the Scientific Field and the Social Conditions for the Progress of Reason." *Social Science Information* 14, no. 6 (1975): 19–47.

Briggs, Asa, and Peter Burke. *A Social History of the Media: From Gutenberg to the Internet.* 3rd ed. Cambridge: Polity, 2009.

Bruns, Axel. *Blogs, Wikipedia, Second Life, and Beyond.* New York: Peter Lang, 2008.

Burke, Peter. "Erasmus and the Republic of Letters." *European Review* 7, no. 1 (1999): 5–17.

Callisen, Christian T., and Barbara Adkins. "The Old Face of 'New' Social Networks: The Republic of Letters as a Virtual Community." Paper presented at the 11th annual conference for the Association of Internet Researchers, Gothenburg, Sweden, October 21–23, 2010.

Dibon, Paul. "Communication in the Respublica Literaria of the 17th Century." *Res Publica Litterarum* 1 (1978): 43–55.

Fumaroli, Marc. "The Republic of Letters." Translated by R. Scott Walker. *Diogenes* 143 (1988): 129–152.

Goffman, Erving. "Felicity's Condition." *The American Journal of Sociology* 89, no. 1 (1983): 1–53.

Goldgar, Anne. *Impolite Learning: Conduct and Community in the Republic of Letters, 1680–1750.* New Haven: Yale University Press, 1995.

Grafton, Anthony. *Worlds Made by Words: Scholarship and Community in the Modern West.* Cambridge, MA: Harvard University Press, 2009.

Haydu, Jeffrey. "Making Use of the Past: Time Periods as Cases to Compare and as Sequences of Problem Solving." *The American Journal of Sociology* 104, no. 2 (1998): 339–371.

Howell, John. *Epistolæ Ho-Elianæ: Familiar Letters Domestic and Forren; Divided into Six Sections, Partly Historicall, Politicall, Philosophicall, Upon Emergent Occasions.* London: For Humphrey Moseley, 1645. *Early English Books Online.* Accessed July 7, 2010. http://eebo.chadwyck.com.

Hunt, Arnold, and Alison Shell. "The Book as Gift in Elizabethan Durham: Barnabe Barnes's *A Divine Centurie of Spiritual Sonnets.*" In *Collaboration and Interdisciplinarity in the Republic of Letters: Essays in Honour of Richard G. Maber*, edited by Paul Scott, 117–133. Manchester: Manchester University Press, 2010.

Knorr Cetina, Karin. "The Synthetic Situation: Interactionism for a Global World." *Symbolic Interaction* 32, no. 1 (2009): 67–87.

Lashmore-Davies, Adrian C., ed. "The Correspondence of Henry St. John and Sir William Trumbull, 1698–1710." Special issue, *Eighteenth-Century Life* 32, no. 3 (2008).

Lee, Kwan M. "Presence, Explicated." *Communication Theory* 14, no. 1 (2004): 27–50.

Maber, Richard. "Knowledge as Commodity in the Republic of Letters, 1675–1700." *Seventeenth-Century French Studies* 27 (2005): 197–208.

———. "Texts, Travel, and Flying Machines: The Lost World of Seventeenth-Century Scholarship." In *Collaboration and Interdisciplinarity in the Republic of Letters: Essays in Honour of Richard G. Maber*, edited by Paul Scott, 229–248. Manchester: Manchester University Press, 2010.

Mauelshagen, Franz. "Networks of Trust: Scholarly Correspondence and Scientific Exchange in Early Modern Europe." *The Medieval History Journal* 6, no. 1 (2003): 1–32.

McNeely, Ian F., and Lisa Wolverton. *Reinventing Knowledge: From Alexandria to the Internet.* New York: W. W. Norton & Co., 2008.

Oxford English Dictionary, online version. Oxford: Oxford University Press, 2010. Accessed December 1, 2010. http://www.oed.com/.

Peters, Benjamin. "And Lead Us Not into Thinking the New Is New: A Bibliographic Case for New Media History." *New Media & Society* 11, nos. 1 & 2 (2009): 13–31.

Scott, Paul, ed. *Collaboration and Interdisciplinarity in the Republic of Letters: Essays in Honour of Richard G. Maber.* Manchester: Manchester University Press, 2010.

Shields, Rob. *The Virtual.* London: Routledge, 2003.

Stegeman, Saskia. "How to Set up a Scholarly Correspondence: Theodorus Janssonius van Almeloveen (1657–1712) Aspires to Membership of the Republic of Letters." Translated by P. J. E. Hyams. *Lias*, vol. 20, no. 2 (1993): 227–243.

Zhao, Shanyang. "Consociated Contemporaries as an Emergent Realm of the Lifeworld: Extending Schutz's Phenomenological Analysis to Cyberspace." *Human Studies* 27, no. 1 (2004): 91–105.

———, and David Elesh. "Copresence as 'Being with.'" *Information, Communication and Society* 11, no. 4 (2008): 565–583.

Part II:

New Media History and Theory

chapter five

Sound Studies for Historians of New Media

D. Travers Scott

Introduction: Histories of Communication Technologies and Hearing Instant Messaging

Sound studies is not solely the study of audio communication technologies, but it is greatly interested in them. Part of this has been an ongoing intervention: studying histories of sound technologies contrasts and counterbalances the dominance, in media and communication studies, of photography, film, computer and TV screens, and other visual media. Sound studies supports an expanded scope of inquiry, new research questions, and productive avenues of investigation for historians of new media not only into neglected histories of audio media but also into the neglected audio of and among all media.

If one defines communication technologies as techniques, mechanical or otherwise, of knowledge production, preservation, and transference, audio technologies are arguably the very first. Vocalization and speech, then the mnemonic techniques of the oral tradition, such as rhyme, alliteration, meter, and music, all present nonmechanical techniques for preserving and transmitting information. Indeed, audio technologies have been studied as prehistories and prototypes of subsequent media. The sound telegraph and radio also served as battlegrounds over which the nature of broadcasting, and hence, the mass-mediated national public sphere, would play out, establishing many aspects of the institutional forms of later media. More recently, digital audio technologies are sites where the sorting out of institutional and economic relationships for media and technologies to come takes place. Telepresence—the real-time splitting of subjectivity across distance that could be directly understood without mediation—has been a popular topic in cyberculture studies yet was first widely engaged and negotiated in audio technologies such as the telephone and telegraphy's Morse code. Audiotape was the first experience for many consumers of productive home audio technologies, perhaps since early read-and-write gramophones, laying the foundation for the shifted roles of producer-consumers we see in today's digital culture of remixes and mashups. DIY, user-created content, such as YouTube videos, are the inheritors of numerous radio plays, pirated broadcasts, analog remixes, oral histories, and documentaries done on reel-to-reel and portable tape recorder—often before home movie or video cameras. Indeed, as Frances Dyson's recent work argues, many of the conceptual concerns and phenomenological attributes associated with new media were first engaged in sound technologies and sound art.[1]

Given the frequent prescience of audio technologies, it is understandable that their study involves several specializations and interest areas, such as the involvement of various mechanical sound technologies in histories of nations, including national defense, border protection and expansion, and interrogation. Another area has been audio technologies' contributions to and unique versions of cultural histories of mass production, reproduction, and consumption, including theorizations of their effects. Much work has been done in new media histories, examining MP3 and other digital audio file formats as a continuation of this process. Whereas histories focused on sound reproduction largely parallel or match reproduction of visual images, sound technologies offer further unique prehistories in their specific examination of mobility, from the transistor radio to portable cassette, CD, and digital audio players.

This gestures only slightly to the full array of media histories of interest to, developed within, or intersecting with sound studies. I will now describe a specific research example of a history of a new medium, but, instead of merely tracing the history of a technology primarily thought of as aural, I wish to extend sounds studies' interest in technological history and argue for attending to neglect, not simply *of* sound technologies, but of the sounds of *all* technologies. I wish to make the case, through this example, of examining *any* communication technology as a *sound* technology, possessing important and neglected aural components. Sound studies encourages a media scholar to examine the neglected aural aspects of all media, such as the audio content of voice communication, embedded or parallel music playback systems, user feedback elements, and ambient machinery noise. Therefore, I will describe approaching a new medium not readily thought of as a sound technology—instant messaging—to suggest the methodological impact sound studies can have on new media history.

Consider a typical history of instant messaging, such as that on Wikipedia.[2] The "History" section of the *Instant Messaging* entry provides a chronological overview familiar in style and structure: from early pre-Internet prototypes in multi-user operating systems such as CTSS and Multics in the mid-1960s; to peer-to-peer, server-based, and Bulletin Board Systems in the 1980s; to early online messaging systems such as Quantum Link for Commodore 64 users; to contemporary, Internet-wide proprietary systems with a graphical user interface, such as AOL Instant Messenger and open source, multi-platform systems such as Jabber, and video conferencing systems, such as Voice Over Internet Protocol (VOIP). In this admittedly brief history, sound is only suggested by the mention of video conferencing. The visual transition from command-line text to graphical interface is noted and even illustrated by screen captures, yet audio elements are absent, a glaring omission for a medium that is about replicating (and early versions of which were named after) the audio communication of "talk."

Sound studies offers ways to listen to a technological history, asking, What did instant messaging *sound* like? How has this changed? This is no more arcane or trivial than the fetishistic litany of inventor names, product models, software releases, and other technical jargon suffusing some media histories. Sound is not merely relevant, it is significant. Arguably the most defining and memorable aspect of e-mail is AOL's auditory salutation, "You've got mail!"—the phrase becoming the title of a 1998 Nora Ephron film and earning modest celebrity for its voiceover artist, Elwood Edwards. What have been equally paradigmatic sounds of instant messaging?

In addition, sound studies argues for consideration of not only sound information carried *by* technologies but the incidental sounds *of* technologies. While some attention has been paid to the sounds of mediation—white noise, tape hiss, vinyl crackle—this too often stops at superficial aesthetics or dismissal as symptoms of fetishizing. More work is to be done: What relations with sense, self, and meaning have imbued cooling-fan hums, transistors' ultrasonic whines, digital-disc stutters, speaker "distortions," or equalizers' factory presets? John Cage's insights into environment and ambience in music and composition await full appreciation and application by historians of new media.[3] Even less considered have been the intentional sounds of design feedback: keyboards and mouses click, keypads beep, software chirps and eeps, ringtones sing and speak, cameras click and whirr, cell phone cameras make artificial shutter snaps, telephone dials click-whirr and sing tones, telegraphs stop and start, TV clickers click. What would it offer to pan sound center in analyses of technology and media effects, aesthetics, or subjectivities? What would it provide to study sound as inherent to rather than augmentation of Instant Messaging? How could one iteration of an IM application—say, Apple's iChat 2.1—be understood in its varied experiences across different desktops, laptops, operating system releases, speakers, headphones, and preference settings?

Such questions call historians of new media toward new challenges: Screen captures of archaic and prototypical technologies, such as Internet Relay Chat, show only the visual aspect of the interface. What were the feedback sounds? User guides and message posts to support groups may provide textual clues—"a beep will alert you"—but critical listening suggests that there are many different types of beeps, with many different connotations. Whether this was a friendly, chirping beep or a stern, dissonant tone is highly relevant to the nature of the medium and the kind of user and usage practices it facilitated or shaped. Sound studies encourages historians and theorists of new media to take more holistic, corporeal, and ethnographic approaches. At what point do CPUs have enough processing capability to play music without interfering with bandwidth? Who turns the sound on or off, and why? Why are audio-off or video-off options still used? In contradistinction to the presumption that more mediation and richer presence are automatically good, consider why instant messaging persists at all in text-only forms, in text-and-audio-only forms. Is it solely a matter of technological access, capability, and skills, or are there unique pleasures and capacities afforded to the user experiences of textual, spoken, and visual communications media, separately and combined? As Charles Acland's collection on residual media demonstrates, "old media" do not disappear.[4] Who then, still uses "old" forms of instant messaging? Who enjoys the silence, and why? Furthermore, how are they combined with other technologies? As should be painfully apparent in an era of home and global networks, the new media historian cannot afford to study technologies in isolation, as this reflects neither their development nor use. This is especially true given how sound waves flow between networked devices: Consider a user running an out of date but preferred IM software iteration with the volume turned off, on the newest Android tablet, playing digitized ragtime cylinder recordings downloaded through the Limewire peer-to-peer network, then using its built-in messaging protocol to ask another user in what archive she found them—all while mousing and typing on her favorite Bluetooth input devices with extra-loud clicks but with many audio user alerts of her operating system silenced so she won't be interrupted by the "tink" of incoming e-mail.

Acknowledging the audio that saturates and washes over all media also implies a larger breaking down of traditional media divisions along perceptual lines, such that distinction of audio or video media becomes irrelevant. This can be applied not only to studies of individual users but also to institutional studies of technologies. Steve Wurtzler, for one, has examined how technologies such as radio, sound film, electric amplification, and phonographs were all inextricably woven together in their development, use, and refinement across various media industries, corporations, and electrical utilities.[5] If traditional separations of screen culture and sound media are disrupted, what other such new, more productive groupings, provocative juxtapositions, research questions, and forms of analysis might appear? How was sound negotiated and divided among researchers and development teams at technology companies developing various forms of Instant Messaging? Why were some features enabled, others disabled? When AOL acquired Mirabilis, the creators of ICQ, how did those employees and teams interface with those who had already developed AOL Instant Messenger, and how were they integrated into subsequent patent applications? What were their interactions, if any, with teams working on streaming audio or music subscription services? When AOL merged with Time Warner, how did audio technology researchers and developers interact with proprietors, custodians, and developers of audio content, such as recording artists and music videos, or radio divisions of news organizations, such as CNN? If there was minimal interface, how were institutional boundaries drawn and defended? How did business and organizational structures and networks affect the development, dissemination, preservation, and creation of sounds? These are some of the research questions to which sound studies lures a media historian.

The Body and Gendered Listening: Theorizing the Persistent Videophone

As Herman Gray reminds us, "Technologies are not neutral but rather are always raced, gendered, and deeply rooted in particular social conditions, histories, and interests."[6] Jonathan Sterne, for example, connects audio recording to *mediate auscultation*, the medical innovation of stethoscope use—a moment deeply gendered, as it was driven in part by modes of propriety that a male doctor should not press his ear directly to a female patient's breast.[7] Indeed, technologies of listening have been studied for their corporeal associations as well as culturally gendered associations and practices. Western dualisms of the literate, mental, or visual and the oral, sensory, or auditory, perhaps summarized as the linguistic/Other, have a long philosophical tradition. The mapping of these dualisms onto gender has been explored, for example, in Hillel Schwartz's historical outline of (and argument against) the devaluation of hearing and the ear, linking them to the feminine.[8] One way of understanding this involves the receptive, penetrative nature of hearing: Listening is an invasion of boundaries, sound waves transgressing and entering an individual's body. While listening, orality, and aurality have been examined as feminine or feminized, there is also a body of scholarship looking at feminine genderings of machines and technology. If technologies can have certain feminine genderings, these are emphasized when they are sound technologies. Sound studies' work on feminized listening, listeners, and technologies can offer theoretical tools for historians of new media grappling with questions such as media adoption or resistance, as I will suggest here in a sketch of a videophone research project.

The 2009 U.S. *Celebrity Apprentice* featured competing teams producing corporate stage spectacles for digital phone service provider ACN to launch their IRIS 3000 videophone. Amid female dancers gyrating with receivers in hand, non sequitur crooning from soul singer Brian McKnight, and comedy by Joan Rivers, user scenarios were presented, such as a deployed soldier seeing loved ones when calling home, a travelling father remotely witnessing his baby's first steps, and a marriage proposal initiated by videophone. That this was far from the first time such "revolutionary" forms of combined audio-video, synchronous, two-way communication have been available to the public was predictably erased in the competitive rapture of announcing the product. Also absent was any acknowledgment of today's relatively easy video-audio communication via instant-messaging or chat software, such as iChat AV, Skype, Windows, AIM, Yahoo Messenger, Gmail, or even web-based Java platforms, such as Userpane, requiring only a browser and webcam, which are often built into computers. Such popular and common technologies make fêting a videophone in 2009 resemble the debut of a self-sharpening straight razor in the era of Bic and Gillette.

Almost two decades ago, in 1992, I trumpeted videophones as an advertising copywriter for several publications of the Sears, Roebuck & Company mail-order catalog. That same year, a social history of telephones would still relegate video telephones to the predictions of futurists.[9] Indeed, while previously futurists had imagined, and manufacturers had attempted to deliver, communication devices that married visual communication with telephony, none had ever been popularly adopted. Experiments in wire transmission of images date back at least to an 1843 British patent application. Technology news reporters breathlessly predicted coming motion-picture telephones in news articles from 1878, 1910, and 1912; the 1938 Walker Report on the telephone industry saw in the new medium of television "the possibility of a nation-wide visual and auditory communication service."[10] From 1936's *Things to Come* and *Flash Gordon* to 1968's *2001: A Space Odyssey* and 2009's *Moon*, the two-way viewscreen has remained a hallmark of sci-fi cinema. In the mid-1960s, AT&T released the Picture Phone, but its failed introduction would come to be seen, along with "loud speaking telephones," as "well-known examples of the danger of too narrowly conceived user groups."[11] A 1981 telephony book tried to sound upbeat while similarly recognizing it as "a technical success but an economic failure; however, we do have Picturephone [*sic*] conference service between conference rooms located in a number of cities. Someday we are sure to have video as an adjunct to much speech in communication."[12] "Someday" hadn't come a decade later, when a *New York Times* article on telephone ubiquity and innovation—including mobility, video, and online networks—included a photo of AT&T's "Videophone 2500," a "full-color, motion picture phone [that] works over existing phone lines. Just plug it in." The article describes how "video phones . . . have made a tentative reappearance in the consumer market in the past year, decades after the doomed Picture Phone gave AT&T its most notorious and painful marketing disaster. The new generation of video phones represents a small victory of technology."[13] Recently, Wendy Chun blamed 1990s hype for videophones as a contributing factor to that decade's overinvestment in fiber-optic cable systems, and a component in telecom accounting scandals, inflated stock prices, and the dot.com bubble.[14]

Whereas there has been popular culture and consumer electronics marketing evidence of persistent desires for telephones with visual capabilities, consumers have remained cool toward the same technology in such a form. Yet, rather than remaining a one-time techno-flop, they reappear. Sound studies offers a way to attune to these recurring reintroductions through theories of gendered listening. As noted previously, numerous scholars from numerous perspectives have argued for a feminine, feminized, or demasculinized gendering in culture of technologies and practices of listening and hearing. Drawing on this, the indefatigable appeal of the videophone can be understood as driven in part by an anxious need to masculinize the most overtly feminine form of communications media, the telephone. However, its lack of widespread adoption attests to strong and persistent pleasures derived from exactly the telephone's audio-only, "feminine" mode of communication. The telephone, which combines all the elements of the phonograph with the added dimension of liveness and an emphasis on orality, listening skills, and verbal culture, can be seen as a paradigmatic example of listening technology and therefore gendered highly feminine.

Several cultural artifacts attest to this anxiety. A common narrative trope is women who transgress boundaries of propriety and privacy via a telephone party line: The gasping biddy overhearing gossip in Norman Rockwell's "The Party Wire," a 1919 cover for *Leslie's* magazine; the eavesdropping gossips who nearly destroy an entire town in the 1935 silent film *Party Wire*; the "nosy old thing" of Hank Williams's country classic "Mind Your Own Business"; the old matron who garners dirty looks at the rural meeting hall in the telephone training film *Dial Comes to Town*; or the aloof blonde who drives a virile man to homosexual masquerade in *Pillow Talk*. Feminine vulnerability, particularly to penetration by knives and other phallic weapons, is seen in the horror movie trope of the victim, typically female, harassed over the phone by a psycho serial killer, as in the *Scream* films, *Halloween*,

When a Stranger Calls, *Don't Answer the Phone*, *Black Christmas*, and many others. Moral panics over obscene phone callers reflect similar concerns. Threatening female desires are conveyed telephonically in representations such as the femme fatale operator of a phone sex line used to lure victims to her serial-killing brother in the 1988 slasher *Party Line,* and the vengeful telephone operator who calls herself, appropriately, "Shiva," and uses her telecom techno-savvy to track, torment, and emasculate a rude male caller in 2000's *The Operator*.

Such examples suggest anxieties around cultural dependence on a too-feminine technology, one that puts masculinity at a disadvantage. Recurring attempts to insert the masculine-gendered qualities of video into telephony can be understood as an expression of anxiety around a utilitarian and ubiquitous technology perceived as in need of gender balance. The presumption would be that introduction of the visual would also entail its secure and familiar dominance: A woman alone and in power is worrisome, so one must introduce a man to keep things in check. Just as the original "telephone boys" of early switchboards were too unruly and difficult to manage, their replacement by female switchboard operators was driven by seeing women as more docile and manageable. Femininity and feminine listening are understood as not only naturally subservient to the visual, but appropriately so. The desire for videophones can be theorized as not merely the expansion of perceptual modes but the reassurance of introducing a dominant masculine visual mode to constrain the feminine listening, to re-create a model of gendered sensory relations that reassuringly reflects gendered social relations.

And yet, the persistent lack of consumer adoption indicates that utilitarian needs and the unique pleasures afforded precisely by a lack of visuality have helped keep the videophone from mass adoption. Indeed, John Shepherd theorizes similarly gendered contradictions and paradoxical desires regarding one form of auditory culture, "music[, which] . . . occupies contradictory positions in the social structures of industrial capitalism that are parallel to those of women."[15] Sound studies also offers tools to theorize what these pleasures might be: empathy, intersubjectivity, and connection rather than detachment. For example, Roland Barthes associates listening with spirituality, intimacy, and constitution of subjectivity: "The injunction to listen is the total interpellation of one subject by another: it places above everything else the quasi-physical contact of these subjects (by voice and ear): it creates transference: '*listen to me*' means '*touch me, know that I exist.*'"[16] By introducing the visual to the telephone, listening threatens to be dominated by, or, at the very least, to share the sensory bandwidth with watching. Perhaps many telephone users have not wished to be listened to, touched, or known to any greater degree. Sound studies' theoretical tools call historians of new media to these questions, which could then lead to more empirical projects, such as archival research into product testing or holding contemporary focus groups of users.

Constitution of Subjectivities: Sounds of and in the *Ring*

At their most literal, audio technologies contribute to the formation of subjects through cybernetic means: transmitting information relevant to understanding a particular subjectivity. Hearing the sounds of a Polish radio station enables listeners to better understand themselves as Polish Americans. Similarly, regional and urban subjects are constituted in part via the technologies of, for example, the Detroit sounds of Motown or Detroit techno, Chicago house and blues, California surf guitar, or Pacific Northwest grunge. Within urban, national, and regional constructs, audio technologies facilitate a complex interplay between past/present, reality/fantasy, geography/essence, and self/Other, as we see in, for example, Josh Kun's work around Tijuana[17] and others' analyses of exotica music.[18] Race and ethnicity have been perhaps one of the most heavily analyzed vectors of sonic subject formation. Organic and mechanical audio technologies have preserved the cultural memory of enslaved and colonized peoples, provided outlets for their cloaked expressions of resistance, and provided modes of healing, negotiation, and memory of this process.

As a research sketch informed by this work on constitution of subjects, I will describe a cultural history of new media that draws on representations of technology in the *Ring* Japanese horror novels, films, and offshoots.[19] A sound studies method recognizes the centrality or at least parallel importance of sound in what are apparently visual narratives; and sound theory suggests understanding these narratives as constitutive discourse of, not racial or gendered subjectivities but technological subjectivity—in understanding oneself and others as users.

To summarize the core narrative: Scientists working on artificial intelligence create an electronic world called The Loop. Although it mirrors our world, it is not a virtual world in the sense of a fake environment we engage but more an electronic Petri dish or terrarium in which sentient digital life forms are born and evolve in an accelerated but parallel path, mirroring human evolution. The Loop is a digital reflection of humanity yet wholly autonomous. At one point in Loop history, a psychic woman is publicly humiliated and commits suicide. Her bastard child, who is intersex or hermaphroditic and has even stronger psychic powers, attempts a career as a stage actress but also suffers humiliations, a sexual assault, and a fatal attempt on her life. Before her death, however, she mentally wills her fury at the world that has hurt her, and at her own inability to have children, through an open television signal frequency and into a recording videotape, creating a series of images on the tape. Viewing this tape kills the viewer within a week if they do not make a copy and show it to someone new, who reproduces the cycle. As the tape-viewing spreads virally, the ghost of the dead daughter, Sadako, manages to impregnate a woman and enter the world of the living. Meanwhile, reporters investigating the fatal videotapes write up the story, which becomes a hit book and movie. However, these mediated versions of the narrative also carry the same viral curse as the original videotapes. Through their spread, and the methods by which Sadako has learned to physically reproduce herself, the world becomes populated by, and eventually taken over by, Sadako clones, snuffing out genetic diversity and killing the human race. However, all of this is only within the electronic world of The Loop. Scientists are able to observe this through watching the virtual world unfold, at its accelerated pace, through computer visualizations. Unfortunately, the ring-virus crosses over from The Loop into the "real" world, unleashing a cancer-like plague that threatens to destroy our world. Eventually, through communication and transfers of characters between the two worlds, Sadako and the ring-virus are stopped, restoring balance to The Loop world, and halting the cancer in ours.

As novels, films, and television shows about a viewed videotape and virtual world, seemingly these are visual narratives. Yet, sound studies readies one to notice how representations of sound function at key moments in the stories. The title's English homonym—"ring" as circle or cycle, wedding band, or hailing tone of a telephone—is not an accident of translation but explicitly noted in the book. In the first cases of ring-virus death, a warning of impending death is announced by a mystery phone call, moments after viewing the tape. The appearance and disappearance of these calls are a crucial clue in geographically uncovering the mystery. The psychic powers of Sadako and her mother, which attract to them their humiliations and sufferings that incite the narratives, are indicated by a high, metallic screech or whine, a sound that recurs in imitation films as death rattles and gasps of telephonic spirits and demons. Sadako's public humiliation, and the ruining of what appears to have been her one chance at happiness, has to do with the inappropriate public playing of audio tapes, implicating betrayal by her one and only potential lover, the theater troupe's sound effects man. Moreover, the telling of this backstory serves in the books and films as what humanizes Sadako from wrathful spirit to a more sympathetic monster, in the classical tradition of gothic horror. Sound, therefore, is not only a signature marker of the series and its villain/heroine, it is central to the inciting events of the narrative, and those are the narratives by which sympathetic, intersubjective understanding of the villain, and thereby her redemption, is achieved.

Jon Cruz describes how sound in the form of slave songs was a crucial empathetic link in the Abolitionist movement[20]: Sound not only provided for expression, community, and identity building among American slaves, it also was a medium by which Whites came to see them as fully human. Such work aids reading *Ring* texts and their representations of new media. Looking for and listening to sound helps one attune to significant moments that might not be noticed if one simply takes them as visual narratives. Indeed, the final image of the book series is intersubjective communion, bereft of visual contact. Significantly, in many *Ring*-inspired films, such as *Phone*, *Dial "D" for Demons*, *One Missed Call* and sequels, and *TxT*, the telephone rises in significance from adjunct to central technology, suggesting the impact of the aural aspects of the *Ring*.

Drawing on work on sound and the production of subjects, sound studies theory asks, What subjects are produced in these narratives? Technological subjects. Bad users who connect indiscriminately to degenerate forces in the network. They are narratives of bad users, abnormal users, and sick users from which we understand and articulate cultural expectations and ideals of healthy users, normal users, and good users. The users of the *Ring* narratives are literally ill, physically and mentally. They watch a tape, receive a call, or read a book and become nauseous, sickened, anxious, emotionally labile, and can literally die. The screech of Sadako and her mother is painful, like extreme tinnitus: In one scene from the films but not the books, patients at a mental hospital become agitated and violent from hearing it. Characters are hospitalized and institutionalized from the traumas associated with all aspects of the ring-virus. Being cursed, haunted, or possessed by evil spirits is one of the oldest etiologies of disease, one that has been with us for centuries and is, indeed, far from gone. Moreover, the books reveal that this is not psychosomatic or a purely ethereal, psychic curse: the ring-virus is a real virus, a hybrid of Sadako's DNA and the smallpox virus, which then becomes cancer. Smallpox is, like sound, crucial to the events of the *Rings*. Sadako's rape and death occur on the site of a former smallpox colony; her rapist is a former doctor there and the last surviving smallpox-infected person in Japan. It is also where the first viewing of the infected tape occurs. Moreover, it is where bad users start the plague: In the novels (unlike the films) there is a patient-zero videotape, an epidemiological epicenter. The tape, as first viewed, has instructions at the end explaining that, to save themselves, they must copy the tape and show it to someone else. The vacationing teenagers who first view Sadako's creation, thinking it a joke, intentionally erase over this section. The Patients Zero of the ring-virus epidemic are technology users who *do not follow the directions*—bad users—and the larger horrors that result are due to their connection to other users: they infect the network, reproducing sick, bad, and abnormal technological subjects. Sound studies method and theory suggest such insights into these historic and globally popular representations of new media.

Conclusion: Challenges for Historians

I conclude suggesting some unique challenges and productive directions they point toward. First is the prickly issue of linguistic representation: talking about sound is notoriously difficult, writing about it even more so. However, rather than a limitation of literary writing, this could provide instead additional impetus for exploring the potentials of multimedia scholarship. Second, for the new media historian, an awareness of and desire to access media sounds underscore the need for technology archives and emulators. Certain shoestring and nascent affairs exist today, such as the Browser Emulator Online, but perhaps our future lies in archives of old machines kept in working order, running archaic operating systems, with period input devices, or modern machines equipped with emulators. These could be housed at facilities staffed by media librarians, with archives of software and user guides, and historian system administrators. Who is preserving knowledge of the bugs, intricacies, troubleshooting, and workarounds for an audio-cassette data drive, a WAP Internet browser on a 2G cell phone, or a computer running NeXT? We need to not only be able to read data on 5 1/4 -inch floppy disks, we need to experience using them, just as we can test out a stereoscope in a junk shop. We need to preserve the current generation of technical experts, document their knowledge and pass it on in training future media archivists, operators, and administrators. Finally, if sound studies is truly about breaking the false binary of sight/sound, with all of its cultural associations and mappings, it is nevertheless difficult to avoid falling into the trap of reifying that very binary by continuing to discuss the two modes in terms of each other—something I may have committed throughout this chapter. Effective binary-busting has been a problem in many fields; queer theory, for example, offers itself to such problems in feminism and gender studies by occupying indeterminable spaces of insistent nonnormativity. Perhaps the task here is simpler, given that, after visual and auditory, three other sensory modes also present themselves: tactile, olfactory, and gustatory. The latter two, in particular, may provoke reflexive giggles or discomfort. I argue that such anxious reactions are often a sign of something well worth investigating. Perhaps the other three senses are simply not developed enough for incorporation into more synesthetic scholarship; perhaps it is merely that their analyses and theorizations have been lacking and await equally useful opportunities ahead.

Notes

1. Dyson, *Sounding New Media.*
2. Wikipedia, *Instant Messaging.*
3. Dyson, *Sounding New Media,* 59–72.
4. Acland, *Residual Media.*
5. Wurtzler, *Electric Sounds.*
6. Gray, *Cultural Moves,* 154.
7. Sterne, *The Audible Past,* 114.

8. Schwartz, "Afterword: The Indefensible Ear."
9. Fischer, *America Calling.*
10. de Sola Pool et al., "Foresight and Hindsight," 136.
11. Ibid., 384n.
12. Pierce, *Signals,* 31–32.
13. Gleick, "The Telephone Transformed," 62.
14. Chun, *Control and Freedom,* 26.
15. Shepherd, "Difference and Power," 59.
16. Barthes, *The Responsibility of Forms,* 251, emphases in original.
17. Kun, *Audiotopia.*
18. Lanza, *Elevator Music;* Taylor, Strange Sounds.
19. Suzuki, *Ring;* Suzuki, *Spiral;* Suzuki, *Loop;* Suzuki, *Birthday.*
20. Cruz, *Culture on the Margins.*

Works Cited

Acland, Charles. R. ed. *Residual Media.* Minneapolis: University of Minnesota Press, 2007.—1

Barthes, Roland. *The Responsibility of Forms.* Oxford, UK: Blackwell, 1986.

Chun, Wendy H. K. *Control and Freedom: Power and Paranoia in the Age of Fiber Optics.* Cambridge, MA: MIT Press, 2006.

Cruz, Jon. *Culture on the Margins: The Black Spiritual and the Rise of American Cultural Interpretation.* Princeton, NJ: Princeton University Press, 1999.

de Sola Pool, Ithiel, Craig Decker, Stephen Dizard, Kay Israel, Pamela Rubin, and Barry Weinstein. "Foresight and Hindsight: The Case of the Telephone." In *The Social Impact of the Telephone,* edited by Ithiel de Sola Pool, 127–157. Cambridge, MA: MIT Press, 1977.

Dyson, Frances. *Sounding New Media: Immersion and Embodiment in the Arts and Culture.* Berkeley: University of California Press, 2009.

Fischer, Claude. *America Calling: A Social History of the Telephone to 1940.* Berkeley: University of California Press, 1992.

Gleick, James. "The Telephone Transformed—Into Almost Everything." *New York Times,* May 16, 1993, 62.

Gray, Herman. *Cultural Moves: African Americans and the Politics of Representation.* Berkeley: University of California Press, 2005.

Kun, Josh. *Audiotopia: Music, Race, and America.* Berkeley: University of California Press, 2005.

Lanza, Joseph. *Elevator Music: A Surreal History of Muzak, Easy-listening and Other Moodsong.* Revised and expanded ed. Ann Arbor: University of Michigan Press, 2004.

Pierce, John R. *Signals: The Telephone and Beyond.* San Francisco: W. H. Freeman and Company, 1981.

Schwartz, Hillel. "Afterword: The Indefensible Ear: A History." In *The Auditory Culture Reader,* edited by Michael Bull and Les Back, 487–502. New York: Berg, 2003.

Shepherd, John. "Difference and Power in Music." In *Musicology and Difference: Gender and Sexuality in Music Scholarship,* edited by Ruth A. Solie, 46–65. Berkeley: University of California Press, 1993.

Sterne, Jonathan. *The Audible Past: Cultural Origins of Sound Reproduction*. Durham, NC: Duke University Press, 2003.

Suzuki, Koji. *Birthday*. New York: Vertical, 2006.

———. *Loop*. New York: Vertical, 2006.

———. *Ring*. New York: Vertical, 2003.

———. *Spiral*. New York: Vertical, 2005.

Taylor, Tim D. *Strange Sounds: Music, Technology & Culture*. New York: Routledge, 2001.

Wikipedia. *Instant Messaging*. Accessed April 13, 2009. http://en.wikipedia.org/wiki/Instant_messaging.

Wurtzler, Steve J. *Electric Sounds: Technological Change and the Rise of Corporate Mass Media*. New York: Columbia University Press, 2007.

chapter six

What if the Internet Did Not Speak English?

New and Old Language for Studying Newer Media Technologies

Zizi Papacharissi and Elaine J. Yuan

Introduction

It has become customary to welcome new media with a narrative that extols their potential for democratization, equality, utopia, and general advancement. This tendency frequently leads researchers to interrogate new media in a manner reflective of Western dogmas of inquiry, possibly resulting in theories and histories of media that contain a Western bias. We argue that the tendency to perceive technology as a liberating force derives from Western canons of social inquiry, reflective of capitalist, imperialist, and neoliberal mentalities. As a result, scholars invest time in search of community, identity expression, citizenship, civility, and democratic ideals that processes of industrialization and postindustrialization have reformed in Western societies and that technologies could somehow revive.

In this chapter, we examine language and metaphors prevalent in understanding the place of technology in contemporary societies. We problematize the cultural and intellectual origins of prominent metaphors and dichotomies and review research to identify non-Western metaphors and language that permit a glocal, cosmopolitan understanding of technologies that are deployed globally. In doing so, we discuss the extent to which English presents the *lingua franca* of the Internet, and how this might shape the conceptualization of research that also employs English as its *lingua franca*. We are interested in what the Internet looks like when it does not speak English, and how we may adjust our terminology to describe that more accurately as researchers. We are thus driven to a different paradigm for examining technological impact, which emphasizes gradual change, adaptation, processes of remediation, and technological affordances that are interpreted differently, based on the cultural context within which they are reified. We conclude with a synopsis of this paradigm, identification of terms and language pertinent to historically and culturally conscious inquiry of the Internet, and methodological suggestions.

Hybrid Vernaculars

The stories that we imagine about technologies reflect corresponding mythologies of our expectations of the new and our disillusionment with the old. Myth does not operate without metaphor. Metaphor permits the comparison of new experiences to past ones. It is employed to capture the meaning of contemporary events and inject elements of continuity to experiences that, without it, appear fragmented and accidental. Metaphors of the past are frequently employed to understand the new, thus contributing to a mythology of the new that bears little relation to reality,[1] or involve "media we do not yet know how to talk about."[2] Similarly, we apply metaphors developed within one culture to the study of technologies that cross cultures, thus developing vernaculars for research that contain inherent bias.

These vernaculars function in ways that are simultaneously emancipatory and restrictive. Utopian and dystopian narratives permit us to incorporate new media into our ethical hierarchies, thus exercising power and ascribing ethical identity to technological artifacts that possess no specific ethos. This is a human "gesture" upon the space suggested by newer media, a way for living beings to make their mark, and then remark, space, actual and imaginary, thus historicizing the relationship between space and technology.[3] Electronic media, in particular, routinely evoke the dominant metaphor of a *new frontier* or a *new world*,[4] a new virtual homestead for community,[5] an electronic frontier for democracy,[6] or a new, alternative *terra nova* for virtual gaming communities.[7]

Several of the English-language metaphors employed to describe net-related technologies aptly capture the elasticity and connectivity of these platforms (web, net, network). As global English evolves into the *lingua franca* of the Internet, it is important to keep in mind that while the majority of the text of the web is written in English, most of the communication on the Internet is conducted in languages other than English.[8] Beyond language, the primarily Western operating logic of the Internet creates cultural conflict for non-Western users who either negotiate cosmopolitan identities so as to navigate online geographies in China[9] and the Arab world,[10] or turn to native, over foreign, language content.[11]

Moreover, global online giants of Western origin, like Google or Facebook, operate on cultural or privacy premises that clash with non-Western social hierarchies and public/private binaries, and also threaten indigenous media industries.[12] Local online companies resist global templates for web content by producing web design and employing language that is friendlier to the cultural context of corresponding cultures,[13] thus providing some examples of what the Internet looks like when it does not speak English. Online governance and domain name administration follow a protocol articulated in English and a structure influenced by Western politics.[14] Metaphors prominently used in portals, like *expert*, *market*, and *community*, are reflective of Western or capitalist hierarchies,[15] and others like *global village* and *global marketplace* serve to legitimate the dominant political order.[16] The medium looks global but is not being used in a global way, as studies indicate that prominent search engines are biased in ways that favor U.S. sites, while Chinese sites are better covered by China-specific search engines.[17] As these tendencies evolve into norms, the history of Internet use becomes expressed in a vocabulary that contains a Western bias.

The bias toward English embedded in the architecture of the Internet may spill over to research that tends to examine English-based content, in the English language or employing English metaphors and terms. English is also the *lingua franca* of several disciplines in the social sciences. Frequently, these research vernaculars contain terms that translate awkwardly across cultures, thus erecting linguistic boundaries in what presents an intercultural history of a technology. For instance, the metaphor of *a new frontier* or *a new world* evokes bitter sentiment for inhabitants of territory that was once considered *new* and was thus subjected to the imperialistic tendencies and political-economic objectives of dominant nations. So, enthusiasm over a new frontier is frequently moderated by historical and cultural context. Moreover, linguistic differences across cultures complicate the use of terms that are employed or referenced in Internet research regularly but translate poorly in languages other than English. For example, the construct of the Public Sphere, or *Öffentlichkeit,* as it was originally expressed in German, is employed frequently to assess the democratic potential of the Internet. Yet, the term translates poorly into several languages, including Greek, which does not contain a similar term. Similarly, the term *community*, central to our understanding of sociality online, connotes different meanings and different forms of social organization when translated into other languages and cultures.[18] To this end, a greater focus on sociality over community may allow for a more pluralized understanding of the variant forms that residential sociality may acquire.[19]

Naturally, definitions and operationalizations of these terms allow us to employ constructs that have shared meaning for all of us, but the question we pose is different: To what extent does the use of terms prevalent in the Western lexicon impose yardsticks that make little sense in the rest of the world? And by employing these metaphors in our research, to what extent does research contribute to a reproduction of an Anglo-based model of sociality, politics, and history of online use? To be fair, the prevalence of the English language online is a necessity having to do with the general social functions of language.[20] An indicator of cosmopolitanism, rather than imperialism, the common language of global standardized English helps emphasize similarities and allows the discussion of differences. Moreover, a multilingual Internet does not guarantee expressional freedom online, nor does it ensure coherent and commonly understood communication. Still, a universal grammar, even if English based, must evolve beyond Western/Anglo-Saxon social and political conventions in order to create *semiotic spaces* or *semiospheres* that make sense to the multilingual publics using the Internet to express themselves and connect.[21]

Hybridity is evident in the manner nonnative speakers of English approach the Internet; they relate to the medium in a manner that affords a layering of multiple cultural identities, ethnic and not.[22] Employing the concept of the vernacular permits the understanding of expressive means that develop dialectically to reflect the inherent attributes of mainstream or subaltern cultures, or, in the context of globalization, translocalities.[23] Hybridity implies that while some of these vernaculars develop in opposition to institutional logic, they frequently contain elements of that logic as a way of introducing their alterity to a variety of publics.[24] An examination of hybrid vernaculars that develop transglobally affords the examination of both indigenous and imported modes of technology use. It also permits an understanding of how indigenous modes shape and are shaped by external cultural influences. A hybrid research vernacular thus permits an examination of cultural alterity and conformity, for all cultures, whether they be defined by technology, nationality, language, or other commonalities and differences. Furthermore, it employs research constructs that carry cultural relevance and resonate with a cosmopolitan spectrum of semiotic spaces.

To establish these vernaculars, we begin by discussing three prominent dichotomies around which vernaculars develop transculturally:

- Individual/Social
- Public/Private
- East/West

This list of conceptual binaries is not exhaustive, but we argue that it is pertinent to identifying where our present research vernaculars for online media fall short, and which vernaculars afford greater hybridity, so as to produce hybrid, rather than hegemonic, history or histories of newer media. These dichotomies are prominent in research about online behaviors and tendencies. By focusing on these, we are able to understand the circumstances around which vernaculars develop and propose language and terms more helpful for future research.

The Individual and Society

The relationship between the individual and society has been a perennial topic of social theory.[25] Georg Simmel and Everett Hughes pointed out that *society* is not merely an abstract concept that represents the realities of individuals drawn into a whole.[26] On the one hand, the individual is articulated and defined by motivations and relationships in changing social contexts.[27] On the other hand, society only has form and effects on people insofar as structure is produced and reproduced in what the individuals do.[28] In essence, "society [shapes] the individuality of its members and the individuals [form] society out of their life actions while pursuing strategies plausible and feasible within the socially woven web of their dependencies."[29]

Social solidarity and individual autonomy have been locked in a permanent state of conflict or uneasy compromise since ancient times.[30] As market-driven industrial economies and capitalism developed, liberal views emphasizing individualism prevailed, affirming the ethical primacy of the individual against the pressures of social collectivism.[31] The state was organized into self-governing republics through demo cratic means on a contractual basis of rights.[32]

The Enlightenment value of individual freedom was further established in the rapid modernization process that followed. Individualism, along with a market economy and democratic polity, was considered a defining dimension of modernity. Individualism celebrated the freedom of the individual from "the tightly knit web of communal dependency, surveillance and enforcement" at early stages of the modern time.[33] As capitalism further progressed, neoliberalism, primarily a theory of society dwelling on an image of the autonomous individual, supposed that social order under market competition would ultimately be disintegrated into individuals confronting each other. As a result, critics of neoliberal policies argue that the market dissolves all forms of social solidarity in favor of individualism and undermines the very idea of community.[34]

The conceptualization of community in recent research reflects our nostalgic memories of intimacy and interdependence. However, it is deemed historically inevitable to lose the spirit of traditional community in the process of modernization. The ideals of community necessarily contrast with the modern social order that is based on impersonal relations among mobile and often anonymous mass participants. Modern society reifies modernism's impact and encroachment upon the traditional community.[35] For instance, Ferdinand Tönnies characterized the transition from community to society as dynamism between *Gemeinschaft*, an organic and intimate life order, and *Gesellschaft*, the instrumentalized structure of modern society.[36] For him, there is no community in or after society.[37]

Furthermore, the development of globalization as a new paradigm has posed new challenges for understanding the reconfiguration of power in the contemporary world.[38] Scholars contend that globalization has led to the retreat of traditional institutions such as nation-state and the family as well as a renewed trend of individualization in Western societies.[39] While some of the properties and functions previously attributed to traditional social institutions have been extensively relocated onto global and transnational organizations, others have been intensively displaced onto the individual.[40]

As a result, "individualization is becoming the social structure of [the] second modern society itself."[41] While individualization grants people unprecedented freedom to experiment with self-identity and ways of living, it also brings the individuals an unprecedented responsibility for dealing with the social consequences of these choices.[42] Consequently, collectivism is deemed a limited and unproductive strategy, for resource-deprived individuals and communities are often expedient, temporary measures that are "fragile and shift erratically from one target to another."[43] Individualization theorists uphold individual creativity as means for the renewal of society under conditions of radical change, suggesting that "[i]n developed modernity, human mutuality and community rest no longer on solidly established traditions, but, rather, on a paradoxical collectivity of reciprocal individualization."[44] The social architectures presented by newer communication technologies reflect these tendencies and tensions, via an infrastructure that further blurs private and public.

Public and Private

The public/private binary provides the cultural context for the theorizing of social behaviors. The distinction between public and private is elusive, as it is culturally formed and sensitive to historical context.[45] For the Greek and the Roman philosophers, emphasis was placed on presence in the public arena, the public affairs, and on leading a good life. The term *public* was thus associated with principles of governance, democracy, and deliberation. Conversely, *private* delineated the locus of the home and related activities. During the nadir of the Roman period, Christianic values positioned private man before God and redefined the essence of what it means to lead a good life. This marked a departure from the Greco-Roman politically based definitions of Virtue (*Areté*) to morally constructed and religious interpretations of virtue as piety. As religious discourse dominated the private sphere and permeated private life, it, along with concurrent political and economic developments, reframed the contours of public and private behaviors.[46] During this period, *private* began to specifically delineate that which is privately owned and impenetrable by public vision. This effectively extended the public/private binary beyond *the political* to domains that are social, cultural, and, in general, behavioral, thus suggesting multiple directions for analytical thought which had, up until that point, treated this mostly in its political context.

Seminal works employ the public and private binary to contextualize the historical progression of human sociality in the Western world. Philippe Ariés's *Centuries of Childhood* maps modernity as the result of a long and complex conversation between religion, political philosophy, the economy, and individual self-interest. The ways in which modernity simultaneously enables solitude and complicates togetherness represent important themes for scholars who employ the public/private distinction. For Tönnies, the distinction between private and public helps construct the conceptual foundation for the concepts of *Gemeinschaft* and *Gesellschaft,* which capture modes of solitary and collective existence, respectively, that are both historically and culturally sensitive.[47] Erving Goffman, on the one hand, focuses on situations created by modern settings to understand, from a dramaturgical perspective, how behavior evolves across public and private social planes.[48] Herbert Gans on the other hand, locates these tensions in the urban setting and examines how the architectural structures of modernity restrict and suggest ways of existing politically and socially for individuals.[49] Richard Sennett compares and contrasts past and present modes of social and political activity to argue for the demise of a way of living structured around the ability to exist, connect, and express oneself in public.[50]

This list is exemplary of thinkers who refer back to the public/private distinction to situate and comprehend socially motivated behaviors. Focusing on the *social,* as an alternative to the bipolar continuum of public and private, Alan Wolfe proposes a trichotomy that collapses the criterion of visibility-collectivity into the realm of the social.[51] Wolfe formulates this trichotomy by distinguishing between (a) "a *private* sector in which we appropriately judge behavior by whether it maximizes individual freedom or self-interest," (b) "a *public* sector in which we make decisions that are meant to apply equally to everyone in the society (even as we recognize the near impossibility of doing this," and (c) "a realm of distinct publics."[52] The social reflects the balance between public and private, and informs the construction of *lifeworlds*, or sociocultural environments where individuals experience life.[53] Conflicting or parallel lifeworlds present the historical context against which the meaning of a technology in a particular era is understood. If we may be permitted the gross generalization of Eastern and Western lifeworlds, for the sake of the limited analysis that may take form in this chapter, it is important to examine how Eastern and Western lifeworlds develop varying vernaculars in response to modernity.

East and West: Multiple Modernities

The conception of modernity has been predominantly grounded on the set of Enlightenment values that were oriented toward the individual.[54] However, the experience of East Asia signifies a new mode of modernity that differs from modernity in Western contexts, in that "[t]he essence of the Asian alternatives is a society built not around individual rights, but around a deeply engrained moral code that is the basis for strong social structures and community life."[55] In fact, the centrality of the state in a market economy, the importance of family values to social solidarity, the rich interplay between communal consensus and personal autonomy, as well as fresh conceptual frameworks defined on indigenous terms to understand a different kind of political and economic dynamics indicate that the modernization process can assume cultural forms different from those identified as characteristically Western.[56]

Weiming Tu has further linked the current economic, political, social, and ethical life of East Asian peoples to the prominent indigenous cultural tradition of Confucian philosophy.[57] Tu points out that the Confucian emphases on "the importance of equality rather than freedom, sympathy rather than rationality, civility rather than law, duty rather than rights, and human-relatedness rather than individualism" suggest a radically different approach to human development.[58] More important, the development in industrial East Asia provides a new perspective for understanding the role of traditions in the process of modernization. East Asian modernity challenges, if not negates, the common thesis that modernity is "either a conscious rejection or an unintended departure from tradition."[59] Because community presents a focal concept in understanding, and historicizing, the cultural relevance of newer media, conversations about how different societies interpret community can help inform hybrid vernaculars of history.

While *community* is conceptualized as "sovereign, limited, and having a horizontal equality among members" connected by voluntary contractual relationships in the West,[60] communal life in the East Asian context features a sense of an organic unity based on primordial ties—the embeddedness of the human condition, as well as a strong sense of duty, "the idea that one is obligated to, and responsible for, an ever-expanding network of human relatedness."[61] Consequently, while Western scholars pronounced that "real community grounded in intimate, personal contact and concrete issues of integration has vanished, replaced by a mental construct,"[62] the continuing role of tradition is sustaining an evolving modernity for East Asia. Indeed, the Confucian doctrines may serve as "political ideology, intellectual discourse, merchant ethics, family values, as well as the spirit of protest" in forming "a spiritual joint venture" with modern Western values.[63] As Tu and others have rightly noted, "these so-called Asian or Confucian values, like Enlightenment values, are universal too."[64] How may research integrate these complex tendencies into a vocabulary of terms and theories that is truly cosmopolitan? We suggest a hybrid set of terms and theories that may advance such a breed of research.

Networked Sociality: A Hybrid Vernacular

We propose the concept of *networked sociality* as a way to understand social and related behaviors that emerge within global, local, and glocal cultural contexts. The theoretical pretext of networked sociality is Manuel Castells's network society,[65] which describes societies organized around networks enabled by information technologies. Networks and social networks have always presented a primary form of organization, for a variety of cultures. For instance, the ancient Chinese practice of *Guanxi* (relationship) has been a form of social networking structure dwelling on the indigenous Confucian culture. In addition to providing security, trust, and social cohesion, it also contributes to the unique trajectory of modernization of the old civilization. Its rich tradition and deep cultural roots contrast with the recent thrust of a social network perspective propelled mainly by the methodological need of sociological analysis and the advent of network technologies in the West.[66] Upon this theoretical premise, networked sociality is best understood in contrast to community, and describes emerging social uses of technology that are a combination of "sociability and experimentation."[67] Andreas Wittel suggests that where community involves "stability, coherence, embeddedness and belonging . . . long and lasting ties, proximity and a common history," networked sociality "stands counterposed to *Gemeinschaft* . . . [and] does not represent belonging but integration and disintegration."[68]

Networked sociality may be defined as a social expression of liquid modernity, wherein "social relations are not 'narrational' but informational. . . fleeting and transient, yet iterative. . . of ephemeral but intense encounters. . . [and] characterized by. . . a combination of work and play."[69] In essence, the construct aims to account for the Western model of modernity, with its highly differentiated spheres of interest as well as that of other distinct societies such as East Asia where the lack of clear boundaries between public and private is the norm.[70] Given that the majority of research on the Internet suggests affordances that enable expression and connection, the concept of networked sociality allows a culturally open and flexible examination of the social character of the Internet. We propose understanding networked sociality by focusing on the following concepts.

Social Ties and Sociality

Research on online social networks examines the formation and maintenance of online networks that support existing and new social ties.[71] The unit of analysis is the interaction or relation between people, measured in terms of ties held by individuals maintaining a relation, the types of exchanges, frequency of contact, strength of ties, intimacy, qualitative elements of relations, size of networks, global or local span of networks, and numerous other variables.[72] Building on this research, scholars have further developed a variety of concepts such as *media multiplexity* (the tendency of more strongly tied pairs to make use of more available media). The construct of social relations as social ties is central to an understanding of the networked sociality that emerges in contrast to community. Affording a variety of strengths, connected individuals, and ritual or purposive communication aimed at sustaining communication, *ties* mark social relations that are flexible, yet central to networked modes of sociality. They also permit an understanding of sociability that translates across cultures and may produce a culturally cohesive historical narrative of newer media technologies.

Affordances of Convergence

The social platforms or spaces sustained by convergent technologies accentuate confluence and flexibility of media content. The convergent properties of media render them both *remixed* and *remixable*: the product of institutions and independent sociocultural agents. The confluent properties of information technologies suggest particular possibilities for interaction, which tend to be structured around the potential for interaction to converge social spheres, remix social resources, and reorganize the time and space contours of sociability. These properties have been characterized as affordances of convergent technological architecture, that is, intrinsic potentialities of technologies that make them "easier to use them for some purposes than for others."[73] Open to reappropriation by individuals, affordances are negotiated and redeployed, characterizing technology that is both "socially shaped and socially shaping."[74] Several studies of social network sites reflect how, in the absence of sufficient relational cues, individuals across cultures actively renegotiate the architectural attributes of websites so as to craft identity performances that are more authentic.[75] Subsequent customizations of space appear to be connected to particular modalities of sociality. The affordances of convergent networked spaces present a meaningful concept for understanding how different cultures make sense of social space created by technology.

Communication and Power

The emphasis on connection over struggle carries important consequences for understanding power in a globalized context. Acknowledging that power is not a constant, but rather, a potential that is discursively negotiated, permits an operationalization of power that is relevant to a variety of cultures.[76] At the same time, structural analyses of power[77] enable us to understand how class struggle is effected on a glocal level, in response to or in appropriation of new technologies. A reconciliation of the structural (fixed) and discursive (flexible) properties of networked power would produce analyses that incorporate a multiplicity of cultural context, and Castells effects such a reconciliation by defining *power* as "the relational capacity that enables a social actor to influence asymmetrically the decisions of other social actor(s) in ways that favor the empowered actor's will, interests, and values."[78] The power that is afforded by the technological architectures of online technologies emerges in networked mode, thus establishing the autonomy of each cultural sphere, as well as the collective power and struggles emerging within conjoined cultural and subcultural spheres. Sharon Strover refers to this reflexively articulated mode of power as "power in the slipstream," to reflect the blurring of the virtual with the geospatial and to describe mutations of power that develop in the shape-shifting and nimble environment of the Internet slipstream.[79] In this networked understanding of power, actors are not perpetually dominating others or being dominated, but rather, power passes through the network and individual cultures that serve as nodes.[80]

Conclusion: A Networked Self

Recognizing that community is not the only means of practicing sociability and attaining sociality permits autonomous, yet connected, agents to converge offline and online spheres of interaction that need not be separate. These spheres of interaction are accessible from spaces domestic, work related, and via nomadic technologies of mobility.[81] The emerging sociability moves beyond community, recognizes individual and collective identity as performance, and defines as culture the converged set of practices of the social, political, economic, work, and personally relevant, as along as they contain a semiology that enables connection. What emerges, then, is a networked self, socially enabled by the affordances of social network sites. We use the term *self* to accent the egocentric character of networks, and to permit culturally variant articulations of selfhood, over individualization. The term *networked self* is conceptually close to John Hartley's "homo nuntius," or the "messaging human," a contemporary species that expresses identity *via* and *as* message, and "*produces* individual *identity* out of social-network *interaction*."[82] In Hartley's words, "Individuals in the species *homo nuntius* don't just 'send' messages as an action ('message' as verb), they *are* a system of messages ('message' as noun); they are both constituted by and productive through messages, which are the process by means of which reason emerges (it is the product of a process, not an input)."[83] Without being specific to a certain culture, the *homo nuntius* is reified in response to local and global cultures.

A networked self, communicated across collapsed and multiplied audiences, seeks social opportunities for expression and connection. Networked and remixed sociabilities emerge and are practiced over *multiplied* places and audiences, which do not necessarily collapse one's sense of place but afford sense of place reflexively. A sense of place is formed in response to the particular sense of self or in response to the identity performance constructed upon that place. This presents the modus operandi for the networked self and the context of newer patterns of sociability and routes to sociality that emerge. The ability to negotiate agency across individual/social, public/private, and East/West binaries lies in the competence of the *homo nuntius* in managing the multiplexity of messages affirming, reproducing, and challenging one's own notion of selfhood. It is the ability to produce but also to edit or *redact* these message-based performances of the self that rises to prominence, across cultures in the new(er) technology environment.[84] Local and translocal performances of identity are constantly edited, retweaked, and remixed to maintain the coherence (or purposeful incoherence) of the performance with varying audiences/publics. The ability of an individual to perform a sense of self that makes sense to multiple audiences and publics while not compromising the authenticity of the performance depends on *redactional acumen*. And applied to researchers conducting work across culturally converged planes of social activity, redactional acumen would gain relevance as the ability to edit one's own cultural leanings in observing and understanding performances of culture across network social planes. Finally, applied to efforts to historicize the progression of newer media, *redactional acumen* refers to the ability to edit out, or recognize, and invite cultural bias as a necessary step in producing hybrid histories of new media.

Notes

1. Carey, "Technology and Ideology"; Marvin, *When Old Technologies Were New.*
2. Peters, "And Lead Us Not," 18.
3. Lefebvre, *Production of Space.*
4. Gunkel and Gunkel, "Virtual Geographies"; Gunkel and Gunkel, "Terra Nova 2.0."
5. Rheingold, *Virtual Community.*
6. Abramson, Arterton, and Orren, *Electronic Commonwealth;* Arterton, *Teledemocracy.*
7. Gunkel and Gunkel, "Terra Nova 2.0"; Consalvo and Miller, "Reinvention through Amnesia."
8. Kramarae, "Language and Nature"; Miniwatts Marketing Group, "Internet World Users."
9. Chen, "Between Three Worlds."
10. Piecowye, "Habitus in Transition?"
11. Guo and Wu, "Media Consumption."
12. Dai, "Towards a Digital Economy"; Zhang, "Media Landscape."
13. Hermeking, "Culture and Internet Consumption."
14. Cogburn et al., "U.S. Role Global Internet"; Hrynshyn, "Globalization, Nationality and Commodification."
15. Pablo and Hardy, "Merging, Masquerading and Morphing."
16. Shah, "From Global Village to Global Marketplace."
17. Liu, "Is There an Alternative?"; Vaughan and Zhang, "Equal Representation."
18. Fox, "New Imagined Community"; Nafus, "Aesthetics of the Internet"; Riegner, "Wired China."
19. Postill, "Localizing the Internet."
20. Dor, "From Englishization."
21. Nöth, "Yuri Lotman on Metaphors"; Ruthrof, "Semiotics of Intercultural Exchange."
22. Straubhaar, "Global, Hybrid or Multiple?"
23. Appadurai, *Modernity at Large.*
24. Howard, "Vernacular Web."
25. Bauman, "Individually, Together"; Beck and Beck-Gernsheim, *Individualization;* Durkheim, *Division of Labor;* Giddens, *Modernity and Self-Identity; Marske,* "Durkheim's 'Cult of the Individual'"; Simmel and Hughes, "Sociology of Sociability."
26. Simmel and Hughes, "Sociology of Sociability."
27. Ibid.
28. Giddens, *Constitution of Society.*
29. Bauman, "Individually, Together," xiv.
30. Bauman, "Individually, Together"; Torbert, *Power of Balance.*
31. Durkheim, *Division of Labor;* Giddens, "Reflections on Durkheim."
32. Marske, "Durkheim's 'Cult of the Individual.'"
33. Bauman, "Individually, Together," 45; Marske, "Durkheim's 'Cult of the Individual.'"
34. Beck and Beck-Gernsheim, *Individualization;* Mansell, "Criticisms."
35. Katz et al., "Personal Mediated Communication"; Tönnies, *Community and Society.*
36. Tönnies, *Community and Society.*
37. Katz et al., "Personal Mediated Communication."

38. Dirlik, "Global Modernity?"
39. Giddens, *Modernity and Self-Identity;* Lash, "Individualization."
40. Beck and Beck-Gernsheim, *Individualization.*
41. Ibid., xxii.
42. Bauman, "Individually, Together."
43. Ibid., xviii.
44. Beck and Beck-Gernsheim, *Individualization,* xxi.
45. Sennett, *Fall of Public Man;* Weintraub and Kumar, *Public and Private.*
46. Ariés et al., *History of Private Life.*
47. Tönnies, *Community and Society.*
48. Goffman, *Presentation of Self;* Goffman, *Behavior in Public Places;* Goffman, *Relations in Public.*
49. Gans, *Urban Villagers;* Gans, Levittowners.
50. Sennett, *Fall of Public Man.*
51. Wolfe, "Public and Private."
52. Ibid., 196.
53. Habermas, *Lifeworld and System.*
54. Gaonkar, "On Alternative Modernities"; Liu, "Is There an Alternative?"
55. Fukuyama, "Primacy of Culture," 12; Liu, "Is There an Alternative?"; Tu, "Implications of the Rise."
56. Tu, "Confucian Traditions."
57. Tu, "Beyond the Enlightenment Mentality"; Tu, "Confucian Traditions"; Tu, "Implications of the Rise."
58. Tu, "Implications of the Rise," 199.
59. Tu, "Confucian Traditions," 24.
60. Katz et al., "Personal Mediated Communication," 310.
61. Tu, "Confucian Traditions," 26.
62. Katz et al., "Personal Mediated Communication," 310.
63. Tu, "Beyond the Enlightenment Mentality," 68.
64. Tu, "Implications of the Rise," 200.
65. Castells, *Communication Power.*
66. Shulman, "Network Analysis."
67. Castells, *Communication Power,* 69.
68. Wittel, "Toward a Network Sociality," 51.
69. Ibid.
70. Tu, "Confucian Traditions."
71. Wellman and Berkowitz, *Social Structure.*
72. Haythornthwaite, "Strong, Weak and Latent Ties"; Haythornthwaite, "Internet in Everyday Life."
73. Buckingham, "Introducing Identity," 12.
74. Buckingham, "Introducing Identity," 12; Williams, Television, *Technology and Cultural Form.*
75. Fono and Raynes-Goldie, "Hyperfriendship and Beyond"; Papacharissi, "Virtual Geographies."
76. Foucault, *Power/Knowledge.*
77. Gramsci, *Selections from the Prison Notebooks;* Poulantzas, *State, Power, Socialism.*

78. Castells, *Communication Power*, 10.
79. Strover, "Power in the Slipstream."
80. de Souza e Silva and Sutko, "Playing Life and Living Play"; Foucault, *Society Must Be Defended.*
81. de Souza e Silva and Sutko, "Playing Life and Living Play."
82. Hartley, "Homo Nuntius," 19.
83. Ibid., 18.
84. Hartley and Rennie, "About a Girl."

Works Cited

Abramson, Jeffrey B., F. Christopher Arterton, and Gary R. Orren. *The Electronic Commonwealth: The Impact of New Media Technologies on Democratic Politics*. New York: Basic Books, 1988.

Appadurai, Arjun. *Modernity at Large.* Minneapolis: University of Minnesota Press, 1996.

Ariés, Phillipe. *Centuries of Childhood: A Social History of Family Life*. New York: Vintage, 1962.

Ariés, Phillipe, Paul Veyne, Georges Duby, and Arthur Goldhammer. *A History of Private Life.* 5 Vols. Cambridge, MA: Harvard University Press, 1987–1991.

Arterton, F. Christopher. *Teledemocracy: Can Technology Protect Democracy?* Thousand Oaks, CA: Sage, 1987.

Bauman, Zygmunt. Foreword: "Individually, Together." In *Individualization: Institutionalized Individualism and Its Social and Political Consequences* by Ulrich Beck and Elisabeth Beck-Gernsheim, xiv–xix. London: Sage, 2001.

Beck, Ulrich, and Elisabeth Beck-Gernsheim. *Individualization: Institutionalized Individualism and Its Social and Political Consequences.* London: Sage, 2001.

Buckingham, David. "Introducing Identity." In *Youth, Identity, and Digital Media*, edited by David Buckingham, 1–24. Cambridge, MA: MIT Press, 2008.

Carey, James W. "Technology and Ideology: The Case of the Telegraph." In *Communication as Culture: Essays on Media and Society* by James W. Carey, 201–230. Winchester, MA: Unwin Hyman, 1988.

Castells, Manuel. *Communication Power*. New York: Oxford, 2009.

Chen, Yanru. "Between Three Worlds: The Internet and Chinese Students' Cultural Identities in the Era of Globalization." *China Media Research* 5, no. 4 (2009): 31–40.

Cogburn, Derrick L., Milton Mueller, Lee McKnight, Hans Klein, and John Mathiason. "The U.S. Role in Global Internet Governance." *IEEE Communications Magazine* 43, no. 12 (2005): 12–14.

Consalvo, Mia, and Toby Miller. "Reinvention through Amnesia." *Critical Studies in Media Communication* 26, no. 2 (2009): 180–190.

Dai, Xiudian. "Towards a Digital Economy with Chinese Characteristics?" *New Media & Society* 4, no. 2 (2002): 141–162.

de Souza e Silva, Adriana, and Daniel M. Sutko. "Playing Life and Living Play: How Hybrid Reality Games Reframe Space, Play and the Ordinary." *Critical Studies in Media Communication* 25, no. 5 (2008): 447–465.

Dirlik, Arif. "Global Modernity? Modernity in an Age of Global Capitalism." *European Journal of Social Theory* 6, no. 3 (2003): 275–292.

Dor, Danny. "From Englishization to Imposed Multilingualism: Globalization, the Internet, and the Political Economy of the Linguistic Code." *Public Culture* 16 (2004): 97–118.

Durkheim, Émile. *The Division of Labor in Society*. New York: The Free Press, 1964.

Fono, David, and Kate Raynes-Goldie. "Hyperfriendship and Beyond: Friends and Social Norms on *LiveJournal*." In *Internet Research Annual, Volume 4: Selected Papers from the AOIR Conference*, edited by Mia Consalvo, and Caroline Haythornthwaite, 91–103. New York: Peter Lang, 2006.

Foucault, Michel. *Power/Knowledge: Selected Interviews and Other Writings, 1972–1977*. Edited by Colin Gordon. New York: Pantheon, 1980.

———. *Society Must Be Defended: Lectures at the College de France, 1975–1976*. Edited by Mauro Bertani and Alessandro Fontana. London: Penguin, 2003.

Fox, Steve. "The New Imagined Community: Identifying and Exploring a Bidirectional Continuum Integrating Virtual and Physical Communities through the Community Embodiment Model." *Journal of Communication Inquiry* 28, no. 1 (2004): 47–62.

Fukuyama, Francis. "Confucianism and Democracy." *Journal of Democracy* 6, no. 2 (1995): 20–33.

———. "The Primacy of Culture." *Journal of Democracy* 6, no. 1 (1995): 7–15.

Gans, Herbert J. *The Levittowners*. New York: Free Press, 1967.

———. *The Urban Villagers*. New York: Free Press, 1962.

Gaonkar, Dilip P. "On Alternative Modernities." *Public Culture* 11, no. 1 (1999): 1–18.

Giddens, Anthony. *The Constitution of Society: Outline of the Theory of Structuration*. Cambridge: Polity, 1984.

———. *Modernity and Self-Identity: Self and Society in the Late Modern Age*. Cambridge: Polity Press, 1991.

———. "Reflections on Durkheim: The 'Individual' in the Writings of Émile Durkheim." *European Journal of Sociology* 12 (1971): 210–228.

Goffman, Erving. *Behavior in Public Places: Notes on the Social Organization of Gatherings*. New York: Simon & Schuster, 1963.

———. *The Presentation of Self in Everyday Life*. New York: Doubleday, 1959.

———. *Relations in Public: Microstudies of the Public Order*. New York: Basic Books, 1971.

Gramsci, Antonio. *Selections from the Prison Notebooks*. New York: International Publishers, 1971.

Gunkel, Ann H., and David J. Gunkel. "Virtual Geographies: The New Worlds of Cyberspace." *Critical Studies in Mass Communication* 14, no. 2 (1997): 123–137.

Gunkel, David J., and Ann H. Gunkel. "Terra Nova 2.0—The New World of MMORPGs." *Critical Studies in Media Communication* 26, no. 2 (2009): 104–127.

Guo, Ke, and Ying Wu. "Media Consumption and Global Visions among Urban Chinese Youth." *China Media Research* 5, no. 4 (2009): 80–94.

Habermas, Jürgen. *The Theory of Communicative Action, Volume 2: Lifeworld and System; A Critique of Functionalist Reason*. Translated by Thomas McCarthy. Cambridge: Polity Press, 1981/1987.

Hartley, John. "Homo Nuntius-messaging Humanity." Faculty working paper, ARC Centre of Excellence in Creative Industries and Innovation, Queensland University of Technology, 2009.

———, and Ellie Rennie. "About a Girl: Fashion Photography as Photojournalism." *Journalism* 5, no. 4 (2004): 458–479.

Haythornthwaite, Caroline. "Introduction: The Internet in Everyday Life." *American Behavioral Scientist* 45, no. 3 (2001): 363–382.

———. "Strong, Weak, and Latent Ties and the Impact of New Media." *Information Society* 18, no. 5 (2002): 385–401.

Hermeking, Marc. "Culture and Internet Consumption: Contributions from Cross-Cultural Marketing and Advertising Research." *Journal of Computer-Mediated Communication* 11, no. 1 (2006): 192–216.

Howard, Robert G. "The Vernacular Web of Participatory Media." *Critical Studies in Media Communication* 25, no. 5 (2008): 490–513.

Hrynshyn, Derek. "Globalization, Nationality and Commodification: The Politics of the Social Construction of the Internet." *New Media & Society* 10, no. 5 (2008): 751–770.

Katz, James E., Ronald E. Rice, Sophia Acord, Kiku Dasgupta, and Kalpana David. "Personal Mediated Communication and the Concept of Community in Theory and Practice." In *Communication Yearbook 28: Communication and Community*, edited by Pamela J. Kalbfleisch, 315–371. Mahwah, NJ: Erlbaum, 2004.

Kramarae, Cheris. "The Language and Nature of the Internet: The Meaning of Global." *New Media & Society* 1, no. 1 (1999): 47–53.

Lash, Scott. Foreword: "Individualization in a Non-Linear Mode." In *Individualization: Institutionalized Individualism and Its Social and Political Consequences* by Ulrich Beck and Elisabeth Beck-Gernsheim, vii–xiii. London: Sage, 2001.

Lefebvre, Henri. *The Production of Space.* Translated by Donald Nicholson-Smith. Oxford: Blackwell, 1974/1991.

Liu, Kang. "Is There an Alternative to (Capitalist) Globalization? The Debate About Modernity in China." *Boundary 2* 23, no. 3 (1996): 193–218.

Mansell, Samuel. "Criticisms of the Theory and Practice of Neo-Liberalism." University of Essex: E-learning Course, 2006. Accessed October 22, 2010. http://74.125.155.132/scholar?q=cache:oJQmsdRlSKEJ:scholar.google.com/+Samuel+Mansell+criticisms+of+the+theory+and+practice+of+neoliberalism&hl=en&as_sdt=400000.

Marske, Charles E. "Durkheim's 'Cult of the Individual' and the Moral Reconstitution of Society." *Sociological Theory* 5, no. 1 (1987): 1–14.

Marvin, Carolyn. *When Old Technologies Were New: Thinking about Electric Media in the Late Nineteenth Century*. Oxford: Oxford University Press, 1988.

Miniwatts Marketing Group. "Internet World Users by Language: Top 10 Languages." *Internet World Stats: Usage and Population Statistics.* Accessed October 22, 2010. http://www.internetworldstats.com/stats7.htm.

Nafus, Dawn. "The Aesthetics of the Internet in St. Petersburg: Why Metaphor Matters." *Communication Review* 6, no. 3 (2003): 185–212.

Nöth, Winfried. "Yuri Lotman on Metaphors and Culture as Self-Referential Semiospheres." *Semiotica* 161, nos. 1–4 (2006): 249–263.

Pablo, Zelinna, and Cynthia Hardy. "Merging, Masquerading and Morphing: Metaphors and the World Wide Web." *Organization Studies* 30 (2009): 821–843.

Papacharissi, Zizi. "The Virtual Geographies of Social Networks: A Comparative Analysis of Facebook, LinkedIn and ASmallWorld." *New Media & Society* 11, nos. 1–2 (2009): 199–220.

Peters, Benjamin. "And Lead Us Not into Thinking the New Is New: A Bibliographic Case for New Media History." *New Media & Society* 11, nos. 1 & 2 (2009): 13–30.

Piecowye, James. "Habitus in Transition? CMC Use and Impacts among Young Women in the United Arab Emirates." *Journal of Computer-Mediated Communication* 8, no. 2 (2003). Accessed October 22, 2010. DOI: 10.1177/1461444808089416.

Postill, John. "Localizing the Internet Beyond Communities and Networks." *New Media & Society* 10, no. 3 (2008): 413–431.

Poulantzas, Nicos. *State, Power, Socialism*. London: Verso, 1978.

Rheingold, Howard. *The Virtual Community*. Reading, MA: Addison-Wesley, 1993.

Riegner, Cate. "Wired China: The Power of the World's Largest Internet Population." *Journal of Advertising Research* 48, no. 4 (2008): 496–505.

Ruthrof, Horst. "The Semiotics of Intercultural Exchange: Ostensive Definition and Digital Reason." *Semiotica* 157, nos. 1–4 (2005): 387–410.

Sennett, Richard. *The Fall of Public Man*. New York: Random House, 1974.

Shah, Nisha. "From Global Village to Global Marketplace: Metaphorical Descriptions of the Global Internet." *International Journal of Media and Cultural Politics* 4, no. 1 (2008): 9–26.

Shulman, Norman. "Network Analysis: A New Addition to an Old Bag of Tricks." *Acta Sociologica* 19, no. 4 (1976): 307–323.

Simmel, Georg, and Everett C. Hughes. "The Sociology of Sociability." *The Amerian Journal of Sociology* 55, no. 3 (1949): 254–261.

Straubhaar, Joseph D. "Global, Hybrid or Multiple? Cultural Identities in the Age of Satellite TV and the Internet." *Nordicom Review* 29, no. 2 (2008): 11–29.

Strover, Sharon L. "Power in the Slipstream: Blurring the Geo-Spatial and the Virtual." Paper presented at the "Internet Turning 40" conference, Chinese University of Hong Kong, Hong Kong, June 17–19, 2010.

Torbert, William R. *The Power of Balance: Transforming Self, Society, and Scientific Inquiry*. New York: Sage, 1991.

Tönnies, Ferdinand. *Community and Society. Gemeinschaft und Gesellschaft*, 1887. Translated and edited by Charles P. Loomis. East Lansing: Michigan State University Press, 1957.

Tu, Weiming. "Beyond the Enlightenment Mentality: A Confucian Perspective on Ethics, Migration, and Global Stewardship." *International Migration Review* 30, no. 1 (1996): 58–75.

———. "Confucian Traditions in East Asian Modernity." *Bulletin of the American Academy of Arts and Sciences* 50, no. 2 (1996): 12–39.

———. "Implications of the Rise of 'Confucian' East Asia." *Daedalus* 129, no. 1 (2000): 195–-218.

Vaughan, Liwen, and Yanjun Zhang. "Equal Representation by Search Engines? A Comparison of Websites across Countries and Domains." *Journal of Computer-Mediated Communication* 12 (2007): 888–909.

Weintraub, Jeff A., and Krishan Kumar, eds. *Public and Private in Thought and Practice*. Chicago: University of Chicago Press, 1997.

Wellman, Barry, and S. D. Berkowitz, eds. *Social Structure: A Network Approach*. Greenwich, CT: JAI Press, 1997.

Williams, Raymond. *Television, Technology and Cultural Form*. London: Routledge, 1974.

Wittel, Andreas. "Toward a Network Sociality." *Theory, Culture & Society* 18, no. 6 (2001): 51–76.

Wolfe, Alan. "Public and Private in Theory and Practice: Some Implications of an Uncertain Boundary." In *Public and Private in Thought and Practice*, edited by Jeff A. Weintraub and Krishan Kumar, 182–203. Chicago: University of Chicago Press, 1997.

Zhang, Yonghua. "Media Landscape in China in the Age of Globalization." *China Media Research* 3, no. 3 (2007): 76–86.

chapter seven

The Evolving Medium Is the Message

McLuhan, Medium Theory, and Cognitive Neuroscience

Teresa M. Harrison

Introduction

Anyone alive for fifty years or more has experienced, within a lifetime, two mighty revolutions in communication media: first, the utter domination of Western cultural life by broadcast and cable television and, second, the invention and global diffusion of computer networking as a new medium for communication. Unprecedented in history, human beings have never before been able to witness both the introduction of a new communication technology as well as the cascading changes in personal and social life that take place in its wake. The rate of technological change now accelerates exponentially, which means, in terms expressed by technology guru Ray Kurzweil, that "it is not the case that we will experience a hundred years of progress in the twenty-first century; rather we will witness on the order of twenty thousand years of progress (at *today's* rate of progress, that is)."[1]

This dizzying rate of technological change makes it possible for communication theorists to take a longer view on the evolution of media technologies, one that simultaneously encompasses both historical and futurist perspectives. We can now compare intentions, predictions, and experiences at the introduction of a new medium with immediate outcomes and with eventual changes in use wrought through incremental adaptation over time. We are increasingly well positioned to anticipate potential trajectories of long-term development and change. The rate of technological change invites us to extend the evolutionary approach to the study of media technologies. Such an approach would begin by understanding media evolution from a historical perspective, as has been the traditional penchant of media theorists but now also invites us to project the consequences of media evolution into the future, since the future takes increasingly less time to arrive. It is indeed critical that we anticipate and understand the implications of media technologies for changes in human social behavior and ensuing transformations in culture and society.

The evolutionary tradition in media studies is also an ecological approach since one of its central premises is that media technologies are more than simply tools used by individuals to accomplish personal goals. Dominant media of the time comprise encompassing environments in which individuals perceive, think, attribute meaning, act, and create social life and the structures that comprise culture. What Lance Strate has called the "media ecology tradition" and its social science analogue dubbed "medium theory" by Joshua Meyrowitz[2] are similar perspectives in that each foregrounds the relatively fixed and idiosyncratic characteristics of a communication medium or class of media, which, through systematic use, and regardless of particular content, create patterns of individual experience and behavior that have far-reaching consequences as they are subsequently reflected in social and cultural life.

While others have joined in,[3] Marshall McLuhan is the best-known scholar elucidating transitions between media and their effects on social and cultural life. McLuhan burst onto the intellectual scene in the 1950s with a challenging set of ideas about the nature of media technology and what it meant to transition from a culture dominated by print media to one dominated by television and other electronic media. McLuhan directed our attention away from the disappointing quality of television programming that galvanized the attention of intellectuals in the 1950s and '60s, to focus instead on the consequences of living in a world in which media consumers were increasingly television viewers, partaking in a constant stream of images and sound almost instantaneously transmitted around the globe.

In perhaps his most famous aphorism, McLuhan proclaimed the "medium was the message," by which he meant that consuming messages conveyed by a medium such as print was far less important a media experience than the persistent effects of consuming alphabet fixed on paper. The consumption of print on paper is a markedly different perceptual experience for the reader, which creates modes of cognition that emphasize the development of linearity, deductive logic, and argumentation, regarded as the *sine qua non* of rigorous thinking, and that give rise to a social order marked by tendencies toward individualistic identities and the growth of nationalism.[4] McLuhan further believed these tendencies were destined for radical change given the alternative experience of television, the use of which would cultivate a quite different set of cognitive capacities and habits and eventually social experiences. The consequences of this alternative media experience would ultimately be reflected in the production of a new social configuration, which he dubbed "the global village" and which he believed would return us to some of the sensory experiences and social conditions of preliterate oral cultures.

Attracting widespread popular interest in the 1960s and '70s, McLuhan's ideas were at the same time vigorously critiqued and even attacked by media theorists of the time. After nearly disappearing from intellectual view by the end of the '80s, his ideas were revived in the '90s, becoming even more influential in helping us to understand the nature and consequences of computer-mediated communication (in which television and radio could be embedded) as well as other new media technologies.

If ever we might be in a position to witness profound shifts in cognition and experience as the result of media use, it is now. Wielding anecdotal observations as well as the latest social science research, it has now become commonplace to compare the intellectual habits, cognitive capabilities, and educational accomplishments of "digital immigrants"—users of new media who have grown up with print and made the transition to electronic media—with those of "digital natives"—users who have never known a media environment not dominated by computer-mediated communication—to use terms coined by Marc Prensky[5] that have become widely adopted. Media pundits, cultural critics, social scientists, and humanists alike are actively debating the significance and merits of changes in visualization, reading, and problem-solving capabilities, as well as attention/distraction tendencies and a variety of other perceptual and cognitive capabilities implicated in interactions with computing technologies.[6]

Although not generally recognized, McLuhan's ideas about the effects of media ecology on perceptual experiences, cognition, learning, and social organization were born of his own familiarity with the physiological processes of the brain.[7] Indeed, he found the hemispheric division of labor in the brain assumed at the time to be evidence for his claims about how media interactions shape cognition. Thirty years after making this connection, breakthroughs in neuroscience imaging technology are now helping us understand how human brains process text and images. These new imaging technologies make it possible in principle to evaluate one of the central premises in McLuhan's thinking, namely to determine whether the human brain changes upon repeated engagement with different media technologies. Entertaining such questions about the effects of new media on cognitive processes enriches our understanding of media evolution and enables us to speculate about the consequences of these effects for social and cultural life in the future.

Unfortunately, it has not been completely obvious how to translate McLuhan's ideas and intuitions about perceptual processes in media ecology into empirical claims about the nature of perception, cognition, and experience as individuals interact with a specific medium. Part of this is due to the way McLuhan wrote. He considered himself an explorer, a provoker, a speculator, emphatically not a scientist. And his perspective on media implied a commitment to other ways of expressing ideas than rigorously logical deductions, which he saw as the legacy of print and worth avoiding. And part of this is simply because not enough was known about neurophysiology and the brain's cognitive processes at the time to formulate more precise claims.

However, it now seems feasible to translate some of McLuhan's ideas about perception and cognition during media experiences into terms that lend themselves to empirical investigation. I have two somewhat more modest goals in this chapter. First, I will show that, although it is not generally appreciated, McLuhan's ideas about media interaction were situated in the sensory experiences of the brain. I will then review some recent developments in contemporary neuroscience that are helping us understand how human brains process text and images and may enable us to explore how brain functioning changes with repeated engagement with new media technologies. I suggest that neuroscience may enable us to move from a predominantly historical perspective in theorizing about media evolution to one that provides us with a purchase on projecting evolution into the future.

McLuhan's Contribution to Medium Theory

From the perspective of medium theory, media evolution is represented by a standardized classification of human societies based on a description of their dominant media technologies.[8] The classification begins with "oral cultures," whose members are connected through spoken language and which give primacy to physical presence, close human relationships, narrative and poetry, and identities forged through one's role within tribal communities. Ancient forms of writing monopolized initially by scribal classes ultimately gave way to the phonetic alphabet, the invention of the printing press, and the availability of printed materials, the combined effects of which were to enable the diffusion of literacy and monumental changes we now associate with "print culture": divisions within community life, the nuclear family, development of the idiosyncratic individual, and the formation of larger social and political units such as nation-states. The invention of telegraphy, radio, and especially television gave birth to the global "electronic culture." New computerized media flesh out the dimensions of global culture in surprising and sometimes troubling ways, since, according to McLuhan, one of the central characteristics of electronic media is a return to some of the key experiential aspects of oral cultures, such as simultaneity of communicative action, but now across larger social groupings.[9]

This classification, and claims about the effects and consequences of media technologies within it, does not lend itself to testing via standard empirical techniques. The central premise, which is that media technologies have "relatively fixed features" that "shape key aspects of the communication on both the micro, single-situation level and the macro-societal level,"[10] is not precise enough for testing. Thus, as Meyrowitz points out, medium theory cannot be assessed through quantitative analysis; its persuasiveness relies on its arguments, its historical analysis, and its ability to discern large-scale patterns in media use and their effects up to the present. The latter renders it particularly susceptible to charges of determinism since it appears to attribute causal force to media qualities that are more accurately understood as inviting, allowing, encouraging, and fostering some behaviors, while discouraging others.[11]

McLuhan and Media Ecology

McLuhan's perspective on media ecology, perhaps the best known and certainly the most ambitious in scope, met with mixed critical reception from fellow media theorists for a number of reasons.[12] For one thing, he did not write like a social scientist or use a conceptual vocabulary as a social scientist would. Instead he was a literary critic who rejected fixed points of view and the logical sequence of a scholarly argument. He used "probes," declarations, and a "fuzzy vocabulary" consisting of familiar words vested with idiosyncratic meanings, puns, and poetry to express his assertions about media.[13]

But more to the point, McLuhan's ideas were seriously at odds with the scholarly zeitgeist of the day. In one of the first of many reassessments of his significance, fellow Canadian Liss Jeffrey calls McLuhan "a catalyst" in the interdisciplinary study of communication because he offered a theory of media transformation that was intended to identify core human symbolizing processes. U.S. scholars, however, still in the throes of defining what might be meant by a social science, were generating linear theories of media as conduits for messages.[14] Thus, "McLuhan worked at a time of ferment, both within the culture at large and within the academy. It became increasingly evident throughout the 1960s that the question of making meaning had been largely abandoned by orthodox social scientists in the study of communications."[15] It is also worth noting that systems approaches to theory construction, which embrace the ideas of recursion, transformation, and evolution, had only just begun to penetrate disciplinary thinking in the 1970s,[16] and potential linkages between media consumption and anything related to the science of the brain were utterly foreign. McLuhan's body of work, taken as a whole, may thus represent a genuine case of paradigm "revolution," in Thomas Kuhn's sense of the term,[17] within communication study.

Thus much of McLuhan's thinking about media has been misunderstood, underappreciated, and, in some cases, simply not taken seriously. Not surprisingly, there have been few attempts to explore it empirically. And yet, upon reconsideration—and scholars have devoted many pages to this enterprise in the past two decades—it becomes clear that, abstruse as he was, McLuhan can be read as making some ambitious and intriguing claims about the interaction between the human brain and media.

McLuhan's Neurophysiological Perspective on Media Transformation

In what follows, I show that McLuhan saw human interaction with media as distinct sensory experiences with a concrete basis in human physiology, although he did not always foreground physiological processes in his explications. McLuhan's fundamental positions on media are expressed in *The Gutenberg Galaxy* and *Understanding Media*, in which very general allusions to physiology are made. In later work, McLuhan connects the perceptual processes he is describing to the operations and functions of the brain.

For McLuhan, media technologies are extensions of human senses. As such, they augment, embellish, and enhance perceptual processes, changing the pace, scale, and/or patterns of sensation experienced in everyday life.[18] McLuhan focuses principally on sight, hearing, and touch; smell and taste receive little attention.

In interacting with a medium, the human senses function in relationship to each other, producing what McLuhan describes as a "ratio," a term he used to express their varying degrees of involvement. Technology "alters sense ratios or patterns of perception steadily and without any resistance."[19] The ratio of sensory involvement between seeing, hearing, and touching depends on which senses figure most heavily in media use. Thus, speech that takes place in face-to-face conditions depends largely on hearing and touch, while the experience of reading print draws heavily on sight and is divorced largely from touch.

The world in which the medium of speech dominates is a nonliterate oral culture in which the sense ratio privileges aurality. This world is described by McLuhan as magical, implicit, hyperaesthetic, discontinuous, and simultaneously "acoustic" and tactile space, characterized by the oral genres of myth, narrative, and poetry.[20]

An alternative medium involves the user in sensory readjustment to create a new ratio or equilibrium. McLuhan makes clear that this is a physiological adjustment, as it is the function of the central nervous system, "the electric network that coordinates the various media of our senses," to maintain an equilibrium among its various organs.[21] Indeed, McLuhan characterizes human interaction with media technology as recursive at the physiological level when he observes that, "physiologically, man in the normal use of technology (or his variously extended body) is perpetually modified by it and in turn finds ever new ways of modifying his technology."[22]

Ancient modes of writing, the alphabet, and especially print on paper each stimulate a readjustment of sense ratios in the consumption of these new information formats. The literate world is intensely visual; print creates a "visual" space through the cultivation of perceptual processes adjusted initially and then habituated to the homogeneity, uniformity, linearity, sequentiality, and repeatability of printed text. Ruth Katz and Elihu Katz express McLuhan's view of this as a neurophysiological process in which "the technologies of alphabetic writing, especially print, trained the brain to process visual information linearly, and such linear thinking—implying determination, causality, logic, detachment, delayed gratification—is then applied to the rest of life."[23]

New media technologies cultivate new cognitive capabilities; for example, literacy makes it possible for individuals to take in an image all at once, in contrast to nonliterate peoples who scan objects and images segment by segment.[24] McLuhan describes the transition from orality to writing in ancient Greece as stimulating the "discovery" of logic, the idea of causes, and an interest in science, while the Romans extended lineality and homogeneity to civic and military life.[25] The "Gutenberg technology," on the one hand, introduces the age of the machine, which is marked by the "principle of segmentation of actions and functions and roles [that] became applicable wherever desired."[26] On the other hand, the affordances of typography make possible the "outering and uttering of private inner experience," enabling the development of individualism and sharing of subjectivity, while at the same time cultivating the seeds of nationalism through the "massing of collective national awareness, as the vernacular is rendered visible, central and unified by the new technology."[27]

Thus, for McLuhan, the physiological structures of the brain interact with the mode of information given by a medium to create perceptual patterns via sense ratios that are extended into and mirrored in the personalities and social systems of the encompassing cultural environment. As media change, a new sense ratio initially presents users with "surprising new worlds,"[28] but then, over time, the entire community comes to absorb and habituate the new ways of perception. This is why sense ratios are not just associated with a particular medium but can also be said to characterize a specific culture. McLuhan viewed Europe in the 1960s as audio-tactile and America as intensely visual.[29]

The extent of sensory involvement differs from medium to medium, some of which McLuhan characterizes as "hot" and others as "cool," based on the degree of cognitive and social participation required by each. Katz and Katz point out (along with numerous other critics) that McLuhan's use of these categories has been frustratingly ambiguous.[30] But more to our purpose is the way McLuhan characterizes this participatory element. Hot media, such as film and print, present information in ways that are well-defined, integral, and intense experiences. But cool media require the viewer to complete the information to construct the experience.[31] For example, as a cool medium, the television image is "visually low in data," presenting a mosaic of some three million dots per second from which only a few dozen are selected by the viewer that he or she "unconsciously reconfigures" into an image.[32] Engagement by the media user may vary from the kind of sensory participation that takes place in television viewing to the dialogic participation that takes place in a seminar.

McLuhan's approach to media transformation thus proceeds on a macro scale from media to societal change, in ways similar to other medium theorists such as Harold Innis.[33] But, unlike Innis and others, McLuhan's unique contribution is to situate the origin of these changes in the human brain and its engagement via the senses with media formats.

In later work, McLuhan maps the locus of visual and acoustic space, as well as the sense ratios of literate and nonliterate cultures, to the functioning of left and right brain hemispheres in the neurophysiology of the day.[34] Invoking the work of Alexander Luria,[35] who found left brain functioning associated with linear sequencing and "hence, mathematics and scientific thinking," McLuhan declared that his observations showed "how the written alphabet, with its lineal structure, was able to create the conditions conducive to the development of Western science, technology and rationality."[36] Following Robert Trotter,[37] who attributes right hemispheric orientation to the nonliterate Inuit society of Northern Canada, McLuhan finds further support for his distinction between oral and literate cultures being founded in neurophysiological interaction with media. Interestingly, McLuhan noted that hemispheric domination did not mean there was no interaction between the two. He was aware that the corpus callosum in the brain bridged the two hemispheres and suggested this might be why Eastern cultures, which he viewed as oriented to the right hemisphere, also manifested tendencies indicative of left hemisphere dominance.

The association of left hemisphere dominance with the visual world and right hemisphere dominance with the acoustic world (of both preliterate and electronic cultures) is one that McLuhan continued to make until the end of his life.[38] His assertions were supported by further references to Luria as well as other scholarly sources of information bearing on hemispheric specialization. However, few of McLuhan's critics or admirers appeared to notice.[39] An exception, on the one hand, is Jonathan Miller, who points out while presenting an overall negative assessment:

> He has done something which very few have done publicly before. That is: to focus attention on the devices through which we obtain knowledge. These aspects have largely been ignored in the past, or at least have been a province of philosophers or else of neuro-physiologists, and I think for the first time what McLuhan has done is to bring the nervous system right into the center of the discussion of ordinary communications and of human knowledge in general.[40]

On the other hand, it is perplexing to find Lewis Lapham casually dismissing McLuhan's knowledge of the central nervous system as "almost nothing" in his introduction to the 1994 edition of *Understanding Media*.[41] McLuhan may not have known much, but there was not much to know at that time and certainly no other media scholars were connecting media experiences to brain processes.

Media Experiences in the Global Electronic Culture

According to McLuhan, manuscript culture gave way to print culture in the 16th-century Renaissance; he believed the next major transition was taking place as he wrote in the 1960s with electronic media remaking the world in the form of a global village.[42] McLuhan speculated that perhaps the shifting sense ratios of earlier media transitions had not been noticed because they happened so gradually. However, in the 1960s, "we experience such a series of new technologies even in our own world, and, besides, have means of observing so many other cultures that only great inattention could now conceal the role of new media of information in altering the posture and relations of our senses."[43] McLuhan believed the introduction of television into Western cultures dominated by print was a "formula for complete chaos"[44] because the sense ratios and behavioral patterns associated with each were so seriously at odds with each other. But by the beginning of the 21st century, an even more profound shift in media usage was taking place, bringing associated changes in habits and preoccupations that some have found disquieting.

We who have straddled the transition between print and television have now become "immigrants" in the new land of digital, computer-mediated communication technologies, including, and perhaps especially, the Internet and World Wide Web. The earliest immigrant scholars—for example, Sven Birkerts, Myron Tuman, and Richard Lanham—have written with great concern about the ways the computer would "destabilize" the "authority of the printed word" and return us to "the process orientation that characterized oral cultures."[45] But their arguments have focused more on the ephemerality of digital text than on the sensory/cognitive experiences of readers consuming print on paper in contrast to text and images delivered on screen.

More recently, media pundits and scholars alike have self-diagnosed new incapacities in reading and writing, linked to habituated use of the Internet and its associated gratifications. Their complaints range from the general difficulty of processing more information, arriving faster than ever, via increasingly plentiful electronic channels,[46] to a cultivated distractibility that interferes with normal writing and reading tasks,[47] to a more profound inability to engage in the kind of "deep" reading that had been hitherto their norm.[48]

For "digital natives" such changes appear to have graver consequences, as young media users have developed behavioral patterns and habits with implications for reading and learning. Among these are the tendency to multitask, which reduces learning abilities and increases susceptibility to irrelevant information;[49] shorter attention spans and distractibility, preferences for immediate experience and gratification, and loss of impulse control fostered by the intense visual environments presented by games;[50] and generalized information overload, with negative consequences for decision making.[51]

Perhaps most worrisome are the increasing indications that young people read fewer texts, preferring media stimulation provided by an assortment of screens (video games, television, DVDs, and the web), and know correspondingly less;[52] read with less proficiency and thus do not understand what they have read;[53] and read in ways that may not cultivate skills associated with rigor and creativity in thinking.[54]

McLuhan would surely view this new array of cognitive experiences as evidence of "the role of new media of information in altering the posture and relations of our senses."[55] The rapidly evolving field of cognitive neuroscience, and its technologies for studying the brain, now provides us with tools to begin to assess such a claim more systematically.

What Can Neuroscience Tell Us About Media Evolution?

As a field of scholarly inquiry, cognitive neuroscience enables us to answer questions about the operations and functions of the brain responsible for producing cognitive or psychological states. The brain science of which McLuhan was aware was then largely in its infancy. Unable to observe the brain in action, the field advanced by examining pathologies caused by brain trauma and illness. Scientists linked cognitive deficits, for example, the inability to speak, to specific locations in the brain marked by lesions, such as what is now known as Broca's area in the left frontal lobe. This gave rise to the idea of "localizationism," which suggested that the brain operates much like a machine comprised of component parts, each of which is responsible for specific functions.[56]

However, recent breakthroughs in imaging technologies, such as positron emission tomography (PET) and functional magnetic resonance imaging (fMRI), now make it possible to view the brain as it functions under normal operations. Studies using these techniques demonstrate that the brain changes dynamically with experience, particularly input that is systematic and prolonged.[57] Indeed contemporary neuroscientists view the functional structure of the brain as "plastic" rather than rigidly fixed, capable of significant reorganization in the face of new environmental demands or by the need to replace or compensate for deficits caused by disease, accident, or deviations at birth from what is considered normal. The loss of one sense may be compensated by increased activity by other senses, along with qualitative changes in their functioning so they become more like the lost sense. For example, when cells in the visual cortex cease to receive signals from the eyes, those cells may be used to process sensation from other senses.[58]

This is not to say there is no regularity or stability in brain structure. There are common structures and basic regularities in brain activation, many of which are still being identified and mapped. "This is how brain mappers can confidently talk of a chart of 'the' brain, rather than 'a' brain," according to Rita Carter.[59] Well before McLuhan's time it was known that functions of the brain are distributed across left and right hemispheres, and regions of the cortex. But we know now that left and right brain hemispheres work together to produce experiences and are not rigidly localized as had been thought previously.[60]

The combination of substantial regularity and ongoing change means it is possible to make generalizations across individuals, while at the same time exploring the effects of changes in the environment and in individual activities on the functioning of the brain. Neuroscientists now use imaging technologies to explore what happens to brains when their owners engage in a wide variety of experiences from listening to music to vigorous exercise, with particular interest in interaction on the computer. In a much-publicized study, researchers compared brain maps for Internet-savvy and Internet-naïve subjects obtained while they conducted Google searches and found major differences between the maps for each group. Even more interesting, maps of naïve subjects became more similar to those of savvy subjects with practice sessions of one hour a day over five days.[61]

Norman Doidge proposes that activities shared within a culture, but not universal to all humans, are "signature activities" that shape the brain and its functional operations in culturally specific ways.[62] Following his own reading of McLuhan, Doidge proposes that reading, writing, computer literacy, and using electronic media are signature activities of the information age, and thus should be compared to determine how they are reflected in differential brain functioning. A study by Erica Michael, Timothy Keller, Patricia Carpenter, and Marcel Adams Just is evocative in this regard. Brain scans taken while subjects listened to or read sentences displayed differences in activation, brain locations, lateralizations, and activity patterns, suggesting that word comprehension does not take place in one center of the brain.[63] Instead "each medium creates a different sensory and semantic experience—and, we might add, develops different circuits in the brain."[64]

A substantial amount of effort has been devoted to studies of brain functioning related to literacy.[65] It is now widely accepted that reading is a cultural invention rather than an evolutionary development of the brain.[66] That is, there is no specific location in the brain that functions to enable reading or writing.[67] Instead, structures preadapted to perform other functions are mobilized in support of the development of new skills. While not explicitly testing McLuhan's ideas about brain functioning and media experiences, research by Alexandre Castro-Caldas and his colleagues with literate and illiterate subjects has been particularly illuminating since its comparisons are similar to those that might be conducted between individuals of oral and print cultures.[68]

Predicated on the assumption of neuroplasticity, Castro-Caldas has explored the possibility that literacy can change the anatomy of the brain using a carefully constructed sample of illiterate and literate subjects from a coastal fishing village in Portugal. The sociocultural conditions of the region reproduced illiteracy since it was common forty or fifty years ago for daughters of large families to perform household duties for much of their early lives, in contrast to younger siblings who were sent to school. Illiterate and literate subjects, in their fifties and sixties at the time of the research and most working at home, were matched for age, gender, sociocultural background, and everyday activities. Those who had learned to read had little more than four years of education.[69]

The two groups were compared in a task involving the repetition of words and pseudowords while being PET scanned. With eyes closed, and words and pseudowords presented via earphones, participants were asked to either repeat the word or, if unable to do so, pass. There were small differences between groups in repeating real words, but significant differences in repeating the pseudowords, with illiterate subjects being less able to do so. The PET images showed substantial differences in activated brain areas between the two groups. The areas activated by literate subjects are thought to be those related to the development of phonological abilities required for reading, that is, the ability to discern that words in a language can be broken down into particular sounds, or phonemes represented by letters.[70] Illiterate subjects could not repeat pseudowords because they "were unable to activate the proper areas of the brain to do so."[71]

Other studies by Castro-Caldas have found differences between groups in hemispheric lateralization, with literate subjects showing considerably more left hemisphere lateralization when listening to and encoding words than illiterate subjects, who show greater right lateralization.[72] These studies also examined the size and structure of the corpus callosum, the region related to the development of neural networks that interconnect hemispheric locations required for literacy. They show that the corpus callosum is thicker, with significantly greater white matter, for literate subjects than for illiterate subjects in those portions that interconnect the parietotemporal regions. The researchers' conclusion is that literacy "influences the functional hemispheric balance in the inferior parietal and parieto-temporal region" and that there are "parallel differences in the white matter related to the mid-body region of the corpus callosum and inferior parietal and parietotemporal regions" suggesting that there "might be a causal connection between reading and writing acquisition, the development of the corpus callosum, and the hemispheric differences reported in this study."[73] Such research thus begins to suggest that learning to read changes both the functional organization of the brain and its anatomy.

Conclusion

It is admittedly a leap to move from the ambiguous "sense ratios" that McLuhan thought were a function of media experiences to what we are now learning about brain organization and anatomy in 21st-century neuroscience. This chapter has not reviewed research related to visual and auditory perceptions that must be located somewhere on the pathway between media consumption and dynamic neurophysiological structures. But this should not keep us from appreciating that research efforts aimed at comparing the brain's interactions with diverse media formats is well within the realm of possibility.

What we already know about brain plasticity supports McLuhan's fundamental intuition that an encounter with a medium new to a user engenders changes in the neurophysiological processes by which the user processes symbols expressed in new forms. The presence of neural networks and specialized circuitry for basic readers, in contrast to their absence for those who are illiterate, invites us to explore further differences between those who are print oriented and those who continue to inhabit an oral world, and ultimately compare them with those who habitually consume new electronic media. Only through such investigations will it become possible to probe the perceptual and cognitive world of digital natives and begin to appreciate the ways in which reorganized neurophysiological processes may be ultimately associated with new ways of learning, new orientations to interpersonal and group life, and emerging social and cultural organization.

This historical rereading of McLuhan has shown that interactions between perceptual/cognitive processes situated in the brain and mediated information rest at the core of media evolution theory. These interactions give rise to perceptual and cognitive patterns, habits, and related behavioral changes that are then thrust outward and mirrored in "the rest of life," as Katz and Katz have commented. McLuhan's particular ways of describing such perceptual/cognitive states, as in changing "sense ratios," may give us starting points for investigation, but these are not nearly as important as the larger idea that we should see as the recursive causal forces that animate medium theory. It is clear that a collaboration between communication studies and cognitive neuroscience presents a fruitful avenue for extending media evolution theory into the future and for helping us as educators to anticipate and appreciate the ways in which media act back upon their users to cultivate new ways of thinking and acting in the future.

Notes

1. Kurzweil, "The Law of Accelerating Returns." I am grateful to Lance Strate of Fordham University for reading an earlier draft of this manuscript and for making comments and suggestions that have improved its final form.
2. Strate, *Echoes and Reflections;* Meyrowitz, "Multiple Media Literacies."
3. See, for example, Ong, *Orality and Literacy.*
4. McLuhan, *The Gutenberg Galaxy;* McLuhan, *Understanding Media.*
5. Prensky, "Digital Natives, Digital Immigrants."
6. For a more detailed discussion of this discourse, see Harrison, "Digital Natives vs. Digital Immigrants."
7. McLuhan, "The Brain and the Media."
8. Meyrowitz, "Medium Theory."
9. McLuhan, *Understanding Media,* 50.
10. Meyrowitz, "Multiple Media Literacies," 103, 104.
11. Meyrowitz, "Medium Theory."
12. See, for example, Stearn, *McLuhan: Hot & Cool* for a range of critical reaction to McLuhan.
13. Meyrowitz, "Canonic Anti-text."
14. Jeffrey, "The Heat and the Light," 23.
15. Ibid., 24.
16. See, for example, Monge, "The Systems Perspective."
17. Kuhn, *The Structure of Scientific Revolutions.*
18. McLuhan, *Understanding Media,* 8.
19. McLuhan, *Understanding Media,* 18; McLuhan, *The Gutenberg Galaxy,* 41.
20. McLuhan, *The Gutenberg Galaxy,* 55, 151.
21. McLuhan, *Understanding Media,* 41–45.
22. Ibid., 46.
23. Katz and Katz, "McLuhan: Where Did He Come from?," 309.

24. McLuhan, *The Gutenberg Galaxy,* 23, 25.
25. Ibid., 58.
26. Ibid., 155.
27. Ibid., 199.
28. Ibid., 23.
29. McLuhan, *Understanding Media,* 45.
30. Katz and Katz, "McLuhan: Where Did He Come from?," 311.
31. McLuhan, *Understanding Media,* 22–32.
32. Ibid., 313–314.
33. See, for example, Innis, *The Bias of Communication.*
34. McLuhan, "The Brain and the Media." See also McLuhan and McLuhan, *Laws of Media.*
35. Luria, "Functional Organization of the Brain."
36. McLuhan, "The Brain and the Media," 55–56. See also McLuhan and McLuhan, *Laws of Media,* 73.
37. Trotter, "The Other Hemisphere."
38. McLuhan and Powers, "Ma Bell."
39. For example, McLuhan's "The Brain and the Media" article is not cited in Levinson's otherwise ambitious extension of McLuhan to digital media. See Levinson, *Digital McLuhan.*
40. Miller, "He Often Opens Doors to Chaos," 235.
41. Lapham, Introduction to *Understanding Media,* xiii.
42. McLuhan, *The Gutenberg Galaxy,* 141.
43. Ibid., 55.
44. McLuhan and McLuhan, *Laws of Media,* 80.
45. See Birkerts, *The Gutenberg Elegies;* Tuman, *Word Perfect;* and Lanham, *The Electronic Word.*
46. Klingberg, *The Overflowing Brain.*
47. See descriptions in Orenstein, "Stop Your Search Engines," 11–12; and Anderson, "In Defense of Distraction."
48. Carr, *The Shallows.*
49. See Ophir, Nass, and Wagner, "Cognitive Control in Media Multitaskers"; and Palfrey and Gasser, *Born Digital.*
50. Greenfield, *I.D.;* Greenfield, "How Facebook Addiction Is Damaging"; Greenfield, "How Computers Can Harm."
51. Palfrey and Gasser, *Born Digital.*
52. Bauerlein, *The Dumbest Generation.*
53. Romano, "Literacy of College Graduates."
54. See Rowlands et al., "The Google Generation"; Wolf, *Proust and the Squid.*
55. McLuhan, *The Gutenberg Galaxy,* 55.
56. Doidge, *The Brain That Changes Itself.*
57. Restak, *The New Brain;* Doidge, *The Brain That Changes Itself.*
58. Small and Vorgan, *Ibrain.*
59. Carter, *Mapping the Mind,* 20.
60. Johnson, *Mind Wide Open.*
61. See Small and Vorgan, *IBrain.*
62. Doidge, *The Brain That Changes Itself,* 290.
63. Michael et al., "fMRI Investigation of Sentence Comprehension."

64. Doidge, *The Brain That Changes Itself,* 308.
65. For a review, see Dehaene, *Reading in the Brain.*
66. Varney, "How Reading Works."
67. Ardila, "There Is Not Any Specific Brain Area for Writing."
68. Castro-Caldas, "Targeting Regions of Interest for the Study of the Illiterate Brain."
69. Petersson et al., "Literacy."
70. Castro-Caldas et al., "The Illiterate Brain."
71. Castro-Caldas and Reis, "The Knowledge of Orthography."
72. See Castro-Caldas and Reis, "Knowledge of Orthography"; Castro-Caldas et al., "The Illiterate Brain"; and Petersson et al., "Literacy."
73. Petersson et al., "Literacy," 797.

Works Cited

Anderson, Sam. "In Defense of Distraction." *New York Magazine*, May 17, 2009. Accessed December 10, 2010. http://nymag/print/news/features/56793.

Ardila, Alfredo. "There Is Not Any Specific Brain Area for Writing: From Cave-Paintings to Computers." *International Journal of Psychology* 39, no. 1 (2004): 61–67.

Bauerlein, Mark. *The Dumbest Generation*. New York: Jeremy P. Tarcher/Penguin, 1999.

Birkerts, Sven. *The Gutenberg Elegies.* 2006 ed. New York: Farrar, Straus, and Giroux, 1994.

Carr, Nicholas. *The Shallows: What the Internet Is Doing to Our Brains*. New York: W. W. Norton, 2010.

Carter, Rita. *Mapping the Mind.* Berkeley: University of California Press, 1998.

Castro-Caldas, Alexandre. "Targeting Regions of Interest for the Study of the Illiterate Brain." *International Journal of Psychology* 39, no. 1 (2004): 5–17.

Castro-Caldas, Alexandre, K. M. Petersson, A. Reis, S. Stone-Elander, and M. Ingvar. "The Illiterate Brain: Learning to Read and Write during Childhood Influences the Functional Organization of the Adult Brain." *Brain* 121 (1998): 1053–1063.

———, and Alexandra Reis. "The Knowledge of Orthography Is a Revolution in the Brain." *Reading and Writing: An Interdisciplinary Journal* 16 (2003): 81–87.

Dehaene, Stanislas. *Reading in the Brain*. New York: Viking, 2009.

Doidge, Norman. *The Brain That Changes Itself: Stories of Personal Triumph from the Frontiers of Brain Science*. New York: Penguin, 2007.

Greenfield, Susan. "How Computers Can Harm Your Children's Future . . . By Damaging Their Brains." *The Daily Mail*, July 4, 2009. Accessed December 10, 2010. http://www.dailymail.co.uk/health/article–1197491/How-computers-harm-childrens-future—damaging-brains.html.

———. "How Facebook Addiction Is Damaging your Child's Brain: A Leading Neuroscientist's Chilling Warning." *The Daily Mail*, April 23, 2009. Accessed October 1, 2010. http://www.dailymail.co.uk/femail/article–1172690/How-Facebook-addiction-damaging-childs-brain-A-leading-neuroscientists-chilling-warning.html.

———. *I.D.: The Quest for Meaning in the 21st Century*. London: Sceptre, 2008.

Harrison, Teresa. "Digital Natives vs. Digital Immigrants: Generational Differences in Media Use, Cognition, and Learning." Paper presented at the annual conference of the National Communication Association, Chicago, Illinois, November 2009.

Innis, Harold. *The Bias of Communication.* Toronto: University of Toronto Press, 1951.

Jackson, Maggie. *Distracted: The Erosion of Attention and the Coming Dark Age.* Amherst, NY: Prometheus Books, 2009.

Jeffrey, Liss. "The Heat and the Light: Towards a Reassessment of the Contribution of H. Marshall McLuhan." *Canadian Journal of Communication* 14, nos. 4 & 5 (1989): 1–29.

Johnson, Steven. *Mind Wide Open: Your Brain and the Science of Everyday Life.* New York: Scribner, 2004.

Katz, Ruth, and Katz, Elihu. "McLuhan: Where Did He Come from, Where Did He Disappear?" *Canadian Journal of Communication* 23, no. 3 (1998): 307–319.

Klingberg, Torkel. *The Overflowing Brain.* Oxford: Oxford University Press, 2009.

Kuhn, Thomas. *The Structure of Scientific Revolutions.* Chicago: University of Chicago Press, 1962.

Kurzweil, Ray. "The Law of Accelerating Returns." Accessed December 10, 2010. http://www/lirzweo;ao/met/the-law-of-accelerating-returns. http://www.kurzweilai.net-/the-law-of-accelerating-returns.

Lanham, Richard. *The Electronic Word: Democracy, Technology, and the Arts.* Chicago: University of Chicago Press, 1993.

Lapham, Lewis. Introduction. In *Understanding Media: The Extensions of Man,* by Marshall McLuhan, ix–xxiii. Cambridge, MA: MIT Press, 1994/1964.

Levinson, Paul. *Digital McLuhan.* London: Routledge, 1999.

Luria, Alexander R. "Functional Organization of the Brain." *Scientific American* 232, no. 3 (1970): 66–72.

McLuhan, Marshall. "The Brain and the Media: The 'Western' Hemisphere." *Journal of Communication* 28, no. 4 (1978): 54–60.

———. *The Gutenberg Galaxy.* Toronto: University of Toronto Press, 1962.

———. *Understanding Media: The Extensions of Man.* Cambridge, MA: MIT Press, 1994/1964.

, and Eric McLuhan. *Laws of Media: The New Science.* Toronto: University of Toronto Press, 1988.

———, and Bruce Powers. "Ma Bell Minus the Nantucket Gam: Or the Impact of High-Speed Data Transmission." *Journal of Communication* 31, no. 3 (1981): 191–199.

Meyrowitz, Joshua. "Canonic Anti-text: Marshall McLuhan's *Understanding Media.*" In *Canonic Texts in Media Research,* edited by Elihu Katz, John Durham Peters, Tamar Liebes, and Avril Orloff, 191–212. Cambridge: Polity Press, 2003.

———. "Medium Theory." In *Communication Theory Today,* edited by David Crowley and David Mitchell, 50–77. Cambridge: Polity Press, 1994.

———. "Multiple Media Literacies." *Journal of Communication* 48, no. 1 (1998): 96–108.

Michael, Erica B., Timothy A. Keller, Patricia A. Carpenter, and Marcel Adams Just. "fMRI Investigation of Sentence Comprehension by Eye and Ear: Modality Fingerprints on Cognitive Processes." *Human Brain Mapping* 13 (2001): 239–252.

Miller, Jonathan. "He Often Opens Doors to Chaos." In *McLuhan: Hot & Cool,* edited by Gerald E. Stearn, 234–239. New York: The Dial Press, 1967.

Monge, Peter R. "The Systems Perspective as a Theoretical Basis for the Study of Human Communication." *Communication Quarterly* 25, no. 1 (1977): 19–29.

Ong, Walter. *Orality and Literacy*. London: Methuen, 1982.

Ophir, E., Clifford Nass, and A. Wagner, A. "Cognitive Control in Media Multitaskers." *Proceedings of the National Academy of Sciences* 106 (2009): 15583–15587.

Orenstein, Peggy. "Stop Your Search Engines: Forcing Ourselves Offline May Be the Path to True Knowledge." *New York Times Magazine*, October 25, 2009, 11–12.

Palfrey, John, and Urs Gasser. *Born Digital: Understanding the First Generation of Digital Natives.* New York: Basic Books, 2008.

Petersson, Karl Magnus, Carla Silva, Alexandre Castro-Caldas, Martin Ingvar, Alexandra Reis. "Literacy: A Cultural Influence on Functional Left-Right Differences in the Inferior Parietal Cortex." *European Journal of Neuroscience* 26 (2007): 791–799.

Prensky, Marc. "Digital Natives, Digital Immigrants, Part II: Do They Really *Think* Differently?" *On the Horizon* 9 no. 6 (2001): 1–8.

Restak, Richard. *The New Brain: How the Modern Age Is Rewiring Your Mind.* Emmaus, PA: Rodale Books, 2003.

Romano, Lois. "Literacy of College Graduates Is on the Decline." *Washington Post*, December 25, 2005. Accessed December 10, 2010. http://www.washingtonpost.com/wpdyn/content/article/2005/12/24/AR2005122400701.html.

Rowlands, Ian, D. Nicholas, P. Williams, P. Huntington, M. Fieldhouse, B. Gunter, R. Withey, H. R. Jamali, T. Dobrowolski, and C. Tenopir. "The Google Generation: The Information Behavior of the Researcher of the Future." *ASLIB Proceedings: New Information Perspectives* 60, no. 4 (2008): 290–310.

Small, Gary, and Gigi Vorgan. *Ibrain: Surviving the Technological Alteration of the Modern Mind.* New York: CollinsLiving, 2008.

Stearn, Gerald E., ed. *McLuhan: Hot & Cool.* New York: The Dial Press, 1967.

Strate, Lance. *Echoes and Reflections: On Media Ecology as a Field of Study*. Cresskill, NJ: Hampton Press, 2006.

Trotter, Robert. "The Other Hemisphere." *Science News* 109 (April 3, 1976): 218–223.

Tuman, Myron. *Word Perfect: Literacy in the Computer Age*. London: Falmer, 1992.

Varney, Nils R. "How Reading Works: Considerations from Prehistory to the Present." *Applied Neuropsychology* 9, no. 1 (2002): 3–12.

Wolf, Maryanne. *Proust and the Squid.* New York: HarperPerennial, 2007.

chapter eight

The Analog History of the "Digital Divide"

Dmitry Epstein

Introduction

The digital divide has been part of the public agenda for over a decade. Although not necessarily the most prominent issue, compared to political drama, military conflicts, or financial crises, the "digital divide" has demonstrated substantial stamina in the public discourse. For years, this term brought together academics, policy makers, industry players, and members of the civil society to advocate, debate, and question its relevance and potential role in impacting socioeconomic and cultural development both on the global and the local scales.

Despite its prevalence in public and scholarly discourses, the question of conceptualization of the digital divide remains an open and continuously challenged topic. Jan van Dijk argues that alongside the need to develop theoretical frameworks for studying the "digital divide," addressing "the lack of conceptual elaboration and definition" is "the most urgent task."[1] Although van Dijk is primarily concerned with operationalizable definitions, his discussion opens up questions raised in earlier writings about the conceptualization of "digital divide" as a social phenomenon, scholarly subject, and object for policy making.[2] From that point of view, the digital divide discourse leads us to conceptualize and understand (and in some cases regulate) the role of media information and communication technologies in the context of societal change with a particular focus on socioeconomic development. As such, we can view the concept of the "digital divide" as emerging from an interaction between three distinctive, but deeply interrelated, domains: the substantive domain, the discursive domain, and the meta-discourse, or theory, domain.

The *substantive domain* refers to the changing technological, political, and social "realities" and the prevailing socioeconomic developmental issues. On the one hand, the media, information, and communication technologies have demonstrated an impressive growth in the past two decades, offering new platforms for communication and continuously opening up new questions about their social role. On the other hand, questions of poverty, dispersion, and socioeconomic underdevelopment remain today as relevant as they were two decades ago. The changes and the challenges imposed by the substantive domain are at the basis of the debate surrounding the "digital divide" and are the driving force behind the attempts to conceptualize it.

The discussion about the role of information and communication technologies (ICTs) in development that is generated primarily by policy makers and practitioners, but also by academics, constitutes the *discursive domain*. This is the domain where power structures in the media, information, and development realms are defined and are continuously negotiated. It produces agendas for the information and communication technologies industry, for public policy, and for perceptions of the social role of communication. As such, the discourse reacts to and feeds back into the substantive domain, as it has the potential to affect the material facts on the ground.

Each of these domains, and the interactions between them, are under continuous scrutiny by their participants and particularly by the members of the research community. These efforts to understand, analyze, and constructively criticize the discourse, and its substance, constitute a meta-discourse or attempts systematically to explain the phenomenon. However, this *theoretical domain* does not exist in a vacuum, as it is in constant conversation with the discursive domain and is tied always to the substantive domain. The resulting picture is that of an interrelated progression of the three domains, as they impact each other, which brings further complexity into attempts to make sense of the "digital divide."

This chapter tracks the evolution of the "digital divide" in recent history. It reviews each one of the domains around the time when first references to the "digital divide" appear in the U.S. public discourse. Although it distinguishes between the domains, it is important to view them as parts of a whole. Discursive, theoretical, and substantive developments did not take place independently and the mutual influences of each are deeply embedded in the others. Following this retrospective, I will discuss the more recent developments in the efforts to conceptualize the "digital divide." I will then highlight how these developments can be understood through the lens of the same three domains. I will conclude with thoughts for further conceptualizing efforts that could incorporate the classic notion of the "digital divide" with contemporary knowledge on media, communication, and socioeconomic development.

Discursive Origins

The exact origins of the term "digital divide" are still being debated, but existing literature allows us to draw a relatively detailed picture. David Gunkel traces the origins of the term to public and political discourse, where it was assigned different meanings by different stakeholders. In 1995, the term "digital divide" was used by *Los Angeles Times* journalists to describe opposing views regarding the potential of information technology to solve the world's problems. Just one year later, the term was utilized by the Clinton-Gore administration to describe the information "haves" and "have-nots" in K-12 education. To make things even more semantically complex, some references during that time used the term "digital divide" to describe differences in technical capabilities, such as interoperability between analog and digital cell phone networks. Other sources used the term to address the lack of racial diversity in the emerging high-tech industry.[3] Nevertheless, there is broad agreement that the term was publicized through a series of reports initiated during the Clinton administration.[4]

The first officially published use of the term "digital divide" can be traced back to a 1999 report by the U.S. Department of Commerce's National Telecommunications and Information Administration (NTIA), titled *Falling through the Net: Defining the Digital Divide*.[5] In this report, the "digital divide" is defined as "the divide between those with access to new technologies and those without."[6] This generic and broad definition, focused on access to physical infrastructure and on the dichotomy between the "haves" and the "have-nots," became one of the main frames of reference to the digital divide, especially in relation to placing this issue in the context of socioeconomic development.

Over time, this policy-based understanding of the "digital divide" as a term that referred to disparity in physical access to infrastructure became a discursive token in both the national and international arenas. In the United States, for example, the Clinton administration praised itself for "bridging the digital divide."[7] Among its achievements, the administration listed tripling funding for Community Technology Centers, which at their peak in 2001 had a budget of almost $65 million and provided access to computers and the Internet in low-income communities across the country.[8] When revising the Telecommunication Act, the Clinton administration also included public schools and libraries within the expanded "universal service" mandate, granting them significant "E-rate" discounts on the costs of building computing and telecommunication infrastructure; the total worth of the benefit was estimated at over $2 billion.[9]

In the international arena, the period of late 1990s to early 2000s was marked by the creation of a series of global efforts aimed to spur greater ICT use in the developing world. For example, in 1996 the World Bank launched its InfoDev program to help finance small-scale projects designed to implement ICTs as part of broader development efforts. In 2000 the UN General Assembly resolved "to ensure that the benefits of new technologies, especially information and communication technologies. . . are available to all" as part of its development agenda known as the "Millennium Goals."[10] Finally, in 2003 and 2006 the International Telecommunication Union (ITU) sponsored the World Summit on the Information Society (WSIS), which aimed to discuss how to bridge the "global digital divide" and to more broadly consider the future of ICTs and development on an international scale.

Some formal analysis of the discourse emerging during that time helps to draw a more detailed picture of the discursive origins of the term. Mark Thompson studied the discourse of the leadership of the World Bank as it carved out a role for ICTs in the arena of development. He viewed the World Bank's incorporation of the debate about information technology as a "developmental land grab," or means for the bank to maintain its authority in the developmental arena. In other words, to remain relevant, the bank could not afford not to incorporate the "digital divide" in its official discourse.[11] In his analysis, Thompson reveals that:

> ICT is represented as a neutral tool of the Bank's experts, the province of "young people," the "new millennium, and the future," and we are repeatedly told that, far from offering alternatives to the existing developmental order, ICT is seen by the Bank as key to its future expansion. Along the way, we have seen examples of the conception of ICT projects within a markedly North American worldview and the use of ICT to export, unchallenged, such cultural assumptions.[12]

In other words the discourse merging ICTs and development is characterized by a belief in the transformative power of technology. In this case, technology is thought to be capable of bringing Western development to the developing world. Moreover, technology is associated with progress and viewed as an essential component of the future.

Siobhan Stevenson found that the framing of the issue as it emerged from the NTIA reports captured the "digital divide" in neo-liberal terms, which placed the burden of catching up on the individual and the market but nevertheless linked socioeconomic development with technology adoption.[13] Her findings highlight a dichotomous division between information "haves" and those who "fell through the net." In their analysis of the U.S. discourse relating to the "digital divide" and economic development, Lesie Tu and Lynette Kvasny have also criticized the notion of a single desired developmental state and the implicit solution in the form of the information "have-nots" having to "catch up."[14] David Gunkel summarized his critique of the "digital divide" as follows:

> The distinction between "information haves" and "information have-nots," for example, is articulated in such a way that the latter is both segregated from, and defined in opposition to, the former. But these two possibilities are not on an equal footing. The "information haves" are not only characterized positively but are presumed to be in the desirable position. The "information have-nots" are defined, quite literally, by what they lack in comparison to the "information haves." They comprise the negative counterpart and undesirable version of their positively defined other.[15]

Numerous studies looking at the digital divide discourse make similar observations about the characteristics of the debate. Moreover, they demonstrate how institutional adoption of this discourse translates discursive frames into operative policy decision, or, in other words, suggests a close interdependence between the discursive and the substantive domains, which will be further discussed below.[16]

Theoretical Origins

Deep conceptual roots support the rhetoric of the "digital divide" as a dichotomous distinction between "haves" and "have-nots" coupled with an underlying belief in the almost revolutionary power of ICTs to bring development. A decade-long tradition of thinking about and practicing socioeconomic development created a notion that there is a single desired state of development. Moreover, this tradition was based on an idea that knowledge, technology, or democratic values can be easily transferable from the developed to the developing.

The post–WW II period is frequently marked as a starting point for generating formal theories of development.[17] Changes in the sociopolitical landscape, such as the formal end of colonization and the emergence of "new" independent states, highlighted the socioeconomic gaps between the Global North and the Global South. A World Bank study showed that in 1960, per capita income in the world's richest countries was 38 times greater than in the poorest countries.[18] Moreover, many of the newly established states, lacking adequate institutions for sustainable statehood, found themselves swamped by political turmoil and civil unrest.[19] Out of this reality emerged a body of research and practice aimed at addressing the developmental needs of the underprivileged societies through export of technological and political know-how from the developed parts of the world. This approach was institutionalized through the establishment of organizations such as the World Bank, International Monetary Fund, and later the UN Development Program.[20]

The dominant developmental paradigm articulated during that time is formally known as the "modernization theory." Built on ideas of modernity,[21] and rooted in the view that economic and technological growth can re-shape social, cultural, and political structures, this perspective remains the dominant approach to international socioeconomic development.[22] In the developmental context, the modernization theory views the Western world as representing the aspirational model for developing nations, both in terms of economic development and in terms of preferred political and cultural value systems.[23] Moreover, this approach implies that development is transferable and developing countries can achieve both economic and political progress through the import of technology, management practices, political institutions, as well as a set of values from the developed world.[24]

The early application of modernization thinking to the information and communication domain can be found in the area of "communication for development," or "development communication." Both research and activism in this area originally built on utilization of media for the mobilization of target audiences, whether these were the communities being developed, the hosting governments, or the specific project facilitators.[25] Communication theories such as "diffusion of innovations," and later the "two-step-flow," constituted the mainstream theoretical frameworks during the early days of development communication. The prevailing approach was that of strong effects and top-down flow of information from the developed to the developing. This was particularly evident in the case of models of innovation diffusion that applied a deterministic perception of how Western technologies should be introduced to the developing world.[26] In this context, communication is viewed as a vehicle that delivers progress from the developed to the developing in the form of technology, know-how, ideology, values, and more. For example, one of the approaches applied in this context is that of "extension," where technological transfer takes place from an expert to the user in a somewhat paternalistic fashion.[27] Such practices clearly resonate with the modernization perspective of a dichotomist division, a clear model of the desired state, and patron-patronized relationship between the developing and the developed.

Even though we can find references to communication as an important element in constituting and changing social structure in the literature on society and state building,[28] the role of communication has never been clearly defined in the developmental process. At most, the modernization approach to development viewed communication as a vehicle for knowledge transfer but more frequently as an exogenous factor in a developmental effort.[29] The "knowledge gap" hypothesis, which was introduced by Phillip Tichenor, George Donohue, and Clarice Olien in

1970, was one of the few approaches that considered communication as an integral part of the developmental process. Building on Robert Merton's observation of the "Matthew effect,"[30] this hypothesis concluded that those belonging to higher socioeconomic strata are in an advanced position to reap the benefits of media, information, and communication technologies. Tichenor, Donohue, and Olien demonstrated that people of higher socioeconomic status have better abilities to navigate the mass media, and contextualize, retain, and recall information when required.[31] In other words, in the context of socioeconomic development, bridging the knowledge gap is in fact equal to development.

Particularly during its early days, the discourse and conceptualization of the "digital divide" can be viewed as an example of modernization thought applied to one particular domain. First, the notion of "divide" implies a dichotomous view of two distinct and dialectically opposed groups of "haves" vs. "have-nots," whether that opposition occurs in terms of access, skills, or attitudes towards technology. Second, there is a clear hierarchy, by which the "have-nots" are inferior to the "haves," who represent the only desired state. In fact, the two states are described in negative, mutually exclusive positions; one cannot belong simultaneously to both groups. Moreover, belonging to the group of "haves" stands not only for ownership of a technological artifact but for ownership of the modern way of life and progress itself. Those on the privileged side of the "divide" are usually wealthier, more educated, more powerful, and overall more "successful." Those who do not belong to the privileged group are excluded from progress or left behind. Finally, the notion of "digital divide" also implies a solution to the socioeconomic disparities; one that is based on access to information technology as a means for development. This point is particularly prominent in the early rhetoric of the digital divide, which focused on physical access to personal computers and later the Internet.

Jan van Dijk draws direct parallels between the "knowledge gap" and the "digital divide" approaches when it comes to unequal "diffusion and development of knowledge and information."[32] The pivotal idea underlying the knowledge gap hypothesis and its link to the digital divide lies in explication of the relationship between communication processes and social inequality. As is the case with mass media, those in the higher socioeconomic strata are in a better position to benefit from ICTs. Moreover, both terms still capture a particular, rather dichotomous, view of the "information haves" vs. "information have-nots," which resonates with the modernization view of the world even if it introduces a more nuanced explanation.

David Gunkel's critique of the digital divide discourse quoted above is very much in line with the critique of modernization. He questions the dualism of the "digital divide" framework as incapable of encompassing the complexity of the phenomenon and the multiplicity of the ways it is expressed in practice.[33] He critiques the implicit hierarchy embedded in the terminology and explains that:

> In defining others as deficient, one does not simply provide a neutral expression of inequality. The very technique by which the discrepancy is articulated necessarily employs an asymmetrical logic that already warrants the position of a privileged minority, and depreciates and simplifies the situation of others.[34]

Finally, Gunkel describes the centrality of technology in the paradigm as deterministic and laments that, "the reports, texts, and discussions of the digital divide do not question this prevailing technological determinism, but exploit it."[35] Similar criticism can be found in Mark Thompson's analysis of the World Bank discourse on ICTs and development.[36]

In the setting of the mid- to late 1990s, when the rhetoric of the "digital divide" was first used by U.S. politicians, the discourse that emerged embodied concepts from the theoretical domain and the long heritage of the debate about development. The early dichotomous definition of the "digital divide" bears clear traces of modernization thinking in terms of two clearly distinctive states of development: a single desired state, and an implied solution in the form of the transfer of knowledge or technology. Even though the digital divide was a multifaceted issue from the outset, the early political and practical solutions to the "digital divide" were built around the idea of providing access to computer equipment and to the Internet; it was assumed that socioeconomic development would follow.

Substantive Origins

In the discussion of the modernization approach to development, we can already see that conceptual frameworks arise in a particular point of time and in light of a particular set of historic events. It is no coincidence that the question of development became a tangible topic in the aftermath of World War II and the end of colonialism. It is also no coincidence that the role of media and communication in the developmental processes gained prominence as the importance of communication technologies such as radio and TV grew in the developed and later also in the developing worlds. What were the substantive conditions that helped to facilitate the discourse and conceptualization of the "digital divide"?

The history of computation technology and the Internet clearly predates the term "digital divide." The first computers date back to the 1940s,[37] and the first account of Internet protocol dates back to 1974.[38] In her extensive analysis of the design documents of the internet infrastructure, Sandra Braman reveals that the designers of the Internet were in fact concerned with a variety of social and political issues, such as spam or privacy, including issues of physical access to the network by people with disabilities.[39] Still, it was not until the commercialization of the

Internet that we witnessed the emergence of the "digital divide" as a developmental issue.

In April of 1995, the National Science Foundation, which had been managing and funding the backbone of the version of the Internet at the time, decommissioned that backbone, thus clearing the way for eventual privatization of the network.[40] Before that, the NSF had spent nearly a decade struggling to fund the infrastructure, which also included encouraging commercial consumers to exploit the economies of scale offered by the network. The network was open to commercial traffic in 1981, and as this traffic grew, the federal funding decreased until it was completely eliminated in 1995.[41] These developments signified a certain maturity of the Internet as infrastructure while they also heralded the coming of the "dot.com bubble."[42]

The period of the "dot.com bubble," which started in 1995 or 1996 (accounts vary), was characterized by high levels of technological optimism.[43] The years 1995–2000 witnessed a massive flow of investment into the Internet market. Between 1998 and 2002 alone, 50,000 new ventures were formed "to exploit the commercialization of the Internet."[44] During the same period, 24,000 firms raised $256 billion from formal and informal investors. At the stock exchange, the earnings from the first day initial public offerings tripled and quadrupled during the dot.com hype,[45] and between 1998 and 2000 alone, the Internet sector earned over 1,000 percent returns on its public equity.[46] All this was accompanied by enthusiastic media coverage that painted a picture of an emerging "information highway" supported by both the government and the private sector.[47]

Privatization and commercialization of the Internet, combined with the optimism of the dot.com period, contrasted sharply with the actual gaps in adoption, both on the national and the international levels. Even before the term "digital divide" was adopted into the official rhetoric, the first of the NTIA *Falling through the Net* reports in 1995, for example, showed that only 4.5 percent of the rural poor in the United States owned a computer and less than a quarter of those owned a modem.[48] Similarly, on the international level, the Internet penetration rate in the U.S. was almost 16 percent in 1999, but in India, for example, this rate stood at only 0.08 percent.[49]

The emergence of the digital divide rhetoric happens against the background of conflicting developments. The growing commercialization of the Internet and the emerging dot.com bubble spurred enthusiasm about the transformative power of ICTs, particularly the Internet. This enthusiasm is in line with one of the core tenets of the modernization approach to development, which places great faith in technology and communication as vehicles for progress. Yet, it seems that not everybody can enjoy the fruits of technology. The striking disparities in ICT adoption, correlated with other social, political, and economic inequalities, led many to believe (and to proselytize on behalf of the ideal) that providing access to ICTs should make the promises of the "dot.com" industry available to those who need them the most.[50]

Recent Developments

The enthusiastic period of ICT industry growth during the dot.com hype coupled with the modernization approach to development can explain the discourse of the digital divide that emerged from the U.S. administration in the mid- to late 1990s. This discourse, and its policy implications, framed the "digital divide" primarily in terms of physical access to technology, with great hopes for socioeconomic development and empowerment once that access is granted. However, since the beginnings of the idea of the digital divide, all three domains that shaped the "digital divide" as a policy and a research topic went through phases of change, review, and adaptation, influencing each other in the process.

The modernization theory came under fire as early as the 1960s. The criticism grew out of the dissonance between theoretical promises of the theory and the results on the ground. Some claimed that modernization brought greater inequality and disparity between the developed and the developing nations.[51] Others criticized modernization for neglecting broader cultural and political processes, while concentrating on the economic mechanisms.[52] The main contribution of the critical theory, labeled also as "dependency theory," was problematization of the developmental process through rejection of the dichotomous view, the idea of a single desired ideal for a state, and the idea that development can be transferred easily from one setting to another. While the modernization theory remains the dominant paradigm, the critical approach expanded the view of development and opened the door for alternative views on the challenges of development and their solutions.

In a similar fashion, the study of the "digital divide" has matured over more than a decade of research.[53] Some scholars suggested the digital divide should be understood as a series of divides[54] or inequalities,[55] while others preferred viewing it as a continuum[56] or spectrum.[57] Others criticized the access framework as determinist, utopian, and naïve, warning that the evident socioeconomic disparities have to do with more than just the presence or absence of technology and do not simply disappear as ICTs and Internet connectivity become more ubiquitous.[58] In other words, we have witnessed a shift from single (divide, access) to plural (divides, accesses) and then the shift from "divide" to "inequality." In fact it was a parallel shift, so the discourse moved from addressing a singular "divide in access" to "inequalities in access and skills."[59] This trajectory of research gives us both a more detailed view of the concept and more sophisticated methods for measuring it.

These developments can be explained through the evolution of theoretical thought but also through changes in the substantive domain. First, there are new, richer, and more comprehensive data available to study the various aspects and the different conceptualizations of the "digital divide."[60] Second, the subject matter has changed substantively. For example, the access gap has narrowed; and Internet penetration grew almost 400 percent between the years 2000 and 2009.[61] Also, the media, whose use is being observed, have evolved. The use of mobile phones became much more widespread, especially in developing countries and communities; the penetration of mobile phones is expected to reach 100 percent of the world's population by the year 2015.[62] The industry also went through the burst of the "dot.com bubble," recovery, and emergence of a new, "Web 2.0" paradigm focused even more on the user and her "empowerment."[63] The high penetration rates of personal computers and other devices for access of the Internet also made the old access paradigm less attractive from the business perspective, which since then has focused on capacity building instead of mere access.

Over the past decade and a half, the policy discourse has also shifted towards focusing on capacity building both in terms of technical capacity of the network and users' skills. Some of these changes are just a different framing of the same access paradigm. In the United States, the NTIA is currently referring to the "digital divide" as the "broadband divide," highlighting that the issue now is not just access but the quality of the online experience;[64] similarly, the FCC has commissioned a report aimed at reviewing policies of advancing broadband deployment and adoption.[65]

Other changes suggest a paradigm shift in conceptualizing the issue behind the "digital divide." Thus for example, in the 2008 presidential campaign, both candidates referred to the need for investment in the development of skills. In the context of the "digital divide," Barack Obama referred to these skills as "math and science education" and John McCain referred to them more broadly as education for "the innovation age" with an explicit emphasis on "degrees in math or science, and the number of computer science majors."[66] On the international level, one can see abandonment of programs such as USAID's Leland Initiative, which was created to develop information infrastructure in Africa.[67] We can also see the enhancement of initiatives such as the ITU Academy, which focuses on human capacity building, as it comes to rely more extensively over the years on distance learning.[68]

Conclusion: Moving Forward

While the conceptual meaning of the "digital divide" has changed over time, the core question has remained more or less the same. "Digital inclusion," "digital inequalities," and "digital divide" are all terms that address the question of the role of media, information, and communication in the formation and transformation of the information society. The question itself is not new, but the variety of forms, particularly the mediated forms, that communication takes in contemporary society, is what distinguishes the questions asked by classic theory regarding how societies function from the questions we are trying to ask by further developing "digital divide" as a concept. Taking on Jan van Dijk's call for further elaboration of the conceptual definition of the "digital divide,"[69] we need to account for the evolution of theoretical thought on society formation, and for the knowledge we have today about the social functioning of media, information, and communication technologies.

For that purpose, I would like to propose the following combination. Considering the evolution of theoretical thought about society formation, the theory of structuration[70] can offer a valuable building block. It builds on the classical contributions of Max Weber and others, yet accounts for contemporary contributions about human agency and highlights the communicative aspects of social processes. The theory of structuration can be applied to understand trends in the substantive domain toward more grassroots-oriented processes of development, bottom-up empowerment, and generation of knowledge. In other words, the "reality" suggests changing the structure through agency. In this aspect, communication is particularly important because the duality of structure is essentially a communication process.

Considering the body of knowledge about the social functioning of media, information, and communication technologies, science and technology studies offer a strong body of scholarship on the social construction of technology and the agency of technological artifacts.[71] Combining these contributions allows us to consider media, information, and communication technologies within the structuration paradigm. This combination may in fact allow us to formulate more concrete questions about the role of media and information technologies in the mutually constituted processes of social structures and human agency.

Understanding the mechanisms that have shaped thought about the digital divide from a historical perspective, including developments that preceded the "digital," is important in continuing the conceptual development of this issue. The primary goal in developing the next generation of conceptual successors of the "digital divide" should be engagement of the multidisciplinary theoretical ideas with empirical work. So far, empirical work has been considered in terms of the currently dominant trajectory in the "digital divide" research. However, strengthening the conceptual trajectory through accounting for the evolution of theoretical thought on society formation and the knowledge about the social functioning of media, information, and communication technologies can open new avenues for inquiry and open doors for additional methodological options.

Notes

1. van Dijk, "Digital Divide Research," 233.
2. Gunkel, "Second Thoughts"; Warschauer, "Reconceptualizing the Digital Divide"; Carvin, "More Than Just Access."
3. Gunkel, "Second Thoughts."
4. van Dijk, "Digital Divide Research"; Gunkel, "Second Thoughts."
5. Klegar Levy et al., *Falling through the Net.*
6. Ibid.
7. See National Archives for the 2000 version of the White House website: http://clinton5.nara.gov/WH/Accomplishments/eightyears-09.html (accessed October 23, 2010).
8. For more up-to-date budget figures, see http://www2.ed.gov/programs/comtechcenters/funding.html (accessed October 23, 2010).
9. See National Archives for the 2000 version of the White House website: http://clinton5.nara.gov/WH/Accomplishments/eightyears-09.html (accessed October 23, 2010).
10. A complete resolution can be found at http://www.un.org/millennium/declaration/ares552e.htm (accessed October 23, 2010).
11. Thompson, "'Discourse,' 'Development' & the 'Digital Divide.'"
12. Ibid., 114.
13. Stevenson, "Digital Divide."
14. Tu and Kvasny, "American Discourses of the Digital Divide."
15. Gunkel, "Second Thoughts," 507.
16. Kvasny and Truex, "Defining away the Digital Divide"; Stevenson, "Digital Divide."
17. Acemoglu, Johnson, and Robinson, "Economic History and Political Science"; Servaes and Malikhao, "Development Communication Approaches"; Przeworski and Limongi, "Modernization."
18. Soubbotina, *Beyond Economic Growth.*
19. Przeworski, "Economic History and Political Science."
20. Cooper and Packard, "Introduction."
21. Emirbayer, *Émile Durkheim;* Kalberg, *Max Weber;* Antonio, *Marx and Modernity.*
22. Servaes and Malikhao, "Development Communication Approaches"; Przeworski, "Economic History and Political Science."
23. Huesca, "Tracing History of Participatory Communication Approaches"; Servaes and Malikhao, "Development Communication Approaches."
24. Servaes, *Communication for Development and Social Change;* Colle, "Threads of Development Communication."
25. Fraser and Restrepo-Estrada, *Communicating for Development.*
26. Fraser and Restrepo-Estrada, *Communicating for Development;* Huesca, "Tracing History of Participatory Communication Approaches"; Servaes and Malikhao, "Development Communication Approaches."
27. Colle, "Threads of Development Communication."
28. Braman, *Change of State.*

29. Acemoglu, Johnson, and Robinson, "Economic History and Political Science."
30. Merton, "The Matthew Effect in Science."
31. Tichenor, Donohue, and Olien, "Mass Media Flow and Differential Growth in Knowledge."
32. van Dijk, *The Deepening Divide,* 126.
33. Gunkel, "Second Thoughts."
34. Ibid., 508.
35. Ibid., 510.
36. Thompson, "ICT, Power, and Developmental Discourse"; Thompson, "'Discourse,' 'Development' & the 'Digital Divide.'"
37. Winston, *Media Technology and Society.*
38. Dalal, Sunshine, and Cerf, "RFC 675: Specification of Internet Transmission Control Program."
39. Braman, "The Interpenetration of Technical and Legal Decision-Making for the Internet."
40. Leiner et al., "A Brief History of the Internet."
41. Bickerstaff, "Shackles on the Giant"; Frischmann, "Privatization and Commercialization of the Internet Infrastructure."
42. Frischmann, "Privatization and Commercialization of the Internet Infrastructure."
43. DeLong and Magin, "A Short Note on the Size of the Dot.com Bubble."
44. Goldfarb, Pfarrer, and Kirsch, *Searching for Ghosts.*
45. Ljungqvist and Wilhelm, "IPO Pricing in the Dot.com Bubble."
46. Ofek and Richardson, "Dot.com Mania."
47. Cukier, Ryan, and Fornssler, "The Rhetoric of the 'Information Highway' in the Media 1992–2008."
48. McConnaughey, Sloan, and Nila, *Falling through the Net.*
49. See ITU Eye for historical statistics of the Internet and other ICT adoption rates at http://www.itu.int/ITU-D/icteye/Indicators/Indicators.aspx (accessed October 23, 2010).
50. Guillen and Suarez, "Explaining the Global Digital Divide."
51. Servaes, *Communication for Development.*
52. Adjibolosoo, *Rethinking Development Theory and Policy;* Hamilton, *Growth Fetish.*
53. For a comprehensive review, see van Dijk, "Digital Divide Research."
54. Barzilai-Nahon, "Gaps and Bits"; Meredyth and Thomas, "Digital Divides."
55. DiMaggio et al., "Digital Inequality."
56. Warschauer, "Reconceptualizing the Digital Divide"; Warschauer, *Technology and Social Inclusion.*
57. Lenhart and Horrigan, "Re-visualizing the Digital Divide as a Dgital Spectrum."
58. van Dijk, "Digital Divide Research"; Gunkel, "Second Thoughts."
59. Epstein, Nisbet, and Gillespie, "Who's Responsible for the Digital Divide?"
60. Barzilai-Nahon, "Gaps and Bits."
61. See Internet World Stats at http://www.internetworldstats.com/stats.htm (accessed October 31, 2010).
62. *World Telecommunication/ICT Development Report,* 2010.
63. See, for example, Scholz, "Market Ideology and the Myths of Web 2.0"; and Treese, "Web 2.0."
64. Strickling et al., *Digital Nation.*

65. FCC, *Connecting America.*
66. The quotations are taken from the candidates' platforms, which were published on their campaign websites. The websites are no longer available.
67. See http://www.usaid.gov/regions/afr/leland/ (accessed October 20, 2010).
68. See http://academy.itu.int/ (accessed October 20, 2010).
69. van Dijk, "Digital Divide Research."
70. Giddens, *The Constitution of Society.*
71. Bijker, Hughes, and Pinch, *The Social Construction of Technological Systems;* Pinch, "The Sociology of Science and Technology."

Works Cited

Acemoglu, Daron, Simon Johnson, and James A. Robinson. "Economic History and Political Science: Clarifying the Questions, Methods and Answers." *The Political Economist* 12, no. 3 (Winter 2005): 4–13.

Adjibolosoo, S.B.-S.K. *Rethinking Development Theory and Policy: A Human Factor Critique.* Westport, CT: Praeger, 1999.

Antonio, Robert. *Marx and Modernity: Key Readings and Commentary.* Blackwell, 2002.

Barzilai-Nahon, Karine. "Gaps and Bits: Conceptualizing Measurements for Digital Divide/s." *The Information Society* 22 (2006): 269–278.

Bickerstaff, Steve. "Shackles on the Giant: How the Federal Government Created Microsoft, Personal Computers, and the Internet." *Texas Law Review* 78, no. 1 (1999).

Bijker, Wiebe E., Thomas P. Hughes, and Trevor Pinch. *The Social Construction of Technological Systems.* Cambridge, MA: MIT Press, 1987.

Braman, Sandra. *Change of state: Information, Policy, and Power.* Cambridge, MA: MIT Press, 2009.

———. "The Interpenetration of Technical and Legal Decision-Making for the Internet." *Information, Communication & Society* 13, no. 3 (2010): 309–324.

Carvin, Andy. "More Than Just Access: Fitting Literacy and Content into the Digital Divide Equation." *Educause Review* 35, no. 6 (2000): 38–47.

Colle, Royal D. "Threads of Development Communication." In *Approaches to Development Communication,* edited by Jan Servaes. Paris: UNESCO, 2003.

Cooper, Frederick, and Randall Packard. "Introduction." In *International Development and the Social Sciences: Essays on the History and Politics of Knowledge,* edited by Frederick Cooper and Randall M. Packard, 1–44. Berkeley: University of California Press, 1997.

Cukier, Wendy, Peter M. Ryan, and Barbara Fornssler. "The Rhetoric of the 'Information Highway' in the Media 1992–2008: Was the Hype Actually Trumped by the Reality?" In *Science and Technology for Humanity* (TIC-STH), 618–623. Tornoto, 2009.

Dalal, Yogen, Carl Sunshine, and Vinton Cerf. "RFC 675: Specification of Internet Transmission Control Program." Internet Engineering Task Force, December 1974. http://tools.ietf.org/html/rfc675.

DeLong, J. Bradford, and Konstantin Magin. "A Short Note on the Size of the Dot.com Bubble." *National Bureau of Economic Research Working Paper Series,* No. 12011, February 2006. http://www.nber.org.proxy.library.cornell.edu/papers/w12011.

DiMaggio, Paul, Eszter Hargittai, Coral Celeste, and Steven Shafer. "Digital Inequality: From Unequal Access to Differentiated Use." In *Social Inequality,* edited by Kathryn M. Neckerman, 355–400. New York: Russell Sage Foundation, 2004. http://www.eszter.com/research/c05-digitalinequality.html.

Emirbayer, Mustafa. *Émile Durkheim: Sociologist of Modernity.* Blackwell, 2003.

Epstein, Dmitry, Erik Nisbet, and Tarleton Gillespie. "Who's Responsible for the Digital Divide? Public Perceptions and Policy Implications." *The Information Society* 27, no. 2 (2011).

FCC. *Connecting America: The National Broadband Plan.* Washington, DC: Federal Communications Commission, 2010.

Fraser, Colin, and Sonia Restrepo-Estrada. *Communicating for Development: Human Change for Survival.* London: I. B. Tauris, 1998.

Frischmann, Brett M. "Privatization and Commercialization of the Internet Infrastructure: Rethinking Market Intervention into Government and Government Intervention into the Market." *The Columbia Science and Technology Law Review* 2, no. 1 (June 8, 2001). http://papers.ssrn.com/sol3/papers.cfm?abstract_id=255423.

Giddens, Anthony. *The Constitution of Society.* Berkeley: University of California Press, 1984.

Goldfarb, Brent D., Michael D. Pfarrer, and David A. Kirsch. *Searching for ghosts: Business survival, unmeasured entrepreneurial activity and private equity investment in the dot-com era.* Working Paper. College Park, MD: Robert H. Smith School of Business, University of Maryland, October 2005.

Guillen, Mauro F., and Sandra L. Suarez. "Explaining the Global Digital Divide: Economic, Political and Sociological Drivers of Cross-National Internet Use." *Social Forces* 84, no. 2 (2005): 681–708.

Gunkel, David J. "Second Thoughts: Toward a Critique of the Digital Divide." *New Media Society* 5, no. 4 (December 1, 2003): 499–522.

Hamilton, C. *Growth Fetish.* Crows Nest, NSW: Allen & Unwin, 2003.

Huesca, Robert. "Tracing History of Participatory Communication Approaches to Development: A Critical Appraisal." In *Approaches to Development Communication,* edited by Jan Servaes. Paris: UNESCO, 2003.

Kalberg, Stephen, ed. *Max Weber: Readings and Commentary on Modernity.* Malden, MA: Blackwell, 2005.

Klegar Levy, Kelly, James McConnaughey, Douglas W Everette, and Taylor Reynolds. *Falling through the Net: Defining the Digital Divide.* Washington, DC: National Telecommunications and Information Administration, U.S. Dept. of Commerce, 1999.

Kvasny, Lynette, and Duane P. Truex. "Defining away the Digital Divide: A Content Analysis of Institutional Influences on Popular Representations of Technology." *Realigning Research and Practice in Information Systems Development: Social and Organizational Perspective* (2001): 399–414.

Leiner, Barry M., Vinton G. Cerf, David D. Clark, Robert E. Kahn, Leonard Kleinrock, Daniel C. Lynch, Jon Postel, Larry G. Roberts, and Stephen Wolff. "A Brief History of the Internet." *ACM SIGCOMM Computer Communication Review* 39, no. 5 (2009): 22–31.

Lenhart, Amanda, and John B. Horrigan. "Re-visualizing the Digital Divide as a Digital Spectrum." *IT & Society* 1, no. 5 (2003): 23–39.

Ljungqvist, Alexander, and William J. Wilhelm. "IPO Pricing in the Dot.com Bubble." *The Journal of Finance* 58, no. 2 (4, 2003): 723–752.

McConnaughey, Jim, Tim Sloan, and Cynthia A. Nila. *Falling through the Net: A Survey of the "Have Nots" in Rural and Urban America.* Washington, DC: National Telecommunications and Information Administration, Dept. of Commerce, July 1995.

Meredyth, Denise, and Julian Thomas. "Digital Divides: Framing the Issues." David C. Lam Institute for East-West Studies, Hong Kong Baptist University, 2002.

Merton, Robert K. "The Matthew Effect in Science: The Reward and Communication Systems of Science Are Considered." *Science* 159, no. 3810 (1968): 56–63.

Ofek, Eli, and Matthew Richardson. "Dot.com Mania: The Rise and Fall of Internet Stock Prices." *The Journal of Finance* 58, no. 3 (June 2003): 1113–1138.

Pinch, Trevor. "The Sociology of Science and Technology." In *21st Century Sociology: A Reference Handbook,* edited by Clifton D. Bryant and Dennis L. Peck, 266–275. Thousand Oaks, CA: Sage, 2006.

Przeworski, Adam. "Economic History and Political Science." *The Political Economist* 12, no. 2 (Fall 2004): 1–12.

———, and Fernando Limongi. "Modernization: Theories and Facts." *World Politics* 49, no. 2 (1997): 155–183.

Scholz, Trebor. "Market Ideology and the Myths of Web 2.0." *First Monday* 13, no. 3 (2008).

Servaes, Jan. *Communication for Development and Social Change.* Thousand Oaks, CA: Sage, 2008.

———, ed. *Communication for Development: One World, Multiple Cultures.* Cresskill, NJ: Hampton Press, 1999.

———, and Patchanee Malikhao. "Development Communication Approaches in International Perspective." In *Approaches to Development Communication,* edited by Jan Servaes. Paris: UNESCO, 2003.

Soubbotina, Tatyana P. *Beyond Economic Growth: An Introduction to Sustainable Development.* 2nd ed. Washington, DC: The World Bank, 2004.

Stevenson, Siobhan. "Digital Divide: A Discursive Move away from the Real Inequities." The *Information Society* 25, no. 1 (2009): 1–22.

Strickling, Lawrence E., Anna Gomez, Daniel J. Weitzner, James McConnaughey, Dennis Amari, Deena Shetler, and Lisa Clement. *Digital Nation: 21st Century America's Progress towards Universal Broadband Internet Access.* Washington, DC: National Telecommunications and Information Administration, February 2010.

Thompson, Mark P. A. "'Discourse,' 'Development' & the 'Digital Divide': ICT and the World Bank." *Review of African Political Economy* 99 (2004): 103–123.

———. "ICT, Power, and Developmental Discourse: A Critical Analysis." *The Electronic Journal on Information Systems in Developing Countries* 20, no. 4 (2004): 1–25.

Tichenor, Phillip J., George A. Donohue, and Clarice N. Olien. "Mass Media Flow and Differential Growth in Knowledge." *The Public Opinion Quarterly* 34, no. 2 (Summer 1970): 159–170.

Treese, Win. "Web 2.0: Is It Really Different?" *NetWorker* 10, no. 2 (2006): 15–17.

Tu, Leslie, and Lynette Kvasny. "American Discourses of the Digital Divide and Economic Development: A Sisyphean Order to Catch up?" *In Social Inclusion: Societal and Organizational Implications for Information Systems,* edited by Eileen M. Trauth, Debra Howcroft, Tom Butler, Brian Fitzgerald, and Janice I. DeGross, 51–65. Boston, MA: Springer, 2006.

van Dijk, Jan A.G.M. "Digital Divide Research, Achievements and Shortcomings." *Poetics* 34 (2006): 221–235.

———. *The Deepening Divide: Inequality in the Information Society.* Thousand Oaks, CA: Sage, 2005.

Warschauer, Mark. "Reconceptualizing the Digital Divide." *First Monday* 7, no. 7 (July 2002).

———. *Technology and Social Inclusion: Rethinking the Digital Divide.* Cambridge: MIT Press, 2003.

Winston, Brian. *Media Technology and Society: A History from the Printing Press to the Superhighway.* New York: Routledge, 1998.

World Telecommunication/ICT Development Report 2010. Geneva, Switzerland: International Telecommunication Union, 2010.

chapter nine

Twenty Years of Unnecessary Forward Slashes

Critiquing Narratives of the Development of the Web

Michael Dick

> Looking at the mechanism alone is like watching half the court during a tennis game; it appears as so many meaningless moves. What analysts of artifacts have to do is similar to what we all did when studying scientific texts: we added the other half of the court.
>
> —Bruno Latour, 1992

Introduction

Working in the tradition of Latour and other theorists who espouse the social construction of technology, the aim of this chapter is to examine competing viewpoints on the future of the World Wide Web by analyzing the theoretical paradigms underlying their trajectories.[1] In doing so, I will endeavor to problematize the commonly accepted modernization paradigm of the technology (one that I argue ascribes to the modernist notion of "progress" within the context of Enlightenment thought and a rigid taxonomical structure) by illuminating areas that I assert do not receive enough consideration in both the academic and practitioner-oriented literature on the evolution, structure, and operation of the web. In the interest of brevity, I will draw special attention to—and frame my discussion on—recent work on the next generations of the web around one very specific transformation within the history of the web, namely the rendering extraneous by end-user communities of the cultural object reflected by the forward slashes one would normally include in the Uniform Resource Identifier (URI).

This vignette is effectively inspired by the October 2009 admission of the web's inventor, Sir Tim Berners-Lee, that the decision to initially require a user to type "http://" before the rest of the address was arbitrary, possibly derived in an attempt to emulate common computing syntax of the time rather than reflecting a distinct raison d'être. The forward slashes, in particular, were a focal point of his admission, noting: "Really, if you think about it, it doesn't need the //. I could have designed it not to have the //. . . . It seemed like a good idea at the time."[2] Although this was, in effect, a minor news story, its place within web studies and within the history of the medium is arguably significant.

The importance can be inferred both through the admission that something affecting so many eventual users of the technology came down to one small, arbitrary, decision effectively made by one person, and also because the story fails to acknowledge the overarching issues raised by the fact that entering the slashes is no longer a requirement. It only acknowledges the fact that most browsers automatically assume this "prefix." Indeed, it is my position that the introduction of this "shortcut" reflects the broader challenges to a unified treatment of the advancement of the technology. More specifically, this anecdote of the "unnecessary forward slashes" can usefully be examined within the framework of two major theoretical perspectives on the web, which I will explore by providing context and a discussion of some of the core technical literature in the remainder of this chapter.

The Slashes in Context: Tim Berners-Lee's Evolving Vision for the Web

Providing a complete cultural history of the web is beyond the scope of this chapter. This said, the origins of the forward slashes as part of the medium's configuration can be traced to the very invention of the technology, which demands further elaboration. Tim Berners-Lee's earliest proposals for a system that resembles the basic structure of today's World Wide Web date back to 1989. At this time, while working as a research scientist at CERN, he formally proposed to his superiors a distributed data management system based on a prior development (his "ENQUIRE" software project written in 1980). Shortly thereafter, in 1990, he revised the proposal to include the concept of "hypertext," wherein what we would now refer to as web pages or websites could be written in HyperText Markup Language (HTML), connected to each other via "hyperlinks," accessed via the HyperText Transfer Protocol (HTTP) and via a Uniform Resource Identifier (URI)—with the "//" intact—and displayed in a browser on the client's machine.

By 1991, the web emerged as a nonproprietary, publicly available service on the Internet, and the subsequent advent of what became the first "popular" graphical web browser in 1993 (Marc Andreessen's "Mosaic') popularized the medium. This chain of events is recounted in the inventor's autobiographical book, *Weaving the Web*.[3] The book also outlines what Berners-Lee terms the "ultimate destiny" of the web, and it is this point that effectively foreshadows the major challenge to the linear paradigm of progression and modernization that has been presented thus far. This is especially poignant in light of the influence Berners-Lee still holds in the development of the technology, due to his position as head of the World Wide Web Consortium (or W3C, the organization he founded in 1993 with the support of MIT and the Defense Advanced Research Projects Agency, or DARPA, upon leaving CERN).[4] Although it would be incorrect to state that all of Berners-Lee's recent work has been related to his position at the W3C, this connection is relevant for the purposes of this chapter.

The Semantic Web

As a specific example of his influence, Berners-Lee has consistently advocated a restructuring of the web, wherein both existing and new data stores are coded in such a way as to allow machines to infer meaning, rather than having markup languages code only for how information is to be displayed on screen. For example, a search for the word "Jaguar" will often return hits related to the car, the animal, and the operating system, since the word appears on various sites as a result of HTML markup that explains to the browser only where (i.e., within the document) and how (e.g., bold, italic, red, black) the word is to be displayed. Berners-Lee proposes that instead, by marking up objects with the Extensible Markup Language (XML) or other XML-based languages, one can effectively code for *semantics* (i.e., by using a "triple structure" in which one can specify the intended structure and meaning, such as "Jaguar is a type of car"), as well as for display criteria.

It is this focus on *both* syntax and semantics that forms the core of Berners-Lee's Semantic Web concept. This has the ultimate aim of transforming the present, human-understandable "Web of Documents" to a robust "Web of Data" that can be leveraged by machines and "intelligent agents" to automate various web-related search tasks.[5] Although this concept is outlined in *Weaving the Web*, its technical details are more fully fleshed out in a 2001 *Scientific American* article authored by Tim Berners-Lee, James Hendler, and Ora Lassila.[6] The material below also addresses the underlying technology and socio-technical implications, while footnotes direct readers to other relevant documents, many of which are primary texts authored by the W3C itself or by scholars who are directly affiliated with it.

Realizing the vision of the Semantic Web can proceed in two ways, both of which are discussed by computer scientists Mark Greaves and Tom Heath and relate to the concept of the "ontology," or the lack thereof[7]: on the one hand, existing and newly created data can be annotated using a prescribed vocabulary that is common to a specific industry; on the other, individuals can annotate data as they see fit and, in doing so, create "folksonomies" (a portmanteau of "folk taxonomies").[8] The latter case has already entered the mainstream through numerous Web 2.0 applications that rely on collective knowledge management, namely the social production that is at the root of a Wiki, a social networking site, or an aggregator of user-generated video content (e.g., YouTube and other sites with a similar focus).

Even with tools that allow a certain degree of automation, creating highly defined technical ontologies is a daunting task, most notably because data remain "trapped" in the various web services databases of organizations, and this material must be "mined" in order to produce the ontologies required to proceed.[9] Strategies to accomplish this are centered on "scrubbing" XML databases (within this so-called Deep Web) so that popular search engines can properly annotate the found data with semantic markup languages.[10] In the literature, this effort is predicted to go beyond the proprietary algorithms utilized by the leading search engines and information retrieval organizations and can be considered more worthy of the "Web 3.0" moniker than the Semantic Web alone. This is because accomplishing it requires that both research tracks on leading-edge web technologies be combined in the pursuit of a new generation of World Wide Web that embraces ubiquitous machine-understandable content.[11]

Facilitating this transition from a web that displays documents to a web that interprets data has been a priority for Berners-Lee and the W3C over the past decade, as demonstrated by the rigorous standards they have set for the approval of new markup languages, and an active research dissemination agenda in computing and engineering journal publications and conference proceedings. In addition to this initiative, Berners-Lee and the W3C have launched other major projects that outline their vision of the web's future: the most notable of these, the Web Science Trust, is intended to promote the Web Science Research Initiative (WSRI), which was undertaken in 2005 to direct the technical and socio-technical research agenda related to the web (i.e., to develop a methodological framework that accommodates positivist studies of the underlying network topologies of the web).

The Web Science Trust

Although annual conferences on the subject have been held since March 2009—in addition to the existence of a dedicated journal for the discipline and the recent emergence of related research institutes and academic programs—the seminal document of Web Science remains, at this time, a set of proceedings that emerged from meetings held by what was then the WSRI (now taken up within the scope of the Web Science Trust, among other things) in 2005 and 2006. Entitled "A Framework for Web Science," the text consists largely of a discussion of engineering issues that are central to the web's decentralized nature.[12] The technical specifics of these issues generally relate to the Semantic Web concept, as previously discussed. Although subsequent chapters do focus on issues of governance and managing the socioeconomic impact of the web, these do not progress beyond broad generalizations concerning security, privacy, and trustworthiness of the data itself at code level.

For example, the authors outline some eventual goals for the discipline with respect to policy (i.e., the perceived need to avoid regulation by the state in order to maintain a sense of democracy online), use of the technology in a way that optimizes social benefit, and outreach activities. This said, an actual action plan for achieving these goals (or at least an agenda for further research) is not included, although a general roadmap does exist on their project website.[13] In other words, while there is an assertion that forming this new discipline is required in order to advance our understanding of the web, this concept document does not actually address anything on a macroscopic level. The fact that a trust has been established to promote the proposed discipline may, however, be expected to enlarge and enhance the Web Science approach in the coming years.[14] Among its other activities, the trust seeks to stimulate further inquiry pertaining to the areas identified within the WSRI's concept document and other work. It also helps foster broader acceptance of the discipline in academic circles, and has so far helped influence the creation of both research institutes and entire academic degree or collaborative programs dedicated to the field of Web Science.[15]

This said, ambiguity surrounding this discipline remains, and this is further aggravated by some of the initial responses to Web Science, particularly in academic literature where I would argue rigor is lacking. As an example, we can consider the Web Science Trust's professed approach to "awaken Computer Science to the interdisciplinary possibilities of the Web's socially embedded computing technology" by conducting existing web-related research under the guise of Web Science.[16] Gestures to other fields outside the purview of computer science are similar in that they seem convincing but are actually supported by limited empirical evidence. For example, consider the perfunctory suggestion to study Web Science's implications on technology enhanced learning, a topic that is presently in vogue within the computing literature.[17] Moreover, investing significantly in Web Science research to find applied solutions to problems like identity theft is presented as a means to "protect our future."[18] Again, Web Science literature is very general in its applications to society because scholarship in this field is emerging and thus requires greater fermentation to produce tangible and measurable results. This said, I assert that scrutiny of both Web Science and the Semantic Web is an appropriate way to begin this dialogue, which is a key motivation in my undertaking this research.

Technological Determinism: Conceptualizing the "Modernization Paradigm"

An important point to note at the outset of an analysis on the recent activities of Berners-Lee and the W3C is the often deterministic nature of their projects. This is due to both the amount of control exercised over the "evolution" of an inherently decentralized system like the web, as well as the reliance on rigid knowledge-representation structures (i.e., ontologies) that are required to provide controlled terminology through which inferences are made in the Semantic Web model. The definition of "determinism" that I am using here is derived from Ben Anderson and Paul Stoneman, who reframe the Marxian perspective of humans as being "enslaved" to machines through the more agnostic reaction they name the "snooker ball method."[19] Essentially, as the analogy goes, thinking in this framework must suggest that the web itself has a direct, causal impact on society (as one snooker ball hitting the other entails an action and a direct reaction). Put another way, this model or analogy reflects Newtonian mechanics extrapolated into the digital, online realm.

In this vein, among the most significant of conclusions that may be derived from this view of determinism is the possibility that the web is somehow "alive," since it is able to create effects on society, even if some are very small. Philip Tetlow provides support for this idea, suggesting that the web is evolving into an organism, supported by the added, artificial intelligence promised by the shift to the Semantic Web.[20] Although Tetlow's framework could be seen as too speculative for Tim Berners-Lee and the web studies community, this should not detract from its value in helping to conceptualize one particular viewpoint on the "ultimate transformation" of the web. Indeed, a separate discipline devoted entirely to studying networks in a similar vein—termed "Network Science"—has emerged in tandem with the work of Berners-Lee and the W3C. Its key proponent, Albert-László Barabási, serves on the Scientific Council of the Web Science Trust and argues that, with developments like the Semantic Web, we are moving towards a "Web without a spider"—that is a web that once set in motion takes on a life of its own.[21] I would argue that Web Science may in fact be recognized as a subdomain of "Network Science," drawing upon similar lines of inquiry that are grounded in the broader tradition of "Systems Theory." However, it is worth repeating that the speculative nature of these theories makes this claim difficult to envision with certainty.

For the purposes of this chapter, "determinism" means that a core group of people drive the technological evolution of the web.[22] Such is the case with the foregoing initiatives, which is why I argue they constitute the dominant "modernization paradigm." Further to this, "determinism" also means there are direct implications upon society, either predicted or occurring. Accordingly, although the idea of "web life" may be far off, more tangible markers of control are occurring today. For example, Thomas Friedman's *The World Is Flat* purports that information and communication technologies (ICTs) like the web have been a direct enabler for the globalization of various industries, especially considering the proliferation of related "flatteners" like the web browser.[23] Unfortunately, what Friedman fails to acknowledge are the negative social and political implications of this, such as the degeneration of local cultures through "cultural imperialism" and outsourcing. Through use of the web, what has resulted is a "flattened" world in terms of the ability of the Global North to dominate the Global South, rather than equal access to the marketplace for all. The web may serve as a democratizing force but only when the means of production are also available in addition to the access itself—in other words, the web must enable a "cultural democracy." This is a requirement we can begin to satisfy through looking at alternatives to determinism and this dominant paradigm.

The Social Constructivist Challenge: Returning to the Forward Slashes

Again, the major challenge to constructivist approaches to modernizing the web is rooted in Berners-Lee's deterministic approach. However, the case for a socially constructed web can still be made. Here, it is vital to consider the role of participatory culture and, concomitantly, the role of the individual user in scholarship concerning the web's evolution and future potential. In reference to the example of user demand negating the requirement to enter the forward slashes into the browser, we are dealing more broadly with the user-generated characteristics of what has been termed "Web 2.0," a development whose various applications (e.g., social networking sites) allow users to "tag" photos and revise encyclopedia entries, among many other things, based on the fluid knowledge representation model encompassed by the "folksonomy."[24] Within cultural studies and Marxist political economy, the latter has frequently been viewed as "emancipatory" because of the potential access to the means of cultural production that can now be provided through the web pursuant to this alternative paradigm. This point is taken up further within the social constructivist framework, and is a central concept to my argument.

As mentioned, society is in the midst of a shift from a "Web of Documents" towards a "Web of Data." This is not an entirely new idea, rather one whose implementation has only recently become technologically feasible. Accordingly, this very purpose-specific modification of the World Wide Web echoes the fact that the Internet (or more generally the network protocols that underlie it) and its predecessor networks like ARPANET were also created for specific means (in this case, national defense and research). For example, Lisa Gitelman and Janet Abbate both discuss at length the centrality of "invention" in literature relating to the Internet and the web, suggesting that "unintended consequences" hold less value here than the manifestations of human ingenuity.[25] It is important, however, to note that the pathway to the creation of the web is more multifaceted than either author, or even parts of this chapter, suggest: for example, the role of predecessor networks and applications like France's Minitel and other related methods of viewing textual data on telephones cannot be ignored.

Additionally, an obvious limit of constructivism is that "unintended consequences" (or at least broader and more multifaceted uses than the web's inventor and the W3C could have predicted or facilitated) *did* determinately move us from the initial web built solely on hyperlinks, on to the interactive elements and services-based architecture characteristic of the web of today (i.e., Web 2.0). However, it can also be argued that computerized machines are unable to replicate the nuanced functions of human intelligence required to effect change. This is, in reality, a position that both helps explain why this view of the evolution of the web is actually a form of constructivism and subsequently challenges further work by centralized authorities, such as the underlying notion of the Semantic Web. This said, I argue overall that it is equally difficult to suggest either a completely determinist or a completely constructivist framework, at least within the context of my usage of the terms as previously discussed. Some sort of "middle range" approach is needed to enhance our understanding of where web studies fits in the scholarly traditions related to ICTs.[26] It is thus my supposition that the Social Construction of Technology (SCOT) theory, as professed in related terms by Latour and in specific terms by his contemporaries, can serve this purpose, because it aptly combines elements of both perspectives.[27] In applying this viewpoint, I would argue that the dominant modernization paradigm relating to the ontology reflects, in some respects, a desire on the part of key personnel involved historically in the development of the web (namely Berners-Lee) effectively to regain the primary position as the driving force behind a comprehensive research agenda focused on the web. It thus reflects the need to "manage" the development of the web, so as to mitigate the negative and unwanted effects on issues related to security, privacy, and trust in transactions, while attempting to stimulate more desirable uses of the technology.

To reiterate, the most immediate theoretical connection that can be made between this perspective and determinist-constructivist approaches involves something in this "middle range" and can be derived from models related to other ICTs: here, studies of the effects of technology on society are still in order, yet they are to be framed with the expectation that at least some of those effects are within the purview of human responsibility and, more specifically, human construction. In other words, and especially given the challenges to the paradigm put forth by the "folksonomy" and user-generated content, a multidirectional model is needed to serve as an analogy for the evolution of the web. The SCOT model effectively fulfills this purpose, as it holds in general that constant feedback from user groups (i.e., identifiable publics within society as a whole in the case of the web) aids developers in refining the medium.[28]

Here, I am dealing with what Anderson and Stoneman have termed an "evolutionary model" of ICT development, in that progress is achieved through feedback mechanisms to ensure a sense of malleability of the technology under investigation.[29] However, the difficulty in using SCOT with the assumption that the model of study is "evolutionary" rests with the bidirectional nature of "evolution" itself—that is to say, one is either evolving or devolving but not necessarily creating peripheral areas for investigation, development, and so forth. The web, with its broad array of constituent research topics, is hardly bidirectional. Indeed, returning to the whereabouts of the forward slashes, anecdotal evidence may suggest a binary existence (i.e., they were either required by browsers or not), but further empirical research is needed to both solidify this point and to explore what other externalities may be relevant here. As a starting point, the hypothesis I raised earlier about influence from elsewhere in the computing domain of the time would be an excellent point for other researchers on this topic to take up in future. For all of its flaws, Web Science may also provide some answers as it develops, though Berners-Lee's influence remains troubling. This is an area that scholars working in this field would be wise to monitor closely; the possibility of actually participating in projects or conferences organized by the Web Science Trust should be considered.

For now, a major assertion which can be made is that a SCOT-oriented model for the web must return to the very core of this paradigm as it relates to the evolution of large technological systems. Here, extrapolating the SCOT theories of Thomas Hughes is useful, in that the author argues social, regulatory, and political economic factors shape technology during the stages of development, innovation, technology transfer, and actual utilization.[30] This thought is further supported by the aforementioned "evolutionary" model of technology; however, it also draws upon a "conditional and co-adaptation" model wherein how human users interface with the web determines what ICTs will engender in future.[31] This is to say that how end-user communities socially construct the various elements of the web is what provides the "progress" and consequences (both intended and unintended) that one then ultimately works to encourage or to mitigate as the circumstances warrant. The actual model utilized is arguably less important, so long as this is achieved.

I will thus ground this user-centered paradigm—which we already observe on a daily basis in our interactions with the folksonomy-driven Web 2.0 environment—within a solid theoretical framework that can then be introduced as a counterpoint to the dominant model of the web based on technical ontologies, which is espoused through the many projects championed by Berners-Lee and the W3C described in this chapter. Therefore, in spite of such a measurable degree of progress that has been asserted over the medium by centralized means, the idea of a viewpoint that negates the technical ontology—that is, in effect, "post-ontological"—has both informed my critique of the state of this track of web studies research as well as the importance of continuing to conduct research on the ways in which the web can achieve and maintain minimal nongovernmental regulation, thus allowing it to be more freely shaped by end-users to the greater benefit of society.[32]

Conclusion

The purpose of this chapter was to introduce two major competing paradigms related to the modernization of the web (in terms of both planned and realized goals), and to situate this work within theoretical discussions of determinism and the social construction of technology, as accomplished both through the framing device of the forward slashes and, more broadly, through some discussion on relevant theoretical perspectives. My intention was simply to review and discuss a small subset of the relevant literature in this area, so as to help provide a firmer foundation upon which new ideas can be generated and subsequently ferment. If this work seems tentative or incomplete, it is because research subjecting the work of Tim Berners-Lee and the World Wide Web Consortium to this degree of analysis from the perspectives of communication and critical studies is an emerging area of inquiry. It is primarily for this reason that I maintain I am only equipped to move readers "toward" a post-ontological viewpoint as of yet.

Moreover, despite the lofty goals of web-related research consortia (such as the Web Science Trust) toward unifying web studies to further social benefits, this particular area remains especially lacking in scholarship regarding pertinent theoretical foundations, along with methods to conceptualize technological progression within this context. As it is now too focused on coding, studies of the web need this to inform the discipline. One major conclusion I would draw from this research, and from considering the vignette concerning the negation of the requirement to include the forward slashes in the URI that began this chapter, is that future studies—and particularly histories and historiographies—of the web should approach it as being an element of ICTs that is heavily constructed by, at times, competing ideologies. Therefore, leveraging a framework that recognizes this, such as theories on the social construction of technology, will prove beneficial in further attempting to understand how best to study and engage with the web, both now and in the future.

Notes

1. Portions of my work have been presented at the International Communication Association's annual conference in 2009, the 2009 IEEE Toronto International Conference—"Science and Technology for Humanity"—and the Canadian Communication Association's annual conference in 2010. I am grateful to the various reviewers, panel chairs, and respondents connected to these venues whose feedback helped guide my revisions and further research. Moreover, I am indebted to Dr. Wade Rowland of York University in Toronto, Canada, for his many helpful edits and insights on an earlier draft of this chapter. Finally, I acknowledge the enduring mentoring, support, and encouragement of my former research supervisor, Dr. Michael Murphy, at Ryerson University in Toronto, Canada.
2. Ahmed, "Backlash."
3. Berners-Lee with Fischetti, *Weaving the Web.*
4. World Wide Web Consortium, "Project Website."
5. In order to ensure relevancy to nonprogrammers, this chapter describes the Semantic Web in largely superficial terms. For a more thorough technical background, consult Warren and Davies, "The Semantic Web."
6. Berners-Lee, Hendler, and Lassila, "The Semantic Web."
7. In the literature reviewed in this chapter, the term "ontology" is used in the technical sense, as a core concept germane to the Semantic Web. However, I acknowledge that some researchers may find this term to be problematic, given its specific meaning within philosophy (and the fact that much of my discussion on the Web here is epistemological rather than ontological). An interesting question arising from my research relates to the W3C's choice of this term within the Semantic Web framework, particularly why such a term was appropriated rather than using something more descriptive and less controversial (e.g., "semantic structure").
8. Greaves, "Semantic Web 2.0"; Heath, "How Will We Interact?"
9. Geller, Chun, and Jung, "Toward the Semantic Deep Web."
10. Wright, "Searching the Deep Web."
11. Additional analysis on this point can be found in Hendler, "Web 3.0: Chicken Farms"; and Hendler, "Web 3.0 Emerging." It is important to note that practitioner-oriented literature related to this discipline lacks a controlled vocabulary; therefore, terms like "Web 2.0" and "Web 3.0" in particular should be taken within the context in which they are used in each respective text.

12. Berners-Lee et al., "A Framework for Web Science."
13. See Web Science Trust, "Creating a Science of the Web (Research Roadmap)."
14. News of the launch of the Web Science Trust (and its relation to the former WSRI and similar initiatives) can be found in Fischetti, "A Science of the Web Begins."
15. Information on the launch of the Web Science Trust Network of Laboratories (WSTNet) can be found in "New Web Research Network." A discussion on an exemplary university-based research unit dedicated to Web Science, the Institute of Web Science at the University of Southampton and Oxford University, as well as information on a degree program in the field can be found in Thomson, "Web Science: Exploring the Network."
16. Shneiderman, "Web Science: A Provocative Invitation." This mandate for the discipline is repeatedly and consistently "professed" across computing literature. For other examples of this, see Berners-Lee et al., "Creating a Science of the Web"; and Hendler et al., "Web Science: An Interdisciplinary Approach."
17. O'Hara and Hall, "Web Science."
18. Shadbolt and Berners-Lee, "Web Science Emerges," or "Web Science: Studying the Internet," 32 or 76. Note that this article was published in two different versions within the cited periodical, hence the alternative title and pagination.
19. Anderson and Stoneman, "Predicting the Socio-technical Future," 6–7. For an example of the "Marxian perspective," see MacKenzie, *Knowing Machines.*
20. Tetlow, *The Web's Awake.*
21. Barabási, *Linked.* For a full account of the Web Science Trust's organizational structure, see "Creating a Science of the Web (Project Website)," and, more specifically, "Creating a Science of the Web (People)."
22. It is important to note that the terms "determinism" and "constructivism" are being used in a slightly unorthodox way within this chapter. More specifically, I have chosen not to completely separate the role of human agency from the operation of computing machinery. Accordingly, "technological determinism" incorporates both the proliferation of particular ideologies on the Web's design and function from people and organizations that serve some kind of regulatory function as well as the theory that the Web takes on characteristics of living organisms; "social constructivism" and the "social construction of technology," as a result, refer to any contradictory perspectives, particularly those that assert the importance of end-user communities in shaping the evolution of the technology. This point is taken up further in the following section.
23. Friedman, *The World Is Flat,* 60–77.
24. For a fuller discussion on online applications that exemplify the user-driven approach, see Runciman, "Like Boiling a Frog."
25. Gitelman, *Always Already New;* Abbate, *Inventing the Internet.*
26. I have adapted this term from Misa, "Retrieving Sociotechnical Change." It is used here within a context similar to its source.
27. A major figure related to this theory is Wiebe Bijker, who co-edited the other papers in the seminal volume containing the Latour text from which this chapter's epigraph was drawn. See also Pinch and Bijker, "The Social Construction of Facts and Artifacts."
28. Pinch and Bijker, "The Social Construction of Facts and Artifacts."
29. Anderson and Stoneman, "Predicting the Socio-technical Future," 11–13.

30. Hughes, "The Evolution of Large Technological Systems"; Hughes, *Human-Built World.*
31. Anderson and Stoneman, "Predicting the Socio-technical Future," 7–11.
32. In my research, discussions on regulation are focused primarily on nongovernmental forms, namely, through what I consider the "determinist" perspectives of organizations like the W3C. I argue that a carefully balanced viewpoint on the Web (where the medium is regulated by nongovernment and government actors only to the extent that it is demonstrably necessary) increases the capacity for economic, social, and technological innovation by end-users.

Works Cited

Abbate, Janet. *Inventing the Internet.* Cambridge, MA: MIT Press, 1999.

Ahmed, Murad. "Backslash: Web Creator Sir Tim Berners-Lee Apologises for His Strokes." *The Times*, October 14, 2009. Accessed March 30, 2010. http://www.technology.timesonline.co.uk.

Anderson, Ben, and Paul Stoneman. "Predicting the Socio-technical Future (and Other Myths)." In *ICT Futures: Delivering Pervasive, Real-Time and Secure Services*, edited by Paul Warren, John Davies, and David Brown, 3–16. West Sussex, England: John Wiley & Sons, 2008.

Barabási, Albert-László. *Linked: How Everything Is Connected to Everything Else and What It Means for Business, Science, and Everyday Life.* New York: Plume, 2003.

Berners-Lee, Tim, with Mark Fischetti. *Weaving the Web: The Original Design and Ultimate Destiny of the World Wide Web.* San Francisco: Harper Business, 1999.

———, Wendy Hall, James A. Hendler, Kieron O'Hara, Nigel Shadbolt, and Daniel J. Weitzner. "A Framework for Web Science." *Foundations and Trends in Web Science* 1, no. 1 (2006): 1–130.

———, Wendy Hall, James Hendler, Nigel Shadbolt, and Daniel J. Weitzner. "Creating a Science of the Web." *Science*, no. 5788 (August 2006): 769–771.

———, James Hendler, and Ora Lassila. "The Semantic Web." *Scientific American* 284, no. 5 (May 2001): 34–43.

Fischetti, Mark. "A Science of the Web Begins." *Scientific American* (November 2, 2006). Accessed April 25, 2010. http://www.sciam.com/article.cfm?id=a-science-of-the-web-begi.

Friedman, Thomas L. *The World Is Flat: A Brief History of the Twenty-First Century.* Vancouver, BC: Douglas & McIntyre, 2007.

Geller, James, Soon Ae Chun, and Yoo Jung. "Toward the Semantic Deep Web." *Computer* 41, no. 9 (September 2008): 95–97.

Gitelman, Lisa. *Always Already New: Media, History, and the Data of Culture.* Cambridge, MA: MIT Press, 2006.

Greaves, Mark. "Semantic Web 2.0." *IEEE Intelligent Systems* 22, no. 2 (2007): 94–96.

Heath, Tom. "How Will We Interact with the Web of Data?" *IEEE Internet Computing* 12, no. 5 (2008): 88–91.

Hendler, James. "Web 3.0: Chicken Farms on the Semantic Web." *Computer* 41, no. 1 (January 2008): 106–108.

———. "Web 3.0 Emerging." *Computer* 42, no. 1 (January 2009): 111–113.

———, Nigel Shadbolt, Wendy Hall, Tim Berners-Lee, and Daniel Weitzner. "Web Science: An Interdisciplinary Approach to Understanding the Web." *Communications of the ACM* 51, no. 7 (2008): 60–69.

Hughes, Thomas P. "The Evolution of Large Technological Systems." In *The Social Construction of Technological Systems: New Directions in the Sociology and History of Technology*, edited by Wiebe E. Bijker, Thomas P. Hughes, and Trevor Pinch, 51–82. Cambridge, MA: MIT Press, 1987.

———. *Human-Built World: How to Think about Technology and Culture*. Chicago: University of Chicago Press, 2004.

Latour, Bruno. "Where Are the Missing Masses? The Sociology of a Few Mundane Artifacts." In *Shaping Technology/Building Society: Studies in Sociotechnical Change*, edited by Wiebe E. Bijker and John Law, 225–258. Cambridge, MA: MIT Press, 1992.

MacKenzie, Donald. *Knowing Machines: Essays on Technical Change*. Cambridge, MA: MIT Press, 1996.

Misa, Thomas J. "Retrieving Sociotechnical Change from Technological Determinism." In *Does Technology Drive History? The Dilemma of Technological Determinism*, edited by Merritt R. Smith and Leo Marx, 115–141. Cambridge, MA: MIT Press, 1994.

O'Hara, Kieron, and Wendy Hall. "Web Science." *Association of Learning Technologies Newsletter*, no. 12 (May 2008).

Pinch, Trevor J., and Wiebe E. Bijker. "The Social Construction of Facts and Artifacts: Or How the Sociology of Science and the Sociology of Technology Might Benefit Each Other." In *The Social Construction of Technological Systems: New Directions in the Sociology and History of Technology*, edited by Wiebe E. Bijker, Thomas P. Hughes, and Trevor Pinch, 17–50. Cambridge, MA: MIT Press, 1987.

Runciman, David. "Like Boiling a Frog: Review of the Book *The Wikipedia Revolution*." *London Review of Books* 31, no. 10 (2009): 14–16. Accessed March 30, 2010. http://www.lrb.co.uk/v31/n10/david-runciman/like-boiling-a-frog.

Shadbolt, Nigel, and Tim Berners-Lee. "Web Science Emerges," or "Web Science: Studying the Internet to Protect Our Future." *Scientific American* 299, no. 4 (October 2008): 32–37 or 76–81.

Shneiderman, Ben. "Web Science: A Provocative Invitation to Computer Science." *Communications of the ACM* 50, no. 6 (2007): 25–27.

Tetlow, Philip. *The Web's Awake: An Introduction to the Field of Web Science and the Concept of Web Life*. Hoboken, NJ: John Wiley, 2007.

Thomson, Rebecca. "Web Science: Exploring the Network without Guesswork." *New Scientist*, May 10, 2010. Accessed May 12, 2010. http://www.newscientist.com.

Warren, Paul, and John Davies. "The Semantic Web—From Vision to Reality." In *ICT Futures: Delivering Pervasive, Real-Time and Secure Services*, edited by Paul Warren, John Davies, and David Brown, 55–66. West Sussex, England: John Wiley & Sons, 2008.

Web Science Trust. "Creating a Science of the Web (Project Website; People; Research Roadmap)." Accessed April 25, 2010, and July 14, 2010. http://www.webscience.org, http://www.webscience.org/people.html, and http://www.webscience.org/research/roadmap.html.

World Wide Web Consortium. "Project Website." Accessed April 25, 2010. http://www.w3.org.

Wright, Alex. "Searching the Deep Web." *Communications of the ACM* 51, no. 10 (2008): 14–15.

Part III:

Comparative Approaches

chapter ten

Interface
History of a Concept, 1868–1888

Peter Schaefer

Introduction

Since the advent of mainframe computers in the early 1960s, "interface" has referred to conduits for data transfer and human-computer interaction. Shortly thereafter the term became nearly synonymous with interpersonal communication. Today, one can just as easily talk about the interface between a lawyer and a client as one can talk about the interface between a lawyer and a laptop. One can be said to interface with a friend and one can interface with a computer, which is to say that interface is a signifier for the idea of communication in a digital age. However, "interface" was used before the 1960s. Victorian-era physicists used the term to describe sites where heat, light, and electricity flowed between different materials. How was the 19th-century conception of interface similar to or different from our contemporary notion? This chapter addresses this question by mapping a twenty-year trajectory of the term starting from its origin in 1868.

Nineteenth-century physicists worked to better understand problems such as the dissipation of energy and the relationship between conduction and signal velocity. In this context, interface was a useful signifier for describing the transfer of energy that could also be used to describe the transmission of information. By the 1880s "interface" wasn't used only to describe theories in the natural sciences but also made appearances in journals associated with the telegraph industry. The study of communication tends to look to the social sciences and the humanities for inspiration, yet the natural sciences "are full of considerations of time, space, signals, distance, contact—central concerns and topics of communication theory."[1] An exploration of the early history of the concept of interface reveals places of overlap between communication history and the history of science. The 19th-century concept of interface is not a discrete prehistory to its conception in the 20th and 21st centuries but rather reflects a shared set of assumptions of what it means to communicate in a modern world.

Science, Industry, and the Thomson Brothers

The etymology of interface begins during a time when individuals from the fields of science and industry worked together to understand circulation, distribution, and transmission on a large and small scale. What are the most efficient ways to send commodities via railroads and waterways? How is temperature diffused within a gas? From a 21st-century perspective, these questions require such different methods of analysis to barely warrant comparison. Yet the conceptual history of interface demonstrates a close connection between such seemingly separate areas of inquiry. The linguistic components of interface give some indication of its relevance to scientific and industrial applications. The prefix of interface suggests linkage, with "inter-" meaning between or shared. The root word, "face," stems from the Latin *facies* to refer to visage as well as surface or front. The term could apply to the metal within a telegraph wire or the site where matter changed from a fluid to a gas. In other words, the idea of an interface was born out of a need to describe forms of connection found in nature and industry.

Two brothers, James and William Thomson, are the figures most responsible for first using and promoting the term "interface." Both men were renowned physicists, born in Ireland and raised in Scotland, who exemplified the unity of science and industry. James studied glaciers and the fluid dynamics of rivers and was quite acclaimed in both areas, serving in a prominent post at the University of Glasgow. William, also known as Lord Kelvin, is by far the more famous sibling because he developed an absolute temperature scale and because his ideas helped popularize the second law of thermodynamics. Historians of communication might be more familiar with William for his work with the transatlantic telegraph, for which he received his knighthood. The two Thomson brothers were mathematical physicists who got their hands dirty with the instruments of the Industrial Revolution. Both men applied their theories to networks: rivers for James[2] and telegraphs for William.[3] They studied material processes of linkage across differences, whether it were dissimilar copper plates for telegraph infrastructure or different densities of water that comprise the flow of a system of rivers.

William Thomson was the first person to use "interface" in a printed publication. The term appeared in an article he authored in an 1874 issue of the journal *Nature*.[4] It wasn't until the 1880s that he used the word to refer to telegraph technology, yet his initial interest in the concept cannot be understood as independent from telegraphy. Like Einstein, whose theories of relativity were shaped by his work with clocks,[5] William Thomson's theoretical approach was formed by his experience with the technologies of the Industrial Revolution. His "was a methodology that grounded mathematical physics in steam-engines, vortex turbines, and telegraph lines."[6] But unlike Einstein, William Thomson was a practical empiricist wedded to classical mechanics, looking for examples that supported his ideas regarding the physical nature of energy. According to Crosbie Smith and M. Norton Wise, William Thomson's work with the transatlantic telegraph was a tremendous influence on his theorizing of natural phenomena, and when looking to understand energy, his metaphorical starting point was from within the telegraph wire.[7] The first published appearance of interface is in the field of thermodynamics, which is not entirely dissimilar to telegraphy, as it refers to conduits and pathways for transmission as they refer to the flow of energy.

Maxwell's Demon: Interface Guard

William Thomson and James Clerk Maxwell proposed influential theories relating to the second law of thermodynamics. William Thomson had a long-standing interest in energy dissipation. In October of 1852, he presented a paper to the Royal Society of Edinburgh that caused quite a stir.[8] In the paper he speculated about the eventual heat death of the universe. Maxwell posed a thought experiment, known as "Maxwell's Demon," that questioned the second law of thermodynamics. First proposed in personal correspondence in 1867 and then published in the first edition of *Theory of Heat*,[9] Maxwell's Demon suggests that the second law was open to chance and limited by a problem of observation. How can one be certain that the entropy of a closed system will increase over time? To illustrate the significance of this question, Maxwell imagined an enclosed space divided into two sections that are kept separate except for a small opening. Both sections are filled with gas molecules, and a tiny creature is stationed at the opening between the two chambers. This creature only will allow the faster, warmer molecules on one side and the slower, colder molecules on the other. This hypothetical scenario would violate the second law of thermodynamics. Maxwell's Demon suggests that one could only say that it is statistically likely that the entropy of a closed system will increase, meaning that the second law of thermodynamics is not an observable condition of nature.

It was William Thomson who gave the name "demon" to the little being who stands guard separating the hot and cold gas.[10] And while the nominal history of Maxwell's Demon is well documented, what is not as well known is that the same article in which William Thomson first refers to the "demon" is also the first published appearance of the word "interface." In fact, the small opening where the demon stands guard is referred to as an "interface." In an article titled "Kinetic Theory of the Dissipation of Energy," Thomson writes: "This process of diffusion could be perfectly prevented by an army of Maxwell's 'intelligent demons' stationed at the surface, or interface as we may call it with Prof. James Thomson, separating the hot from the cold part of the bar."[11] What we see in this quote is that "interface" first appears in the context of the flow of energy. The interface in William Thomson's characterization is a place of connection where certain molecules can pass through.

One can see affinities between William Thomson's interest in heat transfer through a small opening and his work in the previous decade on the transatlantic telegraph. While electricity and heat are different forms of energy, the tenor of the time was to look for unifying forces, ways to explain light, electricity, heat, and magnetism.[12] William Thomson spent the better part of the 1850s and '60s concerned with more practical matters of energy dissipation with regard to the transmission of electricity through a long, thin wire. In 1874 he turned his attention away from transatlantic telegraphy and focused on a tiny aperture in Maxwell's thought experiment where heat was transmitted, calling it an interface. In both cases, the underlying physics concerned energy transmission.

In the pages of *Nature,* William Thomson doesn't take credit for the use of interface. Perhaps in an effort to give publicity to his less-famous older brother, he gives the 19th-century equivalent of a shout-out, writing that his use of interface originates with James Thomson. In fact, it was James Thomson who first used the term in personal notes dating several years before the 1874 publication by William. "Interface" grew out of conversations between James Thomson and Thomas Andrews, a professor of chemistry at Queen's University of Belfast.[13] In late 1868 and early 1869, the two scientists had numerous discussions concerning the change between liquid and gaseous states of matter. They needed a term to refer to pressure differences within a continuous gas, fluid, or liquid, as well as needing a term for a place where the two states bordered each other, or where the transition from one to the other occurred.

James Thomson refers to his previous conversations with Andrews, and uses the word "interface" in a document titled "Notes and Queries—On Gases, Liquids, Fluids." James Thomson writes:

> I shall treat the matter as if from every point in the fluid to every other, no matter how near they be, down to the smallest distances that require consideration for the matters in question, the fluid is continuous as a fluid:—and as if the fluid everywhere possesses an expansive tendency, so that pressure must everywhere be received by the fluid on one side of a dividing surface (or as I call it *interface*) from the fluid, or solid, on the other side to prevent the fluid from expanding indefinitely, or to balance its expansive force.[14]

Based on my research, this is where the historical record begins for "interface." The personal notes were not published until 1912, however. James Thomson's use here refers to the "smallest distances that require consideration for the matters in question." And for James Thomson, an interface measures tiny borderlines. The same is true for William's use in relation to Maxwell's Demon. The interface for James Thomson is an imaginary "dividing surface" for pressure difference within a fluid. Given James Thomson's aquatic interests, there's no surprise that his first use of the term refers to a liquid. However, I should note that it is possible that the original credit for the term goes to Thomas Andrews, not James Thomson. Yet Joseph Larmor credits James Thomson for the origin of interface, as it appears on a "List of Scientific Terms Introduced by Prof. James Thomson,"[15] and I could find no earlier use of interface by Larmor, although that could be due to a dearth of published documentation for Larmor as compared to that of James Thomson. Regardless, the entry of "interface" into published discourse stems from James and William Thomson.

As mentioned previously, William Thomson first publishes the word in 1874 in regard to Maxwell's Demon. In addition, James Clerk Maxwell incorporates interface into a substantially revised section on the second law of thermodynamics in the 1875 edition of *Theory of Heat*.[16] One might think that Maxwell's use of "interface" would have been a result of William Thomson's use of the term in the 1874 article in *Nature*. However, the addition of interface was suggested to Maxwell by James Thomson, as indicated in private correspondence. Maxwell thanks James Thomson in a document titled "Postcard to James Thomson" dated June 25, 1875, where he approves the use of interface.[17] James Thomson finally gets around to using interface in a published form in a paper he presented to the British Association of Glasgow in September of 1876 in an article on fluid dynamics titled "Improved Investigations on the Flow of Water Through Orifices with Objections to the Modes of Treatment Commonly Adopted."[18]

It is worth noting that the historical record for "interface" is a family affair. The *Oxford English Dictionary* is a little slow on the uptake with its etymological report of interface. The *OED* credits a J. T. Bottomley for the first appearance of "interface" in a publication from 1882. As shown, there were numerous uses of the term previous to that. The J. T. Bottomley is James Thomson Bottomley, the nephew of

James and William Thomson. Bottomley used interface in an 1882 book titled *Hydrostatics; or, Theoretical Mechanics Part II,* which explores the behavior of fluids at rest.[19] Bottomley followed in his uncles' footsteps by using the term he coined as well as by researching fluid dynamics. Although James Thomson is given credit for originating the term, it is his brother William who takes the term and runs with it. In interface, William Thomson finds a useful concept that could help explain how light travelled.

An Ethereal Interface for Classical Mechanics

While William Thomson and James Clerk Maxwell collaborated on research concerning the second law of thermodynamics in the 1870s, the two scientists did not see eye to eye on electromagnetic theory. Maxwell had published a series of equations that suggested the existence of electromagnetic waves, but by the 1880s these equations had no supporting empirical evidence. Since there was no proof for Maxwell's theory, William Thomson continued to assert that light was like a compressible fluid, not a wave.[20] Maxwell had eloquent equations with a beauty to their simplicity, but Thomson was on the side of material observation, not believing in theories generated without experiments. William Thomson's work with transatlantic telegraphy provided an experimental basis for his belief about the properties of light.[21] As with his interest in thermodynamics, the telegraph was not an explicit point of reference, but his theory was shaped by the communication technology. Like Thomson's attention to Maxwell's Demon, Thomson's interest was in flows of energy, and the same is true with his interest in electromagnetism. His work on both phenomena relied on the concept of interface.

Working within a Newtonian paradigm, 19th-century scientists like William Thomson assumed that light waves had to travel in a substance. The name they used for this substance was the "luminiferous ether," or light-bearing ether. William Thomson was one of the more esteemed scholars in the late 19th century championing the existence of the ether as a way of explaining electromagnetism using models that moved in step with classical mechanics. The ether was a physical substance, a super medium through which light travelled. In a series of lectures delivered in October of 1884 at Johns Hopkins, now known as the "Baltimore lectures," William Thomson attempted to explain how the ether functioned in relation to electromagnetic theory. These lectures demonstrate an effort to hold on to mechanical models; yet they also reflect a fascinating time in the history of science, as William Thomson's rhetorical maneuvers demonstrate the persistence of mechanics during an age when absolutes were being called into question. In 1884 Thomson stood proud, asserting the existence of the ether and delivering a biting critique of Maxwell's theory of electromagnetic waves.

In his first lecture William Thomson refers to Maxwell's electromagnetic theory of light as a "backward step," stating: "A real matter between us and the remotest stars I believe there is, and that light consists of real motions of that matter . . . in the way of transverse vibrations."[22] The idea of a "real" yet invisible substance points to the rather dubious state of the ether during this time. The ether had to be physical but wasn't visible or palpable. This didn't stop Thomson from providing careful models for how the ether operates. In interface, Thomson found an important concept to convey how there can be a physical connection "between us and the remotest stars." "Interface" appears no less than fifty-four times in his Baltimore lectures, and I take the following quotation as representative of Thomson's use of the term: "Might it not be, it seemed to me, that the luminiferous ether on two sides of the interface at which the refraction and reflection takes place, might differ both in rigidity and in density."[23] As seen in this quote, an interface separates two different sections of ether that have different levels of rigidity. The rigid quality of ether is crucial to William Thomson's ethereal modeling because he believed ether to be an elastic solid that could bear light as a longitudinal wave. For Thomson, an interface is a conduit for light across different qualities of ether, and he makes particular use of the term in lecture eighteen, which concerns the reflection of light. When discussing how light travelled through different substances, interface was crucial to Thomson's effort to explain how light moved through types of matter such as from water to air.

The use of interface by William Thomson in the Baltimore lectures reflects the search for an ever-present, explanatory substance that existed in between two portions of matter or space. Interface worked as a way of describing connections that made possible the transmission of energy, a subject of particular interest on the part of Thomson. Wise argues that William Thomson used the telegraph as an anchor for his theories on electromagnetism, and the telegraph in this context functioned as a mediator between scientific knowledge and culture.[24] Making direct connections between Thomson's work with the telegraph and the Baltimore lectures, Smith and Wise write:

> Electricity and the telegraph actually appear only in isolated remarks in the Baltimore lectures. They play an essential role, however, because they provide Thomson's ground for assuming the existence of longitudinal waves in the luminiferous ether, which justifies his treatment of ether as an elastic solid rather than some sort of substance which would transmit only transverse waves.[25]

William Thomson's previous experience with the telegraph informed his ideas on electromagnetism, and when explaining how light travelled, he relied on a conceptual armature in which interface played an important part.

Something intangible yet fundamentally mechanical was believed to be the stuff through which energy passed. Until 1905, when Einstein broke the ethereal mold with his theory of special relativity, the vast majority of the academic community believed that light travelled through a substance. Once the paradigm shifted, there no longer needed to be a physical medium through which energy travelled, meaning that there was no need for ethereal models for the transmission of electromagnetic waves. However, the term "ether" persisted, becoming a shorthand term for wireless telegraphy and, in particular, broadcast radio during much of the 20th century. The use of interface as a conceptual tool in the Baltimore lectures provides a path from the transatlantic telegraph to broadcast radio. William Thomson served as scientific adviser for the transatlantic cable and invented vital components that made possible electric communication from the Old World to the New. Thomson's work with the transatlantic telegraph, in the words of Smith and Wise, provided a "ground" for Thomson's theories on electromagnetism. In a series of public lectures in which he espoused his theories, he carried the banner for the existence of the ether. In these lectures, Thomson relied heavily on the idea of an interface to explain how ether functioned. While "interface" did not enter into common vernacular with the introduction of broadcast radio, "ether" did. And while interface was not typically used to describe communication technology previous to the introduction of mainframe computers in the 1960s, the arc of William Thomson's scientific theories and his work with industrial practices point to the relevance of interface to 19th-century notions of communication whose vestiges carry through to 20th-century media such as broadcast radio. Although the examples are few, there are instances of direct application of the term "interface" to communication technology, specifically in relation to the telegraph and telephone industry. In the following section, I provide such examples and connect the concept of interface with William Thomson's career with telegraphy.

Interface in Telegraphy

William Thomson did not use the word "interface" to describe telegraph technology until the 1880s. However, Thomson's activities with the transatlantic telegraph show an awareness of issues that would later be subsumed under the contemporary conception of the term. In particular, Thomson worked on ways to improve signal velocity in a conduit for data transfer. Thomson's theories and inventions pertaining to the telegraph could be seen in contemporary terms as ways to improve bit rate by increasing bandwidth. Interfaces were a conceptual concern for him because he was working to improve passages for information, and the great distance travelled by the transatlantic telegraph meant that signal velocity was a particularly thorny issue. In the 1850s, William Thomson was hailed for his theoretical successes that led to technical innovations for increasing transmission speed through submarine telegraph lines. As Charles Bright writes, Thomson "laid down definitely the well-known law for speed through a cable as depending, on the one hand, inversely on the conductor resistance, and also inversely on the electro-static capacity of the system."[26] Yet Thomson's work with telegraphic interfaces was more than just at the level of theory.

Thomson worked closely with the laying of cable in the Atlantic, riding the cable-laying ships, serving as a technical consultant, and building instruments designed to measure signal strength. In 1858 Thomson patented the mirror galvanometer that allowed for sensitive readings of electric current on a long telegraph wire. He joined theory and practice, working to improve submarine telegraphy through mathematical physics, engineering, and direct observation of what worked and didn't work on the arduous journeys across the Atlantic to lay the cable. Signal degradation was a central problem with transatlantic telegraphy because submerged cables did not perform as well as those in the air or ground. Thomson's innovations, such as his invention of the mirror galvanometer, were designed to address the decay of energy transmission.

One can view Thomson's interest in the second law of thermodynamics in relation to his efforts to decrease signal degradation. Thomson had an acute interest in energy loss and the ability to observe it since he worked to make sure an electric signal travelling across a submarine cable remained strong on the long journey across the Atlantic. The telegraph wire encased in gutta-percha was similar to the imagined closed system of Maxwell's famous thought experiment in that both lend themselves to a problem with observing the dissipation of energy. Thomson developed practical measures to overcome the difficulty in determining signal strength, making it possible to have quick communication across the Atlantic Ocean. When working directly with transatlantic telegraphy, William Thomson did not have the term "interface" at his disposal. He would have to wait until the 1870s, after his brother James coined the term, to find a vocabulary to describe sites for the flow of energy. But, by 1874, he employed the term in relation to the flow of energy across a conduit with his linguistic contributions to Maxwell's Demon. In addition to Thomson's effort to solve problems of signal degradation, one of his more notable contributions was on improving conductivity along a telegraph wire.

William Thomson found that the quality of the copper used in a telegraph wire had a tremendous impact on signal strength. As Bright writes, Thomson "made the discovery that the presence of foreign substances, even in minute quantity, reduced the conductivity of copper to a very marked degree, and he pointed out the effect this would have on the speed of signalling [*sic*]."[27] Again, Thomson was using his acute powers of observation to find ways to improve pathways for communication. In this instance, Thomson was concerned with the physical materials that retained the electrical signal across vast distances. The problems identified by Thomson helped shape the refining methods of copper used in telegraphy, leading to the creation of a special category of "conductivity copper." Thomson's concerns for signal velocity now depended on understanding the flow of energy in relation to different types of matter through which the signal travelled. One could say that Thomson wanted to streamline telegraphic interfaces. At the time when he worked most closely with the telegraph industry in the 1850s and '60s, he didn't use such terminology. By the 1880s, however, Thomson had internalized a notion of interface such that he could use the word liberally, referring to an interface in a telegraph and telephone wire.

On May 6, 1882, *The Telegraphic Journal and Electrical Review* printed a transcript excerpt from a legal case regarding patent disputes for telephone apparatuses. William Thomson, by then a highly esteemed figure in 19th-century communication industries, gave an affidavit about conduction between copper plates. Thomson reported: "There is a difficulty in obtaining definite numerical results, but I have no doubt from what I have seen that the effect depends wholly on the area of the interface between the two [copper plates]; the effect would be greater than that in carbon because of its semi-conductive power."[28] When Thomson worked to understand copper conductivity in telegraph wires in the 1850s and 1860s, he didn't have a vocabulary to describe a site where energy flowed. By 1882, however, he now had a way of describing the place where an electrical signal travelled across different copper plates. He called it an interface.

Similarly, in *The Electrical Engineer* published October 5, 1888, William Thomson uses the term "interface" in relation to energy transmission across different materials. Thomson writes: "An interesting and important practical conclusion is that when currents are induced in any way in a solid composed of parts having different electric conductiveness (pieces of copper and lead, for example, fixed together in metallic contact), there must in general be changing electrification over any interface between these parts."[29] In this brief essay on telegraph infrastructure, Thomson uses interface in ways resonant with those mentioned previously. An interface refers to pathways for connection. In the Baltimore lectures, we saw how interface could be deployed to describe the movement of light through dissimilar solids that were physically connected by the ether. Thomson's words show that the movement of electricity across different materials in a telegraph could be called an interface. By 1888, the link is securely established between the concept of interface as employed in relation to the description of natural phenomena and the concept of interface in relation to conduits for communication.

Conclusion

The act of writing history means working at an interface across time. Efforts to shape the past with the resources of the present necessarily entail crossing temporal boundaries to find continuities and discontinuities. Historiography, therefore, shares a contradiction similar to the one inherent to the concept of interface. Interfaces lie in between two things: the interface between the separate chambers in Maxwell's Demon, the interface between different densities of ether, the interface between two different copper plates as a part of a telegraph apparatus, and the interface between a lawyer and a client or a lawyer and a laptop. In other words, an interface is a site of separation and continuity. In this regard, interface can be seen not just as a product of a mid-20th-century revolution in computer technology but rather as an exemplar of the idea of communication in history. The concept of interface was used to describe efforts to bridge gaps, to bring together, and to keep from falling apart. The transcendental hope implicit in the concept of interface is that there is no "inter-." At the same time, "interface" has problems of communication at its very core simply because the term points to difference. There are two faces in play across an interface, which necessarily means that there remain possibilities for miscommunication. To interface via speech or via mouse and keyboard involves communication across a distance, despite our best efforts and best tools for connection. The conceptual history of interface reflects an idea of communication as a vexed endeavor, as an effort to find a seamless conduit for connection. Yet human interaction is never without seams, which is to say that communication is never without an interface.

Notes

1. Peters, "Space, Time, and Communication Theory," 2–3.
2. J. Thomson, *Collected Papers in Physics and Engineering,* v–vii.
3. Smith and Wise, *Energy and Empire,* 445–498.
4. W. Thomson, "Kinetic Theory of the Dissipation of Energy," 442.
5. Galison, Einstein's Clocks, *Poincaré's Maps,* 256.
6. Smith and Wise, *Energy and Empire,* 491.
7. Ibid., 460.

8. W. Thomson, "On a Universal Tendency in Nature."
9. Maxwell, *Theory of Heat,* 308–309.
10. For more on Thomson's interest in energy dissipation and its corresponding terminology, see Leff and Rex, *Maxwell's Demon 2,* 46–49.
11. W. Thomson, "Kinetic Theory of the Dissipation of Energy," 442.
12. Hunt, *The Maxwellians,* 75.
13. J. Thomson, *Collected Papers in Physics and Engineering,* 327.
14. Ibid., 327, emphasis in original.
15. Ibid., ciii.
16. Maxwell, *Theory of Heat,* 4th ed., 95.
17. Maxwell, *The Scientific Letters and Papers,* 225.
18. J. Thomson, *Collected Papers in Physics and Engineering,* 65.
19. Bottomley, *Hydrostatics,* 13.
20. Smith and Wise, *Energy and Empire,* 475.
21. Wise, "Mediating Machines," 77.
22. W. Thomson, *Kelvin's Baltimore Lectures and Modern Theoretical Physics, 9.*
23. Ibid., 15.
24. Wise, "Mediating Machines," 77.
25. Smith and Wise, *Energy and Empire,* 461.
26. Bright, *Submarine Telegraphs,* 81.
27. Ibid., 216.
28. Barney, "Who Is the True Inventor?" 331.
29. W. Thomson, "A Simple Hypothesis," 290–291.

Works Cited

Barney, W. C. "Who Is the True Inventor of the Bell Telephone?" *The Telegraphic Journal and Electrical Review* 7 (May 6, 1882): 331.

Bottomley, James T. *Hydrostatics; or, Theoretical Mechanics Part II.* Glasgow: William Collins, Sons, & Co., 1882.

Bright, Charles. *Submarine Telegraphs: Their History, Construction, and Working.* London: Crosby, Lockwood and Son, 1898.

Galison, Peter. *Einstein's Clocks, Poincaré's Maps: Empires of Time.* New York: W. W. Norton & Co., 2003.

Hunt, Bruce J. *The Maxwellians*. Ithaca, NY: Cornell University Press, 1991.

Leff, Harvey S., and Andrew F. Rex, eds. *Maxwell's Demon 2: Entropy, Classical and Quantum Information, Computing*. Bristol: Institute of Physics Publishing, 2003.

Maxwell, James Clerk. *The Scientific Letters and Papers of James Clerk Maxwell, Volume III 1874–1879.* Edited by P. M. Harman. Cambridge: Cambridge University Press, 2002.

———. *Theory of Heat.* London: Spottiswoode and Co., 1871.

———. *Theory of Heat.* 4th ed. London: Spottiswoode and Co., 1875.

Peters, John Durham. "Space, Time, and Communication Theory." *Canadian Journal of Communication* 28, no. 4 (2003): 397–411.

Smith, Crosbie, and M. Norton Wise. *Energy and Empire: A Biographical Study of Lord Kelvin.* Cambridge: Cambridge University Press, 1989.

Thomson, James. *Collected Papers in Physics and Engineering.* Edited by Sir Joseph Larmor. Cambridge: Cambridge University Press, 1912.

Thomson, William. *Kelvin's Baltimore Lectures and Modern Theoretical Physics; Historical and Philosophical Perspectives.* Edited by Robert H. Kargon and Peter Achinstein. Cambridge, MA: MIT Press, 1987.

———. "Kinetic Theory of the Dissipation of Energy." *Nature* 9 (April 9, 1874): 441–444.

———. "On a Universal Tendency in Nature to the Dissipation of Mechanical Energy." In *Proceedings of the Royal Society of Edinburgh, Vol. 3: December 1850 to April 1857,* 139–142. Edinburgh: Neil and Company, 1857.

———. "A Simple Hypothesis for Electro-Magnetic Induction of Incomplete Circuits; with Consequent Equations of Electric Motion in Fixed Homogenous or Heterogeneous Solid Matter." *The Electrical Engineer* 2 (October 5, 1888): 290–291.

Wise, M. Norton. "Mediating Machines," *Science in Context* 2 (1988): 77–113.

chapter eleven

The Long History of Digital Radio

Old Media in a New Century

Brian O'Neill

Introduction

Radio stands in a curious relationship to the twenty-first-century world of ubiquitous Internet connectivity and immersive digital entertainment. Still a mainstay of everyday life, radio is a medium that has changed relatively little over the course of its history. Originating within the suite of scientific discoveries that produced wired telephony and telecommunications in the late nineteenth century, "wireless" broadcasting seemed to emerge almost as a by-product. Once established, however, it outwardly changed little in the century ahead. A series of technical enhancements to radio—the introduction of FM, stereo broadcasting, RDS—have over the years improved the quality of a medium, the parameters of which were firmly set within the paradigm of a twentieth-century mass communications medium. The essential quality of radio thus defined, characterized by Paddy Scannell as its "listenability,"[1] is as familiar now as the first rudimentary broadcasting experiments that led to the rise of the medium.

Digital radio, which first emerged in the 1980s, stands poised between incremental development of this basic configuration and a more profound and radical transformation of the medium. Proposed by broadcasters and electronics manufacturers as the next-generation platform for radio broadcasting, a swift migration to a fully digital environment was envisaged to match equivalent developments in television, cable, and satellite services. Rival technologies in Europe and the United States, a diversity of regulatory approaches, and the disruptive forces of convergence on the Internet have created a highly fragmented environment in which competing concepts of "newness" and opposing perspectives on the future of the medium collide. Digital radio's credentials as a form of new media are as a consequence uncertain and insecure.

This chapter examines the meaning of digital radio against this historical background. A twentieth-century technology in a twenty-first-century context, digital radio represents the oldest of new media and yet remains an incomplete project. With its fundamental features under negotiation between the pillars of the "listenability" of radio as conventionally received and the "sociability" of interactive and participative forms of networked audio media, digital radio presents a canvas on which many of the unresolved tensions of digitalization can be read and better understood.

The Technological Discourse of Digital Radio

But first, what is digital radio and why was it deemed to be necessary? The digitalization of radio involves transmission of signals in digital form as ones and zeros rather than the traditional approach of modulating the amplitude of a frequency in order to convey information. Broadcasting, as an extension of wireless telephony emerging in the aftermath of World War I, evolved as an efficient one-to-many communications medium with obvious entertainment and mass communication potential to the extent that it was rapidly regulated, commercialized, and, in many instances, nationalized.[2] Technical developments over the course of the past century have sought to enhance the primary function of transmitting in an undistorted form of the original audible signal to the receiver apparatus, thus enabling a simultaneous experience of listening to a (live) acoustic event. Thus, radio's relative simplicity and immediacy have been defining characteristics of a professional ethos that has changed relatively little against the background of a largely invisible technical infrastructure.

Previous innovations in radio broadcasting technology are often seen as a response to the demands for greater audio fidelity and changing listener habits such as the demand for greater mobility.[3] Thus, FM, which was developed initially in the 1930s, and the introduction of stereo in the 1960s offered much less interference and greater audio fidelity. Similarly, transistorized receivers allowed listening to leave the home and become mobile, particularly in cars, thereby extending the reach and the quality of radio programming. Digital radio built on this trend but did so in a more radical way, apparently signaling a break with the past by promising not just new technologies but also new dimensions to radio listening.

In the first instance, when digital radio was first mooted in the 1980s, it appeared to complete a process that had been well established in other parts of the audiovisual production chain and which included digital audio production, processing, and recording techniques.[4] The prevalence of digital technology in professional radio production environments, replacing older analogue production techniques, as well as the wide penetration of digital consumer formats such as MP3 and the compact disc or CD format, had by the mid-1980s made the concept of digital audio and its associated benefits an appealing one. Equivalent developments were in evidence in the telecommunications field where systems such as Integrated Services Digital Network (ISDN) developed a new set of standards for simultaneous digital transmission of voice, video, data, and other network services over the traditional telephone network.

The digitalization of broadcast transmission systems had been an important and ongoing theme of engineering research for an extensive period of time. In the area of sound transmission, developments such as NICAM stereo sound for television in the early 1970s generated significant momentum in the search for replacement technologies for conventional AM and FM broadcasting. The greater efficiency of transmission, resulting in lower costs for broadcasters and transmission networks, as well as greater frequency efficiency, allowing better utilization of spectrum and the ability to provide more services, made the goal of digital broadcasting an important and attractive one for regulators and governments. Similarly, digital transmission of audio signals via satellite, such as Astra Digital Radio or Digital Satellite Services, were also in development but, significantly, were as yet unsuited for reliable mobile reception where, it was claimed, analogue radio transmission suffered most.[5]

But it is in the area of digital audio where a celebratory technological discourse of the digital is most apparent. The rise of the compact disc format in the 1980s as the *de facto* standard for superb audio quality exemplifies the unquestioning belief in the benefits of digitalization and underscores the underlying trend towards a common digital approach to all forms of information and signal processing. Released in 1982, the CD audio standard was the result of collaboration between Sony and Phillips to provide a replacement for the vinyl LP that had dominated the music industry since the 1950s.[6] The hyperbole of the CD's marketing slogan, "Perfect Sound Forever," created the public perception that the goal of perfect digital audio reproduction and fidelity had been attained. Digital radio, it was argued at the time, could be strategically positioned to reproduce the benefits of the newly defined CD-quality audio, therefore completing the picture from the broadcaster's point of view of a stream of digital entertainment services. Complementing the unsurpassed quality of audio now available in digital form, a new type of entertainment was envisaged that could include subscription-based suites of channels offering different genres of music services as well as pay-per-listen cultural and entertainment events. Notably, the broadcast industry was not alone in this view. Cable services and satellite radio services, particularly in North America, were actively developing new home entertainment services. The precursor to Sirius Satellite Radio began life in 1990 as Satellite CD Radio and proposed a digital subscription service similarly based on unlimited access to multiple channels of audio entertainment and exclusive contracts with stars from the entertainment world. In Japan, a rival approach outlined a "digital highway" concept (called Integrated Services Digital Broadcasting or ISDB) in which a single digital broadcast system could be used to deliver all kinds of information including radio and television.[7] This was in contrast to the European concentration on digitalization of individual radio and television networks rather than on an integrated approach to media convergence.

Eureka–147 Digital Audio Broadcasting

The European system of Digital Audio Broadcasting or DAB is the longest established and best known of a number of different digital radio systems. DAB was developed by a consortium comprising some of Europe's leading broadcasters and equipment manufacturers and was intended to develop a global standardized system of digital radio broadcasting that would provide a replacement for analogue AM and FM transmission systems.[8]

DAB began as a collaboration between *Institut für Rundfunktechnik* (IRT), the research and development institute for a number of German broadcasters, and the *Centre Commun détudes de Télédiffusion et Télécommunication* (CCETT), the research arm of France Telecom and TDF. Two essential ingredients of the system were already in development prior to the formal organization of the Eureka consortium: the audio compression or bit-rate reduction system, pioneered by IRT in Germany (MPEG Audio Layer II, originally called MUSICAM), and a new radio frequency modulation system (called COFDM) led by CCETT in France. Initially, an integrated services digital broadcasting system, not specifically dedicated to radio, was envisaged. The DAB bit-stream could in fact be used to transmit all kinds of data including images and slow-scan television.[9] However, with the support of the European Broadcasting Union (EBU) and involvement of leading broadcasting organizations across Europe, including the BBC, the consortium of nineteen proceeded to develop DAB as a successor to AM and FM radio broadcasting.

The Eureka Project 147 was established in 1987, with funding from the European Commission, to develop a system for the broadcasting of audio and data to fixed, portable, or mobile receivers.[10] The Eureka project consisted of developing a formal specification of the digital broadcasting system that was intended to be the definitive global standard for digital radio broadcasting. The technical development envisaged a digitalization of broadcasting distribution, which would produce improved reception compared to FM, particularly mobile reception, and with the potential to offer additional services such as text and other data, conditional access, enhanced traffic services, and picture transmission.[11]

This DAB system was designed for terrestrial, satellite, and hybrid or mixed delivery. Following its adoption by the European Telecommunications Standards Institute (ETSI) in 1993 as the single European standard and its recognition by the International Telecommunication Union (ITU) as a terrestrial and satellite broadcasting system, DAB was widely promoted and demonstrated with regular services being launched in many European countries. In 1995, the European DAB Forum (EuroDAB) was established to coordinate and promote the introduction of DAB services. It became the WorldDAB Forum (WorldDAB) in 1997 and launched a marketing campaign aimed at supporting a consumer launch during that year.

An important element of the overall promotional discourse for DAB was its claims to be the definitive future of radio, underpinned by the certainty that all media would in the future be digital. The dominant trope of mid-1990s technical discourse was the conviction that all traditional media including radio, television, and the press would adopt digitally based delivery systems and that varying elements of convergence between different media would emerge.[12] Through various events and demonstrations, DAB was presented as heralding a new revolutionary era in radio broadcasting. Allied to this was a further belief in the necessity for radio to rapidly embrace digital technology to survive in an increasingly competitive and complex market. DAB, it was claimed, provided the opportunity to keep "radio not only alive but healthy in an increasingly competitive environment."[13] Conversely, it was claimed, radio would be marginalized in the digital era if it remained analogue.[14]

The Architecture of DAB Digital Radio

An examination of the principal features of the DAB system addresses some of the changes it was thought that digital radio might introduce to the medium. The digital radio system developed under Eureka–147, acknowledged to be a highly successful technical feat of engineering and one of the most significant developments since the introduction of FM stereo broadcasting, provided an innovative approach to audio and multimedia broadcasting. DAB offered a wealth of advantages over conventional broadcast systems and was ideally suited, from an engineering perspective, to be a replacement technology for AM and FM radio broadcasting.

Wolfgang Hoeg and Thomas Lauterbach describe the attributes of the Eureka–147 system as follows:

1. *Quality of Service:* The utilization of digital technology to provide listeners with a higher quality of service including superior sound quality, better usability, and perfect reception.

2. *Value-Added Services:* The capability of one multifunctional receiver to include broadcasting services, accompanying programme associated data, additional information services, and still or moving pictures.

3. *A Universal System Layout:* Allowing for the wide availability of the service on fixed, mobile, and portable receivers and across terrestrial, satellite, and cable networks.

4. *Flexible Multiplex Configuration:* A transmission method that enables broadcasters to arrange multiple services in a DAB "multiplex" and to vary the quantity and quality of services through bit-rate adjustment.

5. *Transmission Efficiency:* Offering lower transmission costs for broadcasters and network providers as well as efficient spectrum use through the arrangement of Single Frequency Networks (SFNs).[15]

There are two distinct categories of innovation in DAB digital radio thus described. First, DAB offered technical and engineering improvements aimed at the radio industry including lower running costs, better efficiency, and the potential to offer new services. Second, improved user features and enhanced functionality provided audiences with a better listening experience. DAB's enhancements were widely promoted among diverse audiences and provided the basis for extensive support campaigns in each of the markets in which it was introduced in an effort to win rapid approval and adoption of the new system.

The overriding advantage of Eureka–147, designed to appeal to both consumers and to the industry, was the proposed enhanced quality of transmission and interference-free, perfect reception conditions offered by DAB. The BBC claimed that the consistency of high-quality transmission even in adverse conditions was the single most important reason for considering DAB as the future of radio.[16] So-called multipath interference caused by signal reflections and shadowing due to high buildings, particularly in dense urban areas, had been one of the main problems affecting analogue broadcasting resulting in poor quality reception, fading, and interference. This was particularly problematic for reception in cars and on mobile receivers and was considered a real constraint to further growth of the medium. Previous developments such as stereo FM, introduced first in the 1950s, had been designed for domestic rather than mobile reception—ideally via a fixed, rooftop aerial. Clearly, improvements in receiver design had created acceptable listening FM conditions, which included switching to mono when reception deteriorated, but fundamentally, from an engineering point of view, FM was never designed for mobile and in-car reception. A design parameter for DAB was, therefore, to enable high-quality reception in fast-moving vehicles even in extreme conditions. DAB's innovative solution to the problems of reception was to constructively use multiple- signal reflections in a new modulation system called COFDM (coded orthogonal frequency division multiplex), which successfully combated multipath interference.[17]

A related feature of the COFDM approach was the ability to use a single frequency block with multiple transmitters over an extensive area without mutual interference, allowing broadcasters to plan services in SFNs. Echoing its origins in satellite systems research, DAB's Single Frequency Network approach is such that it is typically optimized for large national or regional areas and offers the greatest spectrum efficiency when deployed in that fashion. The more localized the service required, the more frequencies are needed and the system becomes less spectrally (or economically) efficient. Equally, the optimal solution to ensure the most cost-effective coverage was discovered to be a network of closely spaced, relatively low-power transmitters. As such, planning for digital transmission was conceived on the basis that nationally based or regionally strong networks (such as the BBC) would be primarily responsible for managing the network rather than individual local stations organizing their own transmission.

An additional feature of the DAB transmission system that was unfamiliar to broadcasters at the time was its organization into a service multiplex or ensemble of programme services, of typically up to six stereo channels. The flexibility to dynamically vary the composition of the service according to need, such as splitting a stereo programme into two separate mono channels or providing an additional language channel as required, offered the multiplex operator considerable control over service planning. From the listener's perspective, access to services would be simplified, using an adaptation of the Radio Data System (RDS) whereby text labels identified station tuning and programme content. The multiplex organization would be all but invisible to the listener, who simply had to choose by station or service identification. From the broadcaster's point of view, the organization of programming services into a complex arrangement involving different services represented a significant reconceptualization of the transmission chain. From the relatively simple structure of the radio broadcaster acting as programme provider and feeding final content into the broadcast chain for transmission and distribution, DAB introduced the distinct functions of programme provider, data service providers, and multiplex or ensemble provider. Organizationally, the DAB configuration required effective coordination between each of the elements of the service and as such was optimally suited to the large, multiservice broadcaster with the relevant technical and programming resources to service all aspects of the DAB system. An idealized DAB service provision model, as such, mapped closely to the kind of programme services envisaged by the system's sponsors, the major public broadcasters such as BBC, Danmark Radio, or Bayerische Rundfunk, who could provide suites of diverse programme material, associated programme data, and other listener services under a common brand.

From the listener's point of view, DAB offered a different way to experience radio. The multiplexed nature of the DAB service, combining different forms of information as well as mulitple programme channels, presented a number of challenges for a suitable interface design. Accompanying the main audio service, for instance, DAB included additional information such as alphanumeric text; information on the name of the service (e.g., BBC RI Digital); a programme-type label (e.g., News, Sports, or Classical Music); time and date, for display or recorder control; as well as traffic reports, news flashes, or announcements on other services.[18] A joint project involving WorldDAB, manufacturers including Clarion, Sony, and Bosch, and broadcasters such as BBC, Radio France, and Swedish Radio was established in 1998 to consider various receiver design possibilities based on DAB's possible service applications. The HuMIDAB project examined the "human machine interface" and presented a series of concepts for receiver design that minimized the complex technology underpinning the system. The principle agreed was that DAB radios "should be characterized by *abstraction from technical details* and that service access should be *content based*, so that a listener can 'forget' the technical delivery mechanism."[19] Further designs by the BBC and by Swedish Radio explored various interfaces for in-car systems utilizing touch screen interfaces and Electronic Program Guide (EPG) menu systems as ways to access DAB audio and data information services.

Early market research conducted by broadcasters suggested positive interest among the general public for the features offered by DAB. Three broad market segments or applications for such new services were considered to be particularly important. First, the in-car application was a top priority for the DAB project. Eureka–147 was the first transmission system designed specifically with the motor vehicle in mind and had perfected a system to deliver near-CD quality with no signal loss or fading as a car traversed the country. The major defects of analogue radio, it was claimed, were most apparent in moving vehicles both in urban conditions and on cross national routes. Medium-wave reception was always of low quality, often ruined by interference from electrical equipment or distant stations while FM's reception fluctuated wildly as a vehicle went by buildings, over hills, and down into valleys and had to be retuned as the car moved out of range of one transmitter and into range of another. DAB as a result offered a quality of service never previously attained through its robust reception and linkage to a single frequency network.

The attraction of an all-digital audio entertainment system as well as the potential of high-speed datacasting to vehicles, incorporating GPS navigation systems, traffic management information, and high-quality images, was conceived as potentially DAB's "killer application." The mobility of high-quality digital radio was also envisaged to include an expanded reach for the medium beyond the localism that defines most radio services. An early description conveyed the promise of DAB as *radio sans frontiers*:

> Imagine driving the length of Britain, over the Channel and across Europe, listening all the time to the same radio station. The sound is in digital stereo, which gives it the same quality as that from a compact disc. There is no interference, and none of the fading and fluttering that normally blemish reception as you drive past tall buildings, over hills and down valleys. There is no need to keep retuning the radio because the chosen station remains on the same frequency throughout Europe—although, of course, you could retune to alternative national, international or local stations if you wanted to.[20]

A second market segment envisaged as hugely important and to whom DAB was closely targeted was that of Hi-Fi enthusiasts. As a group of early adopters, audiophiles were considered to be an important means of broadening the consumer market for DAB for both fixed and portable receivers. An assumption of the period was that the advent of digital audio formats such as the CD had created a demand for uniform, high-quality audio in radio. A number of high-end audio receivers were developed building on the wide acceptance of the CD as the bench mark audio standard. This emphasis on DAB's audiophile credentials was an important element of the marketing strategy for digital radio, despite ongoing controversy regarding its implementation, and claims for a radio listening experience of unsurpassed quality were central appeals of the new radio format.

Finally, a further segment identified as an important potential new market for the features offered in DAB was that of personal computer users. PC-card DAB receiver applications targeted at Internet users could better exploit the dynamic programme text capabilities of DAB and had the potential to integrate Internet use with high-quality audio reception. At a time when Internet connectivity was still predominantly based on dial-up connections, DAB receivers as additional modules for PCs could enhance a multimedia experience and offer potential for greater interactivity and e-commerce applications.

The European Context

The development of the Eureka–147 DAB project was to a large extent a specifically European project that both emanated and benefited from the desire of the European Union to play a stronger role in the global competition for innovation in communications technology. With the development of a single European market and emphasis on regulatory harmonization across the continent, the European Commission assumed an enhanced, more centralized role in the communications sector. It initiated a number of measures to support Europe's audiovisual manufacturers in the global competition for communications technologies, in particular against the dominance of the United States and the Far East in consumer electronics.[21] Measures such as the Television without Frontiers Directive established a thriving single European broadcasting market, particularly for trans-frontier satellite broadcasting, while the MEDIA programme was developed to support and protect European audiovisual production and distribution from international competition, including a venture capital programme—the Media Investment Club—to support European audiovisual high technology development.[22]

The Eureka programme, of which DAB was a direct beneficiary, was established in 1985 as an intergovernmental initiative to enhance the competitiveness of European industries and to align them more closely with European Union research and development policies. A particular concern of the period was the increasing dominance of the Japanese consumer electronics industry, threatening Phillips and other European manufacturers, and support for European technological innovation became a priority.[23] Phillips, for instance, having been beaten (along with Sony) in the format war for video cassette recording was determined that it would dominate in the next consumer electronics battleground, that of home digital audio. Hence, the international partnership with Sony to develop the CD standard.

A key objective, then, of European investment in technologies like digital radio, mobile communications, and satellite navigation systems was to enable standardization, first at the European level and subsequently on global terms, in order to create opportunities for world leadership in high technology systems. With regard to digital radio, it was assumed that with the establishment of a common European standard, significant opportunities would be available for the European entertainment electronics industry to develop a whole range of new products for the consumer electronics and automobile sectors. The development of DAB was frequently characterized as an attempt to emulate the success of Global System for Mobile Communications (GSM), the standard for digital mobile phone communication, developed with strong European backing, and which subsequently went on to become the defining global standard.

In addition to the European Commission's support, the European Broadcasting Union (EBU) also played a central role in the development and promotion of the DAB digital radio system. As the representative organization for national public broadcasting organizations across Europe, it had been a key player in its development and coordination. The EBU had initiated the first series of studies on satellite DAB in the mid-1980s and supported the formation of the consortium for Eureka–147. EBU members were the driving force behind the consortium and the EBU's Technical Department actively participated in its various working groups. Crucially, the EBU as an international organization provided the essential logistical support in promoting DAB at the International Telecommunications Union and in the preparations prior to the adoption of DAB as an ETSI standard. EBU members, the public radio broadcasters, were the principal shareholders and proponents of digital radio, providing a level of technical and financial support that commercial broadcasters would be unable or unwilling to do.[24] As such, digital radio in the European context has always been closely associated with and allied to the institutional visions and infrastructure of European public broadcasting in both form and content, and as suggested above, articulated through the actual architecture of a system suited to its needs rather than to other forms of broadcasting.

DAB's claims to be an international standard were founded on the development of a mature technology that had been tested in the field and which offered flexible modes of implementation in a variety of situations for a path to digitalization of broadcasting operations. Prospects for successful adoption would rely, however, on coordinated international action on technology development, spectrum planning, regulatory approaches, and a global marketing of digital radio. DAB did achieve rapid early success in attaining international standardization, for instance with adoption of the basic DAB standard by ETSI in 1993, followed by the ITU-R recommendation of DAB for satellite and terrestrial broadcasting in 1994. The World Administrative Radio Conference (WARC) in 1988 allocated 40 MHz of spectrum in the L-Band for satellite sound broadcasting. At the WARC 1992 conference, a portion of this was allocated primarily for terrestrial digital radio broadcasting, providing a boost to its international standing and supporting international efforts towards its implementation beyond Western Europe. L-Band was in many instances the only available frequency for digital broadcasting even though it was more suited to satellite rather than terrestrial applications. The consolidation of WorldDAB in 1997, now comprising 120 member organizations in 20 countries, confirmed its global status with active DAB trials in countries beyond Europe including China, South Africa, India, Australia, Poland, and Canada.[25] However, despite initial interest in the United States, the DAB platform was rejected in favor of an alternative approach, raising further questions about the viability of a single replacement technology.

The initial reception given to Eureka–147 DAB technology when it was presented in the United States had in fact been very positive. A series of demonstrations at the National Association of Broadcasters' (NAB) Convention in Las Vegas in 1991 and at the NAB Radio Show in San Francisco had been well received following an impressive performance of the technology. However, it was soon recognized that implementation of a DAB-like system would pose significant difficulties for American broadcasters.[26] In contrast to the European notion of a migration of radio to a new frequency band using the Eureka–147 technology, American radio broadcasters favored an in-band, on-channel (IBOC) approach that would deliver digital radio in existing franchise areas without the need for additional frequency allocations.[27] Given the very different conditions for radio in the United States with intense competition in densely populated markets and a strong commitment to localism, the U.S. approach was defined by a gradualism that would ultimately lead to digital radio building on the existing analogue service, offering limited additional content but less disruption to the industry.[28]

Conclusion

The guiding assumption underpinning the development of digital radio, particularly within the European context, was that a robust and mature technology developed within Europe's highly regarded advanced technology research environment would provide an ideal replacement standard for the international radio broadcasting industry. The DAB version of digital radio built on the proud experience of its trusted and oldest broadcasting institutions and looked confidently to an imagined future in which the major broadcasting institutions would continue to provide more content of higher quality and in interactive and multimedia formats. It represented an exemplary model of cooperation among European member states and between public broadcasting organizations and private manufacturers with the guiding and financial support of transnational agencies such as Eureka and the EBU. Its early success in technology design and rapid development of a fully working system suggested that it would be a great success as GSM had been previously, and would contribute further to Europe's leading role in global technology development.

Despite early, promising indicators, the deployment of digital radio stalled and continues to languish in an extended period of early market adoption with both ongoing successes and reversals. Lacking the sense of urgency and political priority given to analogue switch-off for television, radio now contends with a multiplicity of delivery mechanisms, analogue and digital, and has deferred the question of whether AM and FM broadcasting needs to be replaced. Strategies for the introduction of digital radio are characterized by a liberal market approach where it has largely been left to market forces to decide the fate of particular technologies. As with previous technological developments in the sector, this has resulted in long delays in new technology development, competing solutions, confusion for the radio industry and for audiences, and an uncertain environment for future planning.

Given that digital radio now encompasses a wide range of competing formats and derivatives of the original platforms developed in the 1990s, the only truly global standard for receiving digital radio services is in fact via the World Wide Web.[29] It is the Internet that provides the common base, the global platform that increasingly hosts a convergence of content from twentieth-century media. While it may not currently be a replacement for an analogue broadcasting system that has proved remarkably resilient in an era of rapidly changing delivery technologies, the Internet provides the new experimental ground for alternative approaches to radio and audio media, in a way that digital radio formats have failed to do. What examples such as podcasting, personalized audio media, and nonlinear, on-demand radio have illustrated is the potential for redrawing the relationship between content and the audience.[30] Instead of the migration of radio services onto a new platform, new waveband, and a *replacement* delivery technology, Internet radio has evolved as an *alternative* platform on which broadcasters could offer complementary multimedia content under their existing strong brands. Internet radio services have succeeded in augmenting the radio experience in a way in which digital radio platforms have struggled to do, encouraging broadcasters to reshape the medium in favor of more interactive and personalized modes of delivering and sharing audio content. Whether such developments suggest a long-term reconfiguration of radio as a medium remains to be seen, but what has been established is that the digital radio proposition in its first iteration is no longer enough for a twenty-first-century audience accustomed to greater control and audience sovereignty.

Notes

1. Scannell, "The Ontology of Radio," is the foreword to *Digital Radio in Europe,* a collection drawing together extensive research conducted by the Digital Radio Cultures in Europe (DRACE) research group. See www.drace.org for further details.
2. Briggs and Burke, *A Social History of the Media.*
3. Lax, "'A Vision for Radio.'"
4. Maddocks, "Digital Audio Broadcasting (DAB)."
5. Hoeg and Lauterbach, *Digital Audio Broadcasting Principles and Applications.*
6. Immink, "The Compact Disc Story."
7. Ala-Fossi, "Technological Landscapes of Radio."

8. See Kozamernik, "Digital Audio Broadcasting-Radio Now and for the Future"; and Rudin et al., "Digital Audio Broadcasting," for historical sketches of digital radio.
9. Gandy, "DAB: An Introduction," 3.
10. European Telecommunications Standards Institute, *Radio Broadcasting Systems.*
11. Eureka-147, "Eureka Project 147-DAB."
12. Kozamernik, "Digital Audio Broadcasting—Radio Now and for the Future," 3.
13. Witherow and Laven, "Digital Audio Broadcasting," 61.
14. Kozamernik, "Digital Audio Broadcasting—Coming out of the Tunnel."
15. Hoeg and Lauterbach, *Digital Audio Broadcasting Principles and Applications,* 2.
16. Gandy, "DAB: An Introduction," 2.
17. Bower, "Digital Radio."
18. Tuttlebee and Hawkins, "Consumer Digital Radio," 266.
19. Marks, "The Humidab Project," 5, emphasis in original.
20. Fox, "The Perfect Sound Machine," 2. See also Fox, *"Radio Sans Frontiers."*
21. Levy, *Europe's Digital Revolution Broadcasting Regulation.*
22. Collins, "Europe's Digital Revolution."
23. Lembke, *Competition for Technological Leadership,* 212.
24. EBU-UER, *Public Radio in Europe,* 2007, 8.
25. Witherow, "Digital Audio Broadcasting."
26. Hakanen, "Digital Audio Broadcasting."
27. Anglin, "Digital Audio Broadcasting United States Technologies and Systems."
28. Ala-Fossi and Stavitsky, "Understanding IBOC."
29. Ala-Fossi, "Technological Landscapes of Radio," 58.
30. Shaw, "The Online Transformation."

Works Cited

Ala-Fossi, Marko. "Technological Landscapes of Radio." In *Digital Radio in Europe: Technologies, Industries and Cultures*, edited by Brian O'Neill, Marko Ala-Fossi, Per Jauert, Stephen Lax, Lars Nyre, and Helen Shaw, 44–65. Bristol: Intellect Books, 2010.

Ala-Fossi, Marko, and Alan G. Stavitsky. "Understanding IBOC: Digital Technology for Analog Economics." *Journal of Radio Studies* 10, no. 1 (2003): 63–80.

Anglin, Richard L. "Digital Audio Broadcasting United States Technologies and Systems, Terrestrial and Satellite." *Electronics Information & Planning* 23, no. 3 (1995): 129–140.

Bower, Andy J. "Digital Radio—the Eureka 147 DAB System." *Electronic Engineering* (April 1998): 55–56.

Briggs, Asa, and Peter Burke. *A Social History of the Media : From Gutenberg to the Internet.* 2nd ed. Cambridge: Polity, 2005.

Collins, Richard. "Europe's Digital Revolution: Broadcasting Regulation, the EU and the Nation State." *Telecommunications Policy* 24, nos. 10–11 (2000): 981–983.

EBU-UER. *Public Radio in Europe 2007*. Geneva: European Broadcasting Union, 2007.

Eureka–147. "Eureka Project 147—DAB (Imp)." Accessed July 15, 2010. http://www.eureka.be/.

European Telecommunications Standards Institute. *Radio Broadcasting Systems; Digital Audio Broadcasting (DAB) to Mobile, Portable and Fixed Receivers*. Sophia Antipolis Cedex, France, 2006.

Fox, Barry. "The Perfect Sound Machine." *The Times*, October 14, 1994, Friday.

———. "*Radio Sans Frontieres*: By the Mid 1990s, People Driving across Europe Should Be Able to Tune into Their Favourite Radio Programmes in Hi-Fi Wherever They Are." *New Scientist* (1991): 29.

Gandy, Chris. "DAB: An Introduction to the Eureka Dab System and a Guide to How It Works." In *BBC R&D White Paper*. London: BBC, 2003.

Hakanen, Ernest A. "Digital Audio Broadcasting—Promises and Policy Issues in the USA." *Telecommunications Policy* 15, no. 6 (1991): 491–496.

Hoeg, Wolfgang, and Thomas Lauterbach. *Digital Audio Broadcasting Principles and Applications of Digital Radio*. Chichester: John Wiley & Sons, 2003.

Immink, Kees A. Schouhamer. "The Compact Disc Story." *Journal of the AES* 46 (1998): 458–465.

Kozamernik, Franc. "Digital Audio Broadcasting—Coming out of the Tunnel." *EBU Technical Review* no. 279 (1999).

———. "Digital Audio Broadcasting—Radio Now and for the Future." *EBU Technical Review* no. 265 (Autumn 1995).

Lax, Stephen. "'A Vision for Radio': Engineering Solutions for Changing Audiences—from FM to DAB." In *Digital Radio in Europe: Technologies, Industries and Cultures*, edited by Brian O'Neill, Marko Ala-Fossi, Per Jauert, Stephen Lax, Lars Nyre, and Helen Shaw, 69–84. Bristol: Intellect Books, 2010.

Lembke, Johan. *Competition for Technological Leadership: EU Policy for High Technology*. Cheltenham: Edward Elgar Publishing, 2003.

Levy, David A. *Europe's Digital Revolution Broadcasting Regulation, the EU, and the Nation State*. New York: Routledge, 1999.

Maddocks, Michael C.D. "Digital Audio Broadcasting (DAB)—Radio for Tomorrow." Paper presented at the IEE Colloquium on Audio Engineering. London, UK, 1994.

Marks, Bev. "The Humidab Project—Looking at the Human Machine Interface of Digital Radios." *EBU Technical Review* no. 278 (1998).

Rudin, Richard, W. A. Kelly Huff, Gregory Ferrel Lowe, and Graham Mytton. "Digital Audio Broadcasting." In *Museum of Broadcast Communications Encyclopedia of Radio*, edited by Christopher Sterling, 456–462. New York: Fitzroy Dearborn Publishers, 2004.

Scannell, Paddy. "The Ontology of Radio." In *Digital Radio in Europe: Technologies, Industries and Cultures*, edited by Brian O'Neill, Marko Ala-Fossi, Per Jauert, Stephen Lax, Lars Nyre, and Helen Shaw, 11–16. Bristol: Intellect Books, 2010.

Shaw, Helen. "The Online Transformation: How the Internet Is Challenging and Changing Radio." In *Digital Radio in Europe: Technologies, Industries and Cultures*, edited by Brian O'Neill, Marko Ala-Fossi, Per Jauert, Stephen Lax, Lars Nyre and Helen Shaw, 215–236. Bristol: Intellect Books, 2010.

Tuttlebee, Walter H. W., and David A. Hawkins. "Consumer Digital Radio: From Concept to Reality." *Electronics & Communication Engineering Journal* 10, no. 6 (1998): 263–276.

Witherow, David "Digital Audio Broadcasting—on the Way." *EBU Technical Review* no. 270 (1996).

Witherow, D. M. L., and P. A. Laven. "Digital Audio Broadcasting—the Future of Radio." Paper presented at the International Broadcasting Convention, IBC, Amsterdam, Netherlands, September 14–18, 1995.

chapter twelve

New Media in Crises

Discursive Instability and Emergency Communication

Benjamin Peters and Deborah Lubken

Introduction

Over 150 years before the words *new* and *media* became a staple pairing in research on smart phones and social networking platforms, a book review in the inaugural 1838 issue of the *Journal of the Statistical Society of London* applied the phrase to a technology that, from the vantage of the present, seems anomalous. Reporting on the far-reaching repercussions of railways, the reviewer seamlessly articulated the relationship between "these new media of interchange" with face-to-face interaction and communication via pen and ink: "It appears that not only do [railways] facilitate personal intercourse, but create new relations, which give increased activity to correspondence by letter."[1] Although this older example manifests associations between transportation and communication later articulated by, among others, Harold Innis, James Carey, and Wolfgang Schivelbusch, the coupling of *new* and *media* has clearly undergone a semantic shift over the years. Present-day discourse about new media references iPhones and *Second Life*, not railways.

Yet the precise nature of this shift is difficult to specify, perhaps because current scholarly discourse employs the term in multiple, often vague, ways. The most common approach is to leave what is meant by "new media" unspecified, relying on members of common interpretive communities to arrive at shared meanings by sifting through contextual clues. This chapter is, in a way, an indirect attempt to do exactly that: to explore and delimit the contours of new media discourse. After cataloging several uses of the term *new media*, we briefly present two historical case studies in emergency communication. Throughout we advocate an understanding of new media as a complex, layered subject of study, adequately defined by neither novelty nor digital logic, best approached in relation to larger communication systems and cultural contexts.

Reconfiguring the "New" in New Media

At least three general understandings of new media circulate in current media and communication scholarship. The dominant view, drawn heavily from the vocabulary of contemporary computer users, almost wholly equates new media with digital communication technologies that share a numerical base system for delivering data. Lev Manovich has notably led the way in advancing this perspective by positing that new media "objects" exhibit the characteristics of numerical representation, modularity, automation, variability, cultural transcoding, and programmability. Other work has similarly reinforced the association between new and digital media by emphasizing that new media products can be manipulated, networked, compressed, and shared interactively.[2] Taken together, the characteristics commonly ascribed to new media as digital media delineate a relatively narrow subset of computerized technologies; yet, when considered separately, not one of them is unique to the computer age, a point made eloquently by Roger Silverstone in his introduction to the inaugural issue of *New Media and Society*.[3] A less restrictive understanding of digital media as those that coordinate meaning through discrete elements that are often, but not necessarily, numerical opens the domain to a wider range of artifacts and practices that include the abacus, signal fires, semaphoring, and smoke signaling. Digital media may be modern or ancient; they may belong to the twenty-first century c.e. or the fourth century b.c.e. Moreover, purely digital communication is a thing far more likely to inhabit theory than practice. Media—even those meeting the most restrictive definition of digital—create, convey, and manipulate meaning in the context of larger communication systems and processes.[4] In short, while there is value to classifying media by their underlying logic or historical period, we contend that neither method suffices to organize analysis or direct scholarly thought on new media.

A second understanding, favored by media historians, treats new media as emerging media: at some time in the past, every medium was new. This approach rests on the premise that the upheaval of conception affords a unique perspective on social life. The moment before a medium settles comfortably into patterns of production, distribution, and reception is when interested parties jostle for position over "who is inside and outside, who may speak, who may not, and who has authority and may be believed."[5] Although there are advantages to privileging conception as a site of inquiry, recent scholarly interest in the end of television (or newspapers, radio, magazines, etc.) has called attention to other moments when changing circumstances throw a medium's established status into question. The impulse to revisit our understanding of what television is (a radio with pictures in a box? an information service? an audio-visual technical infrastructure? a set of viewing practices? the act of viewing from afar?)—and to ask whether it might be dying—indicates junctures other than when media are first new that might be productively investigated.[6]

Building on this second conceptualization, the third understanding of new media arises out of our taking seriously the observation about new media discourse that began this essay. Namely, that any shared understanding of new media emerges out of discussion and use within an interpretive community. It follows that media can become new again in moments of discursive instability and uncertainty: new media may simply be thought of as media we do not know how to talk about.[7] Changing circumstances—economic, technological, political, institutional—and conversations that attempt to redefine media in response to these changing circumstances are in a reciprocal relationship; asking what a medium has become or assessing developments in its relationship to the larger communication environment is thus a creative act that can take place repeatedly. The inability for talk, let alone the rest of the world, to hold still makes media not only new but renewable. Rick Altman's work on "crisis historiography," for example, although largely focused on the period when cinema emerged, anticipates the concept of media renewability with the remark that the social construction of new technologies "is both *ongoing* and *multiple*. That is, the technology is never socially constructed once and for all."[8] Arising at the confluence of social, cultural, economic, technological, legal, and other transformations, discourse destabilization indexes change that is important but not necessarily revolutionary. Thinking about newness as renewable means that media are potentially, as noted by Lisa Gitelman, "always already new," that is, perpetually available for reinterpretation.[9]

These three ways of thinking about new media—new media as digital media, new media as old media that were once new, and media that become new again when circumstances call for reinterpretation—are not mutually exclusive, but adopting one perspective over another delimits the possibilities for comparative study. In the remaining pages, we juxtapose two case studies of emergency communication systems: the transition from bell-based to telegraph-based fire alarms in nineteenth-century urban America and the strategic development of distributed computer networks in the Cold War nuclear arms race. The first case examines the integration of an existing technology to establish a new system of communication. The second example takes up the attempts to align a relatively recent technology with changing demands for strategic communication. Our case studies, separated in time by almost a century, are strikingly different. Neither bell-based nor telegraph-based fire alarms, on the one hand, were conventionally digital. Networked communication systems for transmitting "go codes," or missile launch commands, on the other hand, combined both analog and digital elements. Both emergency communication systems traded in messages far subtler than simple calls to alarm or quietude. It is the third understanding of new media—one that acknowledges recurrent and under-examined moments of discursive instability—that helps shed insight onto how communities of varying scale make sense of newly reconfigured communication environments and, in turn, use these reconfigurations to make sense of the social world.

Bells to Telegraph: Fighting Fire with the Touch of a Single Finger

Bells remained at the center of complex local emergency communication systems for over two centuries, and their displacement by the fire telegraph in the mid-nineteenth century profoundly influenced how communities responded to and conversed about the threat of fire. The evolution of early American fire alarm systems, as viewed through the lens of New York City ordinances, provides a reference point for evaluating the fire telegraph's introduction to urban centers. New York's first appointed firefighters were charged with immediately responding to their engines whenever alerted to a fire by the City Hall bell or any other means, which included word from the city's watchmen, cries of "fire!" in the streets, and the ringing of church and market bells.[10] Although designated firemen were charged with operating the city's engines and other equipment, extinguishing fires remained largely a community effort well into the nineteenth century. As late as 1817, private residences and businesses were required to maintain leather buckets for public use, and persons remaining indoors during fires were enjoined to illuminate the streets by placing candles in their windows.[11]

As New York expanded, public officials, firemen, and other citizens began to notice and comment on deficiencies in the rudimentary system of emergency communication. By the turn of the nineteenth century, the sound of the City Hall bell no longer reached significant sections of the city, and the Common Council fielded a number of petitions for additional bells at markets and engine houses.[12] The number of church bells also increased with population growth, and the task of notifying sextons and church bell ringers grew increasingly difficult, a problem that motivated local authorities to begin annually collecting ringers' addresses, which were kept in the city's watch houses. In August 1818, sextons requested compensation for the churches' role in sounding fire alarms, prompting an inquiry by the Common Council into the obligation of churches to provide this service. When numerous church bells failed to summon firemen to a blaze a week later, the inquest was carried out with record speed. Church officers assured the investigatory subcommittee that ringing for fires had always been a duty, either express or implied, of sextons, but they also insinuated that the successful execution of this duty depended on timely notification by the city's watchmen.[13] Despite the assurances of church leaders, compelling churches to ring for fires remained a contentious issue, and silent church bells were more conspicuous than negligent watchmen. Less than four months after the meeting between church officers and the municipal subcommittee, for example, the *New York Evening Post* gave bells—not watchmen—first billing when establishing the chain of causality for the destruction caused by a morning fire: "no alarm being given to the city by the ringing of bells, nor any engines arriving at the spot very soon, the conflagration spread fast, altho' very calm, and before it could be mastered, consumed 5 or 6 stores and dwelling houses."[14]

Enlisting the cooperation of churches and installing additional bells on markets extended the range of the general alarm but did not assist firefighters with the increasingly formidable task of finding fires in a crowded, expanding urban environment. Bell towers function logistically, in the sense developed by John Durham Peters, to "arrange people, property, and patterns into time and space."[15] Without supplementary sources of information or prearranged codes, however, it is impossible for a bell to indicate a place other than *here* or a time other than *now*. As early as 1805 the Common Council began considering a "proper method" of ringing the bells that would enable listeners to "distinguish from their sound the place in which a fire happens."[16] Yet the burden of directing firefighters to a specific location continued to rest on the shoulders of the city's watchmen, who could be fined for failing to notify fire officials and bell ringers of a fire's location or for neglecting to specify the street when crying "fire!" for the benefit of the general population.[17] In the 1830s, some of this responsibility was redistributed from watchmen patrolling the streets to watchmen stationed in several towers throughout the city. When a fire broke out, the watchman in the City Hall cupola was required to ring the bell continuously for the emergency's duration and to hang out a light in the direction of the fire. Church bells, market bells, and the bells of other watch houses were to join in until the bell at City Hall stopped ringing.[18] This system was upgraded in 1851, at which time telegraph wires connected the watchtowers to City Hall, and watchmen further specified the location of a fire by tolling the number of the district in which assistance was needed.[19]

New York's use of telegraphy, however, was primitive in comparison with William Channing and Moses Farmer's Fire Alarm Telegraph, a system introduced in Boston in 1852 that soon caught the attention of other communities. Early configurations of the Fire Alarm Telegraph consisted of two primary components: a circuit of signal boxes, installed at regular intervals throughout a city, and an alarm circuit enabling a single operator in the central office to sound bells throughout a city. Both circuits were constructed with duplicate wires, independently routed so that one wire could remain in use even if the other needed repair. Theoretically, even a person unacquainted with a neighborhood might initiate a fire alarm by proceeding to the nearest signal box and reading a notice indicating the location of that box's key. The person responsible for the key could open the box and turn a crank to alert the central operator. By depressing the correct key on the alarm circuit keyboard, the operator would signal the district number of the fire's location on bells throughout the city. At the same time, the operator would tap the number of the signal box from which the alarm originated, and this action would transmit the information to the circuit's signal boxes. Firefighters could ascertain the fire's specific location—to within 250 yards in Boston—by first listening to the bells to learn the district number and then listening to a nearby signal box for the number of the box from which the alarm originated. They could then consult a pocket map for the location corresponding to the correct district and signal box numbers.[20]

Channing and Farmer approached the challenges of emergency communication by attempting to eliminate sources of inefficiency and uncertainty that persisted in older systems, and these were overwhelmingly perceived to stem from the human element. An 1854 promotional circular boasted that the Fire Alarm Telegraph, once installed, would enable a single operator at the central station to ring all of a city's alarm bells "by the touch of a single finger, without the intervention of hands, watchmen or bell-ringers at the belfries or bell-towers."[21] The prospect of eliminating bell ringers—frequently blamed for false alarms and widely considered an undesirable drain on municipal resources—was particularly attractive. Authorities also anticipated that later versions of the fire telegraph, which transmitted the location of a fire directly from the central office to engine houses, would eliminate the need for bells altogether, thereby helping to curtail the rowdy and even criminal behavior associated with fire alarms. The signal indiscriminately broadcast by bells alerted not only firefighters but also thrill seekers and looters. Moreover, volunteer firemen themselves had, over the years, acquired a reputation for disorderly behavior. It is no accident that, in many cities, the introduction of the fire telegraph was accompanied by a reorganization of firefighting labor.[22]

By directing assistance to a fire's precise location, fire telegraph systems markedly decreased emergency response time and, consequently, destruction to life and property.[23] This vast logistical improvement alone was enough to sway public sentiment in their favor, and within twenty years of the Fire Alarm Telegraph's debut, over forty cities had adopted the system.[24] False alarms also decreased, although ordinances to discourage signal box tampering and a series of inventions designed to draw attention to—and even trap—the person initiating an alarm suggest that the problem persisted at some level.[25] Yet neither bells nor bell ringers lapsed into speedy obsolescence. In Boston, Baltimore, and New York human bell ringers served as a source of redundancy to the mechanically sounded bells of the fire telegraph's alarm circuit. Even after automated striking mechanisms superseded hands on bell ropes, the goal of phasing bells out of the system proved difficult to realize.[26] Fires were considered to be public happenings that the public had a right to know about.[27] Moreover, in many communities, the majority of firemen served on a part-time basis, and bells were necessary to summon scattered members of fire companies from their daily activities. When the introduction of steam-powered fire engines and the establishment of smaller, full-time, professional fire departments enabled central operators to quietly transmit a fire's location to specific engine houses, doing away with bells did little to eradicate unruly behavior. Anyone could learn the location of a fire by listening to a call box on the street, and engines speeding to extinguish a fire attracted ample attention on their own.[28]

Instructions distributed to the key keepers of Boston signal boxes prior to the Fire Alarm Telegraph's unveiling provided contingency plans for a variety of mechanical failures: to turn the crank more slowly in the absence of confirmational taps; to proceed to the central office in person if a second attempt proved similarly unsuccessful; and to listen for tapping before initiating an alarm in order to avoid shorting the circuit by sending the signal from multiple boxes.[29] Efforts soon shifted from enlisting humans to compensate for technological shortcomings to eliminating human error through technological innovation. If bell ringers were the scapegoats of earlier times, the man in the street now assumed this distinction. For example, the problem of turning signal box cranks too quickly, too slowly, or at a pace too irregular for the central operator to decipher was addressed first through clearly posted instructions and then through automated signal boxes, which were designed to circumvent this particular form of user error by replacing multiple turns of a crank with the single pull of a hook. Excitement and simple misinterpretation nevertheless persisted in interfering with the successful transmission of signals; the high number of erroneous signals initially received from automated boxes resulted from users pulling the hook, not once as directed, but several times for emphasis—evidence, in the words of one commentator, that "as little as possible should be left to the intelligence of the public."[30] Over time, technological solutions became the favored means of eliminating both human and mechanical sources of inefficiency and uncertainty from modern fire alarm systems.

Go Codes: Fighting the Enemy with the Fear of Fire

In the mid-twentieth century, a new type of emergency communication system came to preoccupy certain elements of American popular cultural and policy debate: the "go code," or a message commanding the launch of a military strike against a distant enemy nation, took on new significance against the bleak geopolitical backdrop of the Cold War nuclear arms race. After the Korean War (a hot proxy for Cold War tensions), both the United States and the Soviet Union began significant nuclear arms buildups. In October 1952, the Americans successfully tested the first thermonuclear device, the H-bomb, delivering a payload exponentially more severe than those that devastated Hiroshima and Nagasaki; in August 1953, the Soviets responded in kind, and then again with a more powerful bomb in November 1955. Under President Eisenhower (1953–1960), the American nuclear arsenal increased nearly eighteen times in size, stocking for the first time intercontinental ballistic missiles (ICBMs) and submarine-based nuclear missiles that made nearly obsolete the looming threat of long-range bombers sent over the Arctic.[31] Later, in the 1960s under Presidents Kennedy and Johnson, strategies such as mutually assured destruction, developed by RAND strategist Herman Kahn and articulated by Secretary of Defense Robert McNamara, underscored the uneasy peace holding the superpowers in check. At the same time that Eisenhower was expanding the American nuclear arsenal, Soviet First Secretary Nikita Khrushchev pushed for a massive military buildup that, while lagging in the overall nuclear warhead tally, succeeded in stalemating the Korean War with the large standing Soviet army in 1953 and later in launching the first Soviet ICBM in 1957. Two months later, on October 4, 1957, Soviet flight command launched Sputnik, the first satellite and potential carrier of nuclear arms to orbit the earth. What had once seemed a distant future suddenly appeared all too present.

Sputnik jolted the United States into response. In February 1958, the Department of Defense created the Advanced Research Projects Agency (ARPA), a special government agency that supported basic, high-risk, long-term research in communication systems and information processing essential for tracking and responding to nuclear threats in the age of Sputnik. Encouraged by an open-ended research environment, ARPA researchers developed several essential computer network innovations including distributed networking, packet-switching, and time-sharing technologies. The earliest design for distributed networks, although not immediately embraced, came about through the request of the U.S. Air Force to build a "survivable" communication network. Drawing on conversations with Warren McCulloch, a founding cyberneticist at MIT who studied how neural networks in the mind could reroute around brain damage, RAND researcher Paul Baran invented a network that—unlike both centralized networks (in which all nodes share a single master hub) and decentralized networks (in which nodes are connected through any mixture of major and minor hubs)—spread out the links between nodes equally, connecting each node to its neighboring nodes.[32] Baran's superiors ignored his advancements, however, until British engineer Donald Davies shared similar, though independently developed, designs with the U.S. government in the mid-1960s.[33] The end result, when combined with packet-switching technology (which allowed message parts to be unpredictably routed around the network and reassembled at the receiving node), was that distributed networks were less vulnerable to disruption than any other available communication systems (radio, telephone, postal system, etc.).[34]

Distributed computer networks, such as the ARPANET, predecessor of the Internet, constituted an important new element of the nationwide emergency communication systems in the 1960s. While cyber enthusiasts have associated the Internet with liberal values of democratic openness, transparency, end-to-end intelligence, and minimum regulation, the discovery of distributed networking came not from a digital revolution but from a military mandate to be able to send a message that would both survive a first strike and execute a ruinous counterstrike.[35] Baran's acclaimed memo *On Distributed Communications*, for example, begins with the chilling invitation, "Let us consider the synthesis of a communication network which will allow several hundred major communications stations to talk with one another after an enemy attack."[36] In other words, the origins of the Internet, or when the ARPANET was new, lie not in the technological triumph of American-centric values so much as in the military motivation that the United States could exact cataclysmic revenge against its enemy.

Although many details remain hidden in closed military archives, some specifics about go codes are known. In the event of a nuclear emergency, the U.S. president, military commanders, and military missile bases needed a network that could sustain "minimal essential communication," or a secure minimum of unidirectional, jam-resistant messages necessary to activate nuclear forces. Initiated by the push of a button, a go code appears on the surface to be a point-to-point message comprised of little more than the command to "go" (i.e., to attack).[37] In addition to the launch command, however, actual go code messages contained a rather complicated timetable and set of target coordinates necessary to deploy a massive counterstrike. The most important function of such a message was to coordinate the trajectories of military personnel and technology across vast reaches of space and very little time. As such the go code—like the practice of sounding district numbers from fire bell towers and, later, more precise fire telegraph systems—belongs to a longer tradition of logistical media that belie traditional dichotomies between transmission and storage, space and time biases, and of which emergency communications are only a subset.

Under ordinary conditions, a go code alone could not launch an attack. Before a military commander could commence the attack, the go code's recipient was obliged, circumstances permitting, to confirm the order by some other secure means of communication. However, a nuclear strike was almost sure to interrupt standard communications, meaning that, in the event of an actual nuclear attack, a single, unconfirmed go code would have to be enough to initiate a rapid counterstrike. The threat of real-time massive retaliation depended on a "survivable" communication system, as the Air Force called it, that could at once coordinate across as well as supersede the national military chain of command and communication. With this, a sort of security paradox resulted: to be truly safe, the military needed to be able to send go codes without any safety checks. Yet such a go code, if incorrectly initiated, might be the most dangerous thing of all.

Popular critics and artists caught wind of this contradiction, and their work animated concerns about scenarios in which human and technological error in a nationwide emergency communication system could combine to precipitate the end of the world as we know it. In Peter George's 1958 little-known novel, *Two Hours to Doom* (published in the United States as *Red Alert*), a psychopathic general launches bombers into the Soviet Union, forcing the world to face the prospect of its own suicide. Four years later, Eugene Burdick and Harvey Wheeler's best-selling novel *Fail-Safe* featured fatal error in the form of humans behaving mechanically: an American bomber pilot unblinkingly attacks Moscow, believing the orders to return to base coming in over the radio to be a ruse by the enemy, even after his commanders enlist the help of his frantic wife who pleads for him to return home.[38] In 1964, in turn, Stanley Kubrick's dark comedy *Dr. Strangelove, or How I Learned to Stop Worrying and Love the Bomb* exploited a combination of maniacal humans, technical failure, and flawed military strategy implicit in the American military communication system. In the farcical storyline of *Dr. Strangelove* (drawn from George's novel and developed in consultation with doomsday strategist Herman Kahn), a psychotic general, Jack D. Ripper, circumvents the nationwide military chain of command and communication by impounding all radios in and barricading his military base from all communication with the outside world. Ripper's attack order results in one lone bomber—whose radio has been damaged, making recall orders impossible—continuing faithfully into Soviet airspace toward its target. At the same time, the Soviet ambassador announces the inauguration of a doomsday device (based loosely on Kahn's 1950 Doomsday Machine), a hypothetical stockpile of computer-triggered hydrogen bombs that, if sprung, would blanket the planet in fallout. In the final scene, the viewer watches as the bomber captain rides the fateful bomb bronco-style as it hurdles toward its target. The movie ends against a backdrop of a mushroom cloud accompanied by the nostalgic tune of Vera Lynn's World War II hit "We'll Meet Again (Some Sunny Day)." Kubrick's satire—with radios, generals, and tactical fail-safe measures all going awry—illustrates one way in which complex emergency communication systems and their fallibilities, combined with the terrible power of nuclear weapons, animated the midcentury imagination of the American public.[39]

In summary, while emergency communication systems have long been of public concern, Cold War interpreters renewed the social significance of computerized communication systems in a militarized nuclear age. Technologists like Baran pursued peace by advancing survivable communication networks that would sustain nuclear stalemate; strategists like Kahn were most concerned when human decision makers refused to cautiously think through the apocalyptic possibilities of the nuclear age; and cultural critics and artists like Kubrick highlighted the double-edged cybernetic fear concerning automated communication systems: the end may come by means not only of machine or human failure but also the fact that humans—presidents, soldiers, and strategists—often successfully behaved like machines. The history and analysis of go codes, in short, serves as reminder that a variety of commentators found the larger social problems besetting the midcentury nuclear arms race freshly reconfigured in emergency communication systems. Like the transition from bell- to telegraph-based fire alarms, the evolution of go codes and distributed networks suggests that the history of reconfigured emergency communication systems is as much about social perceptions of reality as it is about technological innovation. As a case in point, although public agitation over nuclear weapons peaked around the time of the Cuban Missile Crisis, there are currently more nuclear warheads in the world than there were in the 1950s and 1960s. The short history of nuclear emergencies suggests how the fear of nuclear weapons was repeatedly renewed, in part, by changing emergency communication systems: when dropped from radar- and radio-guided bombers on Hiroshima and Nagasaki, the sheer destructive power of nuclear weapons was horribly new; when discovered by satellites in Cuba, the proximity of Soviet nuclear missiles to mainland America came as a shock; human and technological malfunctions at the Three-Mile Island and Chernobyl plants brought the destructive potential of nuclear power into focus in public discussion; and, as stressed above, when coordinated by distributed computer networks, nuclear weapons made a terrifying peace possible in the real-time threat of mutual annihilation. In each example, various social, cultural, political, and historical forces (including chance and error) culminated in some moment of crisis that destabilized, stirred, and renewed discussion about nuclear technologies.

Conclusion

New media are at once those media that we do not know how to talk about as well as those that beg for the most discussion. The chapter in hand has approached new media history from an alternative angle by examining two emergency communication systems in moments of discursive instability, namely, nineteenth-century fire alarms in urban America and missile launch sequences in Cold War America. The first system—anchored initially by bells and later by telegraphy—summoned members of local communities to take collective action against a common but devastating threat. The second system—anchored by distributed computer networks and their game theoretic demands—promised, if activated, to blanket the earth in nuclear fallout and, even if left silent, sent ominous threats meant to deter the enemy from striking the first blow. The significance of both new media configurations lies not in their technological components per se but in how communities made sense of these components in relation to larger communication systems and the broader sociocultural milieu.

The dissimilarities of our case studies are suitable for contrasting. One system fought fires in a defensive mode, the other promised to rain offensive fire down on the enemy; one operated at the municipal level, the other at an international level; and one employed analog technology, the other digital computers. Bells broadcast their signal to what Norbert Wiener called a "to-whom-it-may-concern" audience,[40] and any concerned or curious listener might consult the fire telegraph's signal boxes; go codes streamed across top-secret and secured channels to a known group of military men, and any eavesdropping took place secretly and with significant risk and consequence. Despite these differences, both fire alarm and missile launch systems partook in top-down command-and-control communication that privileged efficiently transmitting information in order to secure public safety in crisis situations. In addition, both systems developed ways over time to reduce the meddling human element, with mixed results: in American cities, bell ringers were replaced by circuit switches and automated striking mechanisms, although not immediately or easily; among nuclear strategists, fully automated doomsday devices were hypothesized, although the military resisted relinquishing direct control over nuclear weapons. Furthermore, although both fire alarm and go code systems transmitted relatively simple messages, neither were point-to-point means of conveying unadulterated information. Instead, both were developed in response to situations that demanded the swift coordination of multiple actors, both human and technological, and the employment of signal redundancy over increasingly great distances and in complex environments.

While different creatures on the surface, fire alarm systems and distributed computer networks belong to a common species of emergency communication systems. A whole cast of other systems—natural disaster warnings, medical and criminal emergency call systems, alert systems for traffic accident and terrorist activity, breaking news media, among many examples from the less recent past—might comprise a fuller register of the ways humans have called one another to assistance and arms. It is worth noting that while it is no surprise that both the emergency communication case studies at hand demonstrate significant advances in reducing the time needed to coordinate actors across increasingly large expanses of space, what may be most essential—in light of the systemic crises besetting the infrastructural failures of an earthquake-torn Haiti and the collapse of global financial markets—is a study of emergency communication that emphasizes the coordination of actors, institutions, and resources over sustained periods of time and local sources of support.[41] Also needed is scholarship that critically assesses the consequences—unforeseen and unadvertised—of logistical improvements.[42]

The substantial contributions of history to the study of new media are evidenced by a subgenre of scholarship addressing the emergence of technologies ranging from facsimile to sound recording; studying old technologies when they were first new has allowed media historians to engage with other disciplines as well as other subspecialties within communication and media studies.[43] Thinking about newness as potentially recurring—as a phenomenon both indexed and generated by discursive instability—presents fresh opportunities for investigating overlooked episodes when audiences have fought and fretted over altered media landscapes. It also opens up previously unexplored avenues for comparative research, which we have attempted to demonstrate with our brief foray into newly reconfigured emergency communication systems of the past. We must seriously—and repeatedly—consider the sociocultural construction of the perception of novelty in working toward a practice of media history that is sensitive to change. Moreover, recognizing that newness is not only detectable *in* discourse but renewed *by* discourse demands reflexivity; in deliberating and researching what makes new media new, we create what we describe.

Notes

1. Review of *The Progress of the Nation*, 29–30. Marshall McLuhan is widely credited with popularizing the phrase in connection with twentieth-century electronic media. See McLuhan, "The Later Innis," 385. We would like to thank David Park, John Durham Peters, Lisa Gitelman, Carolyn Marvin, Andriy Ishchenko, and Jason Lubken for their comments. Early drafts of this exploratory work have benefited from presentation and feedback at the 2008 ICA "The Long History of New Media" pre-conference.

2. Manovich, *The Language of New Media,* 27–47. See also Flew, *New Media;* and Wardrip-Fruin and Montfort, *The New Media Reader.*
3. Silverstone, "What's New about New Media?," 11.
4. See Sterne, "What's Digital in Digital Music?," 98–99.
5. Marvin, *When Old Technologies Were New,* 4.
6. See the September 2009 issue of the *ANNALS of the American Academy of Political* and Social Science, esp. Katz, "The End of Television?" See also Spigel and Olsson, *Television after TV;* and Turner and Tay, *Television Studies after TV.*
7. For an in-depth treatment of this understanding of new media, see Peters, "And Lead Us Not," 17–19.
8. Altman, *Silent Film Sound,* 21. For an application of Altman's crisis historiography to the identity crises of short-lived media, see Gitelman and Pingree, *New Media, 1740-1915,* xii–xiii.
9. Gitelman, *Always Already New.*
10. *MCC, 1675–1776,* 4: 436–440.
11. *Laws and Ordinances,* 78–80.
12. *MCC, 1784-1831,* 3: 188, 667; *MCC, 1784–1831,* 6: 154; *MCC, 1784–1831,* 11: 53, 657.
13. *Laws and Ordinances,* 77; *MCC, 1784–1831,* 9: 585, 763, 774–775.
14. "Fire," *New York Evening Post.*
15. See Peters, "Calendar, Clock, Tower."
16. *MCC, 1784–1831,* 3: 623; *MCC, 1784–1831,* 5: 465.
17. *Laws and Ordinances,* 77–78.
18. *Compilation of the Laws,* 225–226.
19. New York approved the integration of telegraphy into its existing alarm system as early as 1847, but this technology was not implemented until 1851. See *Compilation of the Laws,* 308-309, 325; and *Record of Proceedings,* 78, 111–112.
20. *American Fire Alarm Telegraph,* 3–8.
21. Ibid., 3.
22. Mark Tebeau argues that the reputation of firefighters as ruffians was unfair. Nevertheless, brawls between competing volunteer fire companies received enough attention in the press that the rough image of firefighters was pervasive. See Tebeau, *Eating Smoke,* 15–16, 46.
23. *Record of Proceedings,* 74, 110–111; *Report of the Committee,* 47.
24. *Record of Proceedings,* 6.
25. *Report of the Committee,* 40; *Record of Proceedings,* 167; Bosch, "Historical Sketch," 347.
26. *Record of Proceedings,* 175; Forrest, *Official History,* 189–190; *Annual Reports,* 5, 15–18.
27. *Record of Proceedings,* 209, 251.
28. Kernan, *Reminiscences,* 744–745.
29. *Record of Proceedings,* 189–193.
30. Bosch, "Historical Sketch," 341–344, esp. 344.
31. See McMahon, *The Cold War,* 74–77.
32. Baran, *On Distributed Communications,* 1–4.
33. Baran's role is documented in key works on the history of the Internet including Abbate, *Inventing the Internet;* Aspray and Ceruzzi, *The Internet and American Business;* and Castells,

Internet Galaxy. For a popular narrative of the history, see Hafner and Lyon, *Where the Wizards Stay up Late.*

34. Abbate, *Inventing the Internet.*
35. In fact, most military commands were sent by secured radio, telegraphic, and telephonic networks—which many computer networks continue to use to this day. Before U.S. strategic forces employed computer networks in the 1960s, they experimented with radio towers to relay go codes. While they lacked essential security measures, radio towers did broadcast waves in multiple directions that anticipated the unpredictable message paths of packet-switched networks.
36. Baran, *On Distributed Communications,* 1.
37. See O'Neill, "Interview with Paul Baran"; Brand, "Wired Legends."
38. See Henriksen, *Dr. Strangelove's America,* xiii–xxvi, 303–344.
39. See Weart, *Nuclear Fear,* 273–295.
40. Wiener, *The Human Use of Human Beings,* 70–72.
41. For a rereading of the space-time dialectic played by communication since Innis, see Winkler, "The Geometry of Time." Craig Calhoun has expanded on the need to reconsider long-term relief efforts for Haiti in his introduction to *Haiti, Now and Next.*
42. See, for example, Curry, Phillips, and Regan, "Emergency Response Systems."
43. See Light, "Facsimile"; and Sterne, *The Audible Past.*

Works Cited

Abbate, Janet. *Inventing the Internet*. Cambridge, MA: MIT Press, 1999.

Altman, Rick. *Silent Film Sound.* New York: Columbia University Press, 2004.

American Fire Alarm Telegraph. New York, 1854.

Annual Reports of the Board of Commissioners of the Metropolitan Fire Department, for the Years 1865 and 1866. New York: Baker & Godwin, 1867.

Aspray, William, and Paul Ceruzzi. *The Internet and American Business*. Cambridge, MA: MIT Press, 2008.

Baran, Paul. *On Distributed Communications*. Memorandum RM–3420-PR. Santa Monica, CA: RAND Corporation, 1964.

Bosch, Adam. "Historical Sketch of the Fire Alarm Telegraph." *Transactions of the American Institute of Electrical Engineers* 14 (1897): 335–350.

Brand, Stewart. "Wired Legends: Founding Father: An Interview Conducted with Paul Baran in 1999." *Wired* 9 03 (2001). Accessed March 6, 2010. http://www.wired.com/wired/archive/9.03/baran_pr.html

Calhoun, Craig. "Introduction: When Is Disaster Intolerable?" In *Haiti, Now and Next*, SSRC web forum. January 14, 2010. Accessed August 13, 2010. http://www.ssrc.org/features/pages-/haiti-now-and-next/1338/1347/.

Castells, Manuel. *Internet Galaxy: Reflections on the Internet, Business and Society*. New York: Oxford University Press, 2001.

Compilation of the Laws of the State of New York; Also, of the Ordinances, Resolutions and Orders Established by the Mayor, Aldermen and Commonality of the City of New York, in Common Council Convened, Relating to the Fire Department of the City of New York, from 1812 to 1855. New York: McSpedon & Baker, 1855.

Curry, Michael R., David J. Phillips, and Priscilla M. Regan. "Emergency Response Systems and the Creeping Legibility of People and Places." *Information Society* 20, no. 5 (2004): 357–369.

"Fire." *New York Evening Post*, December 1, 1818.

Flew, Terry. *New Media: An Introduction*. Oxford: Oxford University Press, 2002.

Forrest, Clarence H. *Official History of the Fire Department of the City of Baltimore*. Baltimore, 1898.

Gitelman, Lisa. *Always Already New: Media, History, and the Data of Culture*. Cambridge, MA: MIT Press, 2006.

———, and Geoffrey B. Pingree, eds. *New Media, 1740–1915*. Cambridge, MA: MIT Press, 2003.

Hafner, Katie, and Matthew Lyon. *Where the Wizards Stay up Late*. New York: Simon and Schuster, 2000.

Henriksen, Margot A. *Dr. Strangelove's America: Society and Culture in the Atomic Age*. Berkeley: University of California Press, 1997.

Katz, Elihu. "The End of Television?" *ANNALS of the American Academy of Political and Social Science* 625 (September 2009): 6–18.

Kernan, J. Frank. *Reminiscences of the Old Fire Laddies and Volunteer Fire Departments of New York and Brooklyn*. New York: M. Crane, 1885.

Laws and Ordinances Ordained and Established by the Mayor, Aldermen, and Commonality of the City of New-York, in Common Council Convened, During the Mayorality of Jacob Radcliff. Passed the Fifth Day of May, 1817. New York: T. and J. Swords, 1817.

Light, Jennifer. "Facsimile: A Forgotten 'New Medium' from the 20th Century." *New Media & Society* 8, no. 3 (2006): 355–378.

Manovich, Lev. *The Language of New Media*. Cambridge, MA: MIT Press.

Marvin, Carolyn. *When Old Technologies Were New: Thinking About Electric Communication in the Late Nineteenth Century*. Oxford, U.K.: Oxford University Press, 1988.

MCC. Minutes of the Common Council of the City of New York: 1675–1776. Vols. 1–8. New York: Dodd, Mead and Company, 1905.

MCC. Minutes of the Common Council of the City of New York: 1784–1831. Vols. 1–19. New York: City of New York, 1917.

McLuhan, Marshall. "The Later Innis." *Queen's Quarterly* 60, no. 3 (1953): 385–394.

McMahon, Robert J. *The Cold War: A Very Short Introduction*. Oxford: Oxford University Press, 2003.

O'Neill, Judy. "Interview with Paul Baran." Charles Babbage Institute, OH 182, March 5, 1990, Menlo Park, CA. Accessed March 19, 2010. http://special.lib.umn.edu/cbi/oh/display.phtml?id=110.

Peters, Benjamin. "And Lead Us Not into Thinking the New Is New: A Bibliographic Case for New Media History." *New Media & Society* 11, nos. 1 & 2 (2009): 13–30.

Peters, John Durham. "Calendar, Clock, Tower." In *Deus in Machina: Religion and Technology in Historical Perspective*, edited by Jeremy Stolow. New York: Fordham University Press, forthcoming.

Record of Proceedings before the United States Patent Office: Application for an Extension of Letters Patent No. 17, 355. Granted to William F. Channing and Moses G. Farmer, May 19th, 1857. New York: Kilbourne Tompkins, 1871.

Report of the Committee on a Paid Fire Department, Made to Common Council, May 5th, 1859. Philadelphia, 1859.

"Review of *The Progress of the Nation, in Its Various Social and Economical Relations, from the Beginning of the Nineteenth Century to the Present Time*," Sections III and IV, by G. R. Porter, Esq. F. R. S. *Journal of the Statistical Society of London* 1, no. 1 (1838): 27–33.

Silverstone, Roger. "What's New about New Media?" *New Media & Society* 1, no. 1 (1999): 10–12.

Spigel, Lynn, and Jan Olsson, eds. *Television after TV: Essays on a Medium in Transition*. Durham, NC: Duke University Press, 2004.

Sterne, Jonathan. *The Audible Past: Cultural Origins of Sound Reproduction*. Durham, NC: Duke University Press, 2003.

———. "What's Digital in Digital Music?" In *Digital Media: Transformations in Human Communication*, edited by Paul Messaris and Lee Humphreys, 93–109. New York: Peter Lang, 2006.

Tebeau, Mark. *Eating Smoke: Fire in Urban America, 1800–1950*. Baltimore, MD: Johns Hopkins University Press, 2003.

Turner, Graeme, and Jinna Tay, eds. *Television Studies after TV: Understanding Television in the Post-Broadcast Era*. London: Routledge, 2009.

Wardrip-Fruin, Noah, and Nick Montfort, eds. *The New Media Reader*. Cambridge, MA: MIT Press, 2003.

Weart, Spencer R. *Nuclear Fear: A History of Images*. Cambridge, MA: Harvard University Press, 1988.

Wiener, Norbert. *The Human Use of Human Beings: Cybernetics and Society*. Cambridge, MA: Da Capo Press, 1954.

Winkler, Hartmut. "The Geometry of Time: Media, Spatialization, and Reversibility." Paper presented at the "Media Theory on the Move" conference, Potsdam, Germany, May 21–24, 2009. Accessed August 13, 2010. http://homepages.uni-paderborn.de/winkler/.

chapter thirteen

Pipeline as Network
Pneumatic Systems and the Social Order

Holly Kruse

Introduction

When is an obsolete communication technology not obsolete? When the technology in question is the pneumatic tube, a networked technology that continues to relay information in the digital age. Although pneumatic tube networks used for citywide communication have fallen into disuse since New York City abandoned its system in 1953, Paris stopped using its in 1984, and Prague took its own network out of service after severe flooding in 2002,[1] the pneumatic tube is far from a dead medium. The equivalent of local area networks (LANs) exist in pneumatic form around the world, and the architects of capsule communication systems using pneumatic tubes laid the groundwork for many of today's digital networks.

Thinking of the pneumatic tube as a networked information and communication technology (ICT), with its tangible pipes and capsule carriers, reminds us that networks take physical form. This observation applies to contemporary wireless and wired computer networks, which in the past have been framed in abstract terms, as with the term "cyberspace." Eugene Thacker warns that "discussions of networks—especially in cultural theory—have too often slipped into 'vapor theory,' eliding a specific consideration of the material substrate and infrastructure with the general discussion of links, webs, and globalized connectivity."[2] Therefore, not only should we consider, as Nigel Thrift does, that "this world of flows is not abstract at all—it is the product of and it is produced by people communicating about what is going on,"[3] but that networks are, according to Thacker, "materialized and materializing media," which, in their very materiality play key roles in creating and maintaining power relationships.[4]

As two key thinkers in understanding the formation of information networks, Alexander Galloway and James Beniger demonstrate in their respective research on ICTs that early modern technologies helped create and were created by structures of social and economic relations that persist. They were and are powerful sites of meaning making. Early modern ICTs (like the pneumatic tube) also represent a shift in technology, and indeed in the organization of society, and lay the groundwork for the current era. In his book *Protocol*, Galloway uses periodization theory to argue that we have moved from an era referred to by Michel Foucault as the "disciplinary, or 'modern,' era," which began in the late eighteenth century and lasted into the twentieth century and in which somewhat diffuse structures of power (or "discourses") functioned to regulate people's behaviors, and into what Galloway alternately calls the "postmodern" or "digital" era, or the "control society," in which power is distributed through, and is immanent in, networks rather than being based in one or several hubs.[5] Similarly, Beniger describes a "control revolution" that began in the late nineteenth century to assert control over the complex of quickly expanding social, economic, and technical challenges that emerged as social and economic systems changed during industrialization. The control revolution was comprised of "a series of new technological and social solutions."[6] Specifically, Beniger lists these innovations to be

> a federal postal service (1791), the first turnpike (1795), coastal steamboat travel (1809), mail delivery by steamboat (1813), regular packet service to England (late 1810s), steam railroads and Atlantic clipper ships (early 1830s), local postal delivery service (1836), regular transatlantic steamship service (1838), express delivery using railroad and steamboat (1839), a national turnpike to the West and the first interregional rail line (1840), commercial telegraph (1847), and regular steamboat service to California (1849).[7]

Not included in Beniger's list, however, is another information and communication technology that appeared in the nineteenth century and was used to manage a growing barrage of information; and that, of course, is the pneumatic tube. Capsules in pneumatic tube networks carried mail and telegrams in large cities, transmitted buy and sell orders to stock exchange floors, ferried cash and receipts to and from clerks in department stores, and brought books to librarians in large urban libraries, helping to impose order through explicit rules and implicit protocols in information environments that were then experiencing unprecedented growth.

History

From the moment it appeared in the early nineteenth century, modern pneumatic tube technology has used compressed air, generated by blowers, to propel carriers (usually in the form of canisters or capsules) through tubular conduits. The earliest nineteenth-century pneumatic tube systems relied on steam-powered blowers; later systems used electricity. By the late 1800s, the Postmaster General of the United States, John Wanamaker, urged the development of underground tube systems to convey mail in major cities, starting with Philadelphia in 1893.[8] Boston and New York followed in 1897, and then in the first few years of the twentieth century under the guidance of subsequent Postmaster General Charles Emory Smith,[9] St. Louis and Chicago added pneumatic tube networks. By 1916, postal tube systems were extensive, with New York City hosting fifty-five miles of tubes, while Philadelphia had twenty miles, Chicago had almost twenty miles, Boston had more than thirteen miles, and St. Louis four miles.[10]

These networks were able to move mail in congested cities much faster than horse-drawn wagons. In inclement weather, like a major snowstorm described by New York's Pneumatic Tube Postal Commission in 1914, even though "New York Streets were almost impassable—New York business houses nevertheless received their important mail on time! The pneumatic tubes carried the mails."[11] According to the United States Postal Service, capsules in the tubes could carry up to 600 letters each and were dispatched every six to fifteen seconds, thus transporting about 360,000 letters an hour.[12]

Writers have documented the form and function of the New York City postal tube system particularly well. The far-reaching steel tube network was in operation from 1897 until 1953, and while it was operating, New York City's

> General Post Office, near Pennsylvania Station, served as the nerve center of the tube system. From there, a letter might travel up to Times Square, to Radio City, and so on past several stops at local post offices along the west side of Central Park. The route then passed through Harlem and down Manhattan's East Side, again with several intermediate stops, finally arriving at Grand Central Station, from whence a set of tubes led back to the main office. Alternatively, a missive might continue its journey past yet more stations farther downtown, past another nodal point at Church Street and on to Wall Street and Bowling Green at the island's southern tip. From there, the tubes ran up the island again past Greenwich Village, back to the GPO. Mail for Brooklyn was sent out from Church St., along a branch line that was lifted over the Brooklyn Bridge.[13]

Mail moved at thirty miles per hour, allowing for up to 5 million letters to pass through the system each operating day. E. B. White observed, "When a young man in Manhattan writes a letter to his girl in Brooklyn, the love letter gets blown to her through a pneumatic tube–pfft–just like that."[14] The trip from the General Post Office to 125th Street took approximately twenty minutes. Today it takes a similar piece of mail ninety minutes to make this journey.[15]

Pneumatic message and mail systems were used in North America and also in South America and Australia. Such systems appeared earlier in Europe, in cities including London, Paris, Berlin, Vienna, Munich, Dublin, Rome, Milan, Naples, Marseilles, and Prague.[16] London's network was the earliest, founded in the 1850s, while the sizeable Berlin network commenced operation in 1865 and featured 250 miles of pneumatic tubes.[17] In their earliest years, most of these networks shuttled telegrams, helping relieve street congestion caused by transporting messages between business and financial entities in city centers, and some networks eventually included suburbs. Although the telegraph first went into operation in 1844, within just a few years it had become crucial to efficient functioning in the world's financial centers. The London pneumatic tube system began in 1853 as 220 yards of pipe between the London Stock Exchange and the Electric Telegraph Company. Berlin's network also began as a way to connect its main telegraph office with its stock exchange.[18]

Perhaps the most documented European pneumatic tube system, however, was in Paris, where the network transported mail and messages from 1866 to 1984.[19] The original Paris line was 1 kilometer long and ran between the stock exchange and the main telegraph office; by 1910, the network was 210 kilometers long, and by 1953, it was 450 kilometers long.[20] In 1878 the tube system began carrying pneumatic post messages in addition to telegrams, and in 1931 electrical conducting bands were added to the cylinders used to transport messages so that they could navigate the system automatically, rather than relying on system operators to manually direct the carriers.[21]

These networks allowed well-to-do users to exchange written messages several times a day. Charles Mann describes a series of exchanges that took place in Milan in 1890 between composer Giuseppe Verdi and librettist and poet Arrigo Boito, in which several letters were sent and responded to on the same day. At the time, Milan residents received five mail deliveries a day, in part because of the local pneumatic tube system. Mann describes the process:

> Desk clerks picked up these . . . missives and dropped them into the network of special pneumatic tubes threading through the city. The letters went to a central clearinghouse, where they were quickly routed to another set of tubes that would suck them to their destination. Sometimes the journey took less than half an hour, a period short enough to allow Verdi and the unfortunate objects of his scorn to exchange three or four notes in an afternoon.[22]

Mann notes that the speed and convenience of the system used by Verdi and others was not too different from late twentieth-century communication networks and perhaps was preferable in some ways because of the tangibility of the message sent, allowing for no software conflicts or attachments that couldn't be opened. He adds that these networks were dependent on the growing class of clerks in urban areas:

> Verdi and his confreres could generate correspondence so prolific that we in our electronic era can only marvel because well-to-do Europeans of the day depended on an invisible army of servants and clerks. Servants to run the notes to and from the pneumatic tubes. Clerks to run about the streets of Milan.[23]

In their respective books *Telegraph Messenger Boys* and *The Victorian Internet*, Gregory Downey and Tom Standage chart the growth of communications jobs in the Western workforce in the nineteenth century. Tubes were used within telegraph offices to move messages, and these offices, as Standage explains, were "filled with pneumatic tubes, and staffed by hundreds of people whose sole purpose was to receive messages, figure out where to send then, and dispatch them accordingly."[24] Standage describes the main telegraph office in New York City, where "check-girls" were employed to supplement intra-office pneumatic tubes and delivered messages throughout the building.[25] In 1875, the operator room at the top of the ten-story building was, Downey states, "the nerve center" and housed 290 operators.[26] Once a message made its way out of a central telegraph office and through an urban pneumatic system, it would end up at the satellite telegraph office closest to the recipient, and a messenger would deliver it.[27]

By the 1870s, telegraph wires, tube systems, transoceanic cables, clerks, and messengers were part of a communication network that covered much of the world.[28] The telegraph and the modern postal service, in conjunction with pneumatic tubes, created a variety of white-collar jobs to service these systems. Nineteenth-century American industrialization and corporatization was characterized in part by the growth of the middle class and the number of people aspiring to be middle class.[29] The demand for white-collar workers—office clerks, bank tellers, telecommunication operators, and retail sales people—grew precipitously, especially in the half century after 1870. These jobs represented a chance at upward mobility, of movement into the bona fide middle class, primarily for native-born white male workers. African Americans were mostly excluded from white-collar jobs, and women occupied a small but growing number of white-collar positions by the turn of the century.[30]

Although white-collar work appealed to those aspiring to move into the middle class, workers in low-skill positions often worked in unpleasant conditions for little money. Women comprised a large segment of the clerical workforce. Retail sales work, argues Daniel Graff, "offered white-collar respectability . . . while granting a degree of autonomy not available outside of nursing and teaching."[31] Some clerical jobs, like typist, while originally held by both men and women, became known as feminine professions by the end of the nineteenth century, bringing thousands of women who would not have considered taking factory jobs into the workforce.[32] By the early twentieth century, women also held the majority of retail sales positions.

Whether they were stenographers, telegraph operators, postal workers, or "check-girls," women usually earned significantly less than their male counterparts, and the number of positions available to them was limited, as were the opportunities for advancement.[33] Yet women continued to work closely with communication technology, in telegraph and postal offices, in businesses using typewriters, and later as telephone operators, and in department stores and other retail establishments where pneumatic tubes became popular in the late nineteenth and early twentieth centuries. The first department store in the United States that used pneumatic tubes was, perhaps unsurprisingly, Wanamaker's, which opened in 1876 and was owned by future postmaster general and all-around pneumatic network proponent John Wanamaker. Wanamaker's in Philadelphia installed pneumatic tubes in 1880, a year after the store added electric lights.[34] In New York City, the major department stores—Macy's, Gimbel's, and Altman's—all featured tubes that transported money and sales slips through stores.[35] Although these systems are mostly a thing of the past, Weaver's department store in Lawrence, Kansas, still uses its tube network, which was installed in the 1930s.[36]

A 1903 *Scientific American* article by Day Allen Willey describes how department store pneumatic networks worked, first explaining that the use of

> pneumatic tubes in transmitting money, papers, and parcels of various kinds has become so extensive that the service is considered a necessity in the equipment of the modern mercantile establishment. . . . In the dry goods or department store, for example, it is valuable as a labor saver, dispensing, as it does with the many cash boys, and in some instances cash girls, that have been employed, and performing their work much more quickly, besides avoiding many mistakes which formerly occurred. There is no delay in "making change," as the amount due the customer is usually handed him by the salesman within a minute, sometimes less than a minute, after his money has been taken over the counter.[37]

A clerk making a sale on the floor would write a sales slip, and then put it and the customer's money into a cylindrical carrier and place the cylinder into a sending tube. Carriers arrived at a central office in the store, where another employee checked the sales slip and made change for the customer, both of which were sent back to the sales clerk. A duplicate sales slip was sent from the central office to the bookkeeper, who entered the sale into the store's books. As Willey wrote, "[t]hese operations are usually performed in less time than it takes to read the description."[38] Willey believed that department store pneumatic networks, when combined with postal pneumatic tube systems, offered an ideal way to relay packages to customers. He argued that these networks were

> largely used by merchants for sending parcels to the residence districts where [postal] sub-stations are located . . . the average time required to deliver packages from the main station to any portion reach[ed] by the service is ten minutes, where from forty-five minutes to an hour would be required by the usual method of delivery.[39]

As I will describe in the next section, this kind of practical talk about extensive pneumatic tube networks was not far removed from utopian scenarios in which tubes crossed the globe and reached every home.

Media scholar Shannon Mattern describes a third historical use of pneumatic tubes: transporting book requests in public libraries. In the United States the best-known system is likely the one installed in 1911 at the New York Public Library on Forty-Second Street and used into the early twenty-first century.[40] The library's tubes carried call slips into the stacks, where library assistants read them and pulled the desired books off of the shelves. The books were then sent to the reading room via a conveyor; they were delivered from the most remote corners of the large library to waiting patrons in five to ten minutes.[41] One entrepreneur of the time, Edmond Fordyce, remarked in 1903 that tubes were an "[i]ndispensable part of the mechanical equipment of large public libraries. . . . As messengers, they do their work with all the celerity of the telephone—and do it withal in perfect harmony with the spirit of silence that pervades the atmosphere of the library."[42] Indeed, when the New York Science, Industry and Business Library was being built in New York City in the 1990s at the site of the former B. Altman department store, the library system decided to keep the store's tube network and incorporate it into its operations.[43]

It is constructive to think of these uses, and the ways that workers were positioned in relation to pneumatic tube systems, as contributors to a "control revolution" that emerged in response to industrialization and resulted, in part, in greater bureaucratization of virtually all elements of society—and that, according to James Beniger, "had begun to remake societies throughout the world by the beginning of [the twentieth] century."[44] Pneumatic networks of the nineteenth and twentieth centuries were wide ranging and connected to the most important information and communication hubs in urban areas; and beyond that, to other cities and countries through other control technologies like the railroad, which transported goods but also served as a communication medium in carrying mail across continents, and the telegraph, which conveyed messages locally, nationally, and eventually internationally.

Pipe Dreams

Media scholar Armand Mattelart observes of the history of information and communication technologies that "[e]ach new generation of technology revived the discourse of salvation," such that each new method of communication, "from the optical telegraph to underwater cable, the telephone, the radio, the television and the Internet intended to transcend the spatial and temporal dimensions of the social fabric, brought back the myth of the recovery of the lost agora of Attic cities."[45] The phonograph, radio, television, and Internet were all initially framed by their sponsors as educational tools that would bring the world together in an environment of understanding and shared high cultural tastes. Nineteenth- and even twentieth-century discourses of pneumatic tube networks were no exception; many boosters of the technology believed that it would bring people together, either through physically linking homes and businesses or rapidly transporting people. The success of early pneumatic tube networks encouraged officials, businessmen, and writers to dream big about the networks' future. During the "pneumatic age" in the late nineteenth and early twentieth centuries, all things pneumatic were touted. An 1893 *Washington Post* article claimed, "The present era is likely to be known to history as the pneumatic age. What with the pneumatic tubes and pneumatic tires and pneumatic bells and pneumatic guns."[46]

Most projections of future benefits of tubes focused either on homes connected to each other and to businesses in networks through which messages and goods would be transported, or on pneumatic systems that would transport people. In the case of the former, Postmaster General Charles Emory Smith wrote in the *Brooklyn Eagle* newspaper in 1900 that "[i]t would not be surprising to see . . . the extension of the pneumatic tube system to every house, thus insuring the immediate delivery of mail as soon as it arrives in the city," and further that every house would be connected to other houses by tubes.[47] A few years earlier, poet Ella Wheeler Wilcox maintained that in the next hundred years "the pneumatic tube will be the means of transporting goods." Another writer, Felix L. Oswald, argued that pneumatic tube networks would eventually span oceans and transport mail from one continent to another.[48]

In the last years of the nineteenth century and early years of the twentieth century, the futuristic utopian imaginings of writers H. G. Wells and Edward Bellamy featured large networks of pneumatic tubes. In his 1905 book, *A Modern Utopia*,

Wells wrote of a networked world that resembles our own, though it was networked through pneumatic tubes:

> Here and there, no doubt, will stand quite solitary homesteads, homesteads that will nevertheless be lit and warmed by cables from the central force station, that will share the common water supply, will have their perfected telephonic connection with the rest of the world, with doctor, shop, and so forth, and may even have a pneumatic tube for books and small parcels to the nearest post office. But the solitary homestead, as a permanent residence, will be something of a luxury.[49]

Echoing Wells, many contemporary middle-class Westerners consider the relative quiet of spending time "off the grid" as quite a luxury.

Edward Bellamy's well-known socialist utopian novel of 1917, *Looking Backward, 2000–1887*, prominently features pneumatic tube transport of goods. Bellamy's protagonist, Julian West, falls asleep in 1887 and wakes up in 2000 to a very different world. His guides to Boston in 2000 are Dr. Leete and Leete's daughter Edith. At one point in the book West goes shopping with Edith Leete and is astounded by the role that pneumatic tubes play in this future. Edith tells him:

> But, Mr. West, you must not fail to ask father to take you to the central warehouse some day, where they receive the orders from the different sample houses all over the city and parcel out and send the goods to their destinations. . . . The orders, as they are taken by the different departments in the store, are sent by transmitters to [the dispatching clerk]. His assistants sort them and enclose each class in a carrier-box by itself. The dispatching clerk has a dozen pneumatic transmitters before him. . . each communicating with the corresponding department at the warehouse. He drops the box of orders into the tube it calls for, and in a few moments later it drops on the proper desk in the warehouse. . . . The orders are read off, recorded, and sent to be filled like lightning. . . . The packages are then delivered by larger tubes to the city districts, and thence distributed to the houses. You may understand how quickly it is all done when I tell you that my order will probably be at home sooner than I could have carried it from here.[50]

Of course, no truly lengthy tube networks for transporting goods and messages were developed. By 1920, city postal organizations were switching from pneumatic systems and horse-drawn wagons to motorized trucks for local mail and package transportation.[51]

Despite the shift away from pneumatic tubes in mail delivery, innovation continued in other sectors. It was in 1918 that the New York Stock Exchange introduced a tube system to carry buy and sell orders to and from the trading floor;[52] and as late as the 1930s, inventors were coming up with and even implementing ideas for connecting homes by tube. An article in a 1935 edition of *Modern Mechanix and Inventions* magazine enthused,

> Whizzing at mile-a-minute speed through pneumatic tubes far beneath the streets of Berlin, Germany, are thermos bottles each containing part of some housewife's meal. A phone call is enough to bring, in less than fifteen minutes, a complete meal ready to serve, containing exactly the desired quantity and kind of food for each course.[53]

The experiment allowed housewives in apartment buildings in certain locations to choose meals from an extensive menu book. The magazine predicted that "[n]ewer homes in Berlin will have no kitchens—simply a few pneumatic tube outlets. . . . With the elimination of all stoves and ovens in the home, the fame of German women for tasty cooking may soon pass into obscurity."[54] The subsequent middle-class Western desire for a growing number and variety of elaborate kitchen appliances may well have come as something of a surprise to the writer, although they too tend to be touted as vehicles of greater household efficiency.

Victorian visionaries and their immediate successors might also be surprised to learn that by the early twenty-first century, no pneumatic tube systems for human transportation were in place. Many had been predicted. Some engineers foresaw a transatlantic pneumatic tube that would carry people three thousand miles to and from Europe and North America.[55] In short stories, Jules Verne's son Michel imagined what a transatlantic tube system would be like. A fictional inventor, Colonel Pierce of Boston, accompanies Verne's narrator on a pneumatic tube journey in the story "A Great Transatlantic Subway," and explains that the car in which they are traveling moves at "a trifle over 1,720 miles an hour" and that the "bellows can create and maintain a current of air powerful enough to move a train 3,500 mile[s]—Boston to Liverpool by our route—with nearly the velocity of a cannon ball."[56] In another version of the story, "An Express of the Future," wherein the narrator visits a station for the "Boston to Liverpool Pneumatic [T]ubes Company," he is struck by the realization "that this 'Utopia' had become a reality, and these two cylinders of iron at my feet passed thence under the Atlantic and reached to the coast of England!"[57] Within the tubes passengers sat comfortably in rows of seats contained in carriages, unaffected by the tremendous speed at which they were traveling.

Travel by transatlantic pneumatic tube may not have seemed terribly far-fetched in an age in which telegraph cables on the ocean floor crossed the Atlantic. In fact, a number of inventors attempted to put pneumatic trains into operation. In the United States, Alfred Beach thought that it would be reasonable for New Yorkers to travel underground in a pneumatic subway system. After overcoming technical and political obstacles, Beach unveiled his pneumatic subway in New York City in 1870. The station at the corner of Broadway and Warren was ornately decorated, featuring a grand piano, a fountain stocked with goldfish, damask curtains, and artwork. The tunnel for the subway ended nearby, at Murray Street. Passengers made the brief journey in a well-appointed "tube" car, and this new form of mass transit was a hit. The technology, however, proved impractical, and Beach's subway was not adopted. The size and power of blowers capable of propelling multiple train cars would have been enormous, as would have been the costs. Electric power won out over pneumatic power as the means to propel New York City's fleet of underground trains.[58]

Not all visions of early pneumatic tubes were utopian. E. M. Forster's 1909 science fiction short story "The Machine Stops" depicts a dystopian world in which humans are isolated from one another, communicating only through apparatuses, including the pneumatic post.[59] The articulation of pneumatic tubes, notions of depersonalization, discourses of efficiency, and the extremes of intrusive and mindless bureaucracy were more completely realized later in the twentieth century in Terry Gilliam's 1985 satiric film, *Brazil.* The totalitarian state in Gilliam's movie relies on masses of meaningless documents sent and received through pneumatic tubes by minor functionaries. One might well see these functionaries as updated versions of the clerks and salespeople of Beniger's control society or Foucault's disciplinary modern society who served pneumatic tube networks in Victorian workplaces.

Similarly, in the early twenty-first century television series *Lost*, plane crash survivors are stranded on a mysterious island. They learn of an experimental group—the Dharma Initiative—that was once located on the island. A task apparently required of initiative members at one station was to clandestinely observe other members via closed circuit television, record the actions in notebooks, and send the notebooks through a pneumatic tube. In keeping with the late twentieth-century discursive construction of pneumatic tubes as tools of mindless bureaucracy, crash survivors eventually stumble upon a pile of notebooks at the terminus of the tube, in the middle of nowhere.

The Ghost Is the Machine?

While the imagined pneumatic-tube-centric utopias and dystopias never happened, the pneumatic tube is not a dead technology. Modern pneumatic tube networks are being used to carry money from cash registers to vaults in retail stores, to carry trash from people's homes to dump sites, and to transport messages in corporate headquarters.[60] Indeed, pneumatic technology is experiencing a renaissance as an information and communication medium. It can still be thought of as a control technology that has now been in use for well over a century, a technology created in the modern "disciplinary" era described by Foucault and still used in the "information age." Beniger sees a direct link between these historical periods, noting, "One major result of the Control Revolution had been the emergence of the so-called Information Society. The concept dates from the late 1950s and the pioneering work of an economist, Fritz Machlup, who first measured that sector of the U.S. economy associated with what he called 'the production and distribution of knowledge.'"[61]

As in the nineteenth century, twenty-first-century jobs related to pneumatic networks are largely found in the service sector (and mainly held by women)—particularly in the two areas on which I will focus here: the banking industry and the health care industry. Drive-thru window bank teller is an occupation associated with tubes; the bank is one place where contemporary Americans may have seen and used pneumatic systems. As with the implementation of many technologies in the workplace, banks have used drive-through lanes enabled by pneumatic tubes to increase efficiency. The fewer the number of tellers needed to serve the greatest number of customers in the least amount of time, the better. A 1976 study found that in the case of one bank, expanding from three pneumatic-tube-enabled lanes to five and adding a teller when there were more than three or four cars waiting would mean that "a customer would run less than a five percent chance of waiting more than four minutes."[62] This is certainly the sort of control society job both Beniger and Galloway might envision. The physical environment is one that doesn't allow the teller to leave her position at one end of the pneumatic tubes for any period of time, and efficiency demands that her focus on the tube, its contents, and financial data to be entered into computer networks not waver.

Even more disciplinary in terms of the way they regulate bodies and disembody interaction are innovations in bank services in recent years that have included remote teller systems (RTSs), which combine pneumatic tubes with videoconferencing technology. Customers at RTS kiosks or windows see a teller on a screen and are able to exchange cash and/or documents with the teller via the tube. Although remote systems use screen interfaces, one bank president and chairman claims that "[c]ustomers have reacted very favorably to the greater immediacy versus a traditional drive-in. There, the customer may be looking across three or four lanes to the teller."[63] With the RTS, the tellers are clustered in a workroom elsewhere in the bank; efficiency, rather than a more personal customer experience, is still the main draw. A credit union president states that an RTS "saves on space, moves transactions more quickly, and saves payroll costs because one person can handle two members at the same time."[64]

Greater efficiency with fewer employees is also the goal of installing pneumatic networks in medical facilities. Rather than using staff members to carry materials to and from laboratories and pharmacies in hospitals, employees can send samples and medication by pneumatic tube. The ability to transport solid objects almost instantaneously is an affordance not yet matched by other communication technologies. As Gene Charleton writes in his *Discovery Network* blog, "Try sending a bottle of antibiotics over the Internet."[65] Yet advanced tube technology and computer traffic control have greatly improved the reliability and general utility of contemporary systems, so pneumatic networks are now often also computer networks, connected in a tangibly material way by tubes and wires. At one community hospital in California, a tube network handles up to 1,800 transactions transporting paperwork and medication a day, a workload that would otherwise require fifteen employees.[66] At Columbia-Presbyterian Medical Center in New York City, carriers take biological samples through a network of tubes, allowing samples sent from the emergency room to arrive in the lab in one minute, rather than the ten or fifteen minutes it would take a nurse or clerk to carry the sample from the ER to the lab.[67]

On the West Coast, Stanford University Hospital uses its four miles of tubes to transport lab samples and medication 7,000 times every day. Its network does the jobs of at least twenty people, is computer operated, and boasts 124 pneumatic tube stations (including one at every nursing unit), 141 transfer units, 90 interzone connectors, and 29 blowers. Carriers in the system can travel 1,500 feet—over a quarter of a mile—in less than three minutes. The operation services manager for the hospital's lab says that the network is vital:

> I don't know what we'd do without the tube system, especially when it comes to tests like those that happen in surgery. When arterial blood gases are sent from the operating room, we need to return results in a very short period of time, so physicians know if they need to change settings on a monitor. Years ago, before the tubes, we would get a phone call and we'd have to send somebody. It definitely slowed our turnaround time.[68]

In fact, far from being obsolete, in the early twenty-first century, pneumatic tube sales were growing at the rate of 10 percent a year, largely because of hospitals installing new networks or upgrading existing ones.[69]

Modern, frequently computer-managed, pneumatic networks can be "centralized networks," described by Alexander Galloway as featuring a single center, or host, attached to radial nodes that only connect to the central hub and not to any other host or to each other. This is the sort of network one sees at bank drive-through windows. A hospital network, however, is likely to be a decentralized network, with multiple hubs with their own satellite nodes. In settings like hospitals with numerous labs and procedure rooms, one can even begin to imagine distributed pneumatic networks in which there are no central hosts and only connections between nodes in the network, much like the Internet.[70] One ultimately can then see pneumatic networks as linked via other ICTs to global flows of finance and commerce, of communication and information. They are part of the world described by Armand Mattelart, in which the

> framework of international relations that is emerging relies heavily on technologies of information and is organized according to a reticular logic. The space of globalization is woven together by enterprises structured into corporate networks, "global firms" that interconnect all the sites of their implantation and manage their operations in real time.[71]

At the same time, the very materiality of pneumatic networks demonstrates to us that information flows are not only widespread and global: they are always also local. Jonathan Rutherford reminds us that physical infrastructures and global links that connect urban centers are tied to local and regional practices and processes.[72] We can imagine such connections when we send a check to deposit in a capsule through a tube to a drive-through window teller, who then feeds that information into the bank's computer network, which is linked to regional, national, and international financial flows.

Conclusion

In thinking about, with, or through the pneumatic tube, one thinks at the intersection of the material and meaning. When considering meanings constructed with and around pneumatic tube technology, while some things have changed—certainly pneumatic tubes aren't seen as cutting-edge technology as they once were, and many of their associations are with forecasts that never came to pass—in their quotidian form, they are still tied to lower-paying, nonprofessional white-collar jobs that are viewed as feminine (for instance, bank teller and health care worker), and they are still linked to notions of increased speed and efficiency in the workplace. With the exception of the Roosevelt Island trash system in New York City, pneumatic networks have not become, despite predictions of the delivery of packages and hot meals through tubes, "domesticated," that is, integrated into private space. Over time, the pneumatic tube's meanings have shifted, although the relations in which it is inscribed have not changed that much.

Thus, even though modern-day pneumatic tubes transport, in addition to documents and cash, medication, biological materials, and even, on New York's Roosevelt Island, household garbage, they are still information and communication technologies. Biological systems, as Donna Haraway argues, are information networks; and biology and ICTs are increasingly integrated as our bodies are technologized through cybernetic discipline and the addition of synthetic materials.[73] The pneumatic tube is not, as Mattern claims, an "anachronistic technology," one that is only meaningful in nostalgic contexts, including as an element in the retro "steampunk" universe.[74] It is in fact the apparently rare communication technology that appears obsolete, but isn't. Jonathan Sterne, in his examination of how digital hardware is made obsolete, states, "Some old technologies do make a comeback from the trash heap . . . Some can cross the threshold from 'rubbish' back to 'useful' through successive waves of nostalgic revivals,"[75] thus not accounting for the new production of network technologies that were thought by many to be antiquated.

In light of the shift from disciplinary society to control society in the twentieth century, and because the pneumatic tube has served important functions in both eras, the fact that pneumatic networks remain the province of business and have not, in their latest incarnation, linked private spaces should not be surprising. Roland Wenzlhuemer argues in his comparison of nineteenth-century telegraph networks with contemporary digital telecommunication networks that the patterns of connectivity of the nineteenth-century telegraph and the twenty-first-century Internet are quite similar, with largely the same hubs and cable locations. The reason for this, he states, is the constellation of social practices that are inseparable from technology itself, making structural change in communication networks slow, even as technological change is rapid.[76]

Whether it is a new media technology that takes over many of the functions of its predecessor (for instance, point-to-point telegraph messaging being gradually replaced by the telephone, or television replacing radio as the primary medium for narrative broadcast programming) or an old technology that is adapted in new settings, as with the pneumatic tube, communication networks and systems are, as Lisa Gitelman claims of new media technologies, "socially embedded sites for the ongoing negotiation of meaning."[77] So for instance in examining the case of gender, work, and technology, David Morley's observation that "traditional patterns of gender relations are surprisingly resilient"[78] is an important one.

Pneumatic systems foreshadowed the physical structure of modern communication and information networks: and in the ways that they have been used in local and global flows of information and power, they illustrate how networked technologies have reified relations of control. Regimes of efficiency are paramount in consideration of pneumatic networks. In the early twenty-first century the pneumatic tube sits at the intersection of a variety of social, cultural, and technological relationships, including those of materiality and meaning; of depersonalization and embodiment (of transported objects, at least); of aspirations of class mobility; of the capitalist logic of efficiency; of gendered workplaces; and of the restrictions on autonomy and physical movement represented in the movie *Brazil* and by banks' remote teller systems. Most important, however, it remains a disciplinary technology in the information age, colonizing physical spaces as network sites at and through which information is gathered and flows, and dictating that certain actions and protocols be followed by users. In the end, in its multiple articulations, the pneumatic tube has achieved something rare: it has remained a vital information and communication technology for more than 160 years.

Notes

1. Steenson, "Pneumatic Post in Paris."
2. Cited in the foreword to Galloway, *Protocol,* xiii.
3. Thrift, "A Hyperactive World," 37.
4. Cited in the foreword to Galloway, *Protocol,* xv.
5. Galloway, *Protocol,* 20–27.
6. Beniger, *The Control Revolution,* 13.
7. Ibid., 130.
8. United States Postal Service, *John Wanamaker.*
9. Schaer, "Mail System Down."
10. Ibid.
11. Pogrebin, "Underground Mail Road."
12. United States Postal Service, *John Wanamaker,* 3.
13. Baumgartner, "When the U.S. Mail," 118.
14. Quoted in Thuras and Enemark, "Pneu York, Pneu York."
15. Vescovi, "Underground Mailroad," 118.
16. Standage, *The Victorian Internet,* 97.
17. Levenstein, "A Series of Tubes."
18. Hayhurst, *The Pneumatic Post of Paris.*
19. Steenson, "Pneumatic Post in Paris."
20. Ibid.
21. Hayhurst, *The Pneumatic Post of Paris.*
22. Mann, "E-mail by Any Other Name."
23. Ibid.
24. Standage, *The Victorian Internet,* 98.
25. Ibid., 99.
26. Downey, *Telegraph Messenger Boys,* 68.
27. Standage, *The Victorian Internet,* 99.
28. Ibid.
29. See, for instance, Wiebe, *The Search for Order.*
30. This phenomenon is described in much more detail in sources like Bjelopera, *City of Clerks.*
31. Graff, "Retail Workers."
32. Davies, "Women Clerical Workers and the Typewriter," 33.
33. See Bjelopera, *City of Clerks;* Graff, "Retail Workers."
34. United States Postal Service, *John Wanamaker.*
35. Mattern, "Puffs of Air," 4.
36. Miller, "Airmatic Pneumatic Tube System."
37. Willey, "The Pneumatic Tube System," 206.
38. Ibid.
39. Ibid.
40. Mattern, "Puffs of Air," 1.
41. Ibid., 1–2.
42. Quoted in Mattern, "Puffs of Air," 2.

43. Thuras and Enemark, "Pneu York, Pneu York."
44. Beniger, *The Control Revolution,* 429.
45. Mattelart, *The Information Society,* 23.
46. Mattern, "Puffs of Air," 3.
47. Schaer, "Mail System Down," A15; Thuras and Enemark, "Pneu York, Pneu York"; Pogrebin, "Underground Mail Road."
48. Schaer, "Mail System Down," A15.
49. Wells, *A Modern Utopia,* 218.
50. Bellamy, *Looking Backward,* 107.
51. Pogrebin, "Underground Mail Road."
52. Coval and Shumway, "Is Sound Just Noise?," 1887.
53. "Pneumatic Tubes Shoot Hot Meals to Homes," 41.
54. Ibid.
55. Obermayer, "Pipe Dreams."
56. Verne, "A Great Transatlantic Subway."
57. Verne, "An Express of the Future."
58. Allen, "New York's Secret Subway."
59. Forster, "The Machine Stops."
60. Wofsey, "Back to the Future"; Rueb, "Whoosh!"
61. Beniger, *The Control Revolution,* 21.
62. Foote, "A Queueing Case Study," 35.
63. O'Sullivan, "Tellers Play TV Anchor," 56.
64. Totty, "Branches Get a Tech Tune-Up," 56.
65. Charleton, "Everything's Going Up."
66. Lawson, "Pneumatic Nets Haven't Gone Down the Tubes."
67. Biederman, "This Old Technology."
68. Wykes, "Gone with the Wind."
69. Obermayer, "Pipe Dreams."
70. See Galloway, *Protocol,* 11–12.
71. Mattelart, *The Invention of Communication,* 303.
72. Rutherford, "Networks in Cities," 2403.
73. See, in particular, Haraway, *Simians, Cyborgs and Women.*
74. Mattern, "Puffs of Air," 11.
75. Sterne, "Out with the Trash," 26.
76. Wenzlhuemer, "London in the Global Telecommunication Network," 29.
77. Gitelman, *Always Already New,* 6.
78. Morley, *Home Territories,* 76.

Works Cited

Allen, Oliver E. "New York's Secret Subway." *American Heritage* (Winter 1997). Accessed July 15, 2010. http://www.americanheritage.com/articles/magazine/it/1997/3/1997_3_44.shtml.

Baumgartner, Henry. "When the U.S. Mail Went Down the Tubes." *Mechanical Engineering*, October 2001, 118.

Bellamy, Edward. *Looking Backward, 2000–1887*. Boston: Houghton Mifflin, 1917.

Beniger, James R. *The Control Revolution: Technological and Economic Origins of the Information Society*. Cambridge, MA: Harvard University Press, 1986.

Biederman, Marcia. "This Old Technology Hasn't Gone Down the Tubes." *New York Times*, July 5, 1998. Accessed July 23, 2010. http://www.nytimes.com/1998/07/05/nyregion-/neighborhood-report-new-york-up-close-this-old-technology-hasn-t-gone-down-tubes.html.

Bjelopera, Jerome P. *City of Clerks: Office and Sales Workers in Philadelphia, 1870–1920*. Champaign: University of Illinois Press, 2005.

Charleton, Gene. "Everything's Going up the Pneumatic Tubes." *Discovery Network*, October 1, 2008. Accessed July 23, 2010. http://blogs.discovery.com/guest_spot/2008/10/everything-goi.html.

Coval, Joshua D., and Tyler Shumway, "Is Sound Just Noise?" *Journal of Finance* 55, no. 5 (2001), 1887–1910.

Davies, Margery W. "Women Clerical Workers and the Typewriter: The Writing Machine." In *Technology and Women's Voices*, edited by Cheris Kramarae, 29–40. New York: Routledge & Kegan Paul, 1988.

Downey, Gregory J. *Telegraph Messenger Boys: Labor, Technology, and Geography*, 1850–1950. New York: Routledge, 2002.

Foote, B. L. "A Queueing Case Study of Drive-In Banking." *Interfaces* 6, no. 2 (1976): 31–37.

Forster, E. M. "The Machine Stops." *Oxford and Cambridge Review*, November 1909. Accessed September 15, 2010. http://manybooks.net/titles/forstereother07machine_stops.htm.

Galloway, Alexander R. *Protocol: How Control Exists After Decentralization*. Cambridge, MIT Press: 2004.

Gitelman, Lisa. *Always Already New: Media, History, and the Data of Culture*. Cambridge, MA: MIT Press, 2006.

Graff, Daniel A. "Retail Workers." *Encyclopedia of Chicago*, 2005. Accessed September 9, 2010. http://encyclopedia.chicagohistory.org/pages/1069.html.

Haraway, Donna. *Simians, Cyborgs and Women*. New York: Routledge, 1991.

Hayhurst, J. D. *The Pneumatic Post of Paris*. 1974. Accessed July 18, 2010. http://www.cix.co.uk/~-mhayhurst/jdhayhurst/.

Lawson, Stephen. "Pneumatic Nets Haven't Gone Down the Tubes." *Network World*, May 24, 2004. Accessed August 2, 2010. http://www.networkworld.com/news/2004/0524widernet-tubes.html.

Levenstein, Steve. "A Series of Tubes: Pneumatic Networks Then & Now." *Web Urbanist*, April 11, 2009. Accessed July 18, 2010. http://weburbanist.com/2009/04/11/a-series-of-tubes-pneumatic-networks-past-present-futurama/.

Mann, Charles C. "E-mail by Any Other Name." *Inc.*, March 15, 1995. Accessed July 8, 2010. http://www.inc.com/magazine/19950315/2562.html.

Mattelart, Armand. *The Information Society: An Introduction*. London: Sage, 2003.

———. *The Invention of Communication*. Minneapolis: University of Minnesota Press, 1996.

Mattern, Shannon. "Puffs of Air: Communicating by Vacuum." In *Air*, edited by John Knechtel. Cambridge, MA: MIT Press, 2010. http://www.wordsinspace.net/publications/MatternPneumaticTubesDraft.pdf.

Miller, Harlan. "Airmatic Pneumatic Tube System Still in Use." 2007. Accessed August 5, 2010. http://brassregisters.com/lam/pnumatic/index.htm.

Morley, David. *Home Territories: Media, Mobility and Identity*. New York: Routledge, 2000.

Obermayer, Joel B. "Pipe Dreams." *The Industry Standard*, February 26, 2001. Accessed August 2, 2010. http://findarticles.com/p/articles/mi_m0HWW/is_8_4/ai_71324391/.

O'Sullivan, Orla. "Tellers Play TV Anchor." *ABA Banking Journal*, July 1997, 55–60.

"Pneumatic Tubes Shoot Hot Meals to Homes." *Modern Mechanix and Inventions*, April 1935, 41.

Pogrebin, Robin. "Underground Mail Road: Modern Plans for All-But-Forgotten Delivery System." *New York Times*, May 7, 2001. Accessed July 18, 2010. http://www.nytimes.com/2001/05/07/technology/07TUBE.html.

Rueb, Emily S. "Whoosh! The Trash Can as a Pneumatic Tube." *New York Times*, April 9, 2010. Accessed July 28, 2010. http://cityroom.blogs.nytimes.com/2010/04/09/whoosh-the-trash-can-as-a-pneumatic-tube/

Rutherford, Jonathan. "Networks in Cities, Cities in Networks: Territory and Globalisation Intertwined in Telecommunications Infrastructure Development in Europe." *Urban Studies* 42, no. 13 (2005): 2389–2406.

Schaer, Sidney C. "Mail System Down the Tube." *Newsday*, January 15, 1999, A15.

Silverstone, Roger, ed. *Visions of Suburbia*. London: Routledge, 1997.

Standage, Tom. *The Victorian Internet: The Remarkable Story of the Telegraph and the Nineteenth Century's Online Pioneers*. New York: Berkley, 1998.

Steenson, Molly Wright. "Pneumatic Post in Paris." *Active Social Plastic*, January 12, 2009. Accessed August 18, 2010. http://www.activesocialplastic.com/2009/01/pneumatic_post_in_paris.html.

Sterne, Jonathan. "Out with the Trash." In *Residual Media*, edited by Charles R. Acland, 16–31. Minneapolis: University of Minnesota Press, 2007.

Thrift, Nigel. "A Hyperactive World." In *Geographies of Global Change*, edited by R. J. Johnston, Peter J. Taylor, and Michael J. Watts, 29–42. Malden, MA: Blackwell.

Thuras, Dylan, and Michelle Enemark. "Pneu York, Pneu York." *Curious Expeditions*, May 27, 2008. Accessed July 23, 2010. http://curiousexpeditions.org/?p=321.

Totty, Patrick. "Branches Get a Tech Tune-Up." *Credit Union Magazine*, July 2007, 56–57.

United States Postal Service. *John Wanamaker*, March 2005. Accessed July 18, 2010. www.usps.com/postalhistory/_pdf/PMGWanamaker.pdf.

Verne, Michel. "An Express of the Future." *The Strand*, November 1895. Accessed July 20, 2010. http://www.julesverne.ca/vernebooks/jvexpress.html#express.

———. "A Great Transatlantic Subway." *New York Journal American*, June 19, 1955. Accessed August 2, 2010. http://www.julesverne.ca/vernebooks/jvexpress.html#subway.

Vescovi, James. "Underground Mailroad." *Inc.*, June 15, 1994. Accessed July 23, 2010. http://www.inc.com/magazine/19940615/3277.html.

Wells, H. G. *A Modern Utopia*. New York: Charles Scribner's Sons, 1905.

Wenzlhuemer, Roland. "London in the Global Telecommunication Network of the Nineteenth Century." *New Global Studies* 3, no. 1 (2009): 1–29.

Wiebe, Robert H. *The Search for Order, 1877–1920*. New York: Hill and Wang, 1967.

Willey, Day Allen. "The Pneumatic Tube System of a Modern Department Store." *Scientific American* (March 21, 1903): 206–207.

Wofsey, Michael. "Back to the Future." *Wired*, May 1994. Accessed July 15, 2010. http://www.wired.com/wired/archive/2.05/tubes.html.

Wykes, Sara. "Gone with the Wind: Tubes Are Whisking Samples across Hospital." *Inside Stanford Medicine,* January 11, 2010. Accessed July 24, 2010. http://med.stanford.edu/ism/2010/january/tubes-0111.html.

chapter fourteen

Telephone Media

An Old Story

Gerard Goggin

Introduction

In early 2010, the Australian telecommunications carrier Telstra launched a new product called "T-hub," a home phone that combined favorite Internet sites, YouTube, short message service (SMS), phonebook, and calendar, with traditional directory services. Telstra's advertisement puffed it as the "biggest revolution in home phones since Alexander Graham Bell's creation." In the image for the advertisement (Figure 1), Bell's proud head surmounts a rudimentary version of his telephony instrument with the tableaux preserved in a glass bell jar. Boasting a brass plaque inscribed with his name, Bell's bell jar is juxtaposed with the T-hub, comprising a cordless telephone and an oblong touch screen.

Telstra's ad offers a handy trope of the long history of new media. Customarily regarded as the father of the telephone, the figure of Bell is summoned to accent the point that this new device is something quite different from what he originally had in mind.[1] Preserved in the vacuum of the bell jar, Bell's telephone and its legacy are at a safe remove from its present incarnation.

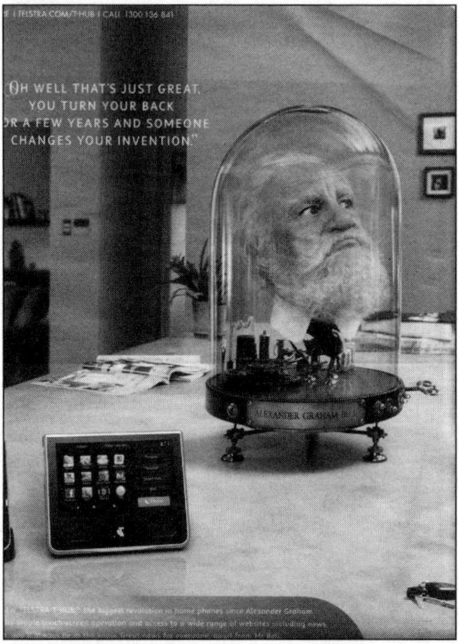

Figure 1: "You turn your back for a few years and someone changes your invention." Telstra Corporation T-hub advertisement, May 2010.

Recall that the bell jar was developed in order to experiment with a vacuum. It demonstrated how once a vacuum was created, the sound from a bell would attenuate because sound could not be propagated without a medium such as air. Telstra's attempt to seal off the histories of the telephone from its new media designs is similarly fraught. The T-hub, we are told, is "sure to become the most useful item in your home." Yet there are quite a few competitors for that title. Not least is the telephone missing from Telstra's ad: the cellular mobile phone. There are two hints about the mobile in the ad. On the bench, right of the home phone and to the front of Bell's jar, lie a set of keys. The other item, beside a wallet or purse that is commonly found on a kitchen bench is, of course, a mobile phone. The mobile phone is missing here, but still leaves its trace—beside the orphaned keys, there is SMS as a feature of the T-hub itself.

As this ad shows, history is replete with its uses, and abuses, so providing contexts for how we grasp what is *new* about media. In this case, a company struggles with its own history, to present itself as decisively breaking from that history, and engaged in epochal acts of reinvention. Its difficulties in doing so are many, which is why I suspect history has been metaphorically put under a glass case, just in case other aspects of telephone history are reanimated, suggesting different trajectories, perhaps with uncomfortable implications.

The telephone has certainly been with us since the last decades of the 19th century, though its histories can be traced back many centuries before that. In this chapter, my particular interest lies in the histories of the telephone *as* media. The telephone has had a shadowy relationship with media, and, until recently, it has not often been thought of as a medium—in the same realm as newspapers, broadcasting, advertising, or other forms thought to exemplify media. After a brief period of experimentation—famously glimpsed from the 1890s through the 1920s in broadcasting of performances and news via the new instrument—the telephone settled into a communication technology *par excellence*. These submerged histories are handy to retrieve, trace, and reactivate, because they serve to think about developments and struggles concerning "new" media, as they play out presently. This is the contemporary moment in which telephone companies—having some time ago become telecommunications carriers—seek to reinvent themselves as media companies. Thus, rather than focussing on the home phone, or the Internet per se, my focus in this chapter is upon the telephone form that has most successfully displaced its predecessor: the mobile phone.

The cellular mobile phone, successor to the landline telephone, has been available commercially since the late 1970s.[2] Sometime in 2010, the number of mobile phone subscriptions worldwide topped the five billion mark, firmly establishing itself as an exemplary cultural technology. The mobile phone recapitulated many of the features, dispositions, and practices associated with the telephone. However, a discourse regarding *mobile media* did not develop until the late 1990s, with the advent of text messaging, mobile Internet, and mobile data, followed in the first years of the new century by full-blown attempts to devise mobile television, mobile games, mobile movies, and mobile news. The attempts of theorists to grasp this framing of the mobile *as* media have led to the remembering and highlighting of the early histories of the telephone, and indeed also of the telegraph, radio, and television. This is evident in the case of mobile television, where promoters and scholars have reactivated earlier media histories to reflect upon this new media form.[3]

In this light, this chapter considers the over-a-century-long history of attempts to create different kinds of telephone media. Such attempts entail great efforts to grasp, promote, and legimitate the telephone—and latterly the mobile phone—as media. I intend to explore not only what are the contexts for understanding "newness" but also to raise fundamental questions about what counts as "media." My argument is that we have not given the concept of the telephone as media sufficient investigation or consideration. If we do so, I wish to tentatively suggest, this will provide us with a much more expansive understanding of these telephone media that will enable us to better theorize their legatees, such as today's mobile media. To develop my argument, I will begin with a review of early experiments with the telephone, from the 1880s onwards, in which the nascent technology appears, resembling, and being assembled as, a media form. Second, I look at the emergence of the cellular mobile phone from the middle of the 20th century until the 1980s and discuss moments where this new portable device was conceived as media. In concluding, I will also make some brief remarks about the appearance of "mobile media" from 2001 onwards, in industry, scientific and technical circles, public discourses, and theory.

Telephone Media Before and After the Fact

The telephone emerges from the confluence of various media forms and many histories. Its main definition—the idea of voice communication at a distance—is a work of some decades. It is difficult to pinpoint exactly the moment when the telephone was "black-boxed,"[4] that is, when the telephone was commonly regarded as a device for point-to-point, interpersonal communication via the public switched telephone network. This is the idea embodied in Robert Hopper's book *Telephone Conversation*: "The sound of telephone conversation is the poem of North American industry, the voiceprint of western culture. . . . The telephone may be our most important communications medium. It is surely the primary electronic medium for interpersonal communication."[5] If the "speaking telephone" did achieve such a status, it would have doubtless occurred at different times and in distinct ways in different places, even if internationally there was certainly a common identity to telephony. Claude S. Fischer's authoritative social history of the telephone is something of a portrait of the high point of this "classic" period, ending as it does in 1940. Fischer examines how the telephone becomes commonplace:

> The absence of press coverage of the telephone in the three northern California towns by the 1930s suggests that it had become an unremarkable part of middle-class American life. The telephone was on its way to becoming an "anonymous" object.[6]

Such an achievement of a stable identity of the telephone telephony involves the interaction of many facts: sufficient diffusion of the device among the population and domestication of the telephone; the concomitant development of collective and individual identities through the telephone; subscribers and communities that are distinct from audiences; stability of the manufacturing, industrial, and economic bases of the telephone industry (that ensure rough agreement about the technical standards of the network and the attributes, features, and capabilities of the cultural object of the telephone that taken together produce its affordances);[7] and differential developments in other communications and media technologies and systems that dictate customary relationships regarding what is transmitted via the telephone as compared to the distributive function that television, radio, and the press serve.

Rich Ling has argued that the mobile phone is what Émile Durkheim terms a "social fact."[8] By social fact, Durkheim means things that "are imbued with a compelling and coercive power by virtue of which, whether he wishes it or not, they impose themselves upon him... it asserts itself as soon as I try to resist."[9] Ling makes a convincing case for the mobile phone as social fact, but the concept is a useful one also to explain the achievement represented by the telephone. In effect, the telephone as it is widely understood and accepted by the middle of the 20th century takes on this kind of social factity. While there are various theoretical issues at play around such a designation, it is a useful heuristic because it highlights the inchoate forms of telephone media that exist before and after the technology of the telephone achieves its firm, classic shape.

When we examine available histories of the telephone, and the narratives of invention about the technology they document, we can discern a wide range of potential visions for the technology evident in its exploratory phases. An influential account is provided by Carolyn Marvin in her history of electric communication in the 19th century. Marvin notes the promotion of the telephone and the education of its potential users by public event and spectacle. She documents occasional uses of the telephone for information and entertainment. These were clearly uses that formed part of media at the time, or which were closely attached to media.[10] As Marvin notes, these "telephone occasions otherwise bear little resemblance to twentieth-century mass media programming."[11] A contrasting example Marvin identifies is the Hungarian Telefon Hirmondó, operating from 1893 until after the First World War, which "for almost a generation transmitted daily programming over telephone wires to supplement the regular telephone service."[12] Indeed such services in Hungary and other countries, such as Italy, were instances of what Gabriele Balbi terms "radio before radio."[13] It may be that there are further examples of such semi-regular use of telephone networks for broadcasting, which may cause us to revise Marvin's judgment, at least to the extent that it may turn out that the telephone was far more deeply involved in broadcasting, and in what become regarded as central forms of 20th-century media, than is widely accepted. For the sake of argument, let us consider some examples drawn from Australian newspaper reports in the 1920s and 1930s.[14]

Early telephone services, forerunners of well-established information services now largely defunct due to online and mobile communications, were described in terms of broadcasting. In 1923, a British telephone service "broadcasting weather reports" was reported in the colonies:

> A new telephone scheme begins in Great Britain on Tuesday by which subscribers may ring up the exchanges between 5 o'clock in the evening and midnight, and learn the weather expected in their district until 6 o'clock the following evening. Rural subscribers will receive the information free, but others will pay the call fee.[15]

Pioneering aspects of the form of radio, such as live concert broadcasts, relied upon relay by telephone lines, something that the public was all too aware. In *The Advertiser* newspaper of Adelaide, Australia, for instance, we find this discussion in 1928:

> The successful broadcast by 5CL in Adelaide of the opera *Thais* from Melbourne, and the unfortunate accidents in connection with the broadcast of the [Dame Nellie] Melba concert at Lilydale previously give rise to a discussion of the question of relaying programmes by telephone lines. There have been a great many programmes from 5CL, brought to the station at Brooklyn Park by telephone lines, and few have not been successful.[16]

To obviate a recurrence of this disappointment in the future, the newspaper recommended:

> There should be a special type of telephone line in use for broadcasting purposes. For speech the ordinary trunk lines are satisfactory; but for the broadcasting of *musical numbers*, especially orchestral items, specially constructed circuits are necessary.[17]

A spectral[18] instance that underlines this point occurred in the New South Wales coastal town of Taree in 1929:

> From about 7.30 o'clock until 11.30 . . . the wireless station of 2FC was heard over the telephone. It was also heard on a long-distance call connected with Taree. . . . Engineers of Amalgated Wireless (A'sia) Ltd explained that the curious effect . . . was probably a product of "cross talk" over the telephone wires. The line, used to relay the program from 2FC, might have become crossed with the Taree circuit, with the result that the station would be heard over both.[19]

The rise of radio sees broadcasting identified with that new media form rather than the telephone. An obscure article in the Queensland *Cairns Post* in 1928 seeks to explain the novel material from the British Broadcasting Corporation by drawing a contrast between the wireless and the gramophone, in which the telephone plays an important explanatory role:

> [The wireless set] has this essential advantage over the gramophone—that the story it tells is not a recorded story but an actual original. Moreover, by being in fact a telephone

and not a musical box there is hardly any limit to what it may be made to reproduce, although always at the will of the sender and not that of the receiver.[20]

Not simply metaphoric, the telephone lingered on as a broadcasting device in the age of the wireless set. Take this 1934 report of how the evils of broadcasting horse races via wireless were held at bay in the state of South Australia:

> Running descriptions of races in other States and from country meetings 100 miles distant may be received by telephone and called to people assembled in registered betting premises, said the chairman of the Betting Control Board (Mr Jelley) yesterday. Mr Jelley added that broadcasting news of races by loud speakers and other mechanical devices was absolutely prohibited.[21]

Rev. B. E. C. Tuck, secretary of the Council of Churches, explained that the Betting Board's decision was the "lesser of the two evils," averring that "broadcasting was the cause of the prolific growth of betting."[22]

A 1937 report discusses the phenomenon of "wired wireless," or the use of radio-telephony in conjunction with ordinary telephone or telegraphy wires.[23] Wired wireless was used in the circulation of broadcast programmes via "existing land-line networks" as a way of reaching "isolated communities and listeners in 'difficult' areas"—and it was argued that it should find wider application, given various successful contemporary uses:

> At the present time there are numerous and often extensive arrangements in some parts of the world by which one or two more programmes are made available by means of lines specially installed for the purpose. In some places ordinary telephone lines when not used for ordinary purposes are used for delivering programmes. In all these cases the programme is distributed in the same way as ordinary telephone conversations.[24]

Wartime provided the motivation for such "wire broadcasting" to be planned for a number of British cities, as reported in 1939, because it is "immune from enemy jamming."[25] The service provided for "three radio programmes, including the Empire short-wave broadcast, as well as the time signal, without interfering with the normal use of the telephone."[26]

Of course, the period of great invention of radio associated with the "wireless" also included the advent of international wireless telephony. From the early 1930s until the late 1950s, when submarine telephone cables took over,[27] this facility allowed users to place (very expensive) telephone calls to other countries.[28] Prior to this, users could transmit messages via wireless telegraphy systems and even pictures but were not able to communicate via voice. It was only later on, however, that the telephone started to take its place with the new system of radio broadcasting. There is the genre of talk radio ("talkback" radio), which allows listeners to call in and converse with announcers, a pervasive and taken-for-granted form of radio broadcasting to this day.[29] The telephone also becomes part of the audience's interaction with television personalities, and their incorporation into program formats (especially game and quiz shows).

Thus far, I have developed a line of argument about rethinking the telephone as media. While further research is really needed, I have tried to point to the manifold ways in which the telephone network articulates with the emergent media broadcasting systems. This is not simply another demonstration of the precedence of the telegraph, postal, and telephone systems to media, which is amply demonstrated by many studies.[30] Rather, I am interested in the profound way in which, very early on, we can see the telephone as media, in a number of senses—continuing indeed through the high-water mark of voice telephony, in which its early and deep links to broadcasting are pushed into the background or forgotten. In the second half of the 20th century, the telephone continued to flourish, with universal service—or close to—not achieved even in the wealthier countries until the 1990s. When we think about the technology of the telephone, however, there is a sense in which its extended aftermath gathers pace with what begins to be called telecommunications. It is here that we see questions of telephone media again being raised, as they were "before" the telephone.

With the development of *telecommunications* in the 1960s and 1970s—that is, the growing sophistication in telephone networks, especially with the additional capacities made possible by computerization, data communications, and digitization—there is recognition of a new force—and new kind—of media.[31] An important moment here is the appearance of audiotext systems, and related videotext and teletext systems.[32] These systems use of extra transmission capacity in television broadcasting systems, as well as the data communications associated with telecommunications networks, to send news, information, and entertainment to viewers conceptualized as part of mass media audiences. This is a moment in which the point-to-point communication capabilities of the telecommunications network—as well as its "technoscientific imaginary"[33]—became marshalled in the transformation of the established broadcasting media, as signalled in discussions of the "new television."[34] The prehistories of such mediations are cannily registered by Robert Larose and David Atkin, who dub audiotext the "reinvention of the telephone as a mass medium."[35] Interestingly, at the same time that the rise of telecommunications occasions talk of media, we also can see the concept of media being broadened to include the now ubiquitous telephone.

Hello Cell Phone

Like the telephone, and other technologies, the mobile phone has various long histories knotted together. Contemplating these, what is of interest to me in the present conjuncture where mobile media are salient are the histories of mobile cellular phones as *telephone media* that might serve as resources for us. So let me explore these briefly, starting with the protean concept of wireless that, as we have seen, has proved so fruitful and constant in the history of the telephone.

Foremost, the mobile phone is a wireless technology that uses radio spectrum. Indeed in the United States the mobile phone is referred to as "wireless,"[36] something that is not such a common label in other parts of the world, where wireless now typically refers to Wi-Fi Internet and other network technologies. The word "wireless" makes plain the links between the mobile and other forms of radio technologies, as previously the word "wireless" was used to refer to the medium of radio (and still is, though mostly now in a consciously archaic sense). The technology most commonly recognized as the mobile phone appeared in the late 1970s and early 1980s. Its obvious predecessors are forms of wireless communications that use radio spectrum—vehicle-based radio communications of different kinds. Due to the evolution of radio-based mobile communications, the mobile was strongly associated with vehicles for some years—the break in design and standards coming with second-generation mobiles.

As the cell phone diffused more and more widely, its role in communication became strongly entrenched.[37] However, it took a little longer for the cell phone to be recognized, and framed, as a kind of new media—especially once the cell phone became a portable technology, a trajectory into which the mobile phone plays is that of the *personalization* of media. This is remarked upon by Tomoyuki Okada in relation to the Japanese *keitai* (cell phone). Like the phones that preceded it, notes Okada, the *keitai* was "originally developed for official uses and for organizational purposes, as manifested by its birth as a shared telephone."[38] As mobiles were adopted during the 1990s, their uses became increasingly personal and individual.[39] Okada also points out that from "the mid-1980s cordless and extension phones were commonly placed in bedrooms as the telephone found its way into the private room of each family member."[40] In this regard, the personalization of the telephone partakes of

> the individualization of television, radio, and other forms of mass media since the 1970s. . . . The popularity of the Walkman [for instance] illustrates this shift away from products used by the whole family to ones used by individuals.[41]

Placing the cell phone alongside other kinds of media is helpful in another way. As we have seen, the sheer scale and scope of the diffusion and take-up of the cell phone placed it inexorably on industrial, commercial, and popular agendas.

Eventually innovations in communicative and cultural practices accompanying the cell phone were acknowledged as media—and new kinds of media at that. The most obvious of these is text messaging. Text messaging could be grasped as a kind of communicative practice with an important social function in particular cultural contexts. A Finnish study of teenagers located text messaging at the heart of mobile phone culture—and of a new facet of friendship, relationships, and social networks.[42] Many studies that followed also documented the ways in which text messaging was involved in the making of youth cultures, new ideas of intimacy, and even new kinds of cultural expression (especially with the much-invoked text language or argot).[43] As text messaging became more widespread, and metamorphized across different countries and settings, its uses proliferated and became recognized as a significant kind of informal media in its own right, bridging interpersonal and group communication, social innovation and entrepreneurship, and community development and business.[44]

With the advent of text messaging, the cell phone takes on some traditional functions of 20th-century media. News, information, and views can now be relatively easily distributed by individual cell phone users, through the viral-like broadcasting function of text message. This is distinct from the use of text messaging by commercial, nonprofit, and governmental organizations that use the facilities of phone companies or content service providers to broadcast messages to users. It is equally distinct from public authorities who establish national alert or emergency warnings that operate via text messaging. Here users themselves generate and snowball messages—as illustrated in the role text messaging has played in public assemblies, such as protest (Manila),[45] times of emergency or disaster (London and Madrid bombings),[46] and riots (Sydney race riots).[47] Text messaging also becomes an important channel for alternative public communication, as has been argued in the case of China where it moves from an interpersonal communication technology to a "quasi-mass communication channel."[48]

My argument, then, is that in the last two decades of the 20th century—the first two decades of the cell phone's rise and rise—the cell phone contributed in a slow and subterranean way to the reconceptualization of media. This happens through the development of what I have called "cell phone culture," and its broadening links with, and commitments to, media in general. It is fair to say that text messaging is perhaps the most distinctive instance of cell phone culture. However, we can point to the fact during the 1990s that there were two large and important areas of media that became strongly associated with the cell phone: music and games.[49] Music on mobiles calls up the history of personal, portable music players such as the transistor radio and the Sony Walkman.[50] However, it is the ringtone—the other signature phenomenon of cell phone culture—through which music on mobiles first becomes popular. The use of the cell phone as a device to collect, store, swap, and play music takes commercial, technical, and user investment before the convergent technology becomes the medium of choice for personal music players. Famously, the Japanese i-Mode ecology features music consumption in the late 1990s, but it takes some years before other countries find ways to make mobile music such a popular service.

Cell phones have been used for games since the mid- to late 1990s, but the distinctive place of mobile gaming has taken some time to become evident.[51] Cell phone gaming has been seen as much more trivial, incidental, and casual[52] than the serious, hard-core gaming on consoles or the Internet. Yet gaming has continued to grow in significance—if, again, like other facets of cell phone culture, not taking the paths expected from earlier media forms and their histories. Both music and games are relatively new kinds of media—latecomers to the predominant definition of media that has the press and broadcasting at its core. Thus it may not be so surprising that the emergence of music and games on the cell phone preceded the explicit discussion of mobiles *as* media.

Recent History of Mobile Media

Until comparatively recently, the cell phone was not explicitly talked about as a type of media. Instances of such talk of the cell phone as a medium are evident from 2001 onwards but rare before then.[53] By 2001, text messaging is well established on cell phones and growing fast. Music and games are also receiving considerable attention. Cell phones are shipping with cameras, and this adds a further dimension to the device's cultural possibilities. New attention is being given to mobile Internet, something that began in the late 1990s, but for most of the world, unlike music and games, was neither attractive to users nor profitable. From roughly 2001 onwards, as the multimedia, multisensory, multilayered affordances of the cell phone grow apace, there is growing interest in designating and creating mobile technologies as a type of media.

The most explicit emergence of mobile media are the articulations between the cell phone technologies and networks and those of media systems. Various kinds of media are directly reconceived for mobiles: television programs are broadcast directly to mobiles; or, failing availability and licensing of spectrum, television content is distributed via the cellular mobile network. Like other new media experiments—the arrival of sound in movies, for instance—such fusing of older and newer media forms is not so straightforward. Mobile television has not developed in the ways that it was envisaged early on—by those who saw it, and laid down standards accordingly—for it to become a thriving species of digital television.[54] While it has certainly found its users, and spawned new genres and viewing habits, in its early years mobile television has fallen well short of the great claims its proponents advanced. Instead mobile television is involved in a complicated set of relations with other media platforms, technologies, and forms—especially downloading of programs via the Internet. Thus mobile television is a number of things, very much involved in the messy transition unfolding in the wake of broadcast television.[55]

The case of mobile television encourages us to look again at the most direct, explicit ways in which the cell phone is framed as media in this post-2001 period. What is clear is that the path towards this kind of telephone media is not at all smooth, as is evident in the range of concepts used to discuss what is occurring in mobiles at this time, such as mobile services, mobile content, and mobile data. Many actors interested in mobiles regard the concept of mobile media as just one gambit among a range of others.

If attempts to inaugurate new media forms for mobiles are fitful, the deep forces at work continue and irrupt. There is a growing acceptance that there is such a thing as "mobiles and online." This recognizes the steady knitting together of the previously separate cellular mobile and Internet platforms. Especially in the case of mobiles, Internet technologies become all the more critical, as a way that mobile media obtain purchase. To give an example: the video camera facility of cell phones is used to some extent to send video via multimedia messaging. Much more common is the uploading of video from a cell phone to an Internet site, such as YouTube to enable a much more pervasive broadcasting experience to occur than would be possible for an individual, amateur user, having only recourse to cellular mobile networks. Moreover, mobile Internet itself for the third time around appears in various countries as a distinctive new kind of experience of both the cell phone and the Internet. Finally, with the appearance of the Apple iPhone in mid-2007, there are new dimensions still to what characterizes mobile media—especially to do with the histories of computing that the "apps" phenomenon brings.

Thus, mobile media are a comparatively recent form in which clear visions of a novel form of media were quickly succeeded by dissolution of such conceptions into a sea of different uses, platforms, and affordances. A threshold problem is that the reframing of mobiles as media is so fresh that it is too early to understand what its "black-boxing" will involve and resemble, should it indeed occur. However, as the discussion here makes plain, another part of the difficulty in tracing the histories at play, and being reactivated, or submerged, lies in the multitude of media potentially inscribed in mobiles—as registered in the term some prefer, "mobile multimedia."[56] The other notable challenge is how to understand what path dependencies, closures, and blockages are decisively shaping mobile media.[57]

Conclusion

The apparent open fecund innovation of mobile media at the present is an appropriate place to rejoin the early history of the telephone as media. In retracing the first few decades of the telephone, it is evident that there were a wide range of possibilities for telephony available before it achieved its "classic" form. This is not surprising, if we regard the histories of many other technologies, or if we hold to the tenets of recent theories of technology that emphasize the contingencies of how technologies are shaped and how systems are constructed, achieve stability, and are reproduced. As part of this development of the telephone towards its classic form, I have noted the work of other scholars, especially Carolyn Marvin, who have suggested that the media aspects of the telephone were foreclosed early in the 20th century. Yet, the appearance of mobile media offers a cue to return and reexamine these histories as Gabriele Balbi, Noah Arceneaux, and others have done. Based on my own brief exploration and analysis in this chapter, I wish to propose the idea of "telephone media" as a way to acknowledge the many crossovers of telephones with other forms more recognizable and dominant as media in the 20th century, notably different forms of broadcasting.

In this light, I contend there is continuity across ideas about and uses for telephones, from the device's inception. This goes directly to the proposition that telephones are as much about media as they are around communications. There are very interesting efforts and experiments in the telephone's early days that frame the telephone as a media form, which would merit comprehensive investigation. These histories of telephone media are scattered across a range of sources and have not yet been brought together—an important task that is beyond the scope of this chapter.

I suspect that the collation of these histories would support the argument that the telephone is an especially unstable media form, far more so than is usually conceded. Certain facets of telephone media are indeed well established and "blackboxed": the role of telephone as carriage, conveying content; the place of telecommunications networks underpinning contemporary media in many facets; the niches that telephony occupies in various media as a tool of media workers (journalists, for instance) or audiences (interactivity, as represented in talk radio, or telephone phone-ins); the rise and rise of the cell phone, prompting us to change our very conceptions of media; the flexibility of text messaging as a low-cost, versatile media form in its own right; and the importance of a range of explicitly mobile media forms, from games and music through video to the burgeoning worlds of mobile Internet. These fertile variations of telephone media lead us to consider the specific histories that belong to each, which, as Larissa Hjorth has suggested in her history of mobile gaming in the Asia-Pacific region, have much to do with local and regional cultures and contexts.[58]

Many other aspects of telephone media were sketched but not realized in the late 19th and early 20th centuries. They recurred as a minor theme, or counterpoint, to dominant narratives of media forms—especially broadcasting and the press—through the 20th century. At various times telephone media surface once more—yet nowhere as insistently as with the development of the mobile phone and the explicit emergence of mobile media in the 21st century. Thus, the future of telephone media is very much open, awaiting in many cases the enlistment of their various supporters. The somewhat quaint and curious concept of telephone media itself could lead us not only to assemble and scrutinize histories of today's new media. The idea of telephone media might provoke us to think, once again, about the very nature of media itself. In this, the putative invention of Alexander Graham Bell, and his counterparts, it appears, is far more open to change by "someone" than telephone companies, media interests, and even historians may care to think.

Notes

1. Beauchamp, "Who Invented the Telephone?"
2. Agar, *Constant Touch;* Farley, "Mobile Telephone History."
3. Balbi and Prario, "Back to the Future."
4. Rosenberg, *Exploring the Black Box.*
5. Hopper, *Telephone Conversation,* xi.
6. Fischer, *America Calling,* 175.
7. See the many histories of the telephone system, including Garnet, *The Telephone Enterprise;* Huurdeman, *A Worldwide History of Telecommunications;* and John, *Network Nation.*
8. Ling, *Taken for Grantedness.*
9. Durkheim, *The Rules of the Sociological Method,* 51.
10. See also Moyal, *Clear across Australia.*
11. Marvin, *When Old Technologies Were New,* 222.
12. Ibid., 223.
13. Balbi, "Radio before Radio."
14. For a definitive account of the first decades of the telephone in Australia, see Moyal, *Clear across Australia;* and Livingston, *The Wired Nation Continent.* On development of wireless in Australia, see Egaña, *Wireless and Empire.*
15. Anon., "British Telephone Service," 8.
16. Anon., "Broadcasting over Telephone Wireless," 8. See also Anon., "Long-Distance Broadcasting."
17. Anon., "Broadcasting over Telephone Wireless," 8. The first use of trunk telephone lines in wireless broadcasting in Australia had occurred three years earlier.
18. Sconce, *Haunted Media.*
19. Anon., "Broadcasting: Messages Transmitted by Telephone," 11.
20. Anon., "Wireless in the Home," 9.

21. Anon., "Race Descriptions by Telephone," 19.
22. Ibid.
23. Anon., "Wireless: Wired Radio Possibilities."
24. Goddard, "Wired Wireless: Use of Telephone Lines," 9.
25. Anon., "Broadcasting by 'Phone Wires,'" 3.
26. Ibid.
27. See Finn and Yang, *Communications under the Seas.*
28. Given, "Talking over Water."
29. See, for instance, Gould, "Cash and Controversy"; Griffen-Foley, "From Tit-bits to Big Brother"; and Tebbutt, "Imaginative Demographics."
30. Among them are Winston, *Media Technology and Society;* and Starr, *The Creation of the Media.*
31. Huurdeman, *A Worldwide History of Telecommunications;* Mansell, *The New Telecommunications.*
32. On audiotext, videotext, and teletext, see Jouët, Flichy, and Beaud, *European Telematics;* Winsbury, *Viewdata in Action;* Woolfe, *Videotex;* and Graziplene, *Teletext.*
33. Marcus, "Introduction."
34. For example, see Gross, *The New Television Technologies.*
35. Larose and Atkin, "Audiotext and the Reinvention of the Telephone."
36. See, for example, Murray, *Wireless Nation.*
37. Katz, *Magic in the Air;* Ling, *The Mobile Connection;* Ling, *New Tech, New Ties.*
38. Okada, "Youth Culture and the Shaping of Japanese Mobile Media," 42.
39. Katz, *Machines That Become Us.*
40. Okada, "Youth Culture and the Shaping of Japanese Mobile Media," 46.
41. Ibid.
42. Kasesniemi, *Mobile Messages.*
43. For instance, see Harper, Palen, and Taylor, *The Inside Text.*
44. Donner, "Mobile Media on Low-Cost Handsets."
45. Pertierra et al., *Txt-ing Selves.*
46. Castells, *Communication Power.*
47. Goggin, *Cell Phone Culture.*
48. He, "SMS in China." See also Yu, "The Power of Thumbs."
49. Goggin, *Global Mobile Media.*
50. Du Gay et al., *Doing Cultural Studies;* Bull, *Sounding out the City.*
51. Hjorth, *Mobile Media in the Asia-Pacific;* Hjorth and Chan, *Gaming Cultures and Place in Asia-Pacific.*
52. Juul, *A Casual Revolution.*
53. The first academic paper using the term "mobile media" that I am aware of is Nilsson, Nuldén, and Olsson, "Mobile Media." It may be that the cell phone is earlier and naturally regarded as a media in some places and not so in others (as, for instance, in the case of Japanese theorists writing about the *keitai* in Ito, Okabe, and Matsuda, *Personal, Portable, Pedestrian*).
54. Goggin, *Global Mobile Media.*
55. See the chapter by Noah Arceneaux in this volume.

56. Koskinen, *Mobile Multimedia in Action.*
57. Goggin, *Global Mobile Media.*
58. Hjorth, "The Place of Mobile Gaming." See also Hjorth and Chan, *Gaming Cultures and Place in Asia-Pacific.*

Works Cited

Agar, Jon. *Constant Touch: A Global History of the Mobile Phone.* Cambridge: Icon Books, 2003.

Anon." British Telephone Service: Broadcasting Weather Reports." *The Mercury* (Hobart), 30 April, 1923, 8.

Anon. "Broadcasting by 'Phone Wires': Value in Wartime." *Courier-Mail* (Brisbane), June 19, 1939, 3.

Anon. "Broadcasting: Messages Transmitted by Telephone." *Sydney Morning Herald,* July 8, 1929, 11.

Anon. "Broadcasting over Telephone Wireless: Successes and Failures." *The Advertiser* (Adelaide), July 14, 1928, 8.

Anon. "Long-Distance Broadcasting: Addresses from Ballarat," *The Argus,* 19 March 1925, 16.

Anon. "Race Descriptions by Telephone: Betting Board Decision—Broadcasting Ban." *Advertiser* (Adelaide), 17 February, 1934, 19.

Anon. "Wireless in the Home: Machine Ousts Fingers." *Cairns Post,* April 3, 1928, 9.

Anon. "Wired Radio Popular." *Advertiser* (Adelaide), 31 August, 1929, 11.

Anon. "Wireless: Wired Radio Possibilities." *Sydney Morning Herald,* 25 October, 1926, 6.

Balbi, Gabriele. "Radio before Radio: Araldo Telefonico and the Invention of Italian Broadcasting." *Technology and Culture* 51, no. 4 (2010): 786–808.

———, and Benedetta Prario. "Back to the Future: The Past and Present of Mobile TV." In *Mobile Technologies: From Telecommunications to Media,* edited by Gerard Goggin and Larissa Hjorth, 161–173. New York: Routledge, 2009.

Beauchamp, Christopher. "Who Invented the Telephone? Lawyers, Patents, and the Judgments of History." *Technology and Culture* 51, 4 (2010): 854–878.

Bull, Michael. *Sounding out the City: Personal Stereos and the Management of Everyday Life.* Oxford: Berg, 2000.

Castells, Manuel. *Communication Power.* New York: Oxford University Press, 2009.

Donner, Jonathan. "Mobile Media on Low-Cost Handsets: The Resiliency of Text Messaging among Small Enterprises in India (and Beyond)." In *Mobile Technologies: From Telecommunications to Media,* edited by Gerard Goggin and Larissa Hjorth, 93–104. New York: Routledge, 2009.

Du Gay, Paul, Stuart Hall, Linda Janes, Hugh Mackay, and Keith Negus. *Doing Cultural Studies: The Story of the Sony Walkman.* Milton Keynes: Open University, 1997.

Durkheim, Émile. *The Rules of the Sociological Method.* New York: Free Press, 1938.

Egaña, Aitor Anduaga. *Wireless and Empire: Geopolitics, Radio Industry, and Ionosphere in the British Empire,* 1918–1939. New York: Oxford University Press, 2009.

Farley, Tom. "Mobile Telephone History." *Telektronikk* 3, no. 4 (2005): 22–34.

Finn, Bernard, and Daqing Yang, eds. *Communications under the Seas: The Evolving Cable Network and Its Implications.* Cambridge, MA: MIT Press, 2009.

Fischer, Claude S. *America Calling: A Social History of the Telephone to 1940.* Berkeley: University of California Press, 1992.

Garnet, Robert W. *The Telephone Enterprise: The Evolution of the Bell System's Horizontal Structure, 1876–1909.* Baltimore: Johns Hopkins University Press, 1985.

Given, Jock. "Talking over Water: History, Wireless and the Telephone." *Media International Australia* 125 (2007): 46–56.

Goddard, N. M. "Wired Wireless: Use of Telephone Lines." *Sydney Morning Herald,* 24 November, 1937, 9.

Goggin, Gerard. *Cell Phone Culture: Mobile Technology in Everyday Life.* London: Routledge, 2006.

———. *Global Mobile Media.* London: Routledge, 2011.

Gould, Liz. "Cash and Controversy: A Short History of Commercial Talkback Radio," *Media International Australia* 122 (2007): 81–95.

Graziplene, Leonard R. *Teletext: Its Promise and Demise.* Cranbury, NJ: Associated University Presses, 2000.

Griffen-Foley, Bridget. "From Tit-bits to Big Brother: A Century of Audience Participation in the Media." *Media, Culture & Society* 26, no. 4 (2004): 533–548.

Gross, Lynne S. *The New Television Technologies.* Dubuque, IA: W. C. Brown Co., 1983.

Harper, Richard, Leysia Palen, and Alex Taylor, eds., *The Inside Text: Social, Cultural and Design Perspectives on SMS.* Dordrecht: Springer, 2005.

He, Zhou. "SMS in China: A Major Carrier of the Nonofficial Discourse Universe." *The Information Society* 24, no. 3 (2008): 182–190.

Hjorth, Larissa. *Mobile Media in the Asia-Pacific: Gender and the Art of Being Mobile.* New York: Routledge, 2009.

———. "The Place of Mobile Gaming: One History in Locating Mobility in the Asia-Pacific Region," 789–795. *Proceedings of DiGRA 2007,* University of Tokyo, September 24–28, 2007.

———, and Dean Chan, eds. *Gaming Cultures and Place in Asia-Pacific.* New York: Routledge, 2009.

Hopper, Robert. *Telephone Conversation.* Bloomington: Indiana University Press, 1992.

Huurdeman, Anton A. *A Worldwide History of Telecommunications.* Hoboken, NJ: Wiley, 2003.

Ito, Mizuko, Daisuke Okabe, and Misa Matsuda, eds. *Personal, Portable, Pedestrian: Mobile Phones in Japanese Life.* Cambridge, MA: MIT Press, 2005.

John, Richard R. *Network Nation: Inventing American Telecommunications.* Cambridge, MA: Harvard University Press, 2010.

Jouët, Josiane, Patrice Flichy, and Paul Beaud, eds. *European Telematics: The Emerging Economy of Words.* Amsterdam: North Holland, 1991.

Juul, Jesper. *A Casual Revolution: Reinventing Video Games and Their Players.* Cambridge, MA: MIT Press, 2010.

Kasesniemi, Eija-Liisa. *Mobile Messages: Young People and a New Communication Culture.* Tampere: Tampere University Press, 2003.

Katz, James E., ed. *Machines That Become Us: The Social Context of Personal Communication Technology.* New Brunswick, NJ: Transaction, 2003.

———, ed. *Magic in the Air: Mobile Communication and the Transformation of Social Life.* New Brunswick, NJ: Transaction, 2006.

Koskinen, Ilpo. *Mobile Multimedia in Action.* New Brunswick, NJ: Transaction, 2007.

Larose, Robert, and David Atkin. "Audiotext and the Reinvention of the Telephone as a Mass Medium." *Journalism Quarterly* 69, no. 2 (1992): 413–421.

Ling, Rich. *The Mobile Connection: The Cell Phone's Impact on Society.* San Francisco, CA: Morgan Kaufmann, 2004.

———. *New Tech, New Ties: How Mobile Communication Is Reshaping Social Cohesion.* Cambridge, MA: MIT Press, 2008.

———. *Taken for Grantedness: The Infusion of Mobile Communication into Society,* 2011.

Livingston, Kevin T. *The Wired Nation Continent: The Communication Revolution and Federating Australia.* New York: Oxford University Press, 1996.

Mansell, Robin. *The New Telecommunications: A Political Economy of Network Evolution.* London: Sage, 1993.

Marcus, George. "Introduction." In *Technoscientific Imaginaries: Conversations, Profiles, and Memoirs,* edited by George Marcus, 1–9. Chicago: University of Chicago Press, 1995.

Marvin, Carolyn. *When Old Technologies Were New: Thinking about Electric Communication in the Late Nineteenth Century.* New York: Oxford University Press, 1988.

Moyal, Ann. *Clear across Australia: A History of Telecommunications.* Melbourne: Nelson, 1984.

Murray, James B. *Wireless Nation: The Frenzied Launch of the Cellular Revolution in America.* Cambridge, MA: Perseus, 2001.

Nilsson, Andreas, Urban Nuldén, and Daniel Olsson. "Mobile Media: The Convergence of Media and Mobile Communications." *Convergence* 7, no. 1 (2001): 34–38.

Okada, Tomoyuki. "Youth Culture and the Shaping of Japanese Mobile Media: Personalization and the *Keitai* Internet as Multimedia." In *Personal, Portable, Pedestrian: Mobile Phones in Japanese Life,* edited by Mizuko Ito, Daisuke Okabe, and Misa Matsuda, 41–60. Cambridge, MA: MIT Press, 2005.

Pertierra, Raul, Eduardo F. Ugarte, Alicia Pingol, Joel Hernandez, and Nikos Lexis Dacanay. *Txt-ing Selves: Cellphones and Philippine Modernity.* Manila: De La Salle University Press, 2002.

Rosenberg, Nathan. *Exploring the Black Box: Technology, Economics, History.* Cambridge: Cambridge University Press, 1994.

Sconce, Jeffrey. *Haunted Media: Electronic Presence from Telegraphy to Television.* Durham, NC: Duke University Press, 2000.

Starr, Paul. *The Creation of the Media: Political Origins of Modern Communications.* New York: Basic Books, 2004.

Steinbock, Dan. *The Mobile Revolution: The Making of Mobile Services Worldwide.* London: Kogan Page, 2005.

Tebbutt, John. "Imaginative Demographics: The Emergence of a Radio Talkback Audience in Australia." *Media, Culture & Society* 28, no. 6 (2006): 857–882.

Winsbury, Rex, ed. *Viewdata in Action: A Comparative Study of Prestel.* New York: McGraw-Hill, 1981.

Winston, Brian. *Media Technology and Society: A History: From the Telegraph to the Internet.* London: Routledge, 1998.

Woolfe, Roger. *Videotex: The New Television/Telephone Information Services.* Philadelphia: Heyden, 1980.

Yu, Haiqing. "The Power of Thumbs: The Politics of SMS in Urban China." *Journal of Asia-Pacific Studies* 2, no. 2 (2004): 31–44.

Part IV:

New Media and Historiography

chapter fifteen

Web Historiography and the Emergence of New Archival Forms

Meghan Dougherty and Steven M. Schneider

Introduction

Noah Wardrip-Fruin uses the phrases "infinite reproducibility," "lossless archiving," and "continual versioning" to frame a skeptical questioning of the nature of the web culture.[1] Rather than assuming this cynical perspective, however, we believe it is precisely these characteristics that reflect some of the most auspicious potentials of digital culture. Digital networked technology would eliminate restrictions on publication and enable documents to be stored efficiently for unlimited periods of time, all the while being continually updated to reflect the most current information. These characteristics underscore skepticism that archives of web objects are necessary at all. There is a common misconception born from these characteristics that the web is itself an archive. While it is indeed a collection of objects organized in multiple ways to guide public access, the objects themselves are continually overwritten, reproduced, reframed, edited, excerpted, and deleted.

On its face, the web feels like an infinitely accessible library, a storehouse of information waiting to be rendered and viewed. These two experiences of the web—the ephemeral and the permanent—struggle for prominence.[2] Objects on the web are continually overwritten, revealing their ephemeral nature, yet we trust in their seemingly reliable presence with bookmarks and saved searches that we repeatedly reference.

While we surf the web, we forget, delete, or overwrite content in certain spaces, while it is remembered, saved, or stored in others. This automatic storage of web elements leads us to believe that many things put on the web can no longer be forgotten.[3] We overwrite old ideas, forget previous posts, delete old versions, and redirect links—all of these things that are of little importance in the everyday activities of the web. When we want to forget, we assume that the simple act of deleting or overwriting has sufficiently enabled us to forget the image, post, e-mail, or other web object. Yet, when we want to remember, we rely on our idealized understanding of characteristics of the technology itself—infinite reproducibility, lossless archiving, continual versioning—to sufficiently enable us to recall those temporarily lost objects later. Documents of past activity on the web are largely irrelevant to what one is seeking on the web now. Indeed, all of that past documentation is often treated like trash to be overwritten, to be tossed in favor of the most current version of content that is more immediately relevant.

As scholars of the web, however, we recognize that it is these very changes that take place within and across web objects that may reveal much about social structure and action online. It is these changes that allow us to understand and develop a more complete history of the web. Web production practices have not evolved in a way that the web itself keeps accessible records for this new type of media history documentation. But web archives can hold snapshots and metadata of developing web structure and content—documentation of web history.

Archives traditionally contain no longer circulating documents that have lapsed. "The archive's formal trappings . . . [function] to tame the trash by turning it into documents of culture and history."[4] In web archives we capture this "trash" to uncover the developmental and co-produced nature of web objects. In web archives we can discover patterns in web structure and trajectories of web action that reveal something about its history. In efforts to capture documentation of development and progress to read history, we borrow from traditional archiving modes. We identify, capture, collect, conserve, index, and catalog. But, as we play with the notion of automatic remembering and forgetting online, as we question the quality of reproducibility, losslessness, and versioning, we must make an effort to examine archiving practice for the web. How do web archivists account for the behaviors of web objects in addition to the objects themselves? How can archiving practices account for the increasingly complex and active objects found online? The dynamism of the web objects we attempt to preserve can be reflected in the practices we use to document and access them in archives.

In this chapter we are interested in the metaphors and modes of archiving engendered by the characteristics of the web objects. We suggest that this activity presents an opportunity to reimagine what an archivist can do, what an archive can preserve, and how history can be written through emerging dynamic modes of archiving. Reimagining how to handle web and new media objects has sparked an emergence of new curation modes.[5] Similarly, this reconsideration of the nature of web objects and their ability to reveal more about the dynamism of web history is sparking an emergence of new modes of archiving. Here we describe an evolution of archival modes in three stages—1.0, 2.0, and 3.0—the final stage of which represents a turn in the definition of objects in which the motivations and experiences of the archivist become a part of the archive. The characteristics of new media demand that we develop new means to capture, conserve, and interface with these archival objects.

Preserving Web Objects

New media challenge outdated modes of information seeking and processing and also challenge the level of engagement they demand from web denizens. New media preservation crosses the boundaries of library sciences within web history. What we see emerging are new approaches to preserving web objects. We see experimentation in different fields with contemporary concepts and approaches, a progression in the concept of an archive itself, and a reinvisioning of the digital archive as an active information space for display and play in writing web history.

The dream of hypermedia as outlined by Ted Nelson and others was to enable actors to read and write most everything from and to a world of connected networks.[6] Everyone would have the ability to produce content and connect it to public content, and access it all as freely. The web was to be the ultimate archive. This dream led to the common misconception that the web itself was an archive when in fact content changes constantly, appearing and disappearing with little documentation.

This leaves us with a landscape that exists constantly in the present. Evaluating structural development or deterioration is difficult if what is out there reflects a permanent present rather than examinable past or predictable future. Amid this ephemeral information-scape, dotted with occasional unreliable elements of permanence, we see a picture of a culture that resembles a primary oral culture rather than an information-literate and networked culture.[7] On the web, we search and retrieve categorizing objects as they are relevant to the next object in a clickstream, shifting our sense of past and future. As a result, production and deterioration of objects on the web can more accurately be described as "unpredictably predictable."[8]

While it is a curious characteristic of the web that it enables us to keep the cultural record constantly up to date, this is not the essence of history. Much of the structure of our online interactions exists in the act of writing over content. We may write recent histories of social action or objects on the web, but our primary sources often disappear as they are overwritten on the live web. This reinforces the idea of the permanent present or at the very least a shallow material past for web culture. As researchers, we examine web phenomena, analyze, and report. There are many structures for archiving our scholarly analyses and reports but very little structure for archiving the web objects we study to produce these reports. Without archiving the objects from which we derive web history, there is no possibility for replication, verification, or long histories of new media. We are limited to what we can study in the time it is live on the web. Depending on the fickle nature of those responsible for serving content on the web, our primary source materials may disappear before our studies can be concluded. As a result, our access to these archives is provided at the whims of those who may not be interested in our results.

Researchers have begun to investigate the potential of material culture of the web as a resource to complement study of the live web. However, there is little agreement on method, few shared practices, and only a small range of common purposes from which to begin grounding web archiving practices. This untethered quality of the nascent field has benefits, as it allows for experimentation in a wide variety of paths resulting in myriad possibilities for future development. It also has drawbacks. Researchers examining the web have little use for archives that are not stabilized, comparable, documented, or accessible. As we conduct studies, we hope that the objects we connect with there will remain in place until the next time we recall them. Rather than "web as archive," a more appropriate description might be "web as unpredictable storage." Web objects must exist online in a stable state for us to view them, and there is a sense of stability in individual web objects. However, this stability depends on many interceding factors: browser compatibility, site owners, expiring domains, or broken links. At any moment, a web object may become unhinged, unlinked, disconnected, or deleted. These resources are therefore not reliable enough to study in real time, and the structure of the web is not stable enough to maintain these objects for retrospective analysis. The documents on which we base our history of the web disappear as we write it.

Web archiving creates reliable collections of reexaminable pasts for evolving and dynamic objects. It is a merger of stewardship methods and scholarly methods and takes on special characteristics of online communication and collaboration modes. Information and cultural artifacts can be reproduced and stabilized online without loss, without having been removed from evolving live web circulation. This kind of reproducibility changes expectations of online permanence, especially for those who use the web as temporary storage or a space for works in progress. It is a great vision to enable all users to contribute to the cultural fabric of the web, to connect, to access, and to add, but there is no equivalent structure to preserve this rich cultural fabric in a similarly distributed fashion. Indeed, the democratizing nature of the web is continually called into question, and yet the distributed ability for individuals to add content departs from that of previous media modes. Beyond enabling individuals simply to contribute to the web, it is an even grander vision that in the future, users would be empowered to create collections of reexaminable pasts in the same mold as the culture they intend to preserve, and with a similarly open sentiment.

The Emergence of New Archival Modes

The artifacts in archives are helpful in retellings of past stories. We can derive much from the material culture left behind. The same is true for the web, though the material culture is captured and impressions made during flurries of activity that produce new and write over existing content online.

Sven Spieker speculates on the nature of archives and posits that archives no longer simply reconnect us with what we have lost or forgotten, explaining that "archives do not record experience so much as its absence: they mark the point where an experience is missing from its proper place, and what is returned to us in an archive may well be something we never possessed in the first place."[9] Archives remind us of stories we may not have told. What is documented in a web archive is not an object removed from live circulation, nor is it always an exact duplicate of the original. The process of web archiving can take time and can introduce errors, producing incomplete traces of original web material, or amalgams of different versions.[10] Web archives may be better described as preserving experience and collective memory as complex objects. The artifacts are shadows of their live equivalents online.[11] Given the nature of the process and the strangeness of objects they wish to stabilize, web archives represent a stage in the evolution of archival forms that reintroduces experience in addition to objects.

The Evolution to Archive 3.0[12]

The developing processes of web archiving represent the most recent step in the evolution of archival forms that moves experience to the center and uses collective memory to parse, interpret, and enable access to archival objects. From the experimentation in web archiving, documentation, and display, we see a transition evolving from earlier modes of archiving practices, a transition in three stages we identify as 1.0, 2.0, and 3.0.[13] Archiving is evolving through versions from early bureaucratic archives, to database-driven search and retrieval structures, to the new forms we see beginning to emerge. Each evolutionary step does not replace the last.

Early archival modes still have value in stewardship practice. Rather, new archival forms are emerging in response to newly mediated information and heritage environments.

Early archives began as bureaucratic entities residing in places of limited access: palaces, government buildings, and houses of worship. They served the purpose of preserving artifacts.[14] Their primary structure reflected 18th-century classificatory tables and specialized schemes for organizing knowledge. Early archiving removed objects from circulation, objectifying and stabilizing documents of past activity. Conserving and preserving these objects places them in a fetishized linear time and historical process. Susan Pearce's description of "souvenir" and "fetish object" collecting styles describes this mode well. These collections can be described as "part of what curators call 'personalia' or 'memorabilia,' and sometimes the personality to which they are attached was sufficiently interesting or notorious to throw a kind of glamour-by-association over the pieces."[15] The motivation behind early Archive 1.0 was to keep and organize pieces of the past; archiving was performed by archivists to capture the glory of the archive patron.

In the next evolutionary step of archiving, Archive 2.0, pieces of the past are not only kept and organized but done so in a way that presents contextual evidence of past activity. What is archivable still loses its status as an object of the present and immediately becomes part of the past. Throughout this evolution, anxiety over disorder and chaos within collections is prevalent in archival literature and research.

Archive 2.0 is motivated by access, search, and retrieval. The 2.0 mode, using database structures as drivers for easy access to archives, has been with us since the 1960s.[16] What constitutes a record of an archival object is expanded to include temporal and spatial context. Contemporary instantiations of Archive 2.0 mechanize access through database structures sometimes including digitized versions of the objects themselves. Classifications and categorizations describe archival objects to facilitate access and retrieval. Categories are typically used as buckets, with items placed into these buckets, and the buckets then organized in a hierarchical or linear structure. This is an excellent scheme for a user who is seeking specific artifacts, and to keep those objects in order and findable again. Keywords are typically used to aid retrieval by search. They simply annotate the item with which they are associated. Cataloging behavior serves the end goal of information retrieval. Cataloging information or objects enables a user to find it again and, depending on the classification strategy and the user, makes this process easy and intuitive. These strategies are useful when the searcher knows precisely what she is looking for, but if she wants to browse beyond the immediate field, she may be left with limited guidance that might come only in the form of broad subject categories. Archive 2.0 rests on a firm foundation of manipulating metadata in databases to point to stabilized artifacts, to search for and retrieve objects. Extant but previously undocumented connections between objects are not captured by the archive, and are therefore not used to further classify objects for search and retrieval purposes. In Archive 2.0, cataloging is performed by archivists for the benefit of archive users.

Archive 3.0 is motivated by access and enrichment.[17] The supporting architecture surrounding the minimally dynamic databases can be extensible, engaging, and social to match the dynamism of objects on the live web. Extant but previously undocumented connections between objects can be captured and used to aid navigation within an archive. Focus on extensible tools to aid access through enrichment would further the reinvention of search from a storage and retrieval paradigm to a strategy for creating multiple paths to artifacts and information. Archive 3.0 no longer treats objects as "moments" torn from the continuity of past actions. What is archivable does not necessarily lose its presence in the present. We include web archiving as a subset of practice developing within this emerging mode. Impressions of web objects are collected and archived while the live objects themselves continue on to evolve on the web.

As researchers begin to take responsibility for preserving the primary documents they use, archives are no longer necessarily compiled for reasons different from those that motivate researchers to consult them. Rather than collecting cabinets of curiosity,[18] these researchers build idiosyncratic archives intended to answer specific research questions. Archives do not simply reconnect us with what we have lost. Instead they confront us with impressions of a fleeting and ever-evolving, rich present. Archive 3.0 is most plainly exemplified by new media art and web archives but is not limited to such collections of objects.

Archive 3.0 is emerging as a compromise or merger between the "ideally . . . naïve" archive,[19] which posits that archives are best constructed free from values of intended use, and the idiosyncratic archive collected to support a particular project. In his academic textbook of archival practice, Theodore Schellenberg explains that to achieve this naïveté, materials in these archives "must be preserved for reasons other than those for which they were created or accumulated."[20] This sentiment is employed in order for the collection processes and motivations of the collector to not interfere with the character of the resulting archive. In contrast, the development of the idiosyncratic archive is directed by a specific purpose of research or event or time.

The idiosyncratic archive is developed to support a specific use but is preserved with the goal of being used for additional, possibly unforeseen, purposes. Idiosyncratic archives in Archive 3.0 reflect the research intentions of the collector. Experimental tools and individual and project-specific annotations can be used to enrich metadata describing the objects in the archive. Traces of web experience left by previous collectors of archives and users of archives enrich the history of objects by showing changes in use or meaning over time. These idiosyncratic archives and annotations, when considered significant for the preservation of digital cultural heritage, can provide the history, texture, and depth that web objects often lack, and furthermore, they can provide rich access points for the writers of web history.

The Archive 3.0 mode is only now coming into its own as archiving and new media curation face a turning point. This turning point serves as a touchstone for some and a point of contention for others. Leading this turning point is a shift in defining the fluidity of objects to include dimensions of activity in the seeking out and collecting of objects by the collector.

Research methods in web studies and web historiography—namely the practices used to stabilize the volatile material culture of the web in order to study it retrospectively—are shifting as scholars and archivists collaborate, and the notion of project-specific and idiosyncratic collection collides with the unintentional ideal of naïve archiving. Researchers examining the web need collections of web material that are stabilized, documented, and accessible. A number of different organizations in different countries are active in this pursuit. The mission and scope of each project depend on the individual organizations that spearhead such efforts. There are massive whole-domain archives, topic- or event-driven archives, project-specific archives, and idiosyncratic archives that reflect isolated activities online. The primary difference between these archives is scope in terms of level of access, what is included and excluded, and the systematic and strategic approach to archiving. All of the different types are influenced by different disciplinary methods and professional practices from library science, computer science, social science, and the humanities.

Archiving web objects is a multifaceted practice evolving in several directions stemming from several communities with different purposes. Starting from the most fundamental need to save web objects, the Internet Archive began capturing and saving web pages by URL. This massive and unorganized collection preserves the objects—sometimes very unreliably—but it does not save the nature of the objects. The Library of Congress and other national archives develop and maintain project-specific but public collections with specific collection development criteria and database-driven accessibility derived from research conducted using the archive. Individual researchers collect small idiosyncratic private archives to serve as evidence and illustration in their studies.[21]

As these different types of archives spawn new practices, new modes of archiving, and new archival research, we call further into question the definition of the web object.[22] Kirsten Foot and Steven Schneider propose "a two-pronged definition of object summed up as object as motive and object as artifact" that suggests a need for additional dynamic structure to capture, document, and display the complexity of web objects.[23] This treatment of the complexity of web objects breaks the cycle of objectification left over from Archive 1.0 and indicates a turn that recognizes the active nature of web objects on several levels.

One aspect of this definition suggests that the motivations associated with the archiving activity be considered as part of the understanding of the object. This notion is drawn from activity theory and suggests that the process of objectification begins with a need on the part of one or more actors and continues through the collection and presentation processes.[24] In this way, the motives and experiences of the archivist become embedded into the archived objects and thus a part of the archive itself. The second perspective on which we focus conceptualizes object as artifact. Our notion of object includes the process of demarcating or drawing boundaries around objects as well as the properties of objects that are shared with other, similar objects. Finally, our notion of object includes an explicit focus on the process by which objects become artifacts and attempts to resolve the tension between the object as "performed" and the object as archived.[25] Jacques Derrida is particularly attuned to this distinction and draws our attention to the impact of the archival act on the impression of the object being viewed.[26] We suggest that objects as artifacts are less fixed and more fluid than some might have initially perceived.[27]

Given these new and expanded definitions of dynamic web objects, we are now asking if simple access is enough. Steve Dietz calls on Hal Foster's idea of an "Archive without Museums" to question whether database access is really anything more than a collection of data for rapid search and retrieval for "a repository of the given."[28] Particularly in regard to web culture—Foster refers to "any dynamic activity"—an archive can be tantamount to "museumification."[29] Many are skeptical that the archiving of dynamic web objects serves only as boxing portions of the participatory and interactive modes driving web culture. Classification schema laid on web objects as structure do not capture the networked essence of objects. These concerns are the motivating factors behind the activity turn driving Archive 3.0 and web archiving.

The rapid evolution of web archiving practices is taking place while archiving practices in general are shifting. To keep up with the rapid pace of content production and subsequent destruction online, preservation practices tend to favor amassing content and ensuring technical accessibility over archival accessibility and accuracy—at least at the software level. This is not a sustainable practice. This practice may be largely successful when considering easily definable and clearly bounded new media art pieces. However, there must be a balance between the two approaches, as they each rely on each other. Finite and bounded new media art objects may be highly networked within but can be plucked from the larger web as distinct objects. This is not true of everyday objects on the web. The objects that are mundane are often overwritten as a normal mode of operation. To study these objects, researchers require archives that preserve and make accessible objects that are stabilized, comparable, and documented.

Enrichment noting the activity of archived web objects is facilitated by the supporting architecture that allows once-static databases to be extensible, engaging, and social. Extensibility and enrichment underline the "complex series of authored stages" of the web archiving process as well as the historiography that develops from those archives.[30] These stages, evident in the selective and iterative nature of web archiving, hold significant implications for historians and their interpretations of archived artifacts, as the process of archiving and the nature of the archival interface are themselves an interpretative model that requires exploration and inquiry.[31]

This progression leads to potential mergers of practices in curation and display to evolve with practices for preserving and making accessible through dynamic archives. We know that the archive is rich with possibilities for social science and humanities research, but we also know that the artifacts are visually compelling in and of themselves. We hope that this progression provides fodder for nontraditional explorations of history by combining practices from multiple disciplines.

The archive should be understood as a "collaboratory," a set of resources for research and experimentation, for aggregating, filtering, and remixing to derive and share meaning. The archive has untapped potential to reinvigorate and redefine the purpose of heritage collection institutions in an era when social relations are shaped by digital and network culture. As a force of activation or animation, the archive becomes not only accessible to broad audiences for broad uses but is also untethered by the uniquely active dimensions of new media and transdisciplinary practices.

Web historiography and web archiving in particular are challenging the boundaries by exploring new archival forms. As web historiography relies on ephemeral, born-digital web objects and increasingly results in ephemeral, born-digital forms of scholarly analysis, the fields of study and the resulting interpretations of those fields are passed over for archiving.

Responses to these challenges are (1) to redefine the object in an archive in a more dynamic way that matches the networked and pliable nature of web culture we seek to preserve and study, (2) to identify and preserve the embeddedness in activity of objects on the web, and (3) to reorient or restructure archiving tools and archival analysis tools for collaboration and dynamism to enable remixing to derive and share meaning. These responses are an effort to remediate or reactivate or animate archives in networked culture, to reimagine archives as dynamic information spaces themselves, which leads to the emergence of Archive 3.0 marked by the activity turn in archiving. In particular, these responses highlight the two-pronged definition of object offered above, drawing attention not only to the lifecycle of archived objects but to the activity—and motivations behind that activity—that have resulted in the object being included in the archive at all.

This is a reincarnation of the archive as a form in network culture as a dynamic information space. The key element to enable this reincarnation of the archive as animated, dynamic, transformable, or remediated is metadata. Lev Manovich describes metadata as data about data that can through widespread use open up possibilities of a "new structure—new interface—new image—new scape."[32] Dynamic metadata placed on objects become the building blocks of a different framework of emergent order. The relational database access of Archive 2.0 is a first step. Moving that from mere access to access and enrichment to incorporate the activity and experience of a complex archival object as collective memory is the essence of emerging Archive 3.0 modes.

The focus on access and enrichment is developing from a merger of archiving literature in different fields. There has been much writing speculating on the digital archive, new media objects, and the impact they will have on curation through the development of new curatorial forms.[33] As archives emerge as dynamic information spaces, with a reimagined sense of object orientation, and as we see new archival forms, with object orientation and digital remixing through access and enrichment, we will begin to see these new archives develop with new historiography and curatorial forms to match the progress in digital curation practice.

Conclusion

We face the digital era by calling for new practices given the potential for connecting, aggregating, filtering, remixing, and sharing experiences to derive meaning. However, our initial actions tend to simply translate traditional archives into a static digital format rather than animating them in a true remediation of networked heritage. Archives have long provided fodder for new interpretations of knowledge, but they have also nurtured the persistent delusion that cultural institutions can somehow gain control of history through a static gridwork repository of documents. Newly animated archives may be able to break the strong hold that past archiving practices have had in previous archival modes.

There are particular differences between communities of practice involved in experimenting with new archival forms to support web historiography. Museum and library culture relies on authoritativeness and selectivity. Within these disciplines, there are movements toward structures to facilitate community-produced content associated with Web 2.0, but it is not a driving force. There are different models to consider that prize bidirectional information flow, multimodal information sources, collaborative filtering, remixing, multiple points of view, transgression of disciplinary boundaries, and the comingling of specialist and nonspecialist. Dynamic archives may help us all to become idiosyncratic archivists, enabling us to discover and write histories not told by traditional preservation institutions.

Perhaps we need to break from the idea of simply archiving the web and consider the large-scale development of collaborative filtering projects as a way to record and preserve web culture. The perspective afforded by Archive 3.0 encourages us to break out of the mind-set of archiving objects as authoritative representations of culture, and engage directly with the objects we archive through collaborative filtering, remixing, interactivity, and dynamism.

Notes

1. Wardrip-Fruin, "Hypermedia, Eternal Life." The authors would like to thank Jamaica Jones, Special Projects Librarian, at the National Center for Atmospheric Research for her contributions to this chapter. Early conversations with her informed our initial conference presentation and manuscript. Her editing and suggestions for rewriting improved later drafts.
2. Foot and Schneider, "Object-Oriented Web Historiography."
3. Mayer-Schönberger, *Delete.*
4. Spieker, *Big Archive,* x.
5. Graham and Cook, *Rethinking Curating.*
6. Nelson, *Literary Machines,* 93.1.
7. Ong, *Orality and Literacy.*
8. Kirsten A. Foot, personal communication, May 28, 2010.
9. Spieker, *Big Archive,* 3.
10. Brügger, "Archiving Websites."
11. Zettl, "Back to Plato's Cave."
12. We developed this terminology while revisiting the September 11 web archive (http://september11.archive.org/) in preparation for the tenth anniversary of the terrorist attacks. It reflects our experiences building the archive and conducting research with other scholars using the archive. The terminology references the social structures in Web 2.0 and Web 3.0, though this progression in archival practice is not a direct corollary. The social qualities typically associated with Web 2.0 are not manifested in archival practice until Archive 3.0 at the earliest. Sociable architectures in archival practice enabling researchers to create and share their own web archives are still developing.
13. Michael Shanks and Christopher Witmore articulate a similar progression in archiving as it relates to archaeological practice. They describe Archive 3.0 broadly as a function of networked architecture surrounding exiting archival material enabling personalization, remix, and democratic access. See Shanks and Witmore, "Memory Practices and the Archaeological Imagination."
14. Derrida, *Archive Fever.*
15. Pearce, *Museums, Objects and Collections,* 69–71.
16. Spieker, *Big Archive.*

17. Dougherty and van den Heuvel, "Historical Infrastructures for Web Archiving."
18. Weschler, *Mr. Wilson's Cabinet of Wonder.*
19. Yerushalmi, "Series Z."
20. Schellenberg, *Modern Archives,* 13.
21. At the time of this writing in 2010, these collections are private and inaccessible because there are few places to serve and share such research resources.
22. Brügger, "Archiving Websites."
23. Foot and Schneider, "Object-Oriented Web Historiography," 64.
24. Foot, "Pursuing an Evolving Object," 132.
25. Schimmel and Stiles, *Out of Actions.*
26. Derrida, *Archive Fever.*
27. Levy, *Scrolling Forward.*
28. Dietz, "The Database Imaginary."
29. Ibid., para. 2.
30. Thomas, "Computing and the Historical Imagination."
31. Ibid.
32. Jacobsen and Søndergaard, *Re_Action,* 103.
33. Paul, *New Media in the White Cube and Beyond.*

Works Cited

Brügger, Niels. "Archiving Websites: General Considerations and Strategies." Accessed August 1, 2010. http://www.cfi.au.dk/publikationer/archiving/pdf.

Derrida, Jaques. *Archive Fever: A Freudian Impression.* Chicago: University of Chicago Press, 1995.

Dietz, Steve. "The Database Imaginary: Memory_Archive_Database v 4.0." 2004. Accessed June 13, 2010. http://databaseimaginary.banff.org/getEssay.php?id=1&t=1.

Dougherty, Meghan, and Charles van den Heuvel. "Historical Infrastructures for Web Archiving: Annotation of Ephemeral Collections for Research and Cultural Heritage." Paper presented at the Massachusetts Institute of Technology "6th Media in Transition" conference, Cambridge, MA, April 24–26, 2009.

Foot, Kirsten A. "Pursuing an Evolving Object: Object Formation and Identification in a Conflict Monitoring Network." *Mind, Culture and Activity* 9, no. 2 (2002): 132–149.

———, and Steven M. Schneider. "Object-Oriented Web Historiography." In *Web History,* edited by Niels Brügger, 61–82. New York: Peter Lang, 2010.

Graham, Beryl, and Sarah Cook. *Rethinking Curating: Art after New Media.* Cambridge, MA: MIT Press, 2010.

Jacobsen, Mogens, and Morten Søndergaard, eds. *Re_Action: The Digital Archive Experience.* Aalborg, Denmark: Aalborg University Press, 2009.

Levy, David. *Scrolling Forward.* New York: Arcade Publishing, 2001.

Mayer-Schönberger, Viktor. *Delete: The Virtue of Forgetting in the Digital Age.* Princeton, NJ: Princeton University Press, 2009.

Nelson, Ted. *Literary Machines 93.1.* Sausalito, CA: Mindful Press, 1993.

Ong, Walter. *Orality and Literacy: The Technologizing of the Word.* New York: Routledge, 1982.

Paul, Christiane, ed. *New Media in the White Cube and Beyond: Curatorial Models for Digital Art.* Berkeley: University of California Press, 2009.

Pearce, Susan M. *Museums, Objects and Collections.* Washington, DC: Smithsonian Institution Press, 1992.

Schellenberg, Theodore R. *Modern Archives: Principles and Techniques.* Chicago: University of Chicago Press, 1956.

Schimmel, Paul, and Kristin Stiles. *Out of Actions: Between Performances and the Object, 1949–1979.* New York: Thames and Hudson, 1998.

Shanks, Michael, and Christopher Witmore. "Memory Practices and the Archaeological Imagination in Risk Society: Design and Long Term Community." In *Unquiet Pasts: Risk Society, Lived Cultural Heritage, and Re-designing Reflexivity*, edited by Stephanie Koerner and Ian Russell. Surrey, UK: Ashgate Publishing, 2010.

Spieker, Sven. *Big Archive: Art from Bureaucracy.* Cambridge, MA: MIT Press, 2008.

Thomas, William G. "Computing and the Historical Imagination." In *A Companion to Digital Humanities*, edited by Susan Schreibman, Ray Siemens, and John Unsworth. Oxford: Blackwell, 2004. Accessed July 15, 2010. http://www.digitalhumanities.org/companion/.

Wardrip-Fruin, Noah. "Hypermedia, Eternal Life and the Impermanence Agent." Paper presented at the "Digital Arts and Culture" conference, Atlanta, GA, 1999.

Weschler, Lawrence. *Mr. Wilson's Cabinet of Wonder: Pronged Ants, Horned Humans, Mice on Toast, and Other Marvels of Jurassic Technology.* New York: Vintage Books, 1995.

Yerushalmi, Josef Hayim. "Series Z: An Archival Fantasy." *European Journal of Psychoanalysis* 3–4 (1997).

Zettl, Herbert. Back to Plato's Cave: Virtual Reality." In *Communication and Cyberspace: Social Interaction in an Electronic Environment*, edited by Lance Strate, Ron Jacobson, and Stephanie B. Gibson, 83–94. Cresskill, NJ: Hampton Press, 1996.

chapter sixteen

The Evolution of Audience Labor

Appropriating Online Activities

Fernando Bermejo

Introduction

The aim of this chapter is to examine the evolving form of media economics through the lens of audience labor. It links the ideas of audience activity and audience labor in order to contrast the work performed by the audience of the cultural and mass media industries with the work of the online audience. It then proceeds to examine recent changes in the process of appropriation of this labor.

In the field of communication studies, the approach proposed here could be considered somewhat unusual in several dimensions: the fact that it incorporates a historical component, that it addresses economic issues, and that it focuses on labor. The first thing I would like to interrogate, however, is the too-frequent assumption that we have entered a "new" era, with "new" media at its center—as opposed to an "old" era with "mass" media at its center—and how this assumption has led to an overemphasis on discontinuities and a disregard of historical contextualizations. But, as David Morley has remarked, "we also need to investigate the continuities, overlaps, and modes of symbiosis between old and new technologies of symbolic and material communications,"[1] and this is only possible through a careful effort to place contemporary developments in historical perspective. Second, the general emphasis on the virtual, the cultural, and the textual that permeates most of contemporary work in communication has relegated issues of material and economic analysis to a somewhat marginal role in our efforts to understand the current media environment. In spite of the contributions of the political economy of communication to our understanding of modern forms of communication, "political economy has tended to foreground corporate and state structures and institutions," and even when it has addressed the issue of commodification, it "has tended to concentrate on its embodiment in media content, to a lesser degree on media audiences, and paid surprisingly little attention to the labor process in the communication industries."[2] As a result, the question of labor "has become marginal for media studies as compared with questions of ownership (within political economy) and consumption (within cultural studies)."[3]

Approaching an analysis of communication media from the point of view of audience labor may also be subject to a general challenge to its very core idea. To what extent can we conceive of what audiences do in relation to media as "labor"? Audiences play and are entertained, they choose and disconnect, they interpret and use. Isn't labor something very different, effortful and compulsory, structured and regulated, involving some kind of wage? No doubt, it is always possible to question the uses of certain complex concepts. Nonetheless, the idea that audiences work is not new. Dallas Smythe contended that "all non-sleeping time of most of the population is work time," and that working as audiences took the lion's share of people's work done outside the workplace.[4] More recently, Shawn Shimpach has pointed out that a "significant but often overlooked site of cultural and creative labor resides within the audience for the mass culture industries. [. . . T]he audience, as a matter of being the audience, performs labor."[5] And Tiziana Terranova has argued that the provision of free labor on the part of consumers of culture, audiences, and online users is not simply "an innovative development of the familiar logic of capitalist exploitation" but, rather, "a trait of the cultural economy at large, and an important, and yet undervalued, force in advanced capitalist societies."[6]

If, in spite of all these views, we still share Vincent Mosco's doubts regarding the appropriateness of applying the term "labor" to what audiences do,[7] we can perhaps help explain and justify the relevance of the approach presented here by relating the idea of audience labor to another idea that has a long-lasting and established tradition in communication research: "audience activity."

Audience Activity and Audience Labor

The idea of audience labor directs our attention to those acts performed by audience members that, because of their economic significance, end up being appropriated by the media and cultural industries. This means that the idea of "audience labor" is necessarily related to that of "audience activity." And it is so on at least two levels. First, debates surrounding the issue of audience labor can help us understand the central topic in communication research that "audience activity" constitutes. As Mosco pointed out, "it is useful to think about analogies between audience activity and the labor process because the latter is a dynamic activity involving complicity and contestation between capital and labor over control of the process and the product" and this process of complicity and contestation parallels the most common characterizations of audience activity—between the inert and passive couch potato and the active producer of meanings and texts.[8] In this sense, the opposing views of audiences as passive or active are similar to the debates regarding the exploitative or pleasurable nature of audience labor. If this is the case, then a proper analysis of the issue of audience labor can make a significant contribution to the long-lasting debate on audience activity by serving as a kind of mirror with which to contrast ideas and approaches.

On a second level, the ideas of labor and activity as they refer to audiences are necessarily linked to the extent that we need a map of audience activity if we want to map audience labor. Audience activity and passivity have probably been the most central issue throughout the evolution of audience research over the past decades. However, the idea of audience activity has rarely been confronted head on and often remains underdefined. It is difficult to find in the audience research literature attempts to catalogue or categorize the different forms of audience activity—and, furthermore, to specify which of the different forms is being addressed at any given moment.[9] Not only would a classification and clarification of the different forms of audience activity be helpful to audience research debates concerning these issues, it would also serve as a guide or map that would allow us to better understand the evolution of those audience activities that can be described as labor. And, since this chapter attempts to map the evolution of audience labor, it might be worth carrying out a preliminary and necessarily sketchy classification of the uses and meanings of "audience activity."

The first type of activity performed by audience members to which we may refer when we talk about audience activity is "perceptual" in nature. Audience members need to apprehend through their senses the information—in the form of light, sound, etcetera—being generated by the media. It is this use of the idea of activity that gave way to Marshall McLuhan's distinction between hot and cool media. In this distinction hot media saturate one of the senses, while cool media leave perceptual gaps that need to be filled in by the audience, and thus McLuhan's assertion that "[h]ot media are, therefore, low in participation, and cool media are high in participation or completion by the audience."[10] It can be argued that this type of activity is almost unconscious and automatic and presents little variability across audience members.[11]

A second use of the concept of audience activity, and the one that has received most of the attention in media and communication studies, can be labelled as "interpretative." In this sense Stuart Hall's "encoding/decoding" model can be considered the canonical recognition of the semiotic activities of audiences.[12] Since then, the issue of interpretation has been central to any understanding of audiences, particularly in the cultural studies tradition. However, as Klaus Krippendorff has plainly stated, "nobody can directly observe or access someone else's understanding," it can only be inferred by someone from observed practices, whether discursive or non-discursive.[13] Therefore, the interpretative activities of the audience can only be known through subsequent communicative acts on the part of audience members or by monitoring their subsequent behavior.

A third conception of audience activity springs from the relationship between audience members' behavior and different media technologies and contents, and can be labelled as "use-related activity." The idea of media use, which has also played a significant role in the history and evolution of audience research, can for our purposes here be divided into two different subcategories. A first type of activities referred to as media use derives from the specific technological characteristics of the media and has to do with the audience's ability to shape the circumstances of media consumption. From this point of view we can say that the television audience of the '90s was, at least potentially, more active than the television audience of the '70s, because through the use of remote controls and video recorders it was able to exert more control over the process of television viewing. Similarly, from this point of view it can be argued that with the pervasiveness of digital devices the audience has the potential to be increasingly active. The second type of activity that can be referred to in terms of use has to do not with the technological characteristics of the medium, but with the psychological and social uses to which media are put by audiences. It is on this idea of media use that the "uses and gratifications" tradition of media research focuses.

Finally, we can distinguish a fourth type of activity—with, in its turn, two subcategories—that we can refer to when we speak of audience activity. In this fourth category, members of the audience perform an action that is either directed at the communication process that "created" the audience or is directed towards an entirely different realm that was somehow involved in the communicative process—we could label this fourth type of activity as "action oriented." The first kind of action-oriented activity, the one that turns back to the very communicative process, consists in the creation of a "text" by a member of the audience that serves as a reply or a continuation of the communicative process that turned her into a member of the audience. Examples of such an activity are a letter to the editor, a call to a talk show, a comment to a blog post, etcetera. In these instances the audience, which is always the receiver, turns into the sender. But the action initiated member might also be directed at a realm that lies outside th process, giving way to the second subcategory of action-oriented a instance, an audience member might, as a result of something viewed on television, decide to join an NGO or start her own organization, or she might go out and purchase the product featured in a commercial.[14]

As we have seen, the idea of audience activity turns out to be a rather multifaceted phenomenon. From the possible uses of "audience activity" discussed above, perhaps the most common ones in the field of audience research are those that look at the audience as interpreter and the audience as user. But our focus here is not on any of these types of activities as such but only on those specific audience activities that may have an impact on media economics, be conceptualized as work, and be appropriated by cultural and media industries—normally in exchange not of a wage but of some content or service. In what follows, this chapter will look at the different audience activities afforded by communication media in their historical evolution and will examine the economic significance of those activities. I will commence my analysis by contrasting the cultural industries—book, music, film—with advertising-supported mass media. I will then examine how the increasing interactivity and flexibility provided by digital media allow for new forms of activities, and, finally, I will examine how this range of activities is being appropriated by online firms in novel ways.

From the Cultural Industries to the Mass Media

Even though we may consider the distant origins of the media audience to reside in the live spectacles of antiquity[15] or in different forms of live communication in which senders and receivers, performers and audiences, gather in a particular space and time, it is probably more relevant to our purposes here to begin with the historical moment when communication started to be technically and materially mediated. When public communication processes became mediated by technology, starting with the printing press and followed by photography, sound recording and film, information in its different forms—the written word, sound, still and moving images—was recorded, captured, imprinted, copied, and distributed in a material container. This process planted the seeds of the cultural industries, since communicative products became commodities that could be manufactured, copied, and sold, while access to them could be restricted and made conditional on the payment of a price thanks both to material barriers—in terms of the ownership of both the means of production and the actual material substrate on which information was recorded—and to the legal scaffolding of copyrights. These physical containers with words, music, or images were but products that could be purchased with the money obtained from waged labor. In this sense, the work of the audience was separated from the process of cultural and media consumption. No doubt, the audience could be active in many ways—though it was not as active as it could be in live performances[16]—but its activities in relation to the communication process did not have much economic relevance to an industry that was mainly concerned with collecting the revenues from the sale of its products.

The advent of the mass media, starting with large-circulation newspapers and following with radio and television, led to a decrease in the importance of the physical container. This made the ability to charge for content more complicated—and in the case of broadcasting, impossible. As a consequence, programmers had to search for alternative forms of revenue. The whole economic dynamic between audiences and producers started to change when advertising became a significant source of revenue for the media industry. However, the meaning of this change with respect to audience work did not become apparent until much later. It was through the work of Dallas Smythe that the role of audiences as an essential element for understanding the economics of communication media gained significant attention. In particular, with his "blindspot" article Smythe placed audiences at the center of our understanding of advertising-supported media. In Smythe's view, the commodity produced by advertising-supported media was not content but audiences. Audiences were attracted by the free lunch of programming, and they were then packaged and sold to advertisers thanks to the work of the ratings industry. In this process, the "work which audience members perform for the advertiser to whom they have been sold is to learn to buy particular 'brands' of consumer goods, and to spend their income accordingly. In short, they work to create the demand for advertised goods."[17] Smythe's view of audience labor focused on its role in the economy at large. However, it did not specify the nature of the work being performed within the communicative process itself to later be appropriated by the media. This is what Sut Jhally and Bill Livant did when they analyzed the process of television viewing. They pointed out that the audience works at "watching extra," at watching what it doesn't want to watch, in other words, the commercials.[18]

Thus, it is possible to conclude from the ideas presented here that in advertising-supported media the audience labors in three related dimensions. In the first instance, it initially works at watching something that it doesn't want to watch—the commercials. If the audience could choose—so the argument goes—it would not watch the commercials. In a second instance, as the audience watches the advertisements, it performs an additional type of work that has to do with interpretation and persuasion: it learns to purchase the advertised products and brands. This learning process culminates in a third act: that of purchasing what was presented in the commercial using the money obtained through waged labor.

Online Labor

The Internet constitutes such a complex and multifaceted phenomenon that any attempt to summarize what it represents always seems simplistic and inadequate. But, in the context of the goals of this chapter, perhaps the best way to address this challenge is by saying that the Internet is a huge system for data collection and storage that allows those who use it to do things with information. This brief description allows us to frame the issue of online labor. First, the variety of actions afforded by digital media is astounding. It includes all possible activities afforded by previous communication media while adding a host of new ones—from reading to writing, from exposure to purchase. Second, those activities leave a trace that can be collected, registered, combined, accessed, analyzed, and used in ways that were not possible before. As a result, the forms of audience labor that characterized legacy media according to the political economy tradition—being exposed to content and learning how to purchase advertised goods—can be supplemented with new forms of labor.

All these new forms of labor can perhaps be grouped under the umbrella of "crowdsourcing," which refers to how "distributed labor networks are using the Internet to exploit the spare processing power of millions of human brains."[19] The concept of crowdsourcing promises to cover the whole range of possible forms of online labor—from online scientific competitions to Amazon's Mechanical Turk, from a marketplace for amateur photography to Wikipedia. But perhaps the most widely discussed feature of the current online environment consists in its ability to blur the distinctions between the consumers and producers of information. As a result, new concepts, such as "produsage," "a new hybrid form of simultaneous production and usage," have been put forth to account for the current online environment, particularly for what has come to be known as Web 2.0.[20]

But the current online environment does something more than merely allow for the possibility of simultaneously being consumers and producers of information. One of the defining features of today's Internet is the double articulation of audience labor: users are producers of content that attracts other users while, at the same time, generating data about themselves that is used to turn them into consumers. It is, therefore, "crucial to understand the new role of users as both *content providers* and *data providers*."[21] This data can and does often include the very content produced as well as the technological use of digital communication tools and covers every single activity performed through the Internet, from the establishment of relationships to the purchase of products. The range of this information and the ways of obtaining it are astounding: login forms, e-mail addresses, IP addresses, persistent cookies, web beacons, flash cookies, etcetera. For the first time in media history, every interaction with the medium is recorded and stored. Technological use, a form of audience activity that had for the most part remained alien to the process of commodification, has become an essential fuel for a digital economy that uses it to improve the process of value generation through increasingly more targeted advertising and marketing.

In sum, while the same types of audience activity that preceded the Internet still have a presence online, others that were somewhat marginal have acquired a growing importance. As a result, new ways of using audience activity for business purposes have emerged, and the labor of online audiences is much more complex than that performed by the audience of other media or cultural industries. Particularly relevant in this context are the appropriation of the content generated by users and the ability to record technological usage—including content creation—and to use this record for advertising and marketing purposes.

Appropriating Online Activity

In the current online environment, the relationship of audiences and users with the websites they visit is regulated by the terms of use drafted by website managers. From the point of view of content production, the work of the audience is appropriated through the use of terms of use in which audience members yield their rights over the content they produce by granting websites "a non-exclusive, transferable, sub-licensable, royalty-free, worldwide license to use any IP content" that they post.[22] Thus, the evolution of audience labor and its appropriation by media firms could be studied by analyzing the rise and evolution of online terms of use.[23] However, it would be difficult to show the contrast between the mass media and the Internet for the simple reason that there were no terms of use that audiences had to agree on before using the mass media. Such agreements did not exist in the world of the mass media, in which the ability of audience members to become producers of information was so constrained by technological and institutional arrangements that there was no need to set the terms of engagement. Since the audience could not participate, there was no need to specify how their participation was going to be used to the media's benefit. But website terms of use, besides referring to rights over content, usually also refer to the issue of the data generated by users' actions on the site. And while these specifications did not exist either in the world of legacy media, the use of data on audience behavior has for decades played a fundamental role in the institutional functioning of the mass media, and this use can serve as a good point of comparison with which to contrast the current process of appropriation of online audience activity.

The use of data on online audiences for commercial purposes has become an essential element for understanding the current state of the Internet. But the commercial use of data concerning audiences is not a new phenomenon; it has a long history in legacy media in the form of audience measurement and ratings. In fact, in the study of the economic role of broadcasting audiences, a key role is awarded to the ratings industry. According to Smythe, the ratings industry exists to reassure the advertising industry that it is getting what it is paying for—audiences of a certain size and profile.[24] The ratings show that audiences are working at "watching extra."[25] This role is so important to the economic functioning of the media that Eileen Meehan stretched the argument further, concluding that ratings are more than just evidence of the existence of the commodity: they *are* the commodity.[26] If ratings are either the proof of the existence of the commodity or the commodity itself, then examining changes in the way ratings are produced, priced, and used offers an excellent entry point into understanding the evolving nature of audience labor.

Metrics

A first possible way to track the changing reality of ratings in order to trace the evolution of audience labor is by looking at the metrics used by online audience measurement and advertising industries and contrasting them with the ones previously used. In the world of print and broadcasting, the metrics used by the ratings industry were directed at linking specific media vehicles and content with the size and profile of the audience exposed to them. In print, two different routes were available. The first dealt with the number of copies of a publication that reached the readers—that is, circulation. The second dealt with the number of readers of a publication—readership. Because broadcasting, unlike print, lacks a physical container, the metrics used to measure broadcasting audiences focused on the number of audience members exposed to specific content, a number that could be expressed as a proportion of the total population—rating points—or of the total number of viewers, or share. The metrics used in the first few years of the online ratings systems combined an interest in the number of times a specific piece of content had been requested—with metrics such as hits or pages—and an interest in the number of people visiting websites or requesting a piece of content, with metrics such as visitors, unique users, or reach. Out of the combination of the two types of metrics grew a new metric that has become central since the late 1990s—the visit—which is neither about the content requested nor about the people requesting it but about both.

In a sense, the metric of the visit constituted the culmination of a process of adaptation of the mass media metrics to the online environment. However, even in the early days of online advertising, a new metric indigenous to the online environment emerged as an industry standard. This was the click. The click is a metric that captures a portion of the technology use afforded by the Internet and that achieved great prominence when Google in 2002 converted its Adwords program into a Pay per Click (PPC) system. Since then, the click has become an essential metric in online advertising, particularly in the context of search engines.

With the increasing relevance of social media in the context of what has come to be known as Web 2.0, the advertising industry felt the need to devise new metrics that could account for the new forms of audience activity facilitated by these media. In 2009, the Interactive Advertising Bureau (IAB) released a report proposing a set of Social Media Ad Metrics Definitions[27] that augmented traditional metrics—such as unique users, visits, or page views—to include a whole new set of metrics aimed at accounting for new modes of audience activity—such as interaction rate, video installs, or relevant actions taken—that could range from games played to comments posted. In relation to the increasing relevance of social media, an additional new metric has been introduced in recent years with the aim of taking into account people's "engagement" with online media. "Engagement" turns out to be an all-encompassing concept that includes a whole range of specific user activities. However, reducing the complexity of users' interactions with online media down to a single metric turns out to be quite a difficult task. For instance, one of the most widely circulated measures of "visitor engagement" proposes to estimate it by adding a click-depth index, a recency index, a duration index, a brand index, a feedback index, an interaction index, a loyalty index, and a subscription index. Clearly, engagement is more multidimensional than it may first appear and may even be more multidimensional than would be useful to many advertisers.

Pricing Models

A second way to look at the evolution of audience labor through the lens of the ratings industry is by looking at the advertising pricing models being used. The traditional way of pricing advertising in the world of mass media prior to the arrival of the internet was the CPM (cost per thousand) or CPRP (cost per rating point). These forms of pricing gave advertisers information on the cost of reaching a certain number of audience members. In its first years, online advertising relied on sponsorship and flat rates, with no clear pricing model beyond a rough estimation of what advertisers were getting in return for their money. But, already in 1995, a host of companies and organizations began offering data on the audience size and composition of different websites. This allowed for the introduction of CPM as a common pricing model for online advertising. The evolution of advertising pricing models would continue with the introduction of performance-based models, that is, pricing that takes into account not only the audience's exposure to content but other audience activities—clicking, typing, requesting information, purchasing, etcetera. In 2001, the availability and use of performance models—whether by click or by action—was small.[28] But just a year later Google would introduce the PPC model in their Adwords program, completely shifting the balance among the different models available. As a whole, performance-only pricing models—including PPC but also other models such as pay per lead, pay per purchase, etcetera, generically referred to as Pay per Action (PPA) models—have steadily grown every year, accounting for 59 percent of the U.S. online advertising market in 2009.[29]

Targeting Strategies

A similar development can be demonstrated if we consider a third possible way to look at the evolution of audience labor in the context of the use of data about users: considering the different targeting strategies followed by the online advertising industry. In order to target ads, the mass media have traditionally relied on the demographic information provided by the ratings industry. In particular, broad socio-demographic variables were usually considered key. This information was usually complemented with, and occasionally replaced by, information about the content next to which the ad was to appear and, when possible, information about the geographic reach of the advertising vehicle. In fact, all these strategies are used in the online world with minor variations, as may occur with the varying difficulty in obtaining accurate socio-demographic data on many websites, or the vagaries of automatization and sophistication of ad placement according to their context (contextual advertising).

In addition to the familiar targeting strategies inherited from the mass media, online advertising has added something new. The most relevant are those connected to user language and behavior. In terms of language, the difference between contextual advertising and the new modes of targeting lies in the fact that the latter rely on the language written by users, not in the language read by them. The most prominent form of this type of targeting, envisioned by Bill Gross in 1998 and fully realized by Google, connects ads with the keywords used in online searches.[30] But it also includes variations such as the placement of ads next to e-mails according to the words used in those e-mails. Behavioral targeting, in turn, has become increasingly prominent since 2005 and relies on the ability to create user profiles that include all kinds of online activities to decide which are the most appropriate ads for a particular user.

In sum, and by looking at the metrics, pricing models, and targeting strategies of the online ratings and advertising industries, it is possible to conclude that within the span of fifteen years there has been a shift from the use of exposure data obtained through research procedures implemented by these industries to the use data on activity—technological use, information posted, purchases made, etcetera—generated by those same users to which the data will be applied.

Conclusion

We can use our review of how audience labor changes with the evolution of the different forms of communication media to try to shed light into at least two main issues. The first one has to do with the appropriation of audience activities and the different business logics of communication media. The second refers to issues of power, inequality, and pleasure and our ability to properly understand how audience labor relates to these concepts.

In the cultural industries, the audience obtained through waged labor the financial means to purchase cultural products, and thus there was a clear separation between labor and communicative products. Audience labor began to achieve relevance in the context of advertising-supported communication media, since in exchange for the free products provided by the media industry, the audience had to work by being exposed to certain commercial messages, learning how to purchase the products advertised in those messages, and by expending their wages according to advertisers' interests. Because of the technological features of print and broadcasting, it was not possible to easily record technological use unless some additional device were inserted in the communication process—and that is why audimeters were introduced. Even with the use of these devices, the only information on media use that could be obtained had to do with the exposure of audience members to a particular media vehicle or content. The advent of digital media completely transformed this process due to the capacity of digital media for recording and storing data on all activities being carried out through them. In addition, the wide range of activities afforded by online media led to a blurring of the distinction between users and producers of content. As a result, the online audience works at producing the content that was previously produced by media industries, while at the same time producing data about their exposure, their technological use, and their purchases. These data are, in the end, turned upon those who produced it in order to extract from them the wages obtained through other forms of labor. In sum, we have moved from a simple transaction that relied on waged labor to take place, to a new relationship in which labor was inserted in the communication process through the use of free content, and to an even more elaborate relationship in which online firms simply serve as conduits that appropriate audience activities at all levels, from exposure, to technological use, to content production, in order to generate purchases.

Beyond this, the need for a better understanding of the increasingly complex forms of the digital economy connects with a second issue that seems worth examining. The question of audience labor, particularly in the digital environment, seems to have a paradoxical component to it. For Terranova, this labor is "[s]imultaneously voluntarily given and unwaged, enjoyed and exploited," and this tension between pleasure and exploitation leads to "the coexistence, within the debate about the digital economy, of discourses that see it as an oppositional movement and others that see it as a functional development to new mechanisms of extraction of value."[31] On the one hand, it is difficult to argue against the pleasurable and voluntary nature of most audience activities. It is also possible to argue that the dependence on audience labor means that the audience obtains some leverage, that there's less stability and predictability for industrial strategies, since audience labor is a type of labor that cannot be managed in the same structured and commanding way as wage labor can. On the other hand, we should not lose sight of issues of exploitation and power.

In applying Michel de Certeau's distinction between the strategies of the powerful and the tactics of the weak[32] to the issue of audience interpretative activities, Morley stated that the "power of viewers to reinterpret meanings is hardly equivalent to the discursive power of centralized media institutions to construct the texts that the viewer then interprets, and to imagine otherwise is simply foolish."[33] And while the long-lasting debate about the interpretative power of audiences confronted with industrially produced texts may lose relevance when audiences themselves are producers of texts, similar debates appear that have to do with the limits of the productive power of audiences, with the rules that govern the production, circulation, and consumption of those texts, and with the overarching logic of those digital communicative environments where audiences interact.

In the end, at the core of the term "audience" there is the idea of asymmetrical relationships. As the concept and the communication process to which this is applied have evolved over time, so has the kind of asymmetry audiences are confronted with: from the stark power imbalance of audiences with political and religious authorities, to the obvious unlevelled communication of the mass media. What we are witnessing today is a new transformation of this asymmetry, now defined by the terms of use, and surrounded by struggles over copyrights and data ownership. In the end, it all boils down to who determines the rules of engagement, the content, and the form of our communication with others.

Notes

1. Morley, "For a Materialistic," 115.
2. Mosco, *The Political Economy,*145.
3. Terranova, "Free Labor." To be fair, since Terranova made her statement, the issue of labor, in part because of the changing dynamic generated by the pervasiveness of digital media technologies, has started to attract increasing scholarly attention. And it has done so both in terms of wage labor in the media industries—see, for example, Mark Deuze's *Media Work*—and in terms of users as producers—see, for example, the special issues of *First Monday* on "Critical Perspectives on Web 2.0" edited by Michael Zimmer, and of the *International Journal of Cultural Studies* on "Co-creative Labour" edited by John Banks and Mark Deuze. This chapter focuses on the latter side of the issue and does not discuss labor from the point of view of media professionals but from the point of view of the work being performed by audiences and of its evolution across different communication media.
4. Smythe, "Communications: Blindspot," 3.
5. Shimpach, "Working Watching ," 343–344.
6. Terranova, "Free Labor."
7. Mosco, *The Political Economy.*
8. Ibid., 149.
9. See Levy and Windahl, "Audience Activity and Gratifications," for a notable exception.
10. McLuhan, *Understanding Media,* 23.
11. And this is why McLuhan is able to draw from this particular conception of audience participation his strand of technological determinism: if there is basically no variation across people, the effects are universal, and if audience involvement works at a preconscious level, then there is no possible defense against media influence.
12. Hall, "Encoding/Decoding."
13. Krippendorff, *On Communicating,* 77.
14. In these instances, the effects perspective and the audience perspective seem to collide in an interesting way. While from the point of view of effects research, a member of the audience who assumes the messages presented to him by the media and reacts according to what they prescribe, would be a passive audience member—uncritical, unable to filter—from the point of view of audience activity, in a broader sense, this member of the audience would actually be quite active.
15. See McQuail, *Audience Analysis.*
16. See Butsch, *The Making of American Audiences,* for a historical analysis of the changing nature of audience activity from live performances to television.
17. Smythe, "Communications: Blindspot," 6.
18. Jhally and Livant, "Watching as Working."
19. Howe, "The Rise of Crowdsourcing."
20. Bruns, "Produsage."
21. van Dijck, "Users Like You?" 47.
22. This particular wording is taken from Facebook's terms of use at http://www.facebook.com/terms.php. Very similar wording is used across the web.

23. See Kienle and Vasiliu "Evolution of Legal Statements on the Web" for a research agenda on and a preliminary analysis of the evolution of online terms of use.
24. Smythe, "Communications: Blindspot."
25. They cannot, however, prove that the audience is working at learning how to purchase the advertised products.
26. Meehan, "Ratings and the Intstitutional Approach."
27. Available at http://www.iab.net/media/file/SocialMediaMetricsDefinitionsFinal.pdf.
28. For a good summary of the state of online advertising pricing models around 2001, see http://www.icondotta.com/online-advertising-models.htm.
29. See the IAB's 2009 "Advertising Revenue Report" at http://www.iab.net/media/file/IAB-Ad-Revenue-Full-Year-2009.pdf.
30. For a detailed examination, see Battelle, *The Search.*
31. Terranova, "Free Labor."
32. de Certeau, *The Practice of Everyday Life.*
33. Morley, "Active Audience Theory," 16.

Works Cited

Banks, John, and Mark Deuze. "Co-creative Labour." *International Journal of Cultural Studies* 12 (2009): 419–431.

Battelle, John. *The Search: How Google and Its Rivals Rewrote the Rules of Business and Transformed Our Culture.* New York: Portfolio, 2005.

Bruns, Axel. "Produsage: Towards a Broader Framework for User-Led Content Creation." In *Creativity and Cognition: Proceedings of the 6th ACM SIGCHI Conference on Creativity & Cognition,* Washington, DC, June 13–15, 2007.

Butsch, Richard. *The Making of American Audiences: From Stage to Television 1750–1990.* Cambridge: Cambridge University Press, 2002.

de Certeau, Michel. *The Practice of Everyday Life.* Berkeley: University of California Press, 1984.

Deuze, Mark. *Media Work.* Cambridge: Polity Press, 2007.

Facebook. "Statements of Rights and Responsibilities." Accessed October 1, 2010. http://www.facebook.com/terms.php.

Hall, Stuart. "Encoding/Decoding." In *Culture, Media, Language: Working Papers in Cultural Studies, 1972–79,* edited by the Centre for Contemporary Cultural Studies, 128–138. London: Hutchinson, 1973/1980.

Howe, Jeff. "The Rise of Crowdsourcing." *Wired* 14, no. 6 (2006). Accessed October 17, 2010. http://www.wired.com.

Interactive Advertising Bureau. "IAB Internet Advertising Revenue Report."Accessed October 1, 2010. http://www.iab.net/media/file/IAB-Ad-Revenue-Full-Year–2009.pdf.

Interactive Advertising Bureau. "Social Media Ad Metrics Definitions." Accessed October 1, 2010. http://www.iab.net/media/file/SocialMediaMetricsDefinitionsFinal.pdf.

Jhally, Sut, and Bill Livant. "Watching as Working: The Valorization of Audience Consciousness." *Journal of Communication* 36, no. 3 (1986): 124–143.

Kienle, Holger, and Crina Vasiliu "Evolution of Legal Statements on the Web." Paper presented at the 10th IEEE International Symposium on Web Site Evolution (WSE 2008), Beijing, China, October 2008.

Krippendorff, Klaus. *On Communicating: Otherness, Meaning, and Information.* New York: Routledge, 2009.

Levy, Mark R., and Sven Windahl. "Audience Activity and Gratifications: A Conceptual Clarification and Exploration." *Communication Research* 11, no. 1 (1984): 51–78.

McLuhan, Marshall. *Understanding Media: The Extensions of Man.* Cambridge: MIT Press, 1964/1994.

McQuail, Denis. *Audience Analysis.* London: Sage, 1997.

Meehan, Eileen. "Ratings and the Institutional Approach: A Third Answer to the Commodity Question." *Critical Studies in Mass Communication* 1, no. 2 (1984): 216–225.

———. "Active Audience Theory: Pendulums and Pitfalls." *Journal of Communication* 43, no. 4 (1993): 13–19.

Morley, David. "For a Materialistic, Non-Media-centric Media Studies." *Television & New Media* 10, no. 1 (2009): 114–116.

Mosco, Vincent. *The Political Economy of Communication.* London: Sage, 1996.

Shimpach, Shawn. "Working Watching: The Creative and Cultural Labor of the Media Audience." *Social Semiotics* 15, no. 3 (2005): 343–360.

Smythe, Dallas. "Communications: Blindspot of Western Marxism." *Canadian Journal of Political and Social Theory* 1, no. 3 (1977): 1–27.

Terranova, Tiziana. "Free Labor: Producing Culture for the Digital Economy." *Social Text* 18, no. 2 (2003): 33–58. http://www.electronicbookreview.com/thread/technocapitalism/voluntary.

van Dijck, José "Users Like You? Theorizing Agency in User-Generated Content." *Media, Culture & Society* 31, no. 1 (2009): 41–58.

Zimmer, Michael. "Preface: Critical Perspectives on Web 2.0." *First Monday* 13, no. 3 (2008). Accessed October 17, 2010. http://firstmonday.org.

chapter seventeen

Digital History and a Register of Websites

An Old Practice with New Implications

Niels Brügger

Introduction: Digital History and the New Media

Ever since the early years of the World Wide Web, historians have debated how the web could be used in historiography. One of the earliest articles on this subject—"Historians and the Web: A Beginner's Guide" from 1996—heralded what was later to become known as "digital history."[1]

Digital history has mainly been concerned with two issues: first, how historians could use the web as a tool to improve their historical research, either as a resource to find, access, search, manipulate, and preserve the sources or as a forum for discussion and collaboration among peers and with a greater audience; and second, how the results of the historian's work should be presented and communicated, for example, in the form of websites, timelines, virtual exhibits, wikis, blogs, and the like.[2] However, very little attention has been paid to the new digital media as historical sources.

This chapter sets out to investigate some of the fundamental methodological issues relating to the web as a source in historical studies. I will focus this general discussion in three ways. First, I will investigate one of the simplest operations when dealing with sources, namely the creation of a register. Second, I will concentrate on a specific branch of historiography, namely media and web history, since this makes it possible to compare the web as a medium with other well-known media types which are often used as historical sources, and from which we have been creating registers for decades. Third, the discussion will be limited to a single type of web publication, namely the subsites of websites (e.g., www.nbc.com/news-sports).

In summary, the overall question is how one of the basic practices of media and web historiography—the creation of a register of websites—can shed new light on the use of the web as a historical source and, thereby, on digital history.

The Register: An Integrated Part of Media History

When writing the history of any medium, old or new, it is important to be able to obtain a chronological and systematic overview of the detailed information which constitutes that history. Historical studies of newspapers, films, or radio and television programs often begin with a register in which relevant information is listed: when and where was the newspaper published and by whom? What was the name of the television program, who made it, and when was it aired? These registers are also often of great relevance for other historians who use media as sources.

There is a long tradition of creating registers and catalogues covering media history, which vary in a number of ways. Some are compiled by an individual scholar or a group of scholars/archivists, while others are produced by archiving institutions, amateurs, or for-profit organizations; some are compiled with a specific research project or book in mind, while others are more general in aim; some are quite simple, while others are very detailed; and some reflect on the creation and limitations of the register, while others do not.[3]

However, this tradition has not yet included the history of the new digital media, such as the history of the web, probably because only a few historical studies of the web have been made at all, and even fewer have required a register.[4]

The Categories of the Register

Usually, a register is created at the interface between, on the one hand, the research question(s) it is designed to answer and, on the other, the specific characteristics of the medium to be registered. The register must be tailored to the research question(s) and must register relevant phenomena in relation to the media type in question. It is not, for instance, relevant to register the director, cast, or principal actors in relation to a newspaper, while it makes good sense to do so in relation to a television drama.

Any register may consist of a number of categories, such as the title, date of publication or transmission, writer, director, and cast. Methodological reflections on the establishment of a register often focus on identifying which categories should be included in the register, and why. For instance: should the title and publication date be included?

Well-Known Categories Reconsidered

The specific characteristics of the medium to be registered are rarely discussed when creating a register. Even though obtaining precise evidence of the title, date of publication, and the like may be difficult, these familiar categories in registration construction do not usually pose any dilemma.

However, the very newness of a medium like the web can in itself call well-known and self-evident categories into question. Are such categories as title and date of publication as self-evident and unequivocal in relation to the web as they are in other types of media? Or do the specific characteristics of the web challenge their necessity, thus forcing us to reconsider and possibly reinterpret them?

Starting from the idea that the web is very different from "old" source material such as newspapers, film, radio, and television, in both their analog and digital forms, I will reconsider some of the categories that normally go unquestioned in the practice of creating a register. First, I will discuss some of the most important categories on a theoretical level. I will then shed light on the general theoretical issues involved by applying them to the practical experience of creating a register of subsites for the website of the Danish national public service broadcaster, DR, dr.dk, from 1996 to 2006. The website dr.dk has been chosen to exemplify the array of potential challenges, since the site is capacious, complex, and has a long history.[5]

A Register of Subsites

In the following, I discuss in more detail how the specific characteristics of the website and its subsites affect four fundamental categories: the naming of the registered object, its spatial extent, its temporal extent, and the various archived versions.

Naming the Subsite

In many cases, the title is the main identifier in a register. In the media of print, film, radio, and television, it is usually simple to determine the title of the registered entities. The name of a newspaper and the titles of the articles in it are supplied by the publisher and are unequivocal, as is the name of a film, or a radio or television program or series. In this sense, it is normally self-evident what should be recorded as the "title" in our register.[6]

This is not the case with a website and its subsites. Although the publisher can name the subsite and often does so, this is not always of help to the researcher who later wishes to register it, since the following three entities, at least, could all be considered the title: first, the name as it appears from the subsite's textual content (using the term "textual" in a broad sense); second, the URL of the subsite as it appears in the location line in the browser window; and, third, the page title that the publisher may have given the web page, and which can be read at the top of the browser window. A subsite may therefore have three nonidentical titles in the register, making it necessary to decide how the problem of possibly equivocal names should be dealt with—such as which of these names should be considered the main entry of the register (if any), and how to handle possible inconsistencies between them, or between different naming policies on different subsites.

In addition, if we wish to use the URL as the name of the website, we face another problem that is specific to the web, namely "redirects": the fact that a URL may not correspond to an actual website but, on the contrary, is merely an "empty" name which immediately redirects the user to another site. A subsite may therefore have more names besides those which constitute part of the opening web page, since all the redirecting URLs may function as a name for the site, thereby multiplying the names of the subsite by an unknown number of "satellite names."

We are familiar with reference systems from other types of media—such as "Read more on page 6" on the front page of a newspaper, or a program announcement in a television flow—but the difference is that these references do not lead directly or unobtrusively to the object of the reference. On the web, the reference directly coincides with what it refers to, in that the redirecting URL and the subsite to which it redirects are de facto the same entity, which simply has two different names.

The existence of redirects has two practical consequences of relevance to the creation of the register. First, it can be very difficult to find the redirecting URLs, since they are not visible on the subsite to which they redirect; and, second, it can be difficult to establish whether a URL corresponds to a website or redirects to another URL and is thus "empty." Consequently, if it has been decided that the URL should be the main entrance to the register, it must be decided whether all of the existing URLs should be registered individually—which risks obtaining a number of "empty" URLs and a very large register—or whether a single URL should be considered the main URL, and redirecting URLs should be registered together with this main URL (the main URL being the URL which does not lead to other URLs).

Finally, this issue becomes further complicated in connection with historical studies, in that redirects are not always identical over a period of time. A redirect which has been observed at a certain point in time may not necessarily have existed before or after this time; it may be that no redirect existed before or after, or other redirects may have existed. Moreover, it is not unusual for a URL which was the main URL of a subsite at a certain point in time to be changed at a later time to a redirecting URL. In other words, the relation between subsite and (redirecting) URLs is ephemeral over time.

All things considered, in a register of a historical source such as a website, one of the most fundamental categories—the title—is in many ways more equivocal and fluid than it is in other media, and in general it is very difficult to reconstruct and document this network of names in the past.

Spatial Extent of the Subsite

The spatial dimension of what is registered can normally be identified without difficulty due to the material or semiotic characteristics of the medium (or combinations of these). A register of printed newspapers or film is based on the material delimitation of each copy, such as separate sheets bound together (possibly sections bound separately, but folded as one publication) or the individual film strip. A register of radio or television programs is based on the semiotic demarcation of programs in the flow by means of transitional markers such as jingles, voiceovers, titles, and credit lines; and a register of newspaper articles is based on both a material delimitation—the individual newspaper copy—and semiotic delimitations within each copy, such as the headings, layout of the text body, and pagination.

A website (and the subsite of a website) is not delimited in the same way as in printed media and film. In some respects it seems closer to broadcast media, as the cohesion of a website—and thereby its outer limits—is established almost solely by semiotic means. But unlike broadcast media, the website does not just unfold in a unilinear dimension with a marked beginning and end; on the contrary, it is more complex than this, and must therefore be delimited by other means.

I suggest that a website may be defined as "a coherent textual unit that unfolds in one or more interrelated browser windows, the coherence of which is based on semantic, formal and physically performative interrelations."[7] In other words, what holds the variety of individual web pages or other web elements together as a website, and thereby establishes its spatial extent, is that they deal with the same subject (semantic cohesion), they resemble each other (formal cohesion), and it is possible to go from one web page/browser window to another (physically performative coherence). By the same token, we can use these criteria to delimit the extent of the subsite. A subsite is thus that part of a website which, on the one hand, shares some of its features (an overall "view of the world," global paratexts such as logo, menu structure, footer, and domain name), but, on the other hand, is differentiated from it in a number of ways (a local view of the world, focusing on, for example, a specific audience, subject, or the like, as well as local paratexts).

To sum up this point: since the website is not delimited in a material way (as are print media) or by the linking of semantic elements in a progressive chain of expression (as are broadcast media), we are dependent on such aspects as semantic cohesion, paratexts, and linking when delimiting the spatial extent of the subsite—and on the consistency of these means of expression over time when trying to trace the same subsite in the past.

Temporal Extent of the Subsite

A register of historical sources such as print media or radio and television programs is based on the rhythm of chronology. Print media have a clearly marked and precise time of publication (month, week, day, and hour), while programs in broadcast media have a precise start time, followed by a transmission time and a precise stop time, all of which are marked in the aired program and possibly also in a program schedule (television series also have a transmission date span). In fact, what defines a broadcast program is that it ends, since if it does not have a clear stop time it is merely an indefinite flow of sounds and/or images, rather than a program.

The subsite cannot be delimited in the same clear-cut manner. It may possess something similar to a time of publication, but in most cases it does not have a narrative structure with a beginning, a story, and an end. The subsite is related to these temporal markers in a more complex manner, which is best characterized as a continuum of publication.

Any website will always have a start time, which is the point in time when it is published on a web server for the first time. However, it can be difficult to determine this start time with certainty, since we cannot expect it to be mentioned on the website in the same way as in a newspaper or a broadcast program. Information about the transmission dates of television programs may be missing, especially in the early years,[8] but websites are rarely provided with a launch date at all. Secondary sources such as program schedules are thereby not an option when we attempt to date the launch of a website, and while press releases may announce a launch date, it is not always possible to determine whether the website was actually launched on the announced date. If our register is based on web archives, the existence of a subsite in a web archive tells us only that the subsite existed at the time of archiving, but not when it was actually launched. In many cases, therefore, the start time is imprecise, since it can be registered only as a period of time rather than a point in time.

If a start time can be established, the temporal extent of the subsite from this point onwards is fundamentally different from that which we know from other media types, since in most cases the website is a continuous publication with no overarching marked temporal subdivisions, such as days or hours/minutes (blog posts and news items on a news page being the exception, but in most cases they are only one element on a web page, and cannot therefore account for the publication time[s] of all the other elements present). In other media types, the temporal subdivisions—such as the publication date of a newspaper, the start and end times of a program—are not placed there by chance; on the contrary, they are intentionally made an inherent part of the media artifact by the publisher, and it would be very unusual to change them afterwards. However, with a continuous publication such as a website, subdivisions of this continuum are in most cases not made by the publisher but must be inserted either by the media researcher or by the archiving institution.[9] Insomuch as these subdivisions are not a function of an inner necessity on the part of the media artifact, they are random; they can be made at any time in the continuum—a day, an hour—and can therefore also be changed. It may cause some problems for the register if the temporal subdivisions are not identical in all archived versions.

When it comes to the stop time of the subsite, we encounter one of the greatest differences between web media and, for example, broadcast media, and thus also one of the greatest challenges. The problem is that although the website has a temporal dimension like a radio or television program, it does not need to have a stop time in order to be a website. A website is a website even if we cannot determine when it ends. But to complicate matters, the stop time of a website may be defined in two different ways. The website can cease to exist either because it has been removed from the web server, or because it is not being updated anymore but remains on the web server.[10] In both cases we face a number of practical problems in determining what has actually happened.

In the first case it is simply difficult to determine when the website has been removed, since we may only be able to register the fact that at a certain point in time it was no longer online. Secondary sources such as press releases or the like are not of much help here, because the closing of a subsite is not usually a news item. Web archives do not help us much, either; if a website no longer appears in a web archive after a certain date, it is difficult to use this information to determine when it was removed from the web server. To compound the problem, the archiving institution may not archive the website anymore (e.g., for technical or archiving strategic reasons).

For the latter case it is difficult to determine whether the website is actually being updated or not. Some websites are simply abandoned, while in others the publisher may write "archive," "not updated," or the like, but very often without giving any precise date. In practice, it can be almost impossible to determine when a website is no longer being maintained, and the consequence for our register may be that at a given point in time, the number of "active" websites registered may be far too high due to an accumulation of abandoned websites. A clear distinction between active and abandoned and/or formally closed websites may, therefore, be difficult to uphold.

Compared to the programs of broadcast media, the web subsite as a whole is often continuous, just as the well-known entities of start and stop times may in themselves form more of a continuum than a point in time, and the website may thus appear to be a historical source that is not only continuous but infinite.

Different Archived Versions of the Subsite

If the register of subsites is based on archived web material, different versions of the same website may exist, even under the same date and time.[11]

On this point, too, the register of subsites differs from registers of other media types. Regardless of who stores a newspaper or a film strip or who presses the record button, archived copies of newspapers, films, and radio and television programs are by and large identical (minor differences may, for instance, include the absence or presence of commercials in archived television programs).[12] This has not always been the case, especially when the media were young. In its very first years, the printed book was usually shipped in the form of individual sheets, without binding, which was a constant source of errors,[13] just as differences in printed copies, followed by "errata," were the order of the day,[14] and differing versions of films have always circulated.[15] But in the main, some kind of standardization generally takes place over time, with the result that the published version will be identical in all archives.

In relation to archived web material, standardization is not a possible solution. To a large extent—and for a number of reasons—the differences between archived subsites are more or less fundamental to their presence in an archive, since any web archiving process creates a unique version rather than an identical copy, and the differences between versions are very difficult to identify.[16] Furthermore, these differences may very well affect the above-mentioned categories—names, spatial and temporal extents—insofar as they may vary, depending on which archived version is used. Accordingly, the differences between archived versions play a crucial role when establishing a register of subsites, which is why it is relevant to register the known archived versions as well as their limitations and deficiencies.

The Register of dr.dk, 1996–2006

I will now compare the theoretical discussion of the four above-mentioned categories with the preparation of a specific register of subsites, namely, the register of dr.dk, 1996–2006. The overall aim of the research project "The History of dr.dk, 1996–2006" is to write the history of the first ten years of the Danish Broadcasting Corporation's (DR) website. The writing of this history is based on a variety of sources, including archived websites, official publications (press releases, annual reports, staff publications), and unpublished material (minutes of meetings, strategy papers, descriptions of subsites, etc.). In particular, the websites constitute an important historical source, on the one hand, as the primary object of study, and on the other, because they contain valuable information about the creation of the website as well as about the broadcaster as an organization. In a historical study of dr.dk it is thus crucial to obtain an overview of the existing subsites, and for this reason, I created a register of dr.dk's subsites from 1996 to 2006.[17]

How to Create a Register of Subsites

The register of dr.dk is based on various sources: the website as it looked when the register was made, archived versions from different archives, and secondary sources, such as official publications and unpublished material.

Since any subsite must be (or has been) located somewhere on the web, it must have a URL, whether on the live web or in a web archive. The URL therefore constitutes one of the principal keys to the creation of the register, and the first task is to re-create a list of all the subsite URLs over the years. However simple this task may appear, this is in fact where the main practical obstacle lies. The publisher of the website may have a record of the URLs of the subsites, but it is probably a "here and now" list, because what happened years ago on the website is not normally of any interest to the publisher today. Moreover, some of the main sources—web archives—are not likely to be of any direct help. Usually, searches for websites in a web archive are conducted by means of URLs that are already known; in other words, we must actually know the result of our search before we start it, since the result of the search is our search term. But the only URL we know is the top-level URL, in this case dr.dk, and nothing beyond that.

However, although web archives may not be useful in a direct manner, they can prove very helpful in an indirect way. When creating the register of dr.dk, it was decided to use the latest existing and largest archived version of dr.dk in the Danish web archive, Netarkivet, as the basis for generating a list of all the URLs following dr.dk, as well as prefixed URLs, such as musik.dr.dk. This resulted in a gross list of the possible subsites. The next step is to "trim" this list by removing duplicates and marking URLs that probably do not correspond to a subsite (such as dr.dk/cgi-bin and the like). The result is a list of URLs that may refer to subsites (either directly or as redirects) for which we can now search in a web archive or on the live web, using our search results to create a basic version of the register. The final step is to complete and verify the register to the greatest possible degree on the basis of reading the archived subsites and any secondary sources.

Although this method provides a key for accessing a web archive's subsites, it also suffers from a number of shortcomings. First, it is very expensive in terms of labor hours, given the amount of work involved in trimming the list of URLs (the gross list for dr.dk included 940 URLs, of which only 339 corresponded to websites), manually searching web archives, and reading secondary sources. Second, a large number of subsites from the past may not be included if the initial archived version on which the list is based does not link to them or if they were removed before this version was archived. To compensate for this incompleteness, more archived versions may be included; however, this strategy makes the register even more expensive in terms of labor hours.

Despite these drawbacks, the creation of a register of subsites provided valuable insights into the practical challenges of this task, and the experience shed new light on the four fundamental categories mentioned earlier in this chapter.

Title

As outlined above, a subsite may have several titles: the name of the opening web page, the URL, or the page title at the top of the browser window as well as a number of redirecting URLs. In cases where more than one of these names appeared among the subsites of dr.dk they were rarely identical, probably due to a lack of standard practice or tradition for this among publishers. In other words: most subsites had more than one title.

It turned out that the use of redirects was very widespread, ranging from variations in upper/lower case (/tv-drama, /TV-DRAMA, /TV-Drama, and /tvdrama for the same subsite) to redirects between levels (/rock redirecting to /musik/rock) and redirects from prefixed URLs to URLs after the domain name (musik.dr.dk to /musik). However, since many URLs in the archive did not work (the material may be incomplete for a number of reasons), it proved in practice to be rather difficult to establish whether a URL was redirecting to something that was not in the archive or to something that actually corresponded to a subsite, which just happened not to be in the archive. Furthermore, as expected, it was difficult to ascertain whether a subsite was pointed to by any redirecting URLs (information on this point was almost exclusively found inadvertently).

In addition, two unforeseen problems were encountered, both of which were related to the URL. First, the URL of some of the subsites had been changed over time. The web address www.sport.dr.dk was, for example, later changed to www.dr.dk/sporten, but the website remained the same. It is not unusual for print media to undergo changes of title,[18] whereas this is not a widespread practice with programs in broadcast media. In any case, such changes will normally be communicated very clearly in the media artifact itself as well as through secondary sources. On the web, however, these name changes often take place unnoticed, and it can therefore be very difficult to establish whether the same subsite has had two different URLs. In addition, if these double names are identified, it must be decided which one to register as the main identifier—the oldest, the most recent, or both?

Second, the same URL may correspond to a subsite at one point in time and later become a redirecting URL. In 2001, for example, /eu was the URL of a subsite, but some years later this only redirected to another, new subsite (/nyheder/temaer/2009/europa). All in all, it became clear that it would be very difficult to compile a complete mapping of the network of URLs at any specific period of time in the past in order to track the changes over time.

Space

In the main, it was possible to delimit each of the registered subsites by focusing on semantic, formal, and physically performative coherence—for instance, by combining the URL with paratexts such as the logo and menu structure.

However, this approach was challenged by a number of subsites that DR created in collaboration with external partners, in the case of websites placed outside of DR's domain name, dr.dk. One example of this was the subsite created for the Olympic Games in Sydney in 2000. DR's official website for the games was produced in association with the National Olympic Committee and Sports Confederation of Denmark and UNICEF and was located at the URL www.ol.dk. It is thus necessary to decide whether such "external subsites" should be included in the register or not. In this particular case, it also turned out that the URL www.ol.dk was actually nothing but a redirect to a subsite at dr.dk, namely, /ol. And to complicate matters even more, in the years following the 2000 Olympics, www.ol.dk no longer redirected to the subsite /ol at dr.dk, but to the website of the National Olympic Committee and Sports Confederation of Denmark. This example illustrates the complex relationship between spatial delimitation, naming, and redirects in historical studies of the web.

Time

As expected, it was generally impossible to determine the launch time of subsites with any certainty. In the majority of cases the start time could only be determined as the date when the subsite appeared in a web archive for the first time. In addition, a further unforeseen temporal inconsistency was encountered: almost every page at dr.dk included a footer with a copyright date (year, month), but when this date was correlated with other information on the same page, or with secondary sources, it often differed from the date in the footer. The earlier date may have resulted from the footer being part of an overall template/CMS (content management system), created before the web page in question, and the later date from the web page being created in a single template/CMS which was subsequently altered. In other words, temporal inconsistencies on the individual web page may make it even more complicated to determine a start time.

Since the register was based exclusively on material from web archives, the temporal delimitations after the start time had to accord with the different ways in which the subsites were delimited in each of the web archives. The Danish web archive, for example, has six versions of some subsites from each day, whereas the Internet archive has only one. In the register of dr.dk it was only necessary to register the start and end times of the subsite, but if what happened between these two dates was to have been registered as well, it is obvious that these differences in "slicing up" the life span of the subsites would have constituted a major challenge.

Concerning subsite end time, the general picture was as expected: it was difficult to determine with certainty if and when subsites ceased to exist. In some cases the subsite simply stopped appearing in a web archive after a certain date, while in others, it continued to appear in the archive, but it was very difficult to determine whether it was still being updated. On rare occasions, the publisher had indicated that the subsite was no longer being updated (for instance, in the form of a watermark, or by inserting "archive" in the URL, or the like). In cases where the register is based on archived versions from an open web archive, such as the Internet archive, we may encounter inconsistencies which make it even more difficult to determine the end time. Even subsites that are not updated anymore may, for example, display today's news, because they contain scripts that are programmed to automatically retrieve the current news headlines from a web server.[19]

Finally, the establishment of the register of dr.dk revealed that the temporal delimitation of a website may extend beyond the start and end times. In connection with the climate conference in Kyoto in 1997, DR launched the subsite "Klima på nettet" [Climate on the Net] at the address /klima, and the site was removed from the server in 1998. But more than ten years later, a new subsite was launched at exactly the same URL in connection with the UN Climate Change Conference held in Copenhagen in 2009. The life cycle of a URL can thus involve birth, death, and resurrection in a new form.

Versions

The various versions of archived subsites in different archives were both helpful and frustrating. On the one hand, having several versions could be helpful when trying to gather information about a subsite's name and spatial and temporal extent, but, on the other hand, it could also increase the uncertainty and confusion about possible inconsistencies. In any case, it also proved important to document the differences in the register.

Conclusion

Taking the specific characteristics of a website into consideration, it becomes evident that a register of subsites is in many ways significantly different from registers of other types of media such as newspapers, films, radio, and television, whether in their analog or digital form. The apparently simple and practical task of creating a register of these historical sources forces us to reconsider well-known categories in a number of ways and to supplement the usual assumptions regarding which categories to include with more fundamental reflections on what we actually understand by each of these categories. In other words: the question is no longer simply whether we wish to include the "title" and "publication date" in our register but also how we wish to *interpret* the terms "title" and "publication date."

With these insights in mind, we may have to reconsider the agenda of digital history. I would suggest that digital history is not limited to questions about how the web can be used in the research process, or how scholarly results can be communicated, but also represents an attempt to bring one of the fundamental aspects of all historiography—the sources—into line with the digital world of today.

The many advantages of digital sources have long been praised within digital history, and with good reason. In the September 2008 edition of *The Journal of American History,* a conversation between scholars entitled "The Promise of Digital History" evoked the hopes and fears associated with historiography in the context of digital media.[20] One commentator stressed the importance of digital sources: "The use of digital sources, in other words, completely changes the landscape of information and transaction costs that historians have traditionally faced." The next participant in the debate followed up on this: "Several million books have been digitized by Google and the Open Content Alliance . . . with millions more on the way shortly; the Library of Congress has scanned and made available online millions of images and documents from its collection; ProQuest has digitized millions of pages of newspapers."[21] All this is, of course, important and true, but the point I would like to make is that this is only the first step into the realm of digital sources. As this conversation reveals, digital history largely equates a "digital source" with a source which was previously analog but has now been digitized. In other words, digital sources have so far been limited to traditional analog sources in digital form.

So the next step will be to recognize that we have been surrounded for almost two decades by another variety of digital sources that are so strange in nature that merely creating an accurate register of them is very difficult. This is important because for some years now, the web has formed such an integral part of our communications infrastructure that it is difficult for us to analyze our contemporary history without including the web as a relevant source. How could we fully understand 9/11, presidential campaigns, or the wars in Iraq and Afghanistan if the web were not included? As Bob Dylan reminded us, "the present now will later be past." Thus the importance of the web as a historical source is likely to increase in the years to come. To investigate the challenges that these new conditions will present for historiography may be one of the tasks for a digital history version 4.0.

Notes

1. McMichael, Rosenzweig, and O'Malley, "Historians and the Web."
2. Cohen and Rosenzweig, *Digital History.*
3. Examples of all these variations can be found in Agger, *Dansk;* Baker and Terris, *A for Andromeda;* Einstein et al., "Source Guide"; IMDb, *The Internet Movie Database;* O'Regan, *Australian National Cinema;* The Paley Center for Media, *The Collection;* and Walravens, *International Newspaper Holdings.*
4. For an overview of historical studies of the web, see Brügger, "Web History: An Emerging Field." A number of web archives exist, but they do not usually create registers of their holdings. Those that most closely resemble registers are the themed web collections, such as the Library of Congress web archives (http://lcWeb2.loc.gov/diglib/lcwa/html/lcwa-home.html), or selective web archives such as the Australian web archive Pandora. In both cases, some information is displayed, but this mainly comprises information about the archiving process.
5. The website dr.dk was launched in 1996, and for a number of years has been among the largest and most frequently visited Danish websites.
6. In the case of radio and television series, however, it must be decided whether the series title alone should be registered, or whether the titles of all the individual episodes should be listed as well; cf. the difference between Einstein et al., "Source Guide"; and Baker and Terris, *A for Andromeda.*
7. Brügger, "Website History and the Website," 122. See also 119–125; and Brügger, *Website Analysis*, 27–49.

8. Cf. Baker and Terris, *A for Andromeda,* xvi.
9. Cf. Brügger, "Website History and the Website," 127–128.
10. Elsewhere I have used the term "ghost website" for this latter type. See Brügger, "The Archived Website," 159.
11. Cf. Brügger, "The Archived Website," 161.
12. Einstein et al., "Source Guide."
13. Febvre and Martin, *The Coming of the Book,* 222.
14. Brügger, "The Archived Website," 173.
15. Thompson and Bordwell, *Film History,* xxxv.
16. Brügger, "The Archived Website," 156; Brügger, "Website History and the Website," 127.
17. The register includes the following information: URL, Name, Start time, End time, Link to archive, Comment, Redirects to, Redirected from, Link to project wiki, Designed by, Produced by, Run by, and Sources. The register is available at http://drdk.dk [in Danish].
18. Cf. Walravens, *International Newspaper Holdings,* viii.
19. Brügger, "The Archived Website," 158–159.
20. Cohen et al., "The Promise of Digital History."
21. Ibid., 455.

Works Cited

Agger, Gunhild. *Dansk tv-drama: Arvesølv og underholdning*. Copenhagen: Samfundslitteratur, 2005.

Baker, Simon, and Olwen Terris, eds. *A for Andromeda to Zoo Time: The TV holdings of the National Film and Television Archive, 1936–1979*. London: British Film Institute, 1994.

Brügger, Niels. "The Archived Website and Website Philology: A New Type of Historical Document?" *Nordicom Review* 29, no. 2 (2008): 155–175.

———. *Website Analysis: Elements of a Conceptual Architecture*. Aarhus: The Centre for Internet Research, 2010.

———. "Website History and the Website as an Object of Study." *New Media & Society* 11, nos. 1 & 2 (2009): 115–132.

———. "Web History: An Emerging Field of Study." In *Web History*, edited by Niels Brügger, 1–25. New York: Peter Lang, 2010.

Cohen, Daniel J., Michael Frisch, Patrick Gallagher, Steven Mintz, Kirsten Sword, Amy Murrell Taylor, William G. Thomas III, and William J. Turkel. "The Promise of Digital History." *The Journal of American History* 95, no. 2 (2008): 452–491.

———, and Roy Rosenzweig. *Digital History: A Guide to Gathering, Preserving, and Presenting the Past on the Web*. Philadelphia: University of Pennsylvania Press, 2006.

Einstein, Dan, Nina Leibman, Randall Vogt, Sarah Berry, Jillian Steinberger, and William Lafferty. "Source Guide to TV Family Comedy, Drama, and Serial Drama, 1946–1970." In *Private Screenings: Television and the Female Consumer*, edited by Lynn Spigel and Denise Mann, 253–276. Minneapolis: University of Minnesota Press, 1992.

Febvre, Lucien, and Henri-Jean Martin. *The Coming of the Book: The Impact of Printing, 1450–1800*. London: Verso, 1998.

IMDb. *The Internet Movie Database*. Accessed July 1, 2010. http://www.imdb.com.

McMichael, Andres, Roy Rosenzweig, and Michael O'Malley. "Historians and the Web: A Beginner's Guide." *Perspectives Online* 34, no. 1 (January 1996). Accessed October 1, 2010. http://www.historians.org/perspectives/issues/1996/9601/9601COM3.CFM.

O'Regan, Tom. *Australian National Cinema*. London: Routledge, 1996.

The Paley Center for Media. *The Collection*. Accessed July 1, 2010. http://www.paleycenter.org/collection.

Thompson, Kristin, and David Bordwell. *Film History: An Introduction*. New York: McGraw-Hill, 1994.

Walravens, Hartmut, ed. *International Newspaper Holdings in German Libraries: A Catalogue of 18,000 Newspapers, Gazettes and Related Periodicals with Locations and Geographical Index*. 2nd ed. München: K.G. Saur, 1993.

chapter eighteen

Placing Location-Aware Media in a History of the Virtual

Adriana de Souza e Silva and Daniel M. Sutko

Introduction

Locative technologies are mobile devices equipped with location awareness (via Wi-Fi, GPS [Global Positioning System], and/or cellular triangulation), allowing users to access place-specific information and interact with other users depending on their geographical location.[1] Originally used to support the development of location-based mobile games (e.g., *Botfighters*, *Mogi*, and *Alien Revolt*), location-aware mobile devices are now used to access location-specific information and to support the development of locative mobile social networks (e.g., *Loopt*, *Brightkite*, *Foursquare*, and *Whrll*) via location-based applications. An important characteristic of location-based applications is that they provide users with a double perception of space: they simultaneously see their physical surrounding spaces, plus a representation of that same space on a map on their mobile devices. This doubling of space creates an "augmented" view of reality, influencing communication and navigation in urban spaces.

Traditionally, mobile phones have been studied as doublers of place that remove users from their physical surroundings or bring distant places and people into the present physical space.[2] These studies generally focused on voice communication, comparing cell phone conversations to traditional telephones. Within this logic, cell phones would allow people to inhabit two places at the same time: the place in which they were physically and the remote place where the other speaking person was. Contrary to this approach, Michel Serres suggested that telephone conversations take place nowhere—they actually happen in a virtual place.[3]

A similar perspective was applied to the early Internet during the 1990s: digital worlds were considered "virtual" because they allowed people to meet in non-physical simulated spaces. Presenting the virtual as a simulation constitutes part of what we call the "technological virtual." One of the consequences of this perspective was the conceptualization of the Internet and digital information as essentially disconnected from physical spaces, a position critiqued by Mark Poster, who observed that, "the great weakness of Baudrillard's effort to theorize VR [virtual reality] is his inability to recognize practices that involve assemblages of humans and machines and account for their differential realizations."[4] Likewise, Rob Shields noted that early theoreticians of cyberspace mapped "the virtuality of digital communications media on to a dichotomy of spirit and matter, with matter fixed firmly in the familiar world of the body."[5] Although David Gunkel critiqued the Platonic dualism of reality/representation,[6] his critique did not go far enough in prescribing an agenda for overcoming this dualism and offered Baudrillard as a potential alternative to Plato, even though Baudrillard is heir to the Platonic tradition, as we demonstrate below. Nowadays, location-aware applications bring these simulated spaces into the physical environment. Moreover, the digital space on the mobile screen often augments a representation of the physical city in which the user is located. Likewise, the physical space itself is a source for digital information (traditionally in the case of GIS [Geographical Information System] and more recently through GPS, restaurant recommendations, and friend location tools). So, mobile devices create a double sense of space that is now attached to location. We argue that the transformation of physical location into digital information and vice-versa highlights an intrinsic process of becoming, which urges us to rethink the meaning of virtual as applied to locative technologies.

With this in mind, we argue there are two primary threads through which we can analyze the development of the concept of virtual and apply these perspectives to location-aware media. The first thread, which considers the virtual as a simulation, has intellectual roots in the Platonic philosophical tradition that conceptualized representation as a copy. The second thread, which views the virtual as potential (and not separate from the real), has intellectual roots in the Aristotelian philosophy that conceptualized representation as *potential* linked to or moving toward *actualization*. In contemporary scholarship, these two trends are developed in very particular ways by theorists such as Jean Baudrillard (as with the first case) and Gilles Deleuze (as in the second case). Finally, we address how N. Katherine Hayles's theory of virtuality[7] emphasizes the materiality of the interfaces that carry digital information, which act as mediatiors of our relationships with digital and physical spaces.

This chapter contributes to ongoing theoretical conversation about the virtual, and in particular to how that conversation relates to communication studies of new media, which address how the Internet, mobile phones, and location-aware technologies mediate the relationships between users and physical spaces, and among users themselves by (1) proposing a new theoretical framework for analyzing location-aware media, and their interconnections with physical/digital spaces, and (2) examining how the articulation between space, mobility, and location transforms the traditional way we think about the relationships between interfaces and information.

The Virtual as Simulation: Representation, Reality, and Physical Spaces

Sherry Turkle observed that the addition of a screen and mouse to the computer, followed by the Graphical User Interface (GUI) developed by Xerox PARC in the early 1980s, indicated a critical shift in information technologies from a culture of calculations to a culture of simulations.[8] In the culture of calculations, code and programming languages were used to interact with computers. In the culture of simulations, everything is taken at interface value. In other words, users became accustomed to interact with computers through a graphic interface that "hides" the code.[9] VPL Research, founded in 1983, was the first company to commercially introduce interfaces such as the data glove and head-mounted display that allowed users to interact seamlessly with digital graphic simulated worlds, which its founder, Jaron Lanier, named "virtual reality."[10]

Turkle defines the term "virtual reality" as "metaphorical spaces that arise only through interaction with the computer, which people navigate by using special hardware."[11] Similarly, Julian Dibbell understands VR as "every technique ever devised for making the shared illusion of representation come more convincingly alive."[12] And Howard Rheingold has suggested that virtual reality would not be "merely" a medium within physical reality but another type of reality.[13] The idea of virtual reality as a simulation (or illusion) of reality opposes the virtual to the real and consists of what we call the "technological virtual." This thought, widespread in the 1980s and 1990s, contributed to popular understandings of VR as representing reality or as something that could be a hyperreality, which could be mistakenly taken as real. Such a perspective is rooted in a Platonically informed theorization of virtuality.

The Virtual as Copy

Plato frames reality within a hierarchy of worlds: ideal, sensible, and represented.[14] While the ideal world was the intangible world of concepts and ideas, the sensible world corresponded to our physical reality. If the sensible world in itself could be considered as a copy of the ideal world, the represented world, by copying the sensible world, was a copy of a copy. According to Plato, representations are copies of a superior reality. Plato explains representation as a reflection or a mirroring and does not differentiate an image in the mirror from the representation of art, poetry, or theater/play, for they are all copies of the sense-world. Representations, for Plato, always have less value than the real itself. Accordingly, the virtual, within the Platonic logic, can be understood as a rhetorical game. Similarly, we can question to what extent the relationship between physical location and digital information as mediated through locative applications is simply another example of the Platonic rhetorical game, in which the representational (mobile map on the cell phone screen) is secondary to the physical (sensible) world. To examine this question, we turn to the locative application *WikiMe*, which connects physical location to digital information.

WikiMe searches for *Wikipedia* entries based on one's location. Using a cell phone, the user is presented with several ways of interfacing with this information. In one view, the user is presented with a list of entries ordered by the distance from the user with a brief name and picture of the location, along with the first sentence or two of the *Wikipedia* entry. Closer entries are listed first and the farthest entries are listed last. This defaulting to distance as the logic for organizing entries begs the question, "what does it mean to list such information by distance?" and illustrates how spatial distance becomes the relevant metric rather than some other quality, such as relevance to the user's interest. Physical space, as represented by distance, becomes the primary interface for that information. Once the user has clicked on a written *Wikipedia* entry, she can also select to see a map view or a photo view of that entry. In the map view, the user sees the location of the entry in relation to other entries. Entries are represented on a map, concentrically oriented around the user's location. Another option for interacting with *WikiMe* is to select a photo view, which lists photos that have been tagged as near that location. *WikiMe* also allows the user to update a *Wikipedia* entry with information about the immediate temporal state of that location and can also take pictures and mark them as being near that location, thereby altering the informational landscape, which becomes tied to the physical landscape through the interface of the mobile. Another possibility is for a remote, online user to make a change to a *Wikipedia* entry, which effectively also changes the info-spatial landscape of that location.

A similar case of attaching information to places can be observed with the locative mobile social application *Whrrl*, which allows users to post location-based updates and location-based photos to a map-like interface. If a user logs into his *Whrrl* account, he will be able to see his friends' posts on a map and see the number and location of different friends' posts. *Whrrl* users are encouraged to develop narratives around particular locations ("What's your story?" is one of their taglines). So, the idea here is that users can share not just brief updates such as "I am here" but can perhaps combine numerous brief updates into a narrative that amounts to "I am here and I did this. Then I went (t)here."

If we analyze *WikiMe* from a Platonic perspective, we might emphasize the pure aesthetic connection to the representative reality. In this sense, the mobile map on which information is displayed corresponds to a stylized representation of the physical/sensible world. Differently from the mirror or realistic painting, which more clearly resembles the original, mobile maps retain from the reality they represent just enough visual information to allow for navigation—digitally, spatially, or narratively. So, according to the Platonic logic, these maps and their accompanying information or stories can be considered even more inferior copies of the sensible world, since they do not have a one-to-one aesthetic relationship to their original. What the Platonic perspective does not allow us to consider, however, is, as German philosopher Eugen Fink notes, how to account for the possible potentiality of these representations,[15] that is, the Platonic logic does not let us take into consideration the dynamic digital information that cannot be found originally in the physical space but becomes attached to that physical space through the map interface. That information may also cause changes to or be changed because of the physical space to which it relates. The Platonic logic ignores the dynamic connection between the physical location of a place and the information about that place that are made available to and editable by other users. Extending Plato's ideas, French philosopher Jean Baudrillard fills this gap by allowing for the significance of the more-than real (i.e., simulated information).

The Virtual as Simulation

Simulation, according to Baudrillard,

> is no longer that of a territory, a referential being, or a substance. It is the generation by models of a real without origin or reality: a hyperreal. The territory no longer precedes the map, nor does it survive it. It is nevertheless the map that precedes the territory—*precession of simulacra*—that engenders the territory, and if one must return to the fable, today it is the territory whose shreds slowly rot across the extent of the map.[16]

Italian scholar Umberto Eco also imagined the instructions for creating a 1:1 map.[17] Eco presents the limitations of the undertaking in a detailed outline of instructions. After all the considerations, Eco concludes that a map that is true to scale is not a logical possibility. When the copy becomes the same as the original, it consequently destroys the original. So, the era of the simulation, according to Baudrillard and Eco, is inaugurated by a liquidation of all references. On the evolution of the simulacra, Baudrillard determines four successive phases of the representational image. The first one, corresponding to Platonic models of representation, reflects a profound reality. The second masks and denatures a profound reality. The third masks the *absence* of a profound reality (as simulation). Finally, the last one, the simulacrum, has no relation to any reality whatsoever. As a result, the power of the simulacrum is to transform the real into its shadow.

According to Baudrillard, the simulacrum tricks us into believing it is real. The idea of simulacrum as something that not only masks reality but also produces it is also constructed by Eco, as hyperreality.[18] "Hyperreality" is defined as what is over or above that which is real. If it is not possible to have the real thing, one fabricates the absolute fake or makes an authentic copy. It is no longer an issue of a false representation of reality but of concealing the fact that reality is no longer real. The construction of reality has been widely discussed in the domain of mass communication media, and until the late 1980s, TV has been most responsible for the dominance of the concept of simulacrum,[19] but more recently, the emergence of VR systems has foregrounded Platonic tensions between real and virtual. Virtual worlds have been envisioned, according to the Platonic legacy, as copies of reality. Moreover, if these "virtual" worlds had no counterpart in physical reality, they were associated with nonphysical and imaginary spaces, and consequently, nonreal spaces—simulacra.

The idea of virtual as simulacrum might also influence how we understand location-aware media. Returning to the *WikiMe* example, when using *WikiMe*, the user stands in a particular location. Say this location is a local museum with a *Wikipedia* entry. Therefore, the user is simultaneously standing at the location of the museum, but also at the location of the information about the musem, as accessed through *WikiMe*. So the original physical location (museum) based on which the information was created is transformed into the marker for that information. Rather than the marker signifying the location of the museum, this logic reverses the signifier/signified relationship: the physical location becomes the marker for that-which-is-not-there, and therefore an example of the simulacrum. This paradox might lead to new relationships between people and urban spaces, such as the case in which the user is in a location not to access that specific location but to access visual and written information about that location. This inversion of the signified (information)/signifier (museum) relationship is achieved through the interface of location-aware media. The map of one's knowledge—*WikiMe*—precedes the territory the user navigates. However, that map of the territory is created dynamically through the interaction between user and physical space, and in turn the user interaction with the physical space is informed by and reflected on the map.

Similarly, consider the Digital Graffiti project. Digital Graffiti, developed by Siemens, the Ars Electronica Center, and the Institut für Pervasive Computing, allowed users to create location-based virtual "walls" on which users may post comments in the form of text messages. The Digital Graffiti project pioneered today's services, such as the iPhone application Graffitio, in which users may post text messages (not to be confused with SMS [Short Message Service]) to any specific location in the real world. In the logic of the simulacrum, is a digital wall created around a physical space or is a physical space created around a digital wall? Assuming the Platonic tradition, we would argue that space cannot be created around a digital wall, because a digital wall is merely representational. It is the ultimate shadow on the wall, except rather than communicating in the absence or presence of light, the digital wall communicates with the absence or presence of electrical current (1s and 0s).

However, location-aware media, especially locative mobile social networks, problematize this perspective, because the physical space actually becomes an interface for information, and information becomes an interface for the physical space. So, following Baudrillard's perspective, location-aware media could actually have the potential to also overcome physical space (its referent). Although traditional maps represent reality, dynamic locative maps work "in connection to" reality, which means that every change in physical space produces a change on the map. Similarly, every change on the map made by users may produce a change in the way others understand, experience, and navigate physical space. This dynamic/mobile connectivity and interdependence between physical and digital spaces is one of the unique characteristics of location-aware media, and an example of a relationship that has no counterpart in Plato's idea of representation or Baudrillard's concept of simulation. In this sense, we might think that location-aware interfaces actually "add" to reality, instead of negating it, replacing it, or being less than it.

But rather than analyzing location-aware media as simulations of reality or as representations without an original (which follows the Platonic model), these applications can also be studied according to the Aristotelian/Deleuzian model of potentiality. This perspective does not oppose virtual and real, for physical spaces become a fold within the virtual. If the real can be unfolded into different possible realities, the virtual and the real are actually synonymous and reality, or physicality, becomes one of the faces of virtual. This statement is unfolded when we look backwards to the origins of the concept according to Aristotle.

The Virtual as Possibility and Potentiality

The Movement from the Potential to the Actual

The Greek philosopher Aristotle initially addressed the idea of potentiality in order to think about movement—not the physical movement of objects in space, but rather the change of a being's state.[20] Movement, in this case, is related to qualitative changes: a green leaf that becomes yellow or an illiterate man who becomes literate. Aristotle thus incorporated movement into each particular being, in contrast to what is defined in modern physics, where movement is relative to an observer.[21]

The act of becoming can be understood, then, as a qualitative change of a specific entity. After Aristotle, the ontological problem was no longer a question of non-being versus being, but a question of actualizing potential in an entity: the entity remained the same, but its attributes could change. For example, when an illiterate man becomes literate, he does not cease to be a man. Simultaneously, this man has in himself the potential to learn, actualized when he becomes literate. This is the difference between the actual and the virtual for Aristotle: the virtual corresponds to potential states, and the actual is the state of that being at an arbitrary spatiotemporal locus, since that being is a becoming.

Consequently, each being can be seen as a multiplicity,[22] for it contains in itself diverse potential qualities, which can be opposed to each other, but might be actualized at specific times. For example, a woman can be a businesswoman and a mother, yet each role is actualized at different times. Contraries exist only in the potential state; once actualized, there can be no opposed qualities in one single being. However, the virtual for Aristotle was not applied to reality as a whole, but only considered for single beings. In the 17th century, the philosopher Gottfried Wilhelm Leibniz used the Aristotelian idea of potentiality and applied it to all of reality through his notion of possible worlds.[23]

Leibniz described a world composed of many incompossible worlds, or scenarios.[24] All of them are possible, although they cannot coexist with each other, since they contain incompatible elements. As with Aristotle, contraries could not exist in the same series of worlds. For that reason, there could be several virtual worlds, although only one could be actualized at a time. In the very moment one world becomes actual, that actuality automatically excludes all other incompatible possibilities.

In "The Garden of Forking Paths," Argentinean writer Jorge Luis Borges goes beyond Leibniz's philosophy.[25] Instead of accepting the existence of one linear series of worlds, the Argentinean writer constructs a model where all possibilities are actualized at the same time. "In all fictional works, each time a man is confronted with several alternatives, he chooses one and eliminates the others; in the fiction of Ts'ui Pên, he chooses—simultaneously—all of them."[26] In this story, there are multiple possibilities that can coexist, with no rules to be actualized. Every time a choice is made, there are several other (incom)possible worlds striving to be actualized all together. For Borges, as for Deleuze, there is no longer a person who chooses among several worlds, as in Leibniz, but a person who is pressured by several selves, which are not masks or appearances (like in Plato) but indeed constitute the same person. This perspective frames the virtual into something that is ready to emerge, to be created, or to transform.

The Virtual as Potential

Gilles Deleuze considers the virtual as desire, as a potential for creation.[27] As such, he suggests that there is more beyond what we see in the world (reality). Therefore, the real encompasses both our actual world and the potential to produce new realities. From this point of view, the virtual is indeed very real. Within Deleuze's logic, there is no point in addressing the opposition between real and virtual. Conversely, we might see the real as an all-encompassing concept, which contains virtual (potential) realities and actual realities.

Deleuze suggests that differentiation is creation.[28] Differentiation is synonymous with actualization, because in the movement from the virtual to the actual an idea or a concept can potentially be differentiated into several actual instances. The potential to be actualized and differentiated into diverse realities is what makes the virtual an important part of the real rather than opposed to it. "The virtual is fully real in so far as it is virtual."[29] The virtual is always ready to emerge, to have actual existence. Deleuze focuses on the process of actualization as acts of differentiation, genesis, or creation.

This movement from the virtual to the actual (actualization) can be used to think about location-aware media. Every location-aware application can be envisioned as a virtual piece, which is differently actualized by each viewer. Therefore, they are per se fully potential entities that can only be completed when the interaction with the user occurs. Each user, in turn, actualizes the application in a different way, revealing some (but not all) aspects of its potentiality. For example, when opening *WikiMe*, a user is able to see all location-based *Wikipedia* articles related to their specific location. If another user logs in from a different place (let's say five miles away), different topics will appear on the mobile screen. None of the users in fact accesses the whole database of articles, which we might think of as this space of potentiality in which all *Wikipedia* articles are stored—the ones that have already been written by users, the ones that are being written right now, and also the ones that will be written in the future.

Also, the choice of interface itself actualizes certain potentialities and leaves others virtual. For example, with *GoogleMaps,* one can choose to see or not see traffic information, yet this says very little about where to eat or where people are. With *CitySense,* the user sees where people congregate in a city, actualizing the social information about a place, yet the user will not know which roads might be the best to take. In using *Yelp*, a user can read the reviews of a place, but there will be many reviews the user ignores. Those reviews are real, yet they remain unactualized for the user. Within this logic, the virtual for Deleuze is distinct from the idea of representation in Plato. According to the representational model, images resemble their originals, and objects resemble the idea (concept) to which they correspond. The virtual for Deleuze is multiple, that is, it can be actualized in many different instances. "Multiplicity" then can be defined in contrast to the Platonic idea of representation, which is generally a one-to-one relationship. The virtual is always absently present, constantly desiring to be actualized and differentiated. Actualization is, then, a genuine act of creation, and it does not result from the limitations of a singular preexisting possibility as with Leibniz. Rather, the virtual is the desire to constitute the real as new. In this context Deleuze considers the virtual as a function of the creative imagination as well as a product of different articulations between art, technology, and science. These articulations can become actualized in different ways, and the magnitude of articulations that can be actualized changes with each interface, such as locative media applications.

Location-aware applications interface between physical space and digital information, so that changes in one are also changes in the other. Recall the earlier example of *WikiMe*, in which a change in a *Wikipedia* entry, such as updating information about a location (e.g., restaurant just awarded four stars; historic building about to be renovated or torn down), could literally mean a change in a physical location for a user. Similarly, a change in physical location leads to accessing different entries, because entries are only displayed within a specific radius of the user location. Therefore, rather than having two spaces that are apparently disconnected or conflicting with each other (what has been formally theorized as the technological virtual—digital simulated computer space—and what we have taken for granted as the real—physical space), the Deleuzian perspective actually allows us to understand both instances as one entity—or two entities that inform each other through the interface of locative media applications. So, from the user's perspective, there is an unactualized virtual articulation between information and physical space or physical space and information; it is an articulation that becomes actual through the interface. Thus, actualization is not a making-real; the real already exists. Actualization is rather one instantiated, particular, immanent, and imminent configuration of the multiplicity of the potential. It is, as Deleuze would say, a creative differentiation: this *Wikipedia* article, this location. The creativity is not in the article or the location, though both are examples of creativity; the creativity is in the particular articulation of the two as accomplished by the user through the interface. The interplay between digital information, urban spaces, people, and location-based mobile interfaces highlights the fact that the material interfaces (in this case, the phone and location-based applications) do influence the way we access and interact with (digital) information. This intrinsic connection between materiality and information is explored by N. Katherine Hayles through her development of the concept of virtuality.[30]

Virtuality: The New Technological Virtual

Hayles uses virtuality to interrogate the connections between material objects and information patterns. According to Hayles, "virtuality is the cultural perception that material objects are interpenetrated by information patterns."[31] Hayles refutes a tradition in information studies and cybernetics, which defines "information" as independent of meaning and of the material substrate that carries it. She emphasizes the importance of material interfaces as media that carry, interpret, and decode (digital) information to users, and moreover, decenter the subject of the user, connecting the user to the machine through the cyborg.[32] However, users do not merely operate machines; machines also operate on users. A separation of user and machine or of information and materiality (which would be another way of putting it) is something Hayles calls an "impossible inversion," which comes from a false duality of information and the material containing that information. Likewise, people do not simply operate in space; space also operates upon people. The container and the thing contained cannot be separated. (Much of Deleuze's theoretical project can also be summarized as trying to push philosophy away from dichotomization, as evinced above by his conflation of the Platonically opposed real/sensible and virtual/ideal.)

N. Katherine Hayles's concept of virtuality is a response to the technological concept of the virtual (addressed in the beginning of this chapter), in which information (in this case, digital information instantiated as virtual worlds) is seen as inherently disconnected from the material interfaces used to access them. Especially during the 1980s and 1990s, the idea that humans could "download" their minds to a computer, and therefore potentially leave their material bodies behind, was strongly represented in sci-fi literature and films, such as *Neuromancer*, *Snowcrash*, *Mind Children*, *The Matrix*, and *The Thirteenth Floor*.[33] In this perspective, as we have stated earlier, (virtual) simulated worlds were represented as better or beyond reality (a sort of hyperreal).

In addition to providing a new way to understand the technological virtual (virtual as simulation), the idea that information patterns cannot be understood as separate from the material interfaces that carry them proves to be relevant to the analysis of location-aware media through the interplay between materiality (as urban spaces/software interfaces) and (location-based digital) information. As users move through space, they act with intention towards applications such as *WikiMe*, *Whrll*, and *CitySense*: loading it, adjusting settings, browsing it, and yet at the same time, the affordances of that program act on the users.

The process of actualizing information as space and space as information mediated by the user in locative media is a strong example of how these two instances are in a constant process of becoming. In today's society, material objects are increasingly interpenetrated by information patterns, as is the case with sensor technologies, mobile devices, and pervasive computing in general. Whereas the previous notion of the technological (simulated) virtual helped to characterize an era in which virtual reality and simulations defined our relationship with digital information and computers, at this point in the 2000s the idea of virtuality, in combination with the Deleuzian logic of virtual as becoming, more accurately defines our interaction with new information and communication technologies (ICTs), specifically mobile and location-aware media.

These location-aware applications and the information they interface with are not outside the physical space, nor is physical material space disconnected from the location-based information now embedded in them: neither is the user purely a mediator between physical space and the application. As Hayles observes, the user and medium become a cyborg, with each informing, expanding, and limiting the other's capacities. Space, digital information, locative applications, and users are all processually bound up together. The removal of one from the relationship changes completely the nature of this relationship, which brings us back to Aristotle, in that the virtual is neither a birth from nothingness nor an elimination of one in favor of the other; rather, the virtual is all of the capacities or potentials therein. These potentials do not exist outside of the individuals, nor are the individuals outside their potential. Although we are writing here of the individual, it would also be accurate to claim the same for any objects. This elimination of interiority/exteriority was also part of Gilles Deleuze and Felix Guattari's theoretical project[34] and can similarly be found in Hayles's criticism of the impossible disconnection between information and materiality.

In our case, location-aware media acquire significance because they actualize different connections between users and their physical surroundings through the interface of their location-aware applications. In this sense, we argue against the unreality of the virtual and posit the actual as the articulation of physical location and information, with actualization as that relational process by which physical location and information are mutually influential on each other.

Conclusion

The emergence and increasing popularity of location-based applications redefine the way we interact both with digital information and urban spaces and therefore require us to rethink the relationship between users, spaces, information, and interfaces. This chapter traces the long philosophical history of virtuality by showing how different traditions of the virtual illuminate or obfuscate connections between representation, simulation, technology, and spaces—connections critical to studying location-aware technologies. We have argued that the concept of the virtual has historically been defined in two distinct but overlapping ways: in relationship with reality and its representation—through Plato and Baudrillard—and in connection to reality (actual) and the real (potential)—through Aristotle, Leibniz, and Deleuze. In the history of Internet studies, more often than not, the virtual has been strictly equated with the digital and with simulation. Such thought is rooted in the Platonic/Baudrillardian tradition that views representations as inferior copies of reality and simulations as "better" than reality. But looking at the virtual as representation/simulation is no longer helpful to understanding the new ways in which we interact with the Internet and digital media. Increasingly, our connection to the Internet depends on where we are. The types of information we access and the people to whom we connect depend on our physical location interfaced through location-aware mobile technologies. Therefore, we combed the history of virtuality for connections that would allow us to understand what's different and what's the same about connecting to the Internet and others through location-aware interfaces.

Because location-aware technologies allow Internet access from many different places, a user's location becomes essential in determining the interaction with and access to digital information. The Platonic tradition does not account for the increasingly palpable imbrication of information/materiality, so we instead proposed the Aristotelean tradition, most recently elaborated by Deleuze and Hayles, as a more relevant framework for theorizing location-aware media. Understanding the virtual no longer as separate from reality—as was frequently the case with the

Platonic tradition—also allows us to reconceptualize the spaces in which we live. Our urban public spaces are no longer comprised of pure physicality and face-to-face interactions. They include both nearby and remote people and information, local and distant connections, all linked to physical location. But the philosophical history above is not meant as some sort of progress narrative. Rather, Deleuze's and Hayles's approaches to information and materiality allow us to investigate questions that we must confront in order to adequately understand the Internet and location-aware media today.

Notes

1. A revised version of this chapter has been published in the journal *Communication Theory* 21, no. 1, under the title "Theorizing Locative Technologies through Philosophies of the Virtual." Also, thanks to Jason Kalin for the titular advice.
2. Moores, "The Doubling of Place"; Katz and Aakhus, *Perpetual Contact;* Plant, "On the Mobile."
3. Serres, *Atlas.*
4. Poster, *What's the Matter with the Internet?,* 136.
5. Shields, *The Virtual,* 78.
6. Gunkel, "Rethinking Virtual Reality."
7. Hayles, "The Condition of Virtuality"; Hayles, *How We Became Posthuman;* Hayles, "Embodied Virtuality."
8. Turkle, *Life on the Screen.*
9. Johnson, *Interface Culture.*
10. Paul, *Digital Art.*
11. Turkle, *Life on the Screen,* 181. By "hardware," Turkle means material interfaces such as head-mounted displays (HMDs), body suits, goggles, and data gloves.
12. Dibbell, *My Tiny Life,* 51.
13. Rheingold, *The Virtual Community.*
14. Plato, *The Republic.*
15. Fink, "Die Spieldeutung der Metaphysik."
16. Baudrillard, *Simulacra and Simulation,* 1.
17. Eco, *How to Travel with a Salmon & Other Essays.*
18. Eco, *Travels in Hyperreality.*
19. Baudrillard, "The Masses"; Boltanski, *Distant Suffering.*
20. Aubenque, *Le Problème.*
21. Ibid.
22. Deleuze, *Difference and Repetition.*
23. Leibniz, *Philosophical Writings.*
24. Leibniz, *Philosophical Writings;* Leibniz, *Monadology and Other Philosophical Essays.*
25. Borges, "Garden of Forking Paths," 19.

26. Ibid., 26.
27. Deleuze, *Difference and Repetition.*
28. Ibid.
29. Ibid., 208.
30. Hayles, "The Condition of Virtuality"; Hayles, *How We Became Posthuman;* Hayles, "Embodied Virtuality."
31. Hayles, "The Condition of Virtuality," 69.
32. Hayles, *How We Became Posthuman.*
33. Gibson, *Neuromancer;* Stephenson, *Snowcrash;* Moravec, *Mind Children;* Warner Bros., *The Matrix;* Emmerich, *The Thirteenth Floor.* Obviously this apparent disconnection from the body was fallacy, since the interfaces used to connect to digital space were very material and indeed connected to the characters' material bodies, and some characters in these works had the ability to freely move in and out of the simulation (for more details, see de Souza e Silva, "From Simulations to Hybrid Space"; Hayles and Gessler, "Slipstream of Mixed Reality"; and Irwin, *The Matrix and Philosophy*). However, the popular perception was that physical and digital spaces (and for this matter, information and materiality) were indeed independent from each other.
34. Deleuze and Guattari, *A Thousand Plateaus.*

Works Cited

Aubenque, Pierre. *Le Problème de L'être chez Aristotle: Essai sur la Problématique Aristotélicienne.* Paris: Presses Universitaires de France, 1962.

Baudrillard, Jean. "The Masses: The Implosion of the Social in the Media." *New Literary History* 16, no. 3 (1985): 577–589.

———. *Simulacra and Simulation.* Ann Arbor: University of Michigan Press, 1994.

Boltanski, Luc. *Distant Suffering: Morality, Media and Politics.* Cambridge, MA: Cambridge University Press, 1999.

Borges, Jorge Luis. "The Garden of Forking Paths." In *Labyrinths: Selected Stories & Other Writings,* edited by Donald A. Yates and James E. Irby, 19–29. New York: New Directions, 1962.

de Souza e Silva, Adriana. "From Simulations to Hybrid Space: How Nomadic Technologies Change the Real." *Technoetic Arts* 1, no. 3 (2004): 209–221.

———, and Daniel M. Sutko. "Theorizing Locative Technologies through Philosophies of the Virtual." *Communication Theory* 21, no. 1 (2011): 23–42.

Deleuze, Gilles. *Difference and Repetition.* New York: Columbia University Press, 1994.

———, and Felix Guattarri. *A Thousand Plateaus: Capitalism and Schizophrenia.* Minneapolis: University of Minnesota Press, 1987.

Dibbell, Julian. *My Tiny Life: Crime and Passion in a Virtual World.* New York: Henry Holt and Company, 1999.

Eco, Umberto. *How to Travel with a Salmon & Other Essays.* New York: Harcourt, Brace, 1994.

———. *Travels in Hyperreality: Essays.* San Diego: A Harvest Book, 1990.

Emmerich, Roland. *The Thirteenth Floor*. Culver City, CA: Columbia TriStar Home Video, 1999.

Fink, Eugen. "Die Spieldeutung der Metaphysik." In *Spiel als Weltsymbol*. Stuttgart: W. Kohlhammer, 1960.

Gibson, William. *Neuromancer*. New York: Ace Books, 1994.

Gunkel, David. "Rethinking Virtual Reality: Simulation and the Deconstruction of the Image." *Critical Studies in Media Communication* 17, no. 1 (2000): 45–62.

Hayles, N. Katherine. "The Condition of Virtuality." In *The Digital Dialectic: New Essays on New Media*, edited by Peter Lunenfeld, 68–95. Cambridge, MA: MIT Press, 2000.

———. "Embodied Virtuality: Or How to Put Bodies Back into the Picture." In *Immersed in Technology: Art and Virtual Environments,* edited by Mary Anne Moser, 1–28. Cambridge, MA: MIT Press, 1996.

———. *How We Became Posthuman—Virtual Bodies in Cybernetics, Literature, and Informatics.* Chicago: University of Chicago Press, 1999.

———, and Nick Gessler. "The Slipstream of Mixed Reality: Unstable Ontologies and Semiotic Markers in *The Thirteenth Floor*, *Dark City*, and *Mulholland Drive*." *PMLA* 119, no. 3 (2004): 482–499.

Irwin, William. *The Matrix and Philosophy: Welcome to the Desert of the Real.* Chicago: Open Court, 2002.

Johnson, Steven. *Interface Culture: How New Technology Transforms the Way We Create and Communicate*. San Francisco: Harper Edge, 1997.

Katz, James, and Mark Aakhus. *Perpetual Contact: Mobile Communication, Private Talk, Public Performance.* Cambridge, MA: Cambridge University Press, 2002.

Leibniz, Gottfried Wilhelm. *Monadology and Other Philosophical Essays.* Indianapolis: Bobbs-Merrill Co., 1965.

———. *Philosophical Writings.* New York: Dutton, 1934.

Moores, Shaun. "The Doubling of Place: Electronic Media, Time-space Arrangements and Social Relationships." In *Media/Space: Place, Scale, and Culture in a Media Age*, edited by Nick Couldry and Anna McCarthy, 21–36. London: Routledge, 2004.

Moravec, Hans. *Mind Children: The Future of Robot and Human Intelligence*. Cambridge, MA: Harvard University Press, 1988.

Paul, Christiane. *Digital Art.* London: Thames & Hudson, 2003.

Plant, Sadie. "On the Mobile: The Effects of Mobile Telephones on Social and Individual Life." In *Motorola Inc.* October 28, 2001. Accessed September 27, 2003. http://www.motorola.com/mot/documents/0,1028,296,00.pdf

Plato. *The Republic.* New Haven: Yale University Press, 2006.

Poster, Mark. *What's the Matter with the Internet?* Minneapolis: University of Minnesota Press, 2001.

Rheingold, Howard. *The Virtual Community: Homesteading on the Electronic Frontier.* Cambridge, MA: MIT Press, 2000.

Serres, Michel. *Atlas*. Lisboa: Piaget, 1997.

Shields, Rob. *The Virtual.* New York: Routledge, 2003.

Stephenson, Neal. *Snowcrash*. New York: Bantam Books, 1992.
Turkle, Sherry. *Life on the Screen: Identity in the Age of the Internet.* New York: Simon & Schuster, 1995.
Warner Bros. *The Matrix*. Burbank, CA: Warner Home Video, 1999.

chapter nineteen

"It's Not Really Our Content"

The Moving Image and Media History in the Digital Archive Age

Simon Popple

Introduction

The history of moving image archiving has a relatively recent digital character. The panacea offered by the "digital" in terms of storage, cataloguing, and virtual access is slowly unravelling as organizations grapple with the complex issues relating to data translation, permanence, intellectual property rights, delivery models, and overload.[1] As Abby Smith notes, digital technologies make content "dismayingly easy to create," while many archives are failing successfully to manage their current pre-"born digital" collections.[2] Constantly expanding bodies of material and associated metadata necessitate a rethinking of some of the key methodological approaches to using digital archives as sources of media history, collection and management, interpretation, access, and engagement. Carl Fleischhauer of the Library of Congress highlighted some of the challenges facing the archive sector when he commented that the

> digitization of moving image content is an emerging area—especially for preservation—and the patterns of technology are not settled. For those that work in the field, the circumstances produce a mixture of exhilaration and anxiety, of engagement and uncertainty.[3]

This chapter examines the moving image as a particular type of historical resource, one that presents issues that confront archivists, academics, and the general public in the face of increasingly available bodies of moving image. I pursue these issues via two case studies—one focussed on issues of access, the other on engagement. The first case study illustrates issues related to access and to the development of standardized practices through collaborative moves made between European states to develop integrated and sustainable approaches to the "uncertainties" of the digital archive. The second case study concerns the case of how a major public sector broadcaster—the BBC—has incorporated some of the possibilities made possible by digital archiving. I offer an assessment of how the BBC interacts with its many public and academic audiences and how it is beginning to use its materials to develop new forms of media history both inside and outside the academy. Central to both case studies is the contention that, in the digital world, we need to look to collaborative and sometimes radically different approaches to the collection, preservation, and interpretation of sources. As a senior BBC executive recently said of their own archive, "This archive is so vast that no one person could ever look at all of it. And even we don't know most of what it contains."[4] This type of admission clearly signals the potential for patterns of collaborative historical analysis that cross traditional boundaries of ownership and disciplinarity, and it represents a certain degree of recognition that the role of the archive itself is increasingly important.

In the recently emergent field of early film studies, the role of the digital archive has become central to disciplinary development, not least because what remains of the historical record is so fragmentary, fragile, and dispersed.[5] Many early film historians have moved away from formative approaches that sought to understand and categorize the development of cinema via a grand narrative. Early film historians are turning to digitized sources to refocus the subfield with a greater emphasis on micro-historical studies dedicated to individual film cultures, filmmakers, exhibitors, exhibition sites, audiences, and scientific and cultural contexts.[6] Working across disciplines and through increasingly accessible archival sources, this revisionist historical approach has radically improved our understanding of early film culture and simultaneously enriched the knowledge and metadata held as part of archival collections. The traditional role of the archivist as gatekeeper has changed to one of collaboration in relation to developing a new "archaeology" of early film. The recent Mitchell and Kenyon early film archiving project provides an effective example of the potency of archival and academic collaboration which has radically changed the interpretation of early film production in the United Kingdom.[7] The partnership between the British Film Institute, the National Film and Television Archive, and media historians has produced a series of outcomes that has led to the preservation of over eight hundred unknown films. It has facilitated these films' digitization and public dissemination online, via a series of commercial DVDs, a major television series, and interdisciplinary collaborations between a range of academics involved in the interpretation of these sources.[8] This is by no means a unique example; it illustrates an increasingly close relationship between traditionally distinct practitioners, between preservation and curatorship, and between multiple fields of historical practice centered on the digital archive.

Whatever our perspective on the idea of the digital, it has by now become commonplace and uncontroversial to observe that the potential for archives to absorb and disseminate "original" historical artifacts via digital platforms increases the franchise for, and uses of, these materials to an extent unimaginable to media historians of the previous generation.[9] Digital archives also have the potential to incorporate new levels of interpretive and contextual sources, to make use of complex and shifting bodies of metadata, and to offer insights into the "mediation" of the events and the media institutions they represent. Such media archives offer a complex and often contested and contestable version of events, shaped by historical accident, as well as by the institutions themselves through collecting policies or managed through interpretive interfaces assembled through institutional, academic, and increasingly public partnerships. The intersection of traditional scholarly and archival practices with a growing public appetite for the raw historical content contained in increasingly digitized vaults places us at a crucial point in the development of archival and historical practice.

For historians of the media, this emerging landscape offers both challenges and opportunities in equal measure. It opens up new vistas of historical inquiry, instant access to sources, and new methods of analysis that draw on interdisciplinary skills and demand progressive collaborative working arrangements. It also offers challenges to the place of academic scholarship within an increasingly open research field where sources are increasingly "democratized" and accessible by all, and where the volume of primary material, metadata, and user-generated content tend to challenge the old nature of universality and grand historical narratives. To seek to illuminate these issues and to suggest positive and developmental approaches, we then need to see how practices in relation to access and engagement with sources and institutions are developing, what role we as media historians can play in these evolutionary processes, what logistical problems mitigate against progress, and where all of this leaves our discipline.

Access, Integration, and Collaborative Working: The European Model

Recognizing many of these challenges and the increasing importance of managing digital assets, the European Commission issued its *Recommendation on Film Heritage* on November 16, 2005. As part of this declaration, it noted that

> [c]inematographic works are an essential component of our cultural heritage and therefore merit full protection. In addition to their cultural value, cinematographic works are a source of historical information about European society. They are a comprehensive witness to history of the richness of Europe's cultural identities and the diversity of its people. Cinematographic images are a crucial element for learning about the past and for civic reflection upon our civilization.[10]

Following this implicit recognition of the historical significance of moving images within society, the European Economic Community began to explore a number of initiatives based on the premise that digitalization, for both access and preservation, was going to be the primary method to secure the longevity of these materials, develop collections, and reach mass audiences.[11] The range of issues relating to moving image sources such as semantic interoperability, copyright, clearance, and metadata standards necessitated cooperation on a scale hitherto unimaginable and reflected the fact that "the challenges of accessing and preserving film—an essentially trans-national medium—cannot be solved at the national level alone."[12]

The first moving image project under the scheme was the development of the Film Archive Online, aimed at the creation of a pan–European Union catalogue of key film archives and collections.[13] This led directly to the development of the European Film Gateway. The EFG is comprised of twenty-one partners from fifteen European nations, and since its inception in September 2008 (for an initial three years), it has outlined a series of work plans to deal with specific alignment activities to ensure a unanimity of practice and with the aim of making over 700,000 films and associated texts available through a single portal.[14] These include specific studies of user needs and service requirements, technical interoperability and access, semantic interoperability, web platform design, management, dissemination, and legal governance.

Moving image-based projects such as this feed into an overarching scheme to develop a Europe-wide digital meta-archive of moving image, sound, and cultural artifacts, all accessible through a single portal known as *Europeana*.[15] *Europeana* offers users access to a current body of 12,000,000 digital sources, ranging from film and television content to photographs, ephemera, and art objects. The scale of the

Europeana project and the problems faced in developing a unified digital architecture and legal framework seemed daunting, but the increasingly integrated European community has so far proved that such a collaborative project is indeed workable. There is clear evidence that while the initial thrust of these projects was more about content, and access to content, the focus is now shifting to a more comprehensive consideration of the value and usability of these resources by audiences. The recently published *A Digital Agenda for Europe* makes great play of the role of what they characterize as creative content and the function it serves in promoting cultural diversity and enabling education. In its action plan it commits to the ongoing deployment of digital resources, particularly those associated with the moving image: "The Commission will. . .[b]y 2012 propose a sustainable model for financing the EU public digital library Europeana and digitization of content."[16]

Again the emphasis here is on access and delivery, but there is also a developing debate concerning the potentialities of moving image resources for both study and online leisure activities which foreground what the consequences are for users:

> In addition to new technologies, societal changes are triggering increasing demand for accessing film heritage. The role of film heritage institutions is evolving from the traditional model of the "sealed box," conserving fragile film materials for posterity in their vaults towards a new "full access model," whereby they become well-springs of film culture.[17]

As audiences become more attuned to the potential of exploring and engaging with digital resources, they are also becoming more sophisticated in their use of materials and questioning of "institutional" interpretive strategies and restrictions based on access, copyright, and content. They are increasingly proficient in using new media tools and are becoming technologically empowered.[18] These evolving public audiences, who are outstripping the traditional "academic" audiences in their use of sources, have been characterized as "professional, amateur, and 'pro/am.'"[19] They have clearly bought into the digital archive revolution of the past decade and are increasingly engaged in reading and remediating historical sources of their own. There are perhaps clear parallels with what Julie Levin Russo has described as the changing relationship between consumers and producers in terms of film and TV fan-generated content, which is blurring the traditional economic and intellectual property hierarchies, commenting that

> [a]s the industry relies on the labor of fans to produce and promote the value of its properties with increasing openness, it becomes increasingly difficult to hold in place the distinctions between owners and consumers.[20]

The use of YouTube as a conduit for clandestine and user-based archive activities has further demonstrated the potential for a new "democratic" and individualized media archive culture. In broad terms of access to material for research purposes, Rob Turnock praises YouTube for providing "a more transnational space for the delivery of television content."[21] But beyond academic interest, the material also fuels what Rick Prelinger has characterized as "Archive Fans," who now "regard once-obscure repositories as exciting, relevant, and culturally hip institutions."[22] As one of the leading lights in this "free archive" movement, Prelinger has demonstrated the potential of open access through his own activities, stimulating what Timothy Wisniewski has characterized as "an increasingly participatory culture, in which access to archival moving images continues to be extended to non-traditional users of archives through digital technologies."[23] As a response, archival organizations are now buying into this form of open access by providing content channels of their own and seemingly de-institutionalizing their own collections.[24] In some respects these user-based initiatives threaten to create a tension between the desire to consume, interpret, and create new works and meanings and the "purity" of the original work or historical source.

Developing secure access and digital preservation strategies alongside models for public and academic engagement is also something that demands new forms of collaboration between public and private sector archives and also between academic communities and a range of public audiences. In the United Kingdom the focus is increasingly more oriented towards the end usage of these materials and allowing for interactive activity. A prime example of this approach comes to us from the BBC's Creative Archive program. The original trial was launched in 2005 to allow users to download and reuse clips provided from consortium members that included the British Film Institute, Channel 4, and the Open University. The premise of the project as outlined by Lord David Putnam was that:

> The Creative Archive License Group exists to ensure public access to public archives is optimised in the digital age. It's quite simple, we all pay for the upkeep of the material in these archives—we should all be able to access them. If we are unable to access most, if not all, of the riches locked up in these treasure troves, then it quite naturally begs the question, "why are we paying for them to be preserved in the first place?"[25]

The project is currently being reconfigured as the Digital Public Space initiative and, if funding is forthcoming, it will herald an important new approach to both access and usage of historical sources. The DPS project is not the only engagement initiative that the broadcaster has been developing, and research in this field is very current.

Engagement and Partnerships: Opening up the BBC Archive

As both a publicly funded organization and commercial broadcaster, the BBC finds itself in an interesting position in that its archive represents one of its most important commodities, while the archive itself also belongs to the public who funded it. The promise made by former BBC director-general Greg Dyke to effectively repatriate its contents to those who paid for it put the BBC ahead of the game in terms of developing a program of mass digitization of analog materials and the immediate dissemination of "born digital" assets. It also demonstrated the inherent problems facing the management and accession of such a vast repository of material. If the organization itself didn't know what it had, how was it going to be possible to open it up? Increasingly the solution would seem to be the gradual introduction of policies and projects that draw on traditionally disparate constituencies of archivists/academics, the general public, and external private and public institutions.

Historically, the BBC has exploited its own archives through broadcast models that combine elements of footage with the "traditional" mode of the academic voice of authority as interpreter of historical sources. This has increasingly been circumvented by factors like the boom in family history, heritage, and "real-time" archaeology, and in the marketing of history as something sexy, participatory, and exciting.[26] In the United Kingdom, broadcasters have moved toward programming that exploits the archive and makes archival interrogation part of the program so that historical inquiry becomes a seemingly open system. The recent rise in the popularity of archive-based programming and the use of new media resources are part of what Kevin Williams has characterized as "a wider revival of media's interest in the past."[27] This is something Williams attributes to the new accessibility of bodies of exploitable sources. As Williams contends, "Digital technology has allowed more access to archives and opened up more than a hundred years of footage to film, documentary and television producers."[28]

The BBC has produced a series of programs where key media archives (largely those held by the BFI and NFTVA) have been the centerpiece, beginning with the *Lost World of Mitchell and Kenyon* (2005), through the *Lost World of Friese-Greene* (2006) and *The Lost World of Tibet* (2008), to *The Wonderful World of Albert Kahn* (2008). In these series the role of the historian presenting the material has changed, and the narrative and interpretation are increasingly related to the sources themselves. The mystique of the academic historian as a lone or class voice of authority has been disrupted, and audiences are engaged in a collaborative, if artificially managed, voyage of discovery with a media-savvy and engaging presenter-historian as guide. This televisual exploration of archival sources and the models of media history which result from this are often facilitated by a well-developed set of online resources provided by the broadcaster where additional materials and often direct access to online archives are provided. We are also seeing a far more self-consciously reflexive use of the archive as a narrative device in its own right within these programs, something mirrored in archive-based documentary and discussed by Jamie Baron when he explores filmmakers' use of the context of the archive as a space to "simulate for the viewer the experience of being in an archive, of following and trying to make sense of fragments and traces."[29]

Reliance on reconstructions or the increasing flamboyance of presenters has been criticized as being part of a supposed process of dumbing-down historical television, whereas these archive-based programs seem to elicit a greater sense of authenticity because we are exposed more directly to the historical sources and can see and explore them for ourselves. However, there are also concomitant dangers, as Pierre Sorlin warned, in the tendency to fail to distinguish between the material and the broader contexts it inhabits.[30]

Beyond the broadcast of archival materials, the BBC is increasingly recognizing the potential of direct engagement through a mixture of commercial and non-commercial platforms. As Jana Bennett, director of BBC Vision, recently said:

> Once people begin to access the archive, we know they'll use it in a huge variety of ways, and find many different kinds of value in it—things we ourselves can't even begin to imagine. . . . The project will be democratic: everyone could be a curator or researcher, a cataloguer or inventor. The archive could turn into a giant apps store. The nature of what could be created and its potential cultural value are almost infinite. The more people get involved the bigger and richer and stronger the archive would become.[31]

Such comments are an affirmation and clear acknowledgment that major media institutions are increasingly unable to cope with their digital assets single-handedly and that collaborative and creative models need to be more than just speculative thinking. There is evidence that a genuinely collaborative and inclusive ethos for archives is developing. Further study needs to be made of how these relationships can be made real. We need to place greater focus on what people want archives for, how they can be encouraged to participate in areas of interpretation, what the new boundaries are likely to be between institutions and the public, and how all of this is likely to affect future developments. It also depends on how far the BBC can go in surrendering the Reithian paternalism of its authorial and institutional voice. Still, we need to accept that we are on the threshold of new forms of broadcasting and collective engagement in content generation and selective scheduling.[32]

A key developmental test bed for many of these issues was the Open Archive Project, which was established in 2007 to study the relationships between content providers (BBC archives) and a range of public and academic audiences. The core of the project was designed to look at how the BBC's regional public audiences might use archival sources and what they actually wanted to do with them. It looked in detail at how they might engage with materials in a way which allowed them to (re)construct historical events and to develop a series of public/academic relationships which would inform future digital accession and contextualization processes, facilitate user metadata, and evolve collaborative academic practice.

As project leader I chose the 1984–1985 miners' strike[33] as the historical case study, as it was the key domestic political event in the United Kingdom of the past quarter century, and the social and political consequences are still highly controversial and contested. It was also primarily a "media event" in which the role of the press and broadcasters was put under detailed scrutiny.[34] The BBC was singled out for criticism due to its uneasy relationship with the then Conservative administration and perceptions that it was taking the government's side. We wanted to explore the feelings and memories that digitized archival sources evoked and use them to provide a number of recommendations to the BBC regarding its archival resources and the potential for public engagement via new media initiatives and programming.[35]

One key focus in this project was the violent confrontation at Orgreave, where the BBC was accused of showing events in the wrong sequence by miners and their supporters.[36] This contested event—one of many—is a clear illustration of the difficulties faced in presenting materials and of the need for effective and sensitive contextualization and historical interpretation of the event and also of contemporary mediated representations.[37] The BBC footage and claims of editorial inaccuracies are framed by a whole series of controversies which still resonate for the institution and explain the current sensitivities surrounding this type of material.[38] Historical debate concerning the BBC's representation of this event and the sense that the archive is compromised also have a bearing on how communities still regard the BBC as an institution and to which it is particularly sensitive. As one striking miner commented after re-viewing footage:

> My mother was disgusted at us throwing stones at police as the BBC showed that first before the baton charge on horseback. In reality the baton charge was first. Ever since then I try and read between the lines of everything I read or see on the news.[39]

The key findings suggested that there was a strong sense that the broadcast material was partial and that individuals had been misrepresented and that the complex and detailed social, political, and historical issues associated with the strike had tended to be simplified and stereotyped in the past. As a consequence, these archival sources required sensitive and detailed contextualization which would be greatly enhanced by academic and public partnership. There was a clear willingness on the part of many participants to talk to archivists and historians and to offer their own views and experiences as a means to represent perspectives which they felt had been ignored or marginalized.[40] Part of this contextualization should, many felt, be directly focused on the circumstances under which much of the material was shot. Users needed to understand BBC technology, editorial policy, and editing processes, as well as the broader social and political contexts which surrounded the material that now constituted this aspect of the archive.

A central theme of many of the exchanges related to the creation of user-generated content and metadata as well as to the archiving of contextual memories that would further deepen the value of the primary sources. Some of the strongest evidence drawn from our participants was a desire to engage directly with content. Participants expressed the desire to be able to interact with, comment on, re-edit, compile, and contextualize archival sources. This strongly accords with current limited user tools like YouTube's Vblog and the developing environment in which

> the technologies being built and tested in the current Internet environment offer a new model for the reimagined moving image archive, which foregrounds the user in the process of creating the archive and strongly encourages the appropriation of moving images for new works.[41]

Working with the public and the BBC, the project importantly allowed me as a media historian to reflect on the nature of my intervention with these materials and the potential of digitized resources to continually renew and revisit key and contested elements of national history while at the same time reading the historical development of the institutions with which I was working. The mediating role I occupied between the archive and the public was both interesting and in some respects uncomfortable. I was concerned that I should at some point remove myself from this interface which led to a follow-up project which has allowed members of the original study to take ownership of the interpretation of digitized sources and to create historical interventions through the production of a series of short documentaries which respond to and frame the original film sources. The *Strike Stories* project, which finished in 2010, allowed the BBC to cede editorial control of its resources not to archivists or historians but to the public and for new voices to contribute.[42]

Within the BBC it is clear that traditional models of programming and gatekeeping roles are being redefined, and as this study has demonstrated, a new participant public is keen to engage with the BBC, not just as passive consumers but as active partners.[43] As content holders, BBC Information & Archives represents a rich resource which could increasingly act as a point of intersection between the organization and its funding audiences and between archivists and media historians. Managing that relationship and the expectations which attend it is perhaps the biggest challenge. As Tony Ageh, current controller of BBC Archive Development, said in a recent interview, the organization's ultimate goal is the "need to work towards permanent availability of every programme we make or have made, through commercial and non-commercial means."[44]

Conclusion

With such major institutions increasingly willing to explore new approaches, and with federal developments in line with the European model, will media historians share the same collaborative enthusiasm? Some will regard such development as anathema, as a diminution of special status and an abrogation of professionalism. Others like those who earlier embraced moving images as historical sources will seize the potential of greater enfranchisement and shared responsibility.[45] Rather than being the primary interpreters with all the attendant responsibilities, perhaps we should, as Megan Norcia suggests, take the opportunity "to change this perception, proposing instead a vision of the scholar as part of an engaged community of learners occupying a nexus between the preservation of archival texts and the production of knowledge about those texts."[46]

Academic and institutional reticence may require a radical realignment of roles and responsibilities, but we can already see some of the positive benefits this could bring to our discipline. For example, the ways in which we approach media history through the archive are changing, as has already been the case in the context of early cinema. We are moving away from broad survey histories and grand narratives, traditions that James Curran identified in his work, to more regional and micro-historical studies, which exist within broader contextualizing frameworks. If Karen Gracy is correct in her assertion that "the meta-archive of moving images seems to be finally within our reach," then we will need to marshal all our resources as historians, archivists, institutions, and public audiences to make sense of this material and to begin that process as soon as possible before the sheer volume of material overtakes us.[47]

The current financial crisis in which the arts and archives sectors are badly exposed may also hasten plans like those on track within Europe. As a result of the crisis, the traditional authoritative partnerships between experts and custodians as the coauthors of archive-based media histories are now under greater pressure than ever and a range of alternative models and relationships are being posited. There are obviously dangers, such as the reliance on user-generated content and user metadata, but these are also the subject of current research, and initial conclusions appear promising.[48] The idea of collaboration, both between the public and institutions and between institutions themselves, is steadily gaining ground, and we seem to have reached an important watershed in terms of testing the willingness of institutions to forgo their authority and embrace collaborative working. As Gracy has asked:

> Will cultural heritage institutions be willing to create systems to acquire and maintain content directly from users, allowing them to define the value of the material through the practices of description, usage, and critical commentary? Does doing so mean that they relinquish curatorial control, and thus have diminished powers as arbiters of value?[49]

In the same way, will we as media historians be able to "relinquish" some interpretive control and respond to and embrace these changing working conditions and benefit from new bodies of content and contextual metadata? For Norcia the jury is still out, as she reflects that "current digital projects promise democratised access to a range of primary source material: to the chagrin or delight of members of the academic community."[50] This "democratising" process, whether real or illusory, implies a sea change in the relationship between "historical" media archives and the audiences they serve. For us as media historians it also necessarily entails a reflection on our own role as mediators and interpreters of such materials and offers different and exciting possibilities.

We can already read the potential of some of these changes in the way in which broadcasters and archives are using their own collections, in the approaches taken to historical interpretation embodying new media content, and in the reframing of the archive as an "open" institution. Rather than a sealed tomb of evidential sources, the digital archive can now increasingly house layers of interpretation and evolving bodies of metadata. New voices can continually be added to contextual and interpretive debate and media histories constantly evolve. As the Open Archive Project demonstrated to me, researching key media-historical events from a finite "dead" set of archival sources could be a thing of the past, and the additional voices of those who were present and who can offer contesting and contextual commentaries open up new historical methodologies which are profoundly exciting. The role played by digital technologies and their impact on how we as historians, sociologists, and communications researchers conduct our own research and stimulate and engage our students are now at a crucial stage and the issues raised by this project might perhaps stimulate debate about the way forward.

Notes

1. The quotation in the title of this essay, "It's not really our content," is from Dyke, Speech at the Edinburgh International TV Festival. See also Crofts, "Digital Decay."
2. Smith, "Valuing Preservation," 9.
3. Fleischhauer, "Keynote."
4. Bennett, "Not Dead, but Diferent." The BBC has an estimated 400,000 TV and Radio programs and an estimated 900,000 hours of content (comprising 600,000 of video/film and 300,000 of audio) dating back to the 1920s. It also has a major ephemeral meta-archive which is also being digitized and put online. See http://www.bbc.co.uk/archive/written.shtml.
5. It has been estimated that less than 10 percent of films from the pre-sound era are now extant.
6. Popple and Kember, *Early Cinema.*
7. As a member of the original research team which worked on the interpretation and preservation of the films, I was concerned that we used a plurality of approaches to developing an understanding of their context and significance.
8. Toulmin, Russell, and Popple, *The Lost World.*
9. The BBC iplayer is a key example increasingly emulated by other PSB and commercial content providers in the UK. It looks likely to be available on a commercial basis worldwide from 2011. See http://www.bbc.co.uk/iplayer/.
10. European Commission, *Recommendation on Film Heritage,* 4–5.
11. The role of the digital in relation to preservation is a deeply contested issue and subject to a recent EC tender under the title "Challenges of the digital era for film heritage institutions."
12. Eckes, Segbert, and Mannghi, "Audiovisual and Film Archives."
13. See www.filmarchives-online-eu.
14. See http://www.europeanfilmgateway.eu/.
15. See http://www.europeana.eu/portal/.
16. European Commission, "Commission Staff Working Document." See also European Commission, *A Digital Agenda for Europe.*
17. European Commission, "Study on the 'Challenges.'"
18. In 2009 the UK government appointed Martha Lane Fox (founder of lastminute.com) as the new UK Digital Champion with the explicit role of getting the entire population online.
19. Smith, "Valuing Preservation," 7.
20. Russo, "User-Penetrated Content," 129.
21. Turnock, "Video Active," 126.
22. Prelinger, "Archives and Access," 114.
23. Wisniewski, "Framers of the Kept," 14, 17. The Prelinger Archives were established by Rick Prelinger in 1983 and grew into a collection of around 60,000 films. See http://www.archive.org/details/prelinger.
24. The British Film Institute operates a popular YouTube channel featuring over 2,000 films and television programs from the National Film and Television Archives. See http://www.youtube.com/user/BFIfilms.
25. Putnam, "The Creative Archive," 7.
26. Hunt, "Reality, Identity, and Empathy."

27. Williams, "Flattened Visions," 127.
28. Ibid., 129.
29. Baron, "Contemporary Documentary," 14.
30. Sorlin, "Historians at the Crossroads."
31. Bennett, "Not Dead, but Different."
32. Ernst, "Between Real Time"; Rubin, "Preserving Digital."
33. The miners' strike of 1984–1985 was one of the bitterest industrial disputes in living memory. It challenged the authority of Margaret Thatcher's Conservative government, threatened to destroy the livelihoods of tens of thousands of miners, witnessed violent conflict between miners and the police, and brought into question the independence and impartiality of the media in the United Kingdom.
34. For example, Guy Cumberbatch's study *Television and the Miners' Strike* was produced by the Broadcasting Research Unit in 1986.
35. The report and recommendations are available at http://www.bbc.co.uk/blogs/knowledge-exchange/leeds.pdf.
36. Orgreave, or as it popularly became known "The Battle of Orgreave," still throws up regular comment. See http://www.guardian.co.uk/media/2007/jul/26/broadcasting.comment.
37. A number of documentaries have been made examining the event and using BBC footage including Yvette Vanson's *The Battle for Orgreave* (1985) and *The Battle for Orgreave—The Sequel* (1991). See http://www.yvettevanson.com/the-battle-for-orgreave.php.
38. The BBC's sensitivity has been heightened by a series of recent controversies over editing malpractice.
39. Questionnaire, 2008.
40. Moseley and Wheatley, "Is Archiving?" 153.
41. Gracy, "Moving Image," 183.
42. The films are available via the Institute of Communications Studies website.
43. One recent example of this is the BBC's Video Nation project. See http://www.bbc.co.uk/videonation/archive/.
44. Ageh, Personal correspondence.
45. Sorlin, "Historians at the Crossroads."
46. Norcia, "Out of the Ivory Tower," 91.
47. Gracy, "Moving Image Preservation," 184.
48. Andreano, "The Missing Link."
49. Gracy, "Moving Image Preservation," 195.
50. Norcia, "Out of the Ivory Tower," 96.

Works Cited

Ageh, Tony. Personal correspondence. September 17, 2010.

Andreano, Keith. "The Missing Link: User-Created Metadata and the Improving Scholarly Access to Moving Image Archives." *The Moving Image* 7, no. 2 (2007): 82–99.

Baron, Jamie. "Contemporary Documentary Film and "Archive Fever': History, the Fragment, the Joke." *The Velvet Light Trap* 60 (2007): 13–24.

Bennett, Jana. "Not Dead, but Different: Public Service Broadcasting in the 21st Century—Safeguarding the Cultural Commons." Speech given at the London School of Economics, October 27, 2009.

Crofts, Charlotte. "Digital Decay." *The Moving Image* 8, no. 2 (2008): 13–35.

Dyke, Greg. Speech given at the Edinburgh International TV Festival, May 2003. Accessed September 19, 2010. http://www.digitalspy.co.uk/tv/feature/a11598/full-text-of-greg-dykes-edinburgh-international-tv-festival-speech.html.

Eckes, George, Monica Segbert, and Paolo Mannghi. "Audiovisual and Film Archives Create Futures: The European Film Gateway." Accessed October 10, 2010. http://www.beliefproject.org/zero-in/zero-in-third-edition 2010.

Ernst, Wolfgang. "Between Real Time and Memory on Demand: Reflections on/of Television." *The South Atlantic Quarterly* 101, no. 3 (2002): 625–637.

European Commission. "Commission Staff Working Document on the challenges for European film heritage from the analogue and digital era." July 2, 2010. Accessed November 11, 2010. http://ec.europa.eu/avpolicy/docs/reg/cinema/report_2/2010_853.pdf

———. "Commission Staff Working Document." June 2, 2010. Accessed November 11, 2010. http://www.europolitics.info/pdf/gratuit_en/276008-en.pdf.

———. *A Digital Agenda for Europe*. Summary section 2.7.3. May 2010. Accessed November 11, 2010. http://ec.europa.eu/information_society/digital-agenda/index_en.htm.

———. *Recommendation on Film Heritage*. November 2005. Accessed November 20, 2010. http://eurlex.europa.eu/LexUriServ/LexUriServ.do?uri-CELEX:32005H0865 EN:NOT.

Fleischhauer, Carl. Keynote for the conference "Audiovisual Archives in the 21st Century," Ghent, Belgium, October 13–14, 2010.

Gracy, Karen F. "Moving Image Preservation and Cultural Capital." *Library Trends* 56, no. 1 (2007): 183–197.

Hunt, Tristram. "Reality, Identity, and Empathy: The Changing Face of Social History Television." *Journal of Social History* 39, no. 3 (2006): 88–102.

Moseley, Rachel, and Helen Wheatley. "Is Archiving a Feminist Issue? Historical Research and the Past, Present, and Future of Television Studies." *Cinema Journal* 47, no. 3 (2008): 152–158.

Norcia, Megan A. "Out of the Ivory Tower Endlessly Rocking: Collaborating across Disciplines and Professions to Promote Student Learning in the Digital Archive." *Pedagogy: Critical Approaches to Teaching Literature, Language, Composition and Culture* 8, no. 1 (2007): 91–114.

Popple, Simon, and Joe Kember. *Early Cinema: From Factory Gate to Film Factory*. London: Wallflower Press, 2002.

Prelinger, Rick. "Archives and Access in the 21st Century." *Cinema Journal* 46, no. 3 (2007): 114–-118.

Putnam, David. "The Creative Archive." Speech by Lord Puttnam of Queensgate, CBE, September 13, 2006. Accessed November 20, 2010. www.bbc.co.uk/creativearchive/pdf/CreativeArchivefinalOctober.pdf.

Rubin, Nan. "Preserving Digital Public Television: Not Just an Archive, but a New Attitude to Preserve Public Broadcasting." *Library Trends* 57, no. 3 (2009): 393–412.

Russo, Julie Levin. "User-Penetrated Content: Fan Video in the Age of Convergence." *Cinema Journal* 48, no. 4 (2009): 125–130.

Smith, Abby. "Valuing Preservation." *Library Trends* 56, no. 1 (2007): 4–25.

Sorlin, Pierre. "Historians at the Crossroads: Cinema, Television . . . and After." In *The Historian and Television History*, edited by Graham Roberts and Phillip Taylor, 25–32. Luton: University of Luton Press, 2001.

Toulmin, Vanessa, Patrick Russell, and Simon Popple, eds. *The Lost World of Mitchell and Kenyon: Edwardian Britain on Film*. London: British Film Institute, 2005.

Turnock, Rob. "Video Active: And the Challenges of Developing Online Access to Compare European Television Programmes from the Archive." *Media History* 16, no. 1 (2010): 125–134.

Williams, Kevin. "Flattened Visions from Timeless Machines: History in the Mass Media." *Media History* 13, no. 2 (2007): 127–148.

Wisniewski, Timothy. "Framers of the Kept: Against the Grain Appraisal of Ephemeral Moving Images." *The Moving Image* 7, no. 2 (2007): 1–24.

Contributors

Barbara Adkins is Associate Professor in Sociology in the Creative Industries Faculty at Queensland University of Technology, Australia. Her research interests include social theory and the philosophy of inquiry with recent focus on the notion of "participation" and its relationship to digital technologies at the level of the micro-processes of everyday use of digital tools, and the broader dynamics of social fields. Papers in this area have been published in journals such as *Australian Journal of Communication*, *Information, Communication and Society*, and *Qualitative Sociology Review*. Her current research focus includes the use of generative arts tools in facilitating participation in the field of culture, and the role of digital technologies with respect to the interests of the subjects of national public apologies such as the recent apology to the "Forgotten Australians." She can be reached at b.adkins@qut.edu.au.

Noah Arceneaux is an Assistant Professor of Media Studies in the School of Journalism and Media Studies at San Diego State University. His research interests include the history of broadcasting, including early radio and television as well as emerging mobile technologies. His work has been published in the *Journal of Broadcasting and Electronic Media*, *Technology & Culture*, *New Media & Society*, and the *Journal of Radio Studies*. He co-edited *The Cell Phone Reader* (Peter Lang, 2006) and is currently working on *The Mobile Media Reader* (Peter Lang, 2012). Prior to joining academia, Arceneaux developed websites for the CBS, ABC, and Fox television networks. He can be reached at Noah.arceneaux@sdsu.edu.

Fernando Bermejo's research focuses on the study and measurement of audiences, online advertising, and communication theory. He is the author of *The Internet Audience: Constitution and Measurement* (Peter Lang, 2007) and editor of *On Communicating: Otherness, Meaning, and Information* (Routledge, 2009). He holds a PhD in Communication from the Universitat Autónoma de Barcelona, and an MA from the Annenberg School for Communication, University of Pennsylvania. He teaches at Universidad Rey Juan Carlos in Spain, and is a Faculty Associate at the Berkman Center for Internet & Society, Harvard University, where he was a Faculty Fellow in residence during the 2009–2010 academic year. He can be reached at Fernando.Bermejo@urjc.es.

Niels Brügger is an Associate Professor at Aarhus University, Denmark, and the director of the Centre for Internet Research at the university. His primary research interest is web history and web archiving, and in 2007 he began to write a history of the Danish Broadcasting Corporation's website entitled "The History of dr.dk, 1996–2006." He has published a number of articles, monographs, and edited books, including *Archiving Websites: General Considerations and Strategies* (The Centre for Internet Research, 2005), *Media History: Theories, Methods, Analysis* (edited with S. Kolstrup, Aarhus University Press, 2002), and *Web History* (edited, Peter Lang, 2010). He is currently co-editing the volume *Public Service Broadcasters on the Web: A Comprehensive History* (with M. Burns, Peter Lang). He can be reached via e-mail at nb@imv.au.dk and the website http://imv.au.dk/~nb.

Christian Thorsten Callisen is a Higher Degree Research student in Brisbane, Australia. His research is concerned with interdisciplinarity and the dissemination of ideas in early modern Europe, and he recently graduated Master of Arts (Research) from Queensland University of Technology with a thesis exploring Georg Calixtus's (1586–1656) relationship to the humanist tradition. Christian's PhD research continues this theme, further considering Calixtus's relationship to the Republic of Letters in light of his extensive unpublished correspondence. He can be reached at christian@callisen.net.au.

Adriana de Souza e Silva is an Associate Professor at the IT University of Copenhagen, at the Digital Culture and Mobile Communication group. Dr. de Souza e Silva's research focuses on how mobile and locative interfaces shape people's interactions with public spaces and create new forms of sociability. She teaches classes on mobile technologies, location-based games, and Internet studies. De Souza e Silva is also faculty at the Department of Communication at North Carolina State University (NCSU), and a faculty member of the Science, Technology and Society Program at NCSU. She can be reached at adriana@souza-esilva.com.

Michael Dick is a doctoral student in the Faculty of Information at the University of Toronto. His research focuses on the historical and cultural context of ICTs, particularly the web. He is also interested in the linkages between media and transportation, as well as technology policy and the social implications of technology. Mr. Dick holds an MA in Communication and Culture from Ryerson and York Universities in Toronto, and an Honours BA in Radio and Television Arts and English, also from Ryerson. He can be reached via e-mail at michaelh.dick@utoronto.ca and the website www.michaeldick.net.

Meghan Dougherty is an Assistant Professor of Digital Communication at Loyola University Chicago's School of Communication. She studies the preservation and interpretation of web culture, collaboration tools to aid knowledge production, and web archiving as an emerging cyberinfrastructure for e-research. She is a researcher for Webarchivist.org, which develops methods for studying action on the web over time.

Dmitry Epstein is a PhD candidate in the Department of Communication at Cornell University. His research focuses on the policy-making processes and the international governance of media, information, and communication, with particular interest in development. He has written about the influence of framing of the "digital divide" on attribution of responsibility for solving the problem and about the duality of nonbinding debates concerning Internet governance. Additional information about Dmitry is available at www.thinkmacro.org and he can be reached via e-mail at de56@cornell.edu.

Gerard Goggin is Professor of Media and Communications at the University of Sydney. His books include *Mobile Technology and Place* (with Rowan Wilken, 2012), *New Technologies and the Media* (2011), *Global Mobile Media* (2011), *Internationalizing Internet Studies* (with Mark McLelland, 2009), *Mobile Technologies: From Telecommunications to Media* (with Larissa Hjorth, 2009), *Mobile Phone Cultures* (2008), and *Cell Phone Culture* (2006). Gerard is undertaking an Australian Research Council-funded project titled *Internet History in Australia and the Asia-Pacific.*

Teresa M. Harrison is Professor in the Department of Communication at the University at Albany, SUNY. Her research focuses on democratic processes in organizations, new communication technologies, and the relationship between democracy and communication technologies. She has served as chair of the Organizational Communication Division of the National Communication Association and chair of the Communication and Technology Division of the International Communication Association. She is managing editor of the *Electronic Journal of Communication* (http://www.cios.org/www/ejcrec2.htm) and serves on the editorial boards of several journals in the field.

Nicholas W. Jankowski is Visiting Fellow at the e-Humanities Group of the Royal Netherlands Academy for Arts and Sciences (KNAW). He has co-edited some half-dozen books. Two recent edited volumes are: *Internet and National Elections: A Comparative Study of Web Campaigning* (2007) and *e-Research: Transformation in Scholarly Practice* (2009). Jankowski is co-editor of the journal *New Media & Society*.

Steve Jones is UIC Distinguished Professor, Professor of Communication, and Research Associate in the Electronic Visualization Laboratory at the University of Illinois-Chicago. His research interests include the social history of communication technology, virtual environments and virtual reality, popular music studies, internet studies, and media history. He was the founder and first president of the Association of Internet Researchers and is co-editor of *New Media & Society*. For more information, see http://stevejones.me.

Holly Kruse is an Assistant Professor in the Department of Communications at Rogers State University. Her research on communication technologies has been published in the journals *New Media & Society*, *Television and New Media*, *Popular Music and Society*, *First Monday,* and others. She is the author of the book *Site and Sound: Understanding Independent Music Scenes* (Peter Lang, 2003) and has a doctorate in communication from the Institute of Communications Research at the University of Illinois.

Deborah Lubken is a doctoral candidate at the University of Pennsylvania. Her dissertation addresses the cultural history of bells in the United States during the late nineteenth and early twentieth centuries. Her broader research interests include the history of communication practices and technologies, auditory culture, public space, and the history of communication and media research. She can be reached at dlubken@asc.upenn.edu.

Brian O'Neill is Head of Research in the College of Arts & Tourism at Dublin Institute of Technology, Ireland. His research interests include digital broadcasting, media literacy, and public interest issues in media and communications. He is co-editor of *Digital Radio in Europe: Technologies, Industries and Cultures* (2010) and co-author of the report *Digital Radio for Ireland: Competing Options, Public Expectations* for the Broadcasting Commission of Ireland. He is a member of the DRACE (Digital Radio Cultures in Europe) research group established under the COST A20 programme. He is also a member of the management committee of COST Action ISO906—*Transforming Audiences, Transforming Societies*—and Vice Chair of the International Association for Media and Communication Research (IAMCR) Audience Section.

Zizi Papacharissi (PhD University of Texas at Austin) is Professor and Head of the Communication Department at the University of Illinois-Chicago. Prior to moving to Chicago, she was Associate Dean for Graduate Programs and Research and Faculty at the School of Communications and Theater, Temple University. Her work focuses on the social and political consequences of new media technologies. Her book *A Private Sphere: Democracy in a Digital Age* (Polity Press, 2010) discusses how we practice politics in a digital age. She also recently edited a volume on online social networks, titled *A Networked Self: Identity, Community, and Culture on Social Network Sites* (Routledge, 2010). She is author of three books, and over forty journal articles, book chapters, or reviews and has studied blogs, online journalism, social network sites, privacy, civility, self-presentation in digital environments, and sociability online.

David W. Park is Associate Professor of Communication at Lake Forest College. He is the founder and past chair of the International Communication Association's Communication History Interest Group, and is the editor, with Jefferson Pooley, of *The History of Media and Communication Research: Contested Memories* (Peter Lang, 2008). His research interests include intellectuals and the media, the history of the study of communication, media history, and internet studies.

Benjamin Peters recently received his PhD in Communications from Columbia University, is currently Golda Meir Postdoctoral Fellow at Hebrew University, and remains, by courtesy, a visiting fellow at the Information Society Project at Yale Law School. His research interests include new media history and theory, critical information studies, and global communication studies, with a special emphasis on Eastern Europe. He posts occasional notes and publications at benpeters.blogspot.c om.

Simon Popple is Senior Lecturer in Cinema at the Institute of Communications Studies at the University of Leeds and co-director of the Louis Le Prince Research Centre for Photography, Film & Television. His main research interests include new media and the archive, popular visual cultures, and media history. He is editor of *Early Popular Visual Culture* and is currently working on research examining the relationships between audiences and broadcast archives of historical film. He has two forthcoming books: *Digging the Seam—Popular Cultures of the Miners' Strike* (with Ian MacDonald) and *Content Cultures: Transformations of User Generated Content in Public Service Broadcasting* (with Helen Thornham).

Devon Powers is an Assistant Professor in the Department of Culture and Communication at Drexel University. Her scholarship focuses on popular music, the history of popular culture, and cultural intermediation and circulation. Along with Melissa Aronczyk, she is the co-editor of *Blowing up the Brand: Critical Perspectives on Promotional Culture* (Peter Lang, 2010), and is currently completing a manuscript on '60s rock criticism at the *Village Voice.* Her most recent article appeared in the July 2011 issue of *Popular Music and Society* and is entitled "Bruce Springsteen, Rock Criticism, and the Music Business: Toward a Theory and History of Hype."

Peter Schaefer is Assistant Professor of Communication Arts at Marymount Manhattan College. His interests concern media theory and the history of technology. His work has appeared in *Critical Studies in Media Communication*. He can be reached at pschaefer@mmm.edu.

Steven M. Schneider is a Professor and Interim Dean of the School of Arts & Sciences at SUNY Institute of Technology, Utica, New York, where he teaches in the Information Design & Technology program. As the co-director of Webarchivist.org, he has organized studies and collections of web objects, including those associated with national elections and the September 11 terrorist attacks, and has designed web archive interfaces in collaboration with libraries and research laboratories. He is the co-author of *Web Campaigning* (MIT Press, 2006) and co-editor of *The Internet and National Elections* (Routledge, 2007). He has a PhD in Political Science from MIT.

Stephanie Ricker Schulte is Assistant Professor of Communication at the University of Arkansas, where she researches communication technologies, media history, media policy, popular culture, and transnational cultural exchanges. She received her PhD in American Studies from George Washington University. Her work has appeared in the *Journal of Television and New Media,* in the *Journal of Transnational American Studies*, and in *Feminist Studies.* She received the American Studies Association (ASA) Ralph Henry Gabriel Prize, the Society for Cinema and Media Studies (SCMS) dissertation prize, and Honorable Mention for the American Journalism Historians Association (AJHA) Margaret A. Blanchard Doctoral Dissertation Prize. You may contact her at sschulte@uark.edu.

D. Travers Scott is an Assistant Professor of Communication Studies at Clemson University in Clemson, South Carolina. His research investigates cultural and historical aspects of media technologies, sound studies, and gender/sexuality studies, with work in *Feminist Media Studies*, *Communication and Critical/Cultural Studies*, and *Westminster Papers in Communication and Culture.* Author of two novels and a short-story collection, he is currently completing a book manuscript on perceived associations between mental and physical illnesses and electric communication technologies. He can be reached via e-mail at scott3@g.clemson.edu and the website http://www.dtraversscott.com.

Daniel M. Sutko is a doctoral student in the Communication, Rhetoric, and Digital Media program at North Carolina State University. His research interests include cultural approaches to media/technology, the social production of spaces and mobilities, and asking what's new about new media. He teaches media history, theory, and criticism in the Department of Communication and is a research assistant in the Mobile Gaming Research Lab. His recent publications focus on locative media, mobility, urban sociability, globalization and media infrastructure, and the philosophy of the virtual. He is co-editor, with Adriana de Souza e Silva, of *Digital Cityscapes: Merging Digital and Urban Playspaces* (Peter Lang, 2009). He can be reached at dmsutko@ncsu.edu.

Elaine J. Yuan (PhD Northwestern University) is an Assistant Professor in the Communication Department at the University of Illinois-Chicago. Her research interests include social and political implications of the new media in China, media convergence, and audience fragmentation and polarization. Currently she is researching issues of online community, privacy, and online journalism within comparative cultural and multiple modernity frameworks. Her recent publications include a variety of topics in these areas, such as online discourse practices on the Chinese Internet and the structuration of China's national television market in *Asian Journal of Communication* and the *Journal of Broadcasting and Electronic Media.*

Index

A

D

Q

R

S

About the Editors

David W. Park is Associate Professor of Communication at Lake Forest College. He is the founder and past chair of the International Communication Association's Communication History Interest Group, and is co-editor of *The History of Media and Communication Research: Contested Memories* (Peter Lang, 2008).

Nicholas W. Jankowski is Visiting Fellow at the e-Humanities Group of the Royal Netherlands Academy for Arts and Sciences (KNAW). He has co-edited some half-dozen books. Two recent edited volumes are *Internet and National Elections: A Comparative Study of Web Campaigning* (2007) and *e-Research: Transformation in Scholarly Practice* (2009). Jankowski is co-editor of the journal *New Media & Society*.

Steve Jones is UIC Distinguished Professor, Professor of Communication, and Research Associate in the Electronic Visualization Laboratory at the University of Illinois-Chicago. He was the founder and first President of the Association of Internet Researchers and is co-editor of *New Media & Society*.

Digital Formations

General Editor: *Steve Jones*

Digital Formations is an essential source for critical, high-quality books on digital technologies and modern life. Volumes in the series break new ground by emphasizing multiple methodological and theoretical approaches to deeply probe the formation and reformation of lived experience as it is refracted through digital interaction. **Digital Formations** pushes forward our understanding of the intersections—and corresponding implications—between the digital technologies and everyday life. The series emphasizes critical studies in the context of emergent and existing digital technologies.

Other recent titles include:

Felicia Wu Song
Virtual Communities: Bowling Alone, Online Together

Edited by Sharon Kleinman
The Culture of Efficiency: Technology in Everyday Life

Edward Lee Lamoureux, Steven L. Baron, & Claire Stewart
Intellectual Property Law and Interactive Media: Free for a Fee

Edited by Adrienne Russell & Nabil Echchaibi
International Blogging: Identity, Politics and Networked Publics

Edited by Don Heider
Living Virtually: Researching New Worlds

Edited by Judith Burnett, Peter Senker & Kathy Walker
The Myths of Technology: Innovation and Inequality

Edited by Knut Lundby
Digital Storytelling, Mediatized Stories: Self-representations in New Media

Theresa M. Senft
Camgirls: Celebrity and Community in the Age of Social Networks

Edited by Chris Paterson & David Domingo
Making Online News: The Ethnography of New Media Production

To order other books in this series please contact our Customer Service Department:
(800) 770-LANG (within the US)
(212) 647-7706 (outside the US)
(212) 647-7707 FAX

To find out more about the series or browse a full list of titles, please visit our website:
WWW.PETERLANG.COM